AF596564

MONEY | GAMES | ECONOMIES

Edited by: Nikolaus Koenig, Natalie Denk, Alexander Pfeiffer, Thomas Wernbacher, Simon Wimmer

Editors: Nikolaus Koenig, Natalie Denk, Alexander Pfeiffer, Thomas Wernbacher, Simon Wimmer

Cover, Illustrations: Constantin Kraus

Publisher: University of Krems Press

Print: tredition GmbH, Halenreie 40-44, 22359 Hamburg

ISBN Paperback: 978-3-903470-14-9
ISBN e-Book: 978-3-903470-15-6

DOI: https://doi.org/10.48341/pwsk-m637

Contact:
Center for Applied Game Studies
Department for Arts and Cultural Studies
University for Continuing Education Krems
www.donau-uni.ac.at/ags
ags@donau-uni.ac.at

Produced with the financial support of the Federal Chancellery of Austria

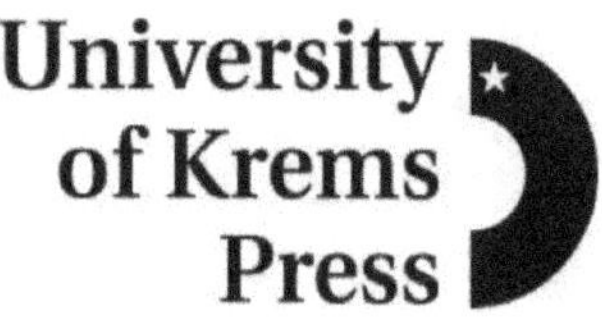

CONTENTS

INTRODUCTION

INTRODUCTION

Nikolaus Koenig, Natalie Denk, Alexander Pfeiffer,
Thomas Wernbacher, Simon Wimmer

Money makes the world go round – and the world of games spins especially fast in this regard. While terms like money, finances, or economy sound much too serious (and to some ears even boring) to be easily associated with games, they describe concepts that are at the very heart of many game-related phenomena. They are the secret ingredient that greases the wheels of the mechanics of play & games themselves.

First of all, there is hardly a game that can do without one or the other kind of in-game money; these currencies might not be called "money" or "dollars" or even "coins", but games are abstract pleasures, and whether we deal in diamonds, teeth (mad, but true), or bottle caps, we can hardly imagine a game in which our efforts are not being translated into some kind of easily tradable mediating resource: a coin by any other name...

But the presence of "money" in games is just the tip of the iceberg: as the various mechanics and practices of turning one resource into another are at the core of the very idea of economy, virtually any game is on some level a game about economy and economic structures, and playing a game is always related to matters of economic thinking and economic behavior.

This begs the question: are games themselves inherently tied to matters of money and economy, or are the logics of capitalism so deeply ingrained in our minds that we cannot but reproduce them even in the games we create and play? Both answers suggest a critical stance towards the ways money and economies are modelled in games – but at the same time, the ease with which games and money intertwine also makes games a potential tool for addressing economic issues, either in the form of educational games aiming to teach financial literacy skills that highlight the opportunities and survival strategies we need to keep in mind when navigating the economic waters of our time; or as a method of economic critique that helps us uncover the downsides of our economic systems, explore alternatives, or ask if (and how) we can even imagine a (game) world in which money or its equivalents do not play any role at all.

At this point, the relation between money and games inverts, as it is only a small step from games as tools of economic critique to viewing economy itself as a game. While this is not a new idea, it has certainly gained some momentum since mathematical game theory has introduced games as a metaphor to the study of economic behavior in social interactions, which has since become a staple of economics itself (with the obvious underlying ideological implications). But just as economies have changed in the age of digital globalization, so have games, and so has our understanding of their complexities and possibilities. What, then, can concepts derived from studying increasingly complex digital games bring to the table when it comes to understanding modern economies?

And the digital age adds yet another layer to the many relations between games & economies: since games have become digital, they have also become a monetary factor themselves. They have become the driving force of a billion-dollar industry, estimated at almost thrice the value of the music and movie business combined. So, games make a lot of money (and quite often it is minors whom they are making money from) – and yet, lack of money is always an issue, either for smaller studios for which raising enough money to make their games and keep their business afloat is a constant challenge, but especially for workers, who often have to balance precarious employment with high-stress working conditions, or are even outsourced laborers or micro-workers altogether. And even paying jobs do not pay the same for everyone, as access to and compensation for jobs in the gaming industry are still notoriously dependent on currencies of class, race, and gender.

And yet, the promise of making money with games does not limit itself to a job in the games industry: the proverbial "kids today" don't seize to astonish their elders with increasingly specialized game-based career plans; job labels like "Gaming Influencer", "Esports Trainer" or "Cosplay Event Manager" might still seem a bit unusual, but they might very well anticipate the working environment of a not so distant future.

But then again, games are often a scapegoat for making money by victimizing unsuspecting (and often underage) customers: especially for younger players, playing is not always an affordable activity, and many players are more than willing to take a seemingly good offer. But what is advertised as free-to-play can quickly turn into a bottomless money pit, and when loot boxes promise the chance to get more than you bargained for (but in a good way!), the question of who's being looted is rarely answered in the players' favor. The uninvited intrusion of hidden costs and costly game-of-chance-mechanics often targets younger players specifically and highlights the necessity to introduce an understanding game-related transactions as a matter of financial literacy – ideally taught in the form of games – bringing us full circle to the beginning. (Well, money does make the world go round after all).

In order to discuss these and other questions revolving around matters of "Money & Games", the 17th Vienna Games Conference "FROG – Future and Reality of Gaming" 2023 – hosted by the Center for Applied Game Studies (University for Continuing Education Krems) in cooperation with the Austrian Federal Chancellery – has invited game scholars, creators, educators, activists and enthusiasts from around the globe to "follow the money" and explore the traces it leaves on the field of games & play. The intellectual investment made by our contributors has paid off, and the profits it has yielded – with interest – can be found in the texts collected in this volume. During this enterprise, four main angles have proved most valuable:

1. The presence of money in games: here, KLEMENS FRANZ takes a look at different types of "toy money", from paper bills to metal coins and the experiences and even communicative functions they can provide to players of analogue games; shifting the question of "lived experiences" to digital games, MARIO DONICK investigates how recent bus simulation games make use of mundane tasks like selling tickets and giving change in order to enhance the games' atmosphere and player immersion; and LEA STELLA SANTNER and WILFRIED ELMENREICH discuss how the dual nature of money as a physical item and an element of an implied monetary systems can pose great challenges on the designers of text adventure games.

2. Economic experiences in games: in this section, KEVIN MERCER explores the "socio-spatial economies" in Dark Souls and Super Mario Bros. Wonders, two games in which – in different ways – players can interact across asynchronously shared virtual spaces, creating economies of meaning, cooperation and mutual care and recognition; using the example of Anno 1800's transition from video to board game, ANDREAS WIESER shows how even when monetary capital is completely removed from a game, giving it the appearance of emerging from a non-capitalist attitude, capitalist logics can still persist in the simulation of economic growth and player competition as key features of the game system; FIONA S. SCHÖNBERG uncovers the procedural rhetoric underlying contemporary roleplaying games in which the accumulation of money is not only a diegetic goal in itself, but also a means of self-improvement, reflecting and reproducing real life capitalist/libertarian ideologies; MICHAELA WAWRA and

ALEXANDER PFEIFFER examine the inclusion of women in EA's FC24 Ultimate Team and its impact on the virtual economy driven by loot boxes, specifically analyzing how community reactions evolved from skepticism prior to the game's release to a more nuanced and increasingly positive acceptance in the endgame phase.

3. Dark patterns in and beyond games: the starting point of this section is SONJA GABRIEL's attempt to give a structured overview of strategies to teach financial literacy through games, including a discussion of whether and why games might be especially equipped to raise awareness for the risks and complexities of keeping your money together in a digital age; complementing this discussion of financial literacy, RALPH J. MOELLER provides an in-depth examination of a case where a lack of such literacy leads to financial loss and quite a bit of family drama, highlighting the dangers of dark patterns in seemingly "free to play" games – but not without some suggestions on how you might get your money back after all; MARGARETE JAHRMANN, THOMAS BRANDSTETTER and STEFAN GLASAUER tackle dark patterns from a different perspective: they show how their low interaction game KOPFGELD - in the artistic tradition of "dark play" - intentionally engages us in forms of non-consensual play, providing us with an opportunity to experience what the future of pervasive gaming might have in store for us.

4. Opportunities for the gaming industry: the question if and how money can be made by using Artificial Intelligence tools for game development is at the center of BENJAMIN HANUSSEK's and YARASLAU KOT's paper, in which the promises of new technologies are opposed to challenges such as the potential for job displacement and quality issues; AHMAD KALATIANI, MAGDALENA M. STROBL and WILFRIED ELMENREICH present a case study exploring the potentials and limitations of using 3D printing technologies as a production tool in game development, using the example of a heist board game, and specifically highlighting the technology's benefits for heightening accessibility for the visually impaired; LINDA RUSTEMEIER showcases the online simulation game ScrumSimPlan, in which players can engage in a virtual scrum-team and explore a simulated scrum process, enabling them to understand the scrum framework and employ scrum and agile methods to overcome obstacles, as a time-saving and cost-effective method of preparing students for the requirements of their potential employers; instead of focusing on careers in the game industry in the stricter sense, PRATAMA WIRYA ATMAJA, SUGIARTO, HENDRA MAULANA, DHIAN SATRIA YUDHA KARTIKA and YISTI VITA VIA ask how careers in the near future might be fueled by what we can learn from games and

game design, assessing the potential of "ludonarrative professions" as key elements in an increasingly "ludonarratified" society based on multiverse structures.

5. The commodification of games and its costs: in this section, EDUARDO LUERSEN and BIBIANA DA SILVA DE PAULA address the problem of cloud gaming infrastructures and their environmental effects by discussing the complex relations between gaming, sustainability efforts, geo-distributed cloud-based infrastructures and economic interests, and highlight the necessity of increased intersectoral research on cloud infrastructures as a prerequisite for addressing an urgent problem of global scale; MAXIMILIAN STEFAN MOHR examines what happens when players' enthusiasm for a game is no longer in balance with the economic interests of copyright holders: using the example of Super Mario 64's legacy, he explores the ways nostalgic players (and scholars) use technological and social means to hold onto a game that can no longer rely on market mechanisms to keep it "alive"; and finally, SIMON HUBER aims to overcome the often stated rift between viewing games as an art form and treating them as an economic commodity, avoiding the temptation to favor one side over the other, but instead choosing a ludological approach to evade binary distinctions, oriented on the ways game scholars have dealt with the ambiguities of the Ludology vs. Narratology debate.

Please note that in what is becoming a FROG tradition, the authors were free to choose the citation style they deemed most suited for their papers and topics; the resulting variety is not an editorial oversight, but a design choice - a feature, not a bug.

Let us conclude our business by expressing our gratitude to those who have contributed to this volume, and by giving special credit to Herbert Rosenstingl for his fixed interested in the FROG conference. But most importantly, our books would not be in order without appreciating our valued members of the FROG community, who are, and always will be, the greatest asset to this enterprise.

I. THE PRESENCE OF MONEY IN GAMES

REAL. FAKE. ANALOGUE.

THE JOY OF PLAYING WITH REAL PEOPLE AND FAKE MONEY.

Klemens Franz

In ancient times money and play met for the first time initiating a fruitful tradition of gambling. Since then, (toy) money has become an integral part of analogue games, serving not only as a means to bet but also as a gameplay element, components, rules, and mechanisms.

Through four main examples this paper seeks to highlight the distinct qualities in which analogue games incorporate money—in most cases differently than their digital counterparts. Money is more visibly tangible and requires direct management by players. It can serve as a component to visualize growth and value or occupy spaces affecting spatial prices. Money may take various forms, including paper currency, cardboard coins, or even luxurious metal coins—meeting aesthetic preferences and enhancing the overall experience at the table. Moreover, money in analogue games fosters social interaction, acting as a medium for communication. Players have to be greedy, engage in deception, bribery, guessing, and bluffing. Analogue games always have to abstract reality, unable to achieve the level of simulation seen in their digital counterparts. But in doing so, they use their components—material and players—in innovative ways. And maybe this sometimes seemingly raw approach can be an inspiration for digital games too.

Keywords: Philosophy, Philosophy of Language, Freedom, Agency, Normativism

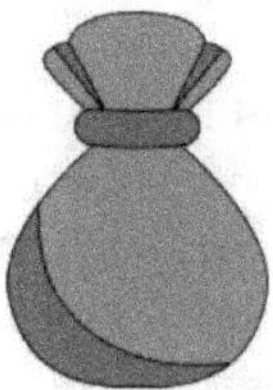

1. What this paper is not about

This paper won't be discussing the intricate relationship between money and games, and how the introduction of money did and still can disrupt the immersive experience often referred to as the *magic circle* [1] of games. This concept suggests that games exist within their own enclosed world, separate from reality, as people engage with them during play [2]. The introduction of real-world money with its real-world impact can indeed blur and even dissolve this boundary, affecting the game's dynamics and player experiences [3].

[1] In general, the concept of the *magic circle* was extensively discussed by the Dutch historian Johan Huizinga in his seminal work *Homo Ludens*. This influential and frequently referenced book explores the fundamental nature of play and its significance in human culture. The term *magic circle* is used to describe a figurative or literal space where the usual norms and rules of the everyday world are temporarily set aside, replaced by a distinct set of rules that govern the game world (Huizinga 77). Within this defined space, players engage in activities that are governed by the internal logic and dynamics of the game, creating a system with its own unique parameters and constraints. This concept of the *magic circle* highlights the independency of play, allowing individuals to enter into a realm of imagination and creativity where they can explore new possibilities and experiences free from the constraints of reality. At least in theory.

[2] Beat Suter argues that "A game is always a dynamic system composed of different formal and dramatic elements combined into a working structure" and that "The game world is clearly separated from the real world" (19). Despite the romantic notion of the *magic circle* being a closed system, it is a fragile construct, as players inevitably carry elements from the game into the real world and vice versa. This includes the experience of winning or losing, observing other players' reactions, understanding the game's ruleset, or even tokens that can be exchanged for real-world money.

[3] The distinction between open and closed systems offers valuable insights when examining games and their real-world implications. While the concept of the *magic circle* suggests a closed system, those theoretical models are not feasible in reality (Luhmann 70). Nevertheless, analyzing games and observing the flow of elements between the game world and its surroundings can provide essential perspectives: Salen and Zimmerman illustrate this with the example of Chess, which can be perceived as a closed system from a formal standpoint, yet appears quite open when viewed as a cultural system (53). When considering an analogue game that incorporates money as a component, whether the system is open or closed largely depends on whether the money involved is toy currency or real-world currency. However, this distinction may vary depending on one's perspective. For instance, the formal system of playing *Poker* for money differs significantly from the social system of playing *Poker* for money.

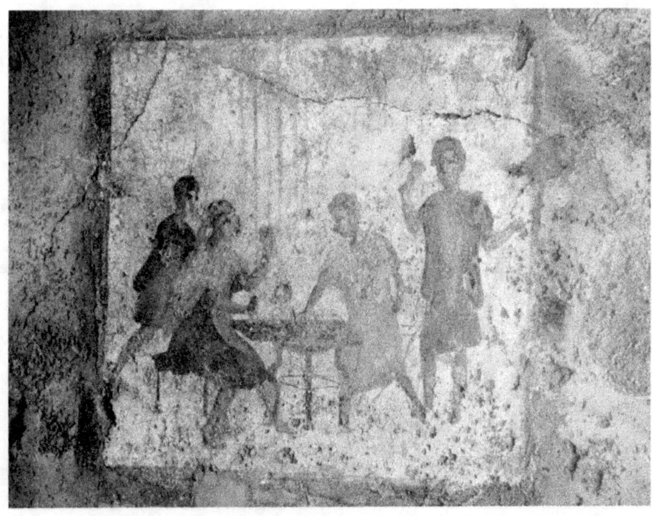

Figure 1. Dice players fresco from the Osteria della Via di Mercurio (Raddato)

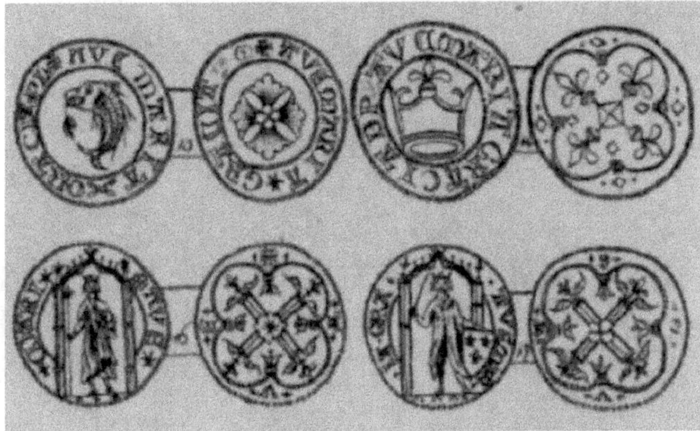

Figure 2. Ancient jettons or counters as depicted in Thomas Snelling's book (17)

However, it's worth noting that comprehensive historic publications discussing these topics are available, offering valuable insights into the intersection of money and gaming, money for play [4], as well as toy money in general [5].

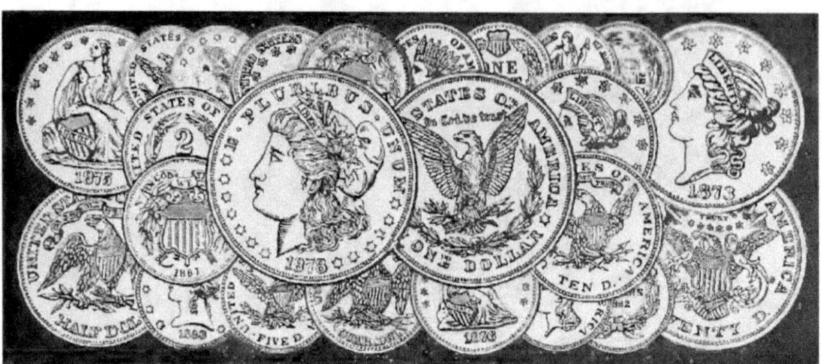

Figure 3. Educational toy money from the catalogue of Milton Bradley (11)

Toy money originated in the 19th century when imaginative play scenarios like pretend shopping were used to teach practical life skills to children in a

[4] In the book *Playing with Money*, which accompanied an exhibition of the same name at the British Museum in 2019, Robert Bracey provides a comprehensive overview of the concept of playing money in analogue games. The discussion ranges from earliest examples like *Bourse*—or *Pit*, as it is called in the Parker Brothers edition from 1904 (13ff)—to contemporary examples like *Bohnanza* (Rosenberg), where the backsides of the cards serve as money (96), as well as *Citadels* with plastic tokens (96), and *Alhambra* with its four different currency types. (111 ff)

[5] *Play Money of American Children* by Richard F. Clothier is an extensive collection of toy coins illustrating the wide thematic range, from coins featuring the *Joker* and *Batman* from 1966 (8) to *Pooh's Lucky coins* from 1976 (35). Based on Clothier's collection and research, it appears that metallic play money emerged around 1900 in America (5). Paper money and cardboard coins, mostly for educational purposes, were introduced to kindergartens around 1880 by the Milton Bradley Company through their set called Educational Toy Money (Milton Bradley Company 11) (see figure 3).

supposedly[6] fun and engaging manner. These toy shops originated in dollhouses and were available in a wide range of themes[7].

I won't be discussing *Monopoly* (Darrow) either, which introduced the concept of toy money to the people playing analogue games. While *Monopoly* holds a significant place in gaming history, there are valid criticisms of its game design, as highlighted in the insightful and quite entertaining video *You Should NEVER Play MONOPOLY again*[8].

Conversely, the original *The Landlord's Game* (Magie), from which *Monopoly* originates, had the appropriate framing and narrative to support its theme of the problematic situation of rental costs during its time[9]. However, it still falls short, from our contemporary game design perspective, as a good game in many ways.

---

[6] In the short chapter on Toys in Roland Barthes' *Mythologies*, the critique of preparing young people through play is quite pronounced. Barthes writes that toys "are all reduced copies of human objects, as if the eye of the public child was, all told, nothing but a smaller man, a homunculus to whom must be supplied objects of his own size" (53). From Barthe's perspective, industrially produced toys aim at future consumers not only by consuming the toy itself but also by training to consume through play scenarios. However, role play and pretending to be someone else are integral forms of play—we need only look at Callois' categories of play, where mimicry described as "one can also escape himself and become another" (19), is one of them.

[7] The field and history of toy shops is extensive and complex. One of the earliest known dollhouses was commissioned by *Duke Albrecht V of Bavaria* in 1558 for his daughters (Kutschera 124). From dollhouses, toy shops developed in parallel with the liberalization of the real-world economy in the 19th century (Bachmann 25), which—unlike dollhouses—could be played with by both genders (Bachmann 45). In addition to miniature cash registers, the different shops also featured slots for inserting play money (Maß 222).

[8] John Perkins' criticism can be boiled down to one essential point: *Monopoly* does not offer players any meaningful decisions. The course of the game is solely determined by the result of the dice roll. This means that *Monopoly* theoretically can last indefinitely, and thus, an arc of suspense cannot be maintained. Additionally, the destructive goal of the game—driving opponents into financial ruin—cannot be pursued deliberately. Monopoly "takes the joy out of being mean" (5:48).

[9] Elizabeth Magie Phillips patented *The Landlord's Game* game in 1904, making it the first patented board game (Tönnesmann 23). It seems that the thematic embedding of the game

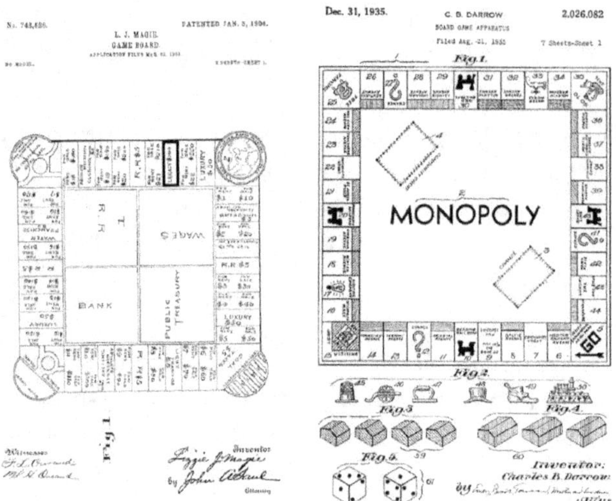

Figure 4. Left: The patent for *The Landlord's Game* (Magie). Right: The patent for *Monopoly* (Darrow).

Furthermore, I won't delve into the intricacies of currency systems in games like *Orongo* (Knizia), where players utilize shells or other tokens as a form of currency [10]. These thematically charged components essentially are money-in-disguise and sometimes contribute little to the game design beyond their aesthetic appeal [11].

---

is a combination of two factors: firstly, Maggie was a Quaker, which is why there are no churches or theaters in the game (Tönnesmann 28). On the other hand, she may have been a follower of the economic teachings of Henry George. The New Yorker criticized primarily the large gap between the rich and the poor (Tönnesmann 24). And so, in *The Landlord's Game*, players are forced to pay taxes to alleviate social distress (Tönnesmann 28).

[10] *Orongo* is a board game designed by Reiner Knizia, a renowned game designer known for his elegant and strategic designs. In *Orongo*, players take on the roles of Polynesian tribes competing to construct monumental stone statues, known as Moai, on the remote island of Rapa Nui. In the game the shells are the currency in which players bid for spaces on the playing field. Furthermore, the same shells are placed on the playing field to mark used spaces.

[11] Ham distinguishes between assets and resources in his work. Assets are elements that provide a benefit to the player possessing them. Resources, on the other hand, are a specific

Lastly, I won't be discussing complex games like the *18XX* series either. These games blend elements of railroad management and stock market speculation [12]. They often require extensive calculations, with players even utilizing external tools such as tablets or laptops to manage the intricate financial aspects of gameplay.

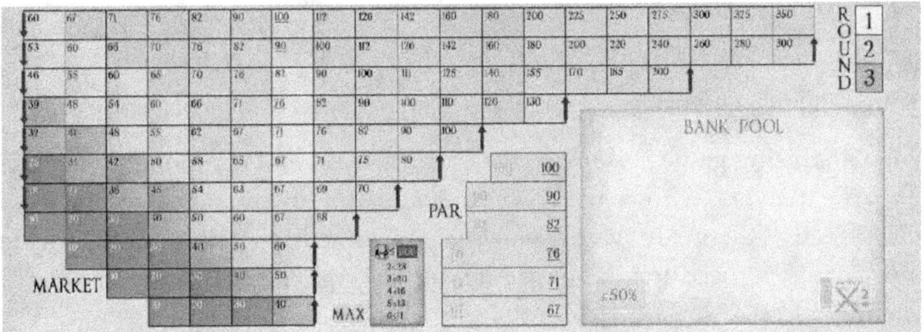

Figure 5. The stock market from the new edition of *1830* (Tresham).

2. What this paper is about

What I want to delve into instead is the concept of games viewed as systems and discuss a few examples that I find particularly unique in terms of how and what they do with their components. This exploration will highlight the distinctions between analogue games—board games, card games, tabletop games, and other variation played on or around a table—and digital games.

---

type of asset characterized by their generic quality and interchangeability with others of the same type (214). To further expand on this concept and summarize, money can be categorized as currency, which falls under the classification of resources, ultimately making it an asset.

[12] The games developed by British designer Francis Tresham in the late 1970s, particularly *1829* and *Civilization,* exerted a significant influence on European analogue game designers (Woods 36). *1829,* a game focusing on simulating railway expansion and corresponding stockholding management, spawned an entire sub-genre of games known as the *18XX* series. Tresham's creation served as a template, inspiring an open-source-like concept for analogue games. According to the online database boardgamegeek,com, a total of 282 games are listed within this series.

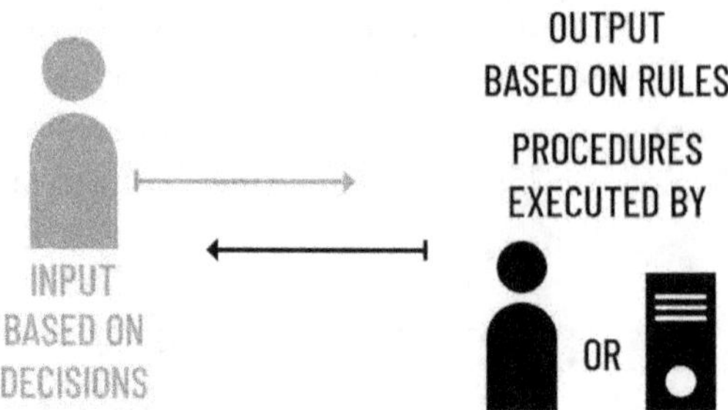

Figure 6. Input by the player an output based on rules executed by players or computers.

When analyzing game systems [13], we encounter several components. Firstly, we have the players who actively participate and interact within the system. Additionally, there are various elements comprising the system, including components, procedures, and a rule set that governs their interaction and function [14].

Interaction within game systems manifests in two primary directions. On one hand, players engage with the system by making strategic moves, choices, and providing input. On the other hand, the game itself responds to these actions by providing feedback to the players (see figure 6). Digital games excel in this aspect, featuring an automated process where outcomes are calculated within the game's programming, invisible to the players. For instance, in a role-playing game, attacking an enemy can be as simple as pressing a button, with all calculations performed automatically in the background. In contrast, analogue

[13] According to Niklas Luhmann, a system as a entity that operates mostly independently of its environment. In his work, he emphasizes that a system consists of elements, relations between these elements (30-32), and a boundary that distinguishes it from its environment. These elements interact within the system according to specific ruleset, producing outputs that loop back into the system, influencing its behavior (Luhmann 154). Furthermore Luhmann emphasizes the autonomy of systems, highlighting their ability to self-organize and adapt to changes in their environment (76).

[14] When examining games as systems, Järvinen describes three categories of game elements (55): Systemic, compound, and behavioral. The systemic elements encompass components and the environment, representing the physical dimension of the game. Compound elements are defined by the ruleset, theme, and interface of the game. Lastly, behavioral elements refer to the players and their context within the game. Moreover, Järvinen analyzes each element in terms of its ownership: whether it pertains to oneself, another player, or the game itself (57). Money in games, much like in the real world, can change ownership according to the flow of the game.

games require players to physically interact with and manipulate components, such as rolling dice and performing calculations, thereby exposing the inner mechanics of the system during gameplay. Those actions executed by the players for the system are called procedures [15].

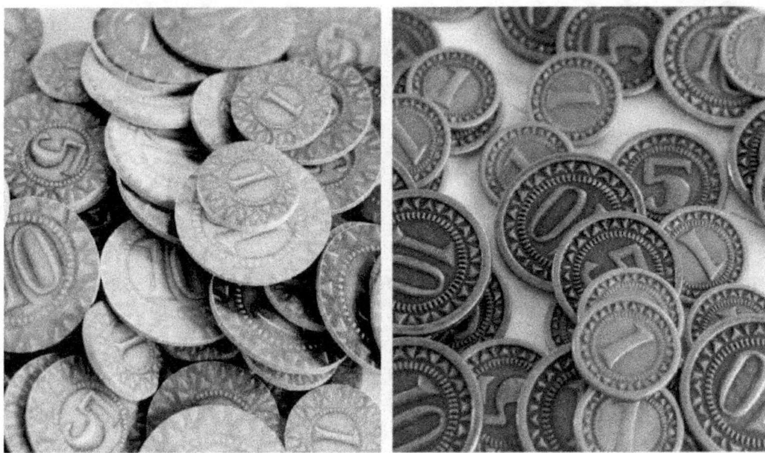

Figure 7. Cardboard and metal coins in comparison for the game *Orléans* (Stockhausen).

Understanding the unique underlying characteristics of board games is essential for grasping their appeal and functionality. Consider the role of money in board games as an example: Money can assume diverse material forms, ranging from wooden tokens to cardboard or metal coins. The popularity of metal coins correlates with the rise of crowdfunding platforms like *Kickstarter*, as players are willing to invest in tactile experiences that enhance immersion [16].

---

[15] Järvinen defines procedures as actions taken by the game system to assign value to different game states and outcomes by handing out rewards or penalties to the players. And for managing the interrelations of game elements. So in general procedures handle the flow and manipulation of information within the system (Järvinen 71). In an analogue game this could mean that when a player encounters a specific situation an event card is drawn, triggering a particular chain of events and potentially altering the game state. This chain of events is managed by a procedure outlined within the rule set of the game.

[16] There are numerous examples of *Kickstarter* campaigns that offer metal coins as an in-game currency, usually as an optional upgrade for an additional pledge. These upgrades

It's worth noting that paper money, although more common in analogue games in the United States, sees less use in Europe[17]. A similar but more stable alternative to thin and hard-to-handle paper money is the reverse side of cards. They, or even the cards themselves, can also function as a form of currency within board games. In general, the tangible nature of money holds significance; it encourages physical interaction among players and interaction inherent to the game, enriching the overall gameplay experience.

The concept of money in board games serves multiple purposes. It acts as a medium through which players interact, execute rules, and assign values. Moreover, it can contribute to storytelling within the game. In essence, money in board games embodies the essence of gaming itself—it's not just a means of exchange but also a fundamental component and a medium through which players interact. The concept of money can enrich the gameplay experience due to its weight and importance, connected to real-world concepts. In analogue games, money is always interpreted in ways that people have learned in the real world.

2.1 Diamonds Club

Diamonds Club (Dorn) is a game about wealthy individuals in the 19th century encompassing purchases, investments, wealth accumulation and gardening. In the game, plastic coins serve as both: a currency and an asset to visualize occupation. The core mechanic requires players to place a coin on an action space to activate it, with each action space requiring one coin as the basic cost. If a player wishes to activate an action space adjacent to one already occupied by a coin, they must pay one additional coin for each adjacent coin. These coins are stacked on the game board.

---

are usually designed to resemble the cardboard coins found in the basic edition game. These coins may reference historical currency, such as the metal coins in *Wayfarers of the South Tigris* (Macdonald and Phillips), or they may be futuristic creations, like the triangular metal coins available for *Xia: Legends of a Drift System* (Miller).

[17] Since the 1990s, there has been a decline in the use of paper money in games (Bracey 6). Bracey highlights the absence of paper money in so-called euro-games, a genre primarily originating in Germany and Europe. He attributes this to the better handling of cardboard coins compared to paper money. Paper money crumples, tears, and can even be blown away by movements (99).

This mechanic serves to visualize the cost of specific spaces on the game board and introduces a spatial element [18]. As the game progresses, the cost of spaces increases, reflecting the growing investment required to access certain actions and/or areas. At the end of each round, the game board may be filled with coins, illustrating the three-dimensional economic landscape of the game.

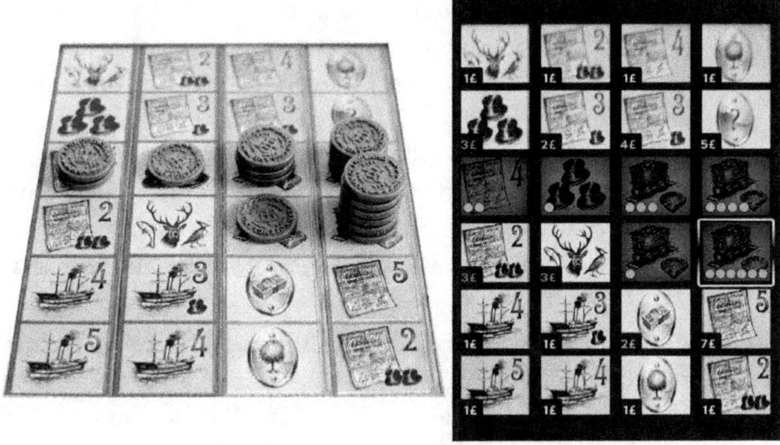

Figure 8. Comparison of the physical game (Dorn) and the digital mockup.

To demonstrate the contrast between the physical and digital approaches within games, a mockup was created. In the digital version, players can observe the price of each space and witness immediate adjustments in surrounding spaces' prices [19]. While the underlying mechanics remain the same, the visual representation highlights the difference between manual coin placement and automatic adjustments in a digital environment. Where the analogue version creates a scenery of three dimensionally growing money piles the digital mock-

[18] In this regard, *Diamonds Club* takes on a rather abstract quality. Its visuals even evoke the aesthetics of games like *Checkers* or *Nine Men's Morris,* with discs being moved around and stacked on the game board.

[19] This is another example for the idea how to apply procedures with as little additional bookkeeping work for the players as possible. The prices for the different actions fields do not have to be calculated on the fly but are visible through the adjacent stacks of coins. Players keep track of the prices by placing their coins to activate the action. Of course players have to add those coins but the calculation is simple and the height of the stacks is giving an intuitive idea of what is expensive and what not.

up takes away that aspect for clear visuals—in other words: the real world fun of stacking money is taken away by a much needed visual clarity.

2.2 Lions of Lydia

The *Lions of Lydia,* minted under the rulership of *King Croesus,* marked an important early point of coinage in history as the first standardized gold coins used for payment[20]. Remarkably, there exists a game centered around this historical event. In *Lions of Lydia,* (Pac) players begin with only traders who exchange goods—placing their pawns at different spots earns them corresponding goods of various colors. As the game progresses, merchants emerge, represented by golden pawns. Interacting with these merchants players now have the opportunity to exchange goods for money, which serves as a wild card and is even needed for purchasing specific valuable cards in the game.

The appearance of these merchants later in the game signifies a shift from a currency-less start to the introduction of a new gameplay element, opening up new possibilities within the game[21]. It's a fascinating method of storytelling through the change of the game's inherent structure[22], allowing players to feel the shift in gameplay by expanding options.

---

[20] Coinage originated from the use of naturally occurring metal nuggets. The Lydians in Asia Minor stamped these with various symbols. From these marked pieces emerged what we now understand as coin images. *King Croesus* introduced the first gold coins as we understand them today—featuring the motifs of a lion and a bull (Jungwirth 7).

[21] This is the central thematic metaphor of *Lions of Lydia* and it deepens the players experience by incorporating various levels of gameplay: The available pieces change, the options increase, the rhythm changes and the amount of player interaction changes (Schipp 22). For Shipp "metaphoric mechanics differ from metaphoric actions in that metaphoric mechanics are broader concepts that can be applied to the game as a structural whole." (21)

[22] As Arnaudo describes in his book *Storytelling in the Modern Boardgame,* it is the "inner dynamic of the represented event [...] when the game pieces behave to an extent like they would in the fictional reality they present." (23) In *Lions of Lydi*a the game pieces not only behave similarly to their real-world counterparts—even if it is on an abstracted level—but they also change and thereby alter the structure of the game in a manner modeled after reality.

2.3 Isle of Skye

The basic concept of *Isle of Skye* (Pelikan and Pfister) combines elements of tile laying, reminiscent of games like *Carcassonne* (Wrede), with a unique pricing system. Players have tiles at their disposal and secretly assign a value to each tile[23]. In the pictured example (see figure 9), the axe tile indicates that the tile leftmost will be removed, with the other one tile priced at two coins and the one on the right side at seven coins.

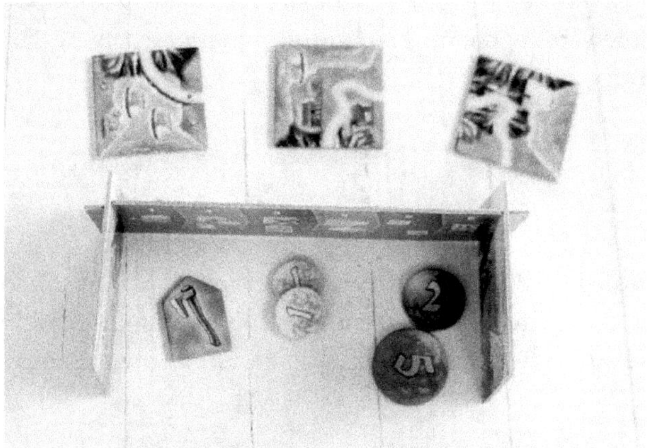

Figure 9. Hidden price and the axe to remove the tile on the left side in *Isle of Skye* (Pelikan and Pfister).

In this system, if a player wishes to acquire a tile, they must pay the designated price. In the example, this would mean that for the cheaper tile, the offering player would receive two coins and additionally get back his own two coins,

[23] *Isle of Skye* incorporates various layers of imperfect information. Players randomly draw tiles from a bag and must set their prices without knowing the values set by others or which tiles will return to the bag. Imperfect information involves revealing the game state gradually, and Björk and Holopainen discuss when and how this information is unveiled to players (124). In *Isle of Skye* there are two key moments involving imperfect information. One is more intimate: drawing tiles from a bag. The other is a group experience: after all players set their prices, they simultaneously reveal their offerings by lifting their player screens. This moment evokes a combination of emotions as players react to excluded—but desired—tiles or exceptionally high prices, and simultaneously assessing the situation to make their subsequent decisions.

which defined the price. If a tile remains unsold, the player who priced it must forfeit that amount to keep the tile.

Essentially, this game employs a variation of the *I cut, you choose*[24] concept, where one player divides a resource into two parts, and the other player selects which part they want. This dynamic encourages players to strive for a common language, akin to the norming, storming, and performing phases of group dynamics observed in team-building exercises[25]. Through the duration of 60 to 90 minutes, players as a group establish their own valuation system for the various tiles they trade, creating an individual and evolving language of value within the game.

3. QE

The last example is called *QE* (Birnbaum), which stands for quantitative easing, a term referring to the response of central banks during the banking and financial crisis of 2007-2008, where they injected money into the economy to stimulate it (Joyce, et al. 271).

What's particularly fascinating about this game—once again—is its mechanics for defining value: players bid for companies represented by discs placed in the center of the table. One player acts as the auctioneer, publicly stating the amount they wish to bid, while all other players secretly write down their own bids for the same company. The auctioneer then collects all the bids, compares them, and

---

[24] This technique of splitting something is one often used by parents when dividing something sweet. The underlying idea is to ensure fairness, as the person dividing knows the other will choose the larger piece (Engelstein and Shalev 326). In *Isle of Skye* this concept is expanded into a strategic dimension: How much am I willing to pay for this tile, and how high is the price I am willing to let it go for? It becomes a meaningful decision regarding the threshold of ownership.

[25] The model of group development known as forming–storming–norming–performing was initially introduced by Bruce Tuckman in 1965. He argues that these phases are unavoidable for a team to progress, confront challenges, address issues, devise solutions, organize tasks, and achieve outcomes. Tuckman emphasized that these inevitable phases played a crucial role in the growth and advancement of teams (66). *Isle of Skye* with its dynamic pricing system, effectively simulates this process within a brief timeframe, particularly evident when played with a new group for the first time.

awards the disc to the highest bidder[26]. What makes this intriguing is that the actual amounts bid remain undisclosed, adding an element of mystery. Furthermore, there are no limits to the bidding amounts—players can bid any sum, ranging from thousands to billions, reflecting the potential of banks and countries to create money out of nothing. However, the twist comes at the game's end: the player who has spent the most money overall is eliminated from the game and cannot win. *QE* combines hidden information, psychological depth, and a sense of mistrust among players, fostering discussions and negotiations that lead to a shared understanding of the value of assets within just 20 minutes of gameplay and a minimal ruleset.

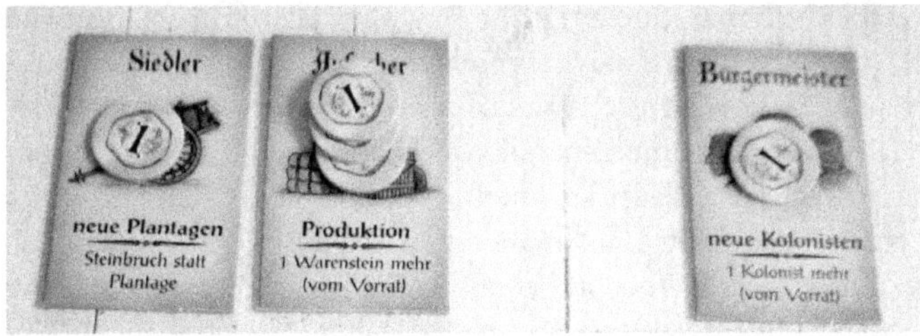

Figure 10. Action spaces getting more valuable through stacks of coins in *Puerto Rico* (Seyfarth).

4. The qualities of money in analogue games

All of these four examples demonstrate unique ways of incorporating the concept and the qualities of 'money' into analogue games. Initially, the requirement for analogue games to be highly transparent due to their non-digital, non-responsive nature—where players must manually execute

[26] In QE, a variation of blind bidding is used, or more precisely, a first-price sealed bid auction, where "potential buyers submit sealed bids and the highest bidder is awarded the item" (McAfee 702). In analogue games, various bidding systems can be found, each with its own emotional impact. The direct competition and the empathic guessing of other players' actions create a unique tension, contrasting the silent decision-making process—referred to by Ewary as the "inner opera" (108)—with the evaluation of outcomes. Unlike in a real auction for an object, the outcome is never static but serves to change the game state, thereby influencing enabling subsequent meaningful decisions.

procedures for the gaming system [27]—may seem like a disadvantage. However, this absence of digital automatism actually opens the door for creative and distinctive uses of money in games. On one hand, the component may be utilized in ways beyond just serving as a currency [28]. On the other hand, players, with all their flaws and unpredictability, become an integral part of these gaming systems and the design process [29]. Money, as a medium of economics, serves as

---

[27] Interface quality: Since players are required to manage money, it makes sense from an interface design perspective to either streamline the handling process as much as possible or enrich it with additional functions. The first approach primarily considers materiality and how much and how often a player's money supply changes. If the changes are frequent but small, a money track with a scoring token makes sense—as seen in *Grand Austria Hotel* (Gigli and Luciani). If the game generally deals with resources and money is just one of them, it's more practical to represent money as cardboard coins in various values. The second approach—enriching the material with additional functions—can lead to interesting spatial aspects, as seen in games like *Diamonds Club*. Another example is *Puerto Rico* (Seyfarth), where unused action spaces become more valuable—each round, an additional coin is placed. The value becomes visible and tempting to players (see figure 9). It's evident how difficult it is to separate qualities, as the mechanism is integrated into the system and works through a visual stimulus, but also evokes emotional reactions like temptation and greed.

[28] Systemic quality: Essentially, money as an asset always has an impact on the system. The question is therefore how it is integrated into the game. Is it used as currency, as seen in games like *Orléans* (Stockhausen), or as a material wildcard, as in *Lions of Lydia*? Or is the emergence of prices and values a central element, as in *Pirates of Maracaibo* (Pfister)? In this game, various goods have dynamic values based on their availability, which players can manipulate, enabling forms of indirect interaction: if a player obtains resources of a certain type, their value decreases for all players. This allows players to influence each other's victory point standings. Often, there are also hybrid forms, such as in *Bohnanza,* where money is found on the back of the cards. This not only saves material but also carries systemic aspects: when a certain type of beans is harvested in the game, a certain amount of these resources—here: beans—is turned to the backside, revealing the money side. As a result, players receive money, but a corresponding amount of beans is also removed from the game, causing noticeable changes in availability.

[29] Social quality: The deep sociocultural embedding of money in our society also enables various forms of interaction in games: bidding, bribing, bluffing, and many more. These actions, often associated with significant risks in reality, create compelling situations for players. In *Bohnanza* players trade beans that can be converted into money—money primarily represents victory points but can also be spent. Tresham's *Civilization* combines

a means through which people communicate—not just in terms of numbers. Analogue games, due to the visible and integral role of humans, excel at incorporating these dynamics of communication media. This necessity arises because a complex simulation is simply not feasible.

Furthermore, money represented within the game as real tactile components and labeled as 'money' inherently carries specific connotations projected onto the components by players[30]. Being labeled as 'money' imparts a multitude of attributes automatically attached to the components by players[31]. This label fundamentally alters real people's perceptions. The idea and understanding of what for and how money in the real world is used creates a mental framework that (hopefully) is embedded by the game itself to create the feeling of a smooth and natural gameplay. Even if the money is fake.

---

a trading mechanism—which also inspired *Bohnanza*—with the elimination of unwanted cards: players must truthfully announce only the total value of the cards they offer, without revealing which cards are actually in the set. The resulting emotional situations revolve around deception, trickery, schadenfreude, and frustration. Similarly, in *Sheriff of Nottingham* (Halaban and Zatz)players attempt to bribe the titular sheriff to smuggle goods. The sheriff never knows which goods are actually being smuggled, whom to trust, or how much to demand for leniency.

[30] The already mentioned physical quality cannot be emphasized enough. While it can be enjoyable to handle cardboard coins—as in *Machi Koro* (Suganuma)—or paper money—as in *Grand Cru* (Blum)—this experience is heightened by using heavy metal coins. The sensation of holding and playing with weighty and even noisy objects, whether it's pirate gold or ancient coins, is difficult to replicate and consistently evokes a remarkable reaction from players.

[31] Narrative quality: Naturally, interactions with players through money create exciting situations that are rich in drama and essentially tell a story. Particularly, games with a high social quality in integrating money evoke such situations. When the *Sheriff of Nottingham* is cunningly deceived, these are moments that are especially memorable. The other dimension is the one pursued by *Lions of Lydia* which actually sets a point in the game where the game state changes significantly—intentionally placed by the game designer at precisely that moment. A final example that combines different qualities of money is *Architects of the West Kingdom* (Macdonald and Phillips). Here, players can decide for themselves how righteously they want to play. Those who buy from the black market or steal lose virtue. This results in being excluded from building the cathedral, which yields victory points, but also not having to pay taxes anymore. It's a conscious decision by the players on how they want to handle money, which directly affects their options in the game.

About the Author

Klemens Franz studied *Information Management* in Graz and *Digital Games Research and Design* in Tampere, Finland. He worked as an assistant for new media technologies at the FH Joanneum. In 2006 he founded the atelier198 where he has worked on over 300 analogue games as an illustrator, graphic designer and editor. In the last couple of years he started to talk about analogue games and his experience with their visuals. He worked on the interactive aspects of exhibitions, held game-design workshops and wrote about gaming culture. He teaches *Digital Imaging* and *Media Theory* at the FH Joanneum.

Bluesky: @atelier198.bsky.scoial
Website: https://www.atelier198.com

References

Arnaudo, Marco. Storytelling in the Modern Board Game: Narrative Trends from the Late 1960s to Today. McFarland, Incorporated, Publishers, 2018.

Bachmann, Manfred, and Wolfram Metzger. Vom Marktstand zum Supermarkt: der Kaufladen in Puppenwelt und Wirklichkeit. Info Verlagsgesellschaft, 1992.

Barthes, Roland. Mythologies. Vintage, 1993.

Bjork, Staffan, and Jussi Holopainen. Patterns in Game Design. Charles River Media, 2005.

Bracey, Robert. Playing with Money. Spink and Son, 2019.

Caillois, Roger. Man, Play, and Games. University of Illinois Press, 2001.

Clothier, Richard F., Play Money of American Children. Richard F. Clothier, 1985.

Darrow, Charles B. Board Game Apparatus. US2026082. United States Patent Office, 1935.

Engelstein, Geoffrey, and Isaac Shalev. Building Blocks of Tabletop Game Design: An Encyclopedia of Mechanisms.
CRC Press, 2022.

Erway, Scott. Loving Eurogames: A Quest for the Well Played Game. Griffin Creek Press, 2018.

Fittà, Marco. Spiele und Spielzeug in der Antike: Unterhaltung und Vergnügen im Altertum. Konrad Theiss Verlag GmbH, 1998.

Ham, Ethan. Tabletop Game Design for Video Game Designers. CRC Press, 2015.

Huizinga, Johan. Homo Ludens: A Study of the Play-element in Culture. Routledge, 1998.

Järvinen, Aki. Games Without Frontiers: Theories and Methods for Game Studies and Design. University of Tampere, 2008.

Joyce, Michael, and David Miles, and Andrew Scott, and Dimitri Vayanos. Quantitative Easing and Unconventional Monetary Policy – An Introduction. The Economic Journal Vol. 122, No. 564, pp. 271-288. 2012.

Jungwirth, H. Erfolgreich Sammeln von Münzen. Pinguin Verlag, 1972.

Kutschera, Volker. Die Welt im Spielzeug. Ellert & Richter, 1995.

Luhmann, Niklas. Systemtheorie der Gesellschaft. Suhrkamp Verlag, 2017.

Maß, Sandra. Kinderstube des Kapitalismus? Monetäre Erziehung im 18. und 19. Jahrhundert. De Gruyter, 2017.

McAfee, R. Preston, and John McMillan. Auctions and Bidding. Journal of Economic Literature Vol. XXV, pp. 699-738. 1987.

Magie, Lizzie J. Game-Board. US748626. United States Patent Office, 1904.

Milton Bradley Company. Catalogue of Games, Sectional Pictures, Toys, Puzzles, Blocks and Novelties.
Milton Bradley Company, 1889.

Perkins, John. Why You Should NEVER Play MONOPOLY Again. Youtube. 8 February 2017,
https://www.youtube.com/watch?v=tL9wCYTWTDw.

Raddato, Carole. Dice players fresco from the Osteria della Via di Mercurio (VI 10,1.19, room b), in situ wall fresco, Pompeii (14880010983).jpg. https://commons.wikimedia.org, 2014.

Salen, Katie, and Eric Zimmerman. Rules of Play. MIT Press, 2003.

Shipp, Sarah. Thematic Integration in Board Game Design. CRC Press, 2024.

Snelling, Thomas. A View of the Origin, Nature, and Use of Jettons Or Counters. T. Snelling, 1769.

Suter, Beat. Rules of Play as a Framework for the magic circle. Games and Rules: Game Mechanics for the magic circle,
edited by Beat Suter, Mela Kocher, René Bauer. transcript Verlag, 2018.

Tönnesmann, Andreas. Monopoly: das Spiel, die Stadt und das Glück. Wagenbach, 2011.

Tuckman, Bruce W. Developmental Sequence in Small Groups. Group Facilitation: A Research and Applications Journal - Number 3, edited by Sandor P. Schuman. 2001.

Woods, Stewart. Eurogames: The Design, Culture and Play of Modern European Board Games. McFarland, Incorporated, Publishers, 2012.

Analogue games

Birnbaum, Gavin. *QE*. Strohmann Games, 2022.

Blum, Ulrich. *Grand Cru.* Eggertspiele, 2010.

Darrow, Charles B. *Monopoly.* Parker Brothers, *1935.*

Dorn, Rüdiger. *Diamonds Club.* Ravensburger Verlag GmbH, 2008.

Faidutti, Bruno. *Citadels.* Hans im Glück Verlags-GmbH, 2000.

Gigli, Virginio, and Simone Luciani. *Grand Austria Hotel.* Lookout Spiele GmbH, 2015.

Halaban, Sérgio, and André Zatz. *Sheriff of Nottingham.* Arcane Wonders, 2014.

Henn, Dirk. *Alhambra.* Queen Games, 2003.

Knizia, Reiner. *Orongo.* Ravensburger Verlag GmbH, 2014.

Macdonald, S J, and Shem Phillips. *Architects of the West Kingdom.* Garphill Games, 2018.

Macdonald, S J, and Shem Phillips. *Wayfarers of the South Tigris.* Garphill Games, 2022.

Miller, Cody. *Xia: Legends of a Drift System.* Far Off Games, 2014.

Pac, Jonny. *Lyons of Lydia.* Spielefaible, 2021.

Pelikan, Andreas, and Alexander Pfister. *Isle of Skye.* Lookout Spiele GmbH, 2015.

Pfister, Alexander. *Pirates of Maracaibo.* dlp games, 2023.

Rosenberg, Uwe. *Bohnanza.* AMIGO Spiel + Freizeit GmbH, 1997.

Seyfarth, Andreas. *Puerto Rico.* Ravensburger Verlag GmbH, 2002.

Shelley, Bruce, and Francis Tresham. *1830.* English second edition. Mayfair Games, 2011.

Stockhausen, Reiner. *Orléans.* dlp games, 2014.

Suganuma, Masao. *Machi Koro.* Franckh-Kosmos Verlags-GmbH & Co., 2014.

Tresham, Francis. *1829.* Hartland Trefoil Ltd., 1974.

Tresham, Francis. *Civilization.* Hartland Trefoil Ltd., 1980.

Wrede, Klaus-Jürgen. *Carcassonne.* Hans im Glück Verlags-GmbH, 2000.

THE ROLE OF MONEY FOR ATMOSPHERE IN BUS SIMULATION GAMES

Mario Donick

In bus simulation games, players operate buses to transport passengers. Usually, the main focus of these games is driving the vehicle itself – for relaxation, or for matching a schedule. However, in recent releases like "The Bus" and "Bus Simulator 21", additional tasks are included – such as selling tickets, processing payments, giving change money, and controlling passengers for tickets. Money in such games is depicted as made of certain materials (coins made of metal, bank notes made of paper, debit cards made of plastics, and smartphones made of plastics and glass). This supports a specific atmosphere which can be perceived with the lived body ("Leib", in the neophenomenological meaning). The goal of this paper is to show how money enhances atmospheric details of the situation, and thereby facilitates the player's incorporation and playful identification with the role.

Keywords: Money, Simulation, Atmosphere, Lived Body, Felt Body, Neophenomenology

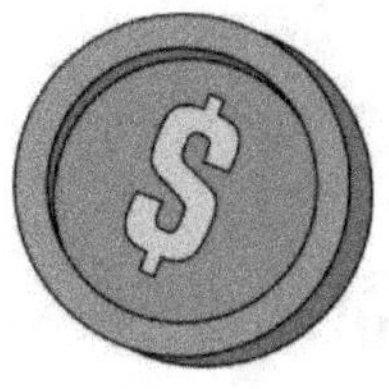

1. Introduction

Public transport simulation games are a sub-genre of both vehicle simulations and career simulations. In bus simulation games, players take on the role of a bus driver. They steer a bus through cities, transport passengers from A to B, try to keep to a tight schedule, but still make the ride comfortable for their passengers. But players do not just drive. They also sell tickets for money, and they control if passengers really have a ticket.

This paper discusses observations about the ticket selling aspect of such games from a mostly neophenomenological point of view (cf. Schmitz 2011, Böhme 1995). This view is interested in the player's subjective perceptions of the gaming situations, especially in the sense of the felt body (lived body; "Leib" in German) in contrast to sensations of the measurable, Cartesian body ("Körper" in German).

This paper discusses money in "The Bus" (TML/Aerosoft, 2021, still early access) and, to a lesser extent, "Bus Simulator 21" (Still Alive Games/Ascaron, 2021). The main focus of these games is driving the bus. "The Bus" offers a large part of the German capital Berlin as playground; the city center of Berlin is modeled very detailed, as are the busses themselves. "Bus Simulator 21" has also busses based on reality, but they are driven in two entirely fictional cities, one supposed to be at the U.S. west coast and one to be in some version of Austria. While "The Bus" offers real-world routes and -schedules, "Bus Simulator 21" allows players to create their own routes and traffic schedules, thereby extending the economic aspect.

2. Money in "Bus Simulator 21" and in "The Bus"

Selling tickets to passengers is a part of both games (fig. 1). When players stop at the bus stop and open the front door, passengers step inside the bus and often ask for a specific ticket (like student ticket or regular ticket) and pay some amount of money. The player selects the correct ticket in the bus on-board computer and prints it. If the passenger pays a too large amount of cash, the player has to give the correct amount of change money by pressing buttons of a coin dispenser.

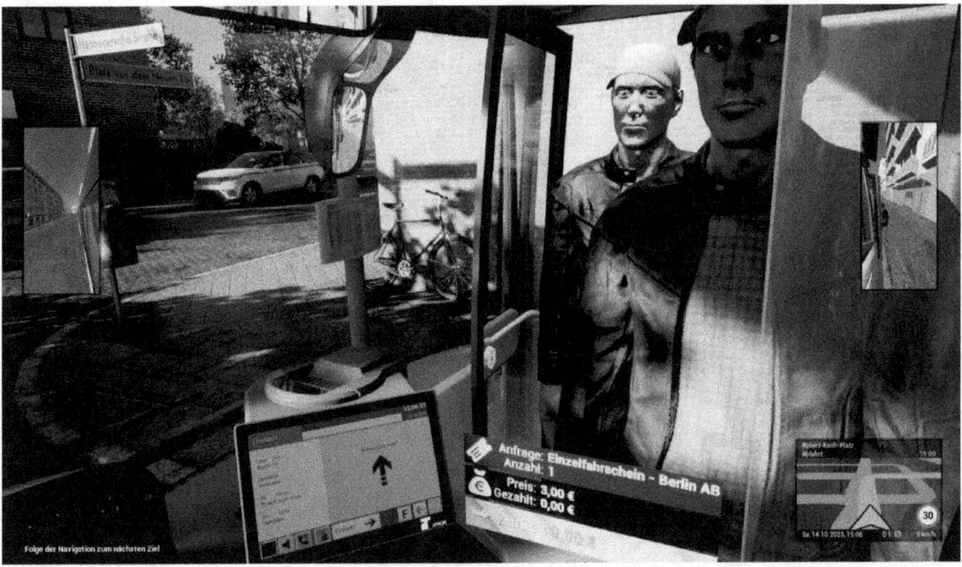

Figure 1. Simulated passengers in "The Bus" buy tickets from the bus driver (= the player). Players must use the on-board computer to select and print the correct ticket, as well as taking different steps to process the payment.

"Bus Simulator 21" models this process in a simplified and abstract way; ticket types are generic, and money is not visible, even if it is modeled internally. "The Bus", on the other hand, is quite realistic in this regard – the available ticket types and pricing zones match the city of Berlin; the user interface of the on-board computer resembles its real-world counterpart; the passengers use different means of paying – and if they pay in cash, actual coins and bank notes are visible and must be taken by clicking on each coin and note.

The ticket selling process is, in terms of game mechanics, very trivial. However, it adds to the atmosphere of the games in some ways, and it increases the immersion in the played role of a 'traditional' bus driver, who is still responsible for ticket selling at many places. This role play situation uses certain game mechanics, and it also has some narrative aspects (like the narrative of a typical shift in the job as a bus driver, as in "The Bus", or the narrative of a little bus company which grows over time and must be managed, besides the mere driving, as in "Bus Simulator 21" [1]). As players, we seek both the mechanics and narratives of the "dream job" bus driver, but we may also seek a certain atmosphere which associate with that job.

3. The Neophenomenological Perspective

3.1 Atmosphere

"Atmosphere" is a term that is often used intuitively without any further definition. For example, we can perceive the focused tense atmosphere of an interesting conference session, and the lively relaxed atmosphere of a conference dinner. In the same way, players can also perceive a world in a computer game as atmospheric – maybe as "dense" (without further specification), maybe as "exciting" (like in a sports game), as "frightening" (like in a horror survival game), or as "stressful" (like in a bus simulator where a tight schedule must be kept).

In this paper, the term "atmosphere" is used in a phenomenological perspective, although there are different takes on atmospheres in various varieties of phenomenology. Especially the question if an atmosphere can be made intentionally (created with specific means by designers or artists), or if an atmosphere is 'just there' is a point of discussion, because the answer to that question decides if we can talk about atmospheres only in a reception-oriented

---

[1] In addition to driving busses and handling money during ticket selling, "Bus Simulator 21" includes a (simple) economic simulation. Players need to create routes to connect the various parts of a fictional city, and buy the busses used for serving the routes. Busses currently not driven by the players are driven by NPC drivers. Successful routes with many passengers generate income used for paying the ongoing costs of the bus company, for extending the route network, for buying additional busses, for upgrading bus stops, or for replacing Diesel-powered busses by electric busses. The money paid by the individual passengers to the bus driver is part of that income – the game shows that money is necessary for the simulated bus company to operate. The economic simulation is very forgiving, though. Unlike real-world public transport companies, the bus company in "Bus Simulator 21" usually never struggles financially, and it is next to impossible to go bankrupt.

aesthetics, or if also a production-oriented view (how to 'create' a specific atmosphere as designer) is possible.

According to Gernot Böhme, atmospheres can be created by work on objects (Böhme 1995, 35f). He gives the examples of landscape parks and stage design (ibid.). When this view is taken, it's reasonable to assume that game designers can arrange certain design elements to achieve a certain atmosphere as well, and that emerged atmospheres can be traced back to certain design elements. [2]

In contrast to a production-oriented view, Hermann Schmitz sees atmospheres as free-floating and not emitted by objects: "An atmosphere […] is a borderless, indivisible, extended occupation of a surface-less space [own translation]" (Schmitz 2011, 89). From this point of view, it may be questioned whether atmospheres can be created at all, and whether we can identify specific elements in games related to the creation of atmospheres. Schmitz' take is rooted in his very comprehensive works on the felt body, which also offers a specific vocabulary to facilitate speaking about felt body perceptions.

This paper follows a pragmatic approach: The player perception of a game and the felt atmospheres during play can be described with terms suggested by Schmitz (see the next sections [3]), while at the same time it is reasonable to assume that specific design elements of the game add to the atmosphere perceived by players.

---

[2] The field of game studies is studying atmospheres since several years, most notably the works collected in Huberts/Standke (2014) and the work by Jung (2023). A particularly comprehensive example on how to study atmospheres is Felix Zimmermann's work on atmospheres of the past (Zimmermann 2023). Zimmermann develops and presents a method to identify elements in digital games involved in creating atmospheres which are perceived as 'authentic' by players. Such atmospheres can be quite powerful, and this becomes a problem if more specific contents of the game (such as narratives, motifs, or facts) contradict the felt authenticity.

[3] For more detailed examples on how to analyze game situations with neophenomenological terminology, cf. Donick/Schwelgengräber 2024 and Donick 2022. Helpful for a broader understanding is also Schwelgengräber (2022), who provides detailed analyses on television and movie perceptions.

3.2 Perceptions of the lived/felt body

The player perspective is strongly related to the concept of "Leib" or, in English, "lived body" or "felt body", in contrast to the physical, measurable "Körper" or "body". Böhme (2019) gives the following definition: "body is human nature in external experience; lived body is human nature in self-experience [own translation]" (Böhme 2019, 41). The external experience is related to the scientific view on the body, as in anatomy, physiology and medical sciences (ibid.), whereas self-experience is our own, subjective view on ourselves.

In everyday life, we don't separate both terms, of course; experiences of both the body and the lived body are related. Also, the "Leib" is not a distinct 'thing'; the term is more of a shorthand to refer to those perceptions near the region of the body which cannot be clearly assigned to one of physical senses. A simple example for phenomena felt by the "Leib" is our ability to move among a group of people without collision – without the need of constantly looking out for others and without the need for analyzing measurable distances. Schmitz gives a similar example for this "intelligence of the lived body [own translation]" (Schmitz 2021, 87): our immediate ability to intuitively and very quickly evade a danger, such as preventing an imminent car accident (ibid.).

Schmitz provides a vocabulary to facilitate speaking about perceptions of the lived body. Particular importance is given to the terms narrowing and widening, as these are central to the so-called "vital drive [own translation]" ("vitaler Antrieb", Schmitz 2011, 16). Schmitz writes: "Being physical means [...] first and foremost: standing in the middle between narrowness and width and not completely breaking away from either one or the other [own translation]" (Schmitz 1987, 273). In our everyday world we constantly have experiences affecting the vital drive; for example, we may feel tense moments as tightening, and relaxed moments as expanding.

Sensations of narrowness and expansion can also arise when perceiving media, which is something everyone knows who has ever slipped back and forth in their chair while watching an exciting film, tense and contracted, and then sank back and relaxed into their seat when the exciting scene dissolves (cf. Schwelgengräber 2022). Gaming situations are even more intense in this regard, because in games players are usually actively engaged with the situations.

3.3 Situations and Constellations

According to Schmitz, a situation comprises of facts, problems and programs (Schmitz 2011, 75). Facts are *what is*, problems are *what is meant to be* (ibid.). Programs are norms, wishes, ideas, etc. that influence how we perceive, judge and deal with the situation with regard to the problem (ibid.). However, situations do not appear step by step, and the three mentioned aspects can not be separated. Situations appear to us suddenly and holistically. Therefore, a situation's 'meanings' cannot be explained in detail (the attempt to identify single elements of a situation would lead to mere constellations of single elements, but still not grasping the essential aspects of the situation); situations are, as Schmitz says, "internally diffuse [own translation]" ("binnendiffus", ibid. 118).

The problem and program terms are therefore a bit different than the everyday use of these words suggests. In everyday life a problem is an undesirable state which has to be transformed into a desired state, whereby a barrier must be overcome during the transformation (cf. Dörner 1984). The steps of such a transformation would usually be viewed as the program: First I do this, then I do that, etc., in order to achieve the desired state.

However, from a neophenomenological point of view, the focus is not on doing something, but on perceiving the situation. That's why the term "problem" (in this perspective) should not be misunderstood as something to be 'solved'. Similarly, the term "program" should not be misunderstood as a step-by-step solution – programs are the norms and desires which are the background for our decisions and acting.

In every-day life, we are constantly reducing the complexity of holistic situations into workable constellations. It's a necessity for survival (Schmitz 2021, 87). Many digital games are designed to provide workable constellations as well. They want us to tackle very specific problems and reward us for being successful. Games use atmospheres as a means of enriching and contextualizing their problem-posing situations. To better understand this, it can be worthwhile to single out elements comprising the situation and analyze them as constellations. Zimmermann (2023) does this in order to learn how historic atmospheres are made by game designers. In a somewhat related manner, in the remainder of this paper I ask how money in bus simulations is related to the atmosphere of the simulated situations.

4. Situation, Material, Atmosphere, and Money in Bus Simulations

4.1 Playing Situation and Played Situation

When playing a bus simulation, we are in a complex situation which consists of both in-game and 'real' aspects. If we tried to split this overall situation into sub-situations, we could come up with (1) our own playing situation as players, and (2) the simulated situation of our played character:

1. The player's playing situation:

   a. Fact: The player plays the simulation game and perceives all its elements together, at once: the movement, the sounds, the other traffic, the signs, the people, the weather, while at the same time being the 'real' world's space with all the other elements of that space to perceive, and all the contexts which influence the playing.

   b. Problem: The player may use the game for several reasons, for example: Relaxing or seeking escapism; exploring a virtual city; remembering the last vacation in the depicted city; achieving a high score (being on time, earning lots of money with the bus company, …), learning something about the job of a bus driver or the technology; or just creating chaos in the city.

   c. Program: Players play the game based on their own values and goals (which also define the problem), for example as a serious simulator, a driving game for the sake of driving, a tool for learning about the job, a tool for learning traffic rules, etc.

2. The bus driver's simulated situation:

   a. Fact: The bus driver has to follow a schedule and transport passengers in a comfortable way to their destination.

   b. Problem: The bus driver has to navigate the city, not crash, obey traffic rules, care about ticketing, be on time, …

c. Program: Is the schedule more important than traffic rules? Are rules more important than the schedule? Is safety more important than the schedule? Or is there an equilibrium between schedule, rules, and safety?

During play (to emphasize this again) we perceive *one* situation with aspects of both, and we perceive it at once and holistically; it is internally diffuse. The attempt to split the situation in a playing situation and a played situation leads can not grasp this situation fully. It leads to a constellation and is an attempt to tackle the whole complex for the purpose of analysis.

When the player is focused on the game, their overall situation is influenced by what is shown on the screen. Due to the player's ability to playful identification ("spielerische Identifizierung", cf. Schmitz 1977, 465), aspects of the presented situation are incorporated in the player's lived body ("Einleibung", cf. Schmitz 2011, 38) and become part of their situation.

The norms, goals and wishes of the programs influence how the problems are tackled – if being on time is a dominant norm in the player's simulated situation (and maybe their real life as well), they may disobey traffic rules (like being faster than allowed or crossing a red traffic light). If safety or passenger comfort is the dominant norm, they may sacrifice punctuality for that. If the player takes the game very seriously and tries to accomplish all goals at once – being on time, no accidents, no rule breaks, fast ticketing – they may feel a form of stress. The game may feel as work – like the job it tries to depict.

In the dynamics of the vital drive, players may feel the stress while processing the tickets as a "narrowness" within their "Leib" (and maybe even their body). This can happen, for example, when the player knows they are already late and each passenger without a ticket delays them further (especially those passengers who dare to pay with lots of small coins or large bank notes which both takes more time to process, in contrast to handing the exact ticket price, cash-less payment methods, or no need for ticket purchase at all).

Contrary, the player may feel a relaxed body tension and an expansion of the lived body when just a few or no passengers buy tickets, because they can save time this way, which makes it easier to adhere to the other norms. The player may also feel an expansion when they can change to a special bus lane or an empty street with only green traffic lights. The empty street functions as a motion suggestion ("Bewegungssuggestion"), thereby motivating faster, uninterrupted driving. This allows to drive less stressed and to catch up with the schedule.

If the norm "keep the schedule" is not an important part of the player's problem and program (because the player just enjoys the driving experience), the player may just drive in a relaxed way, safely, within the speed margins, and just be happy with the ticketing process, the sound of the coins, giving change money, the sound of printing the ticket, etc.

4.2 Material and Atmosphere

The ticket selling process is about money and handling money – taking coins and bank notes and giving change money using the coin dispenser or processing wireless payment methods used by the passengers. The modeling of this process is referencing material aspects of the payment methods which we know from the real world. Proverbs like "money doesn't stink" or "the scent of money" address the material character of money. The proverbs are positive statements about money; they frame money as something desirable, regardless from where it comes from.

Of course, if you ever hold your nose near a stack of old bank notes that have gone through lots and lots of other hands before yours, or if you ever smelled at your hands after you held a bunch of coins, you probably noted that money *can* have a scent and that it is not always positive. The scent is a mixture of the coin's and bank notes' own materials (the different kinds of metal, the paper and its structure), and the traces of lots of other people and their environments. Modern payment methods, like debit cards or payment apps on your phone, are different, but also made of a material – plastics and glass, with a certain feel.

For phenomenology, the sensory input of a material is not sufficient to describe how we perceive it. Böhme (1995) points out that feeling a material as having some quality (like its warmth) is neither explained by analyzing it physically, nor by using it as (part of) an object, but by perceiving the material as an atmosphere (Böhme 1995, 54).

According to Böhme, materials emit atmospheres, which we absorb in our perception and feelings. For example, a cheap mobile phone made of plastic emits a different atmosphere than an expensive mobile phone made of metal and glass – and we may associate one with a low-income and the other one with wealth (and we may even buy the expensive one even if we can't afford it, just to present ourselves as wealthy). Material and social meaning are connected (ibid., 55f.).

Böhme considers materials a combination of both so-called synesthetic characters and social characters (ibid., 53):

- Synesthetic characters means that two or more qualities are perceived together (ibid., 54). For example, the material of an object can be perceived as having a warm color (or emitting a warm atmosphere), because several qualities are perceived together, such as its color, its shape, or its softness. We could add that also the context in which the perception happens can have an influence – context like our personal disposition for felt body perceptions ("leibliche Disposition", cf. Schmitz 1987, 274) in a certain situation, as well as other materials with which the item may be arranged.

- Social character refers to the association of a material's atmosphere with certain ways of life. For example, an expensive golden watch with a leather strap may feel warm due to its colors, and therefore be associated with a wealthy way of life (cf. Böhme 1995, 52).

In digital games, the visuals and sounds of objects are means of transporting material qualities. They transport a specific atmosphere. An expensive leather seat in a business jet is associated with other synesthetic and social characters than a hard passenger seat in a city bus. Simulations of these types of vehicles convey these qualities as atmospheres. [4]

Regarding money in bus simulation games, we can think of the visual and audible qualities of the coins and bank notes passenger use to pay in "The Bus", and the typical "coin" sound emitted when pressing the coin dispenser to give change money (which sounds a bit like money coming out of a gambling machine). The "cash register" sound in "Bus Simulator 21" is similar; it is played

---

[4] In a bus simulator, NPC passengers can support a specific atmosphere as well, for example by clothing styles (cheap looking or expensive looking?), behavior (sitting calmly? Disturbing others with loud music? Specific small talk topics?) or by riding the bus with or without ticket. Thanks to the reviewers for this remark.

when players take the role of a ticket inspector and find passengers without ticket (fig. 2).

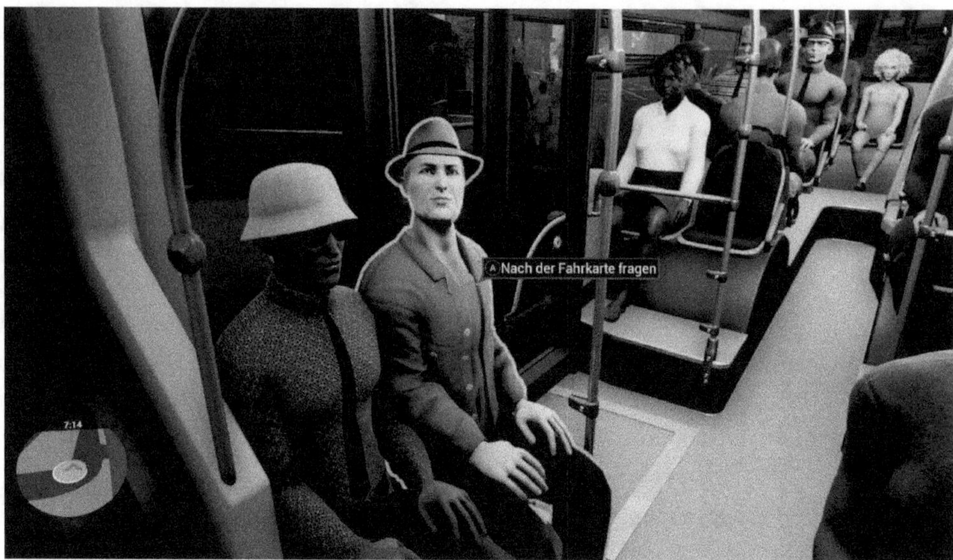

Figure 2. Players of "Bus Simulator 2021" can also work as ticket inspectors. When passengers without a ticket are found, a cash register sound is played by the game.

4.3 Payment Types and Materials in "The Bus"

In "Bus Simulator 21", change money is only audible, but not visible. Payment given by the passengers and change money returned is visually abstracted into a message field shown next to the money dispenser.

In contrast, "The Bus" tries to convey a very haptic feeling of the money (fig. 3).

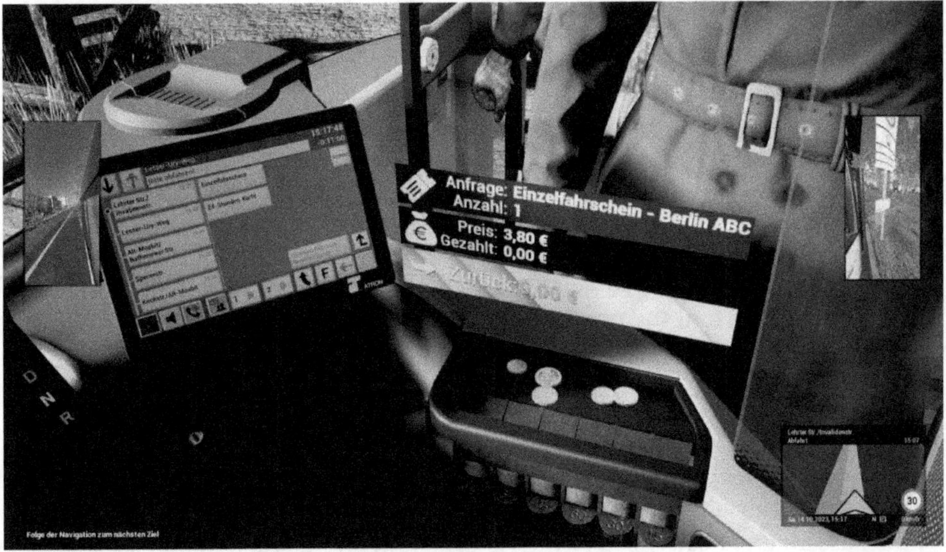

Figure 3. Paying in "The Bus" is simulated in great detail. Each single coin is clickable, and change money is given by pressing the buttons of the coin dispenser. Cashless payment methods are also being used by the simulated passengers.

Several payment types are depicted in this game – people pay with coins, with bank notes, with debit cards, and with their mobile phones. So, when the virtual people pay, they use payment means of different materials. The synesthetic characters of the materials can be associated with social characters, which can lead to a lot of interpretations:

- **Paying cash with coins:** typical coin sounds; hard, metallic, heavy, warm look (golden color, copper color) or cool look (silver color). Traditionally, lots of coins were associated with wealth (many coins = lots of money), but nowadays, coins may also be associated with either traditional people still sticking to cash (maybe sceptics of newer payment methods) or with people who may not be wealthy enough for payment methods other than coins.

- **Paying cash with bank notes:** soft, warm (paper); similar associations as coins, but possibly wealthier (e.g. using a 20 EUR bank note for paying a 3 EUR bus ticket).

- **Paying with debit card:** hard, warm (plastics); the card shows that the person has a bank account, i.e. the person conforms to certain norms. The person maybe also prefers efficient payment methods.

- **Paying with mobile phone:** smooth, glassy, both cold (visually) and warm (battery warmth, CPU warmth); similar associations as debit card, but possibly a younger person used to modern internet services and electronic payment options, and wealthy enough both to afford such a device and to be a customer of online payment providers.

The modeling of different payment types supports immersion in the played role (as bus driver). It becomes part of the felt atmosphere of the game, it adds detail to the situation, and thereby facilitates incorporation and playful identification. This, though, is possible also because we know from our everyday lives that public transport services cost money, and how ticket selling situations are typically structured. We can re-live such situations in and with the game.

If a player considers themselves a somewhat grumpy bus driver, they may tell the passenger: "Really, you pay the short trip with a 20 EUR note?", because they don't like to press the coin dispenser buttons a lot for giving change money. The player may also ask: "Seriously, you have to pay with so many small coins?", where they have to pick and possibly count the money, which on the one hand is strangely satisfying (because of the atmosphere that transports the haptics of the virtual money), but on the other hand is wasting time when the player's main interest is driving, not interacting with passengers, and the player mainly want to keep the schedule.

5. Outlook: Free Bus Rides

Ticket selling and identifying passengers without tickets integrate money into the driving simulation. Besides an enhanced atmosphere, due to a more complex situation, the inclusion of money makes players aware that passengers were not able to drive the bus if they had not any money – which, in the real world, is a big problem for many people, who are sometimes even criminalized.

By default, bus simulators depict this status quo with the inclusion of money related tasks. The implicit resulting message of the game is: "public transport is only for those with money". This is the norm. When a person pays, they adhere to the norm. If the person pays with a debit card or phone, the person presents themselves as financially solvent, able to use (i.e. to pay for) modern technology. When the person pays with lots of small coins, in a society where cashless payment is the norm, the person sticks out. Therefore, the different means of payment divide people into groups.

The settings of both "The Bus" and "Bus Simulator 21" allow players to adjust the probability of passenger ticket buying, down to 0 if players just want to drive without interruption. This basically means that players can simulate that everybody has already a ticket, or that rides are free.

The immediate effect of moneyless simulation is that everything feels smoother and the whole atmosphere is more relaxed. The stress level is lower, because it's much easier to keep the schedule. On the level of the lived body, the changes from expansion to narrowing are less hard. It is easier to devote oneself to the movement suggestions induced by the streets and the vehicle. Stopping at bus stops does not interrupt the flow of driving that much. The game loses the infantile "playing with money" aspect (the coins, their sounds), but the rhythm of playing the game – the vital drive we can perceive as narrowing and expanding in the phenomenological sense – is much smoother.

I can only imagine, without any proof or study, that a similar positive effect could occur if free public transport would become the norm in the real world. Bus simulation games may be a way to estimate possible effects.

About the Author

Mario Donick has studied German language & literature, and history, and has a PhD in communication studies. Since 2015 he is, besides other jobs, working as a freelance author.

Social: @mariodonick.bsky.social
Website: https://ueberstrom.net

References

Böhme, G. (1995). Atmosphäre. Essays zur neuen Ästhetik. Suhrkamp.

Böhme, G. (2019). Leib. Die Natur, die wir selbst sind. Suhrkamp.

Donick, M. (2022). Zum leiblichen Erleben fantastischer Situationen in Spielen. In: PAIDIA – Zeitschrift für Computerspielforschung. 15.02.2022, https://paidia.de/zum-leiblichen-erleben-fantastischer-situationen-in-spielen [24.04.2024]

Donick, M. / Schwelgengräber, W. (2024). Urbaner Ruinen-Tourismus: Enge und Weite in Fallout 4 und Elex 2. In: Görgen, A. / Inderst, R. T.: Old World Blues. „Fallout" und das Spiel mit der Postapokalypse. transcript.

Dörner, D. (1984). Denken, Problemlösen und Intelligenz. Psychologische Rundschau, Band XXXV, Heft 1 (1984), S. 10–20.

Huberts, C. / Standke, S. (eds.) (2014): Zwischen|Welten: Atmosphären im Computerspiel. Hülsbusch.

Jung, A.: Stealth, Immersive Sim und Atmosphäre(n): Eine wechselseitige Infiltration. Illustriert an ‚Hitman 3' und ‚Thief 2: The Metal Age'. In: PAIDIA – Zeitschrift für Computerspielforschung. 17.05.2023, https://paidia.de/stealth-immersive-sim-und-atmosphaeren-eine-wechselseitige-infiltration-illustriert-an-hitman-3-und-thief-2-the-metal-age [24.04.2024]

Schmitz, H. (1977). Das Göttliche und der Raum. System der Philosophie III, Teil 4. Bouvier.

Schmitz, H. (2011). Der Leib. De Gruyter.

Schmitz, H. (1987). Der vergessene Leib. Phänomenologische Bemerkungen zu Leib, Seele und Krankheit. Zeitschrift für Klin. Psych. Psychopath. Psychother., 35 (1987) Heft 3, S. 270–278.

Schmitz, H. (2021). Sich selbst verstehen. Ein Lesebuch. Ausgewählt und eingeleitet. von Michael Großheim und Steffen Kluck. Verlag Karl Alber.

Schwelgengräber, W. (2022). Wer sehen will, muss spüren. Warum uns manche Serien und Filme berühren und uns andere kaltlassen. Springer.

Zimmermann, F. (2023). Virtuelle Wirklichkeiten. Böhlau.

II. ECONOMIC EXPERIENCES IN GAMES

MONEY SYSTEMS IN TEXT ADVENTURES AND THEIR DESIGN CHALLENGES

Lea Stella Santner, Wilfried Elmenreich

Text adventure games, also known as interactive fiction, allow players to engage with the game world by typing commands. These games often feature intricate puzzles that necessitate correct actions and the combination of specific objects to progress. Although the concept of money is infrequently encountered within these games, there are instances where a single coin becomes instrumental in operating machinery or serves as part of a puzzle. Incorporating a monetary system into text adventures presents a formidable challenge to the genre. The introduction of money can disrupt puzzle complexity, enabling players to bypass cumbersome acquisition tasks by simply purchasing necessary objects. Despite these hurdles, some text adventures have implemented functional money systems. This paper addresses the intricate design and implementation challenges associated with introducing money systems into text adventure games. This leads to discussions about its impact on narrative choices, such as deciding between spending or retaining money, and how these decisions influence the overall storyline, as well as to technical questions regarding the implementation of the concept using a typical programming language for interactive fiction, such as Inform. As a case study, the implementation process of a money system using the Inform 6 programming language and the PunyInfom Library is presented.

Keywords: Interactive Fiction, Text Adventures, Game Engineering

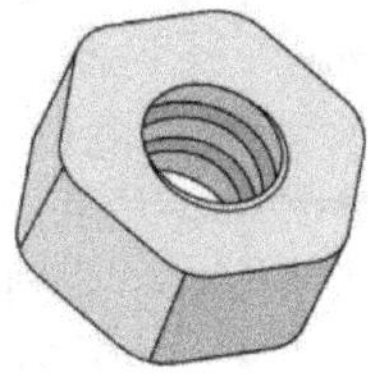

1. Introduction

A text-based adventure game is a genre of computer games within the wider area of interactive fiction. While interactive fiction also includes systems where the user can make inputs via selections without entering text, the interface to the player in a text-adventure takes place by entering a text string that contains the players' intended action to the game. Will Crowther's game "Adventure" (Crowther, 1976) is considered the first text adventure and was released in 1976 for the PDP-10 mainframe computer. The game, later renamed Colossal Cave Adventure, was massively popular among the computer community in the later 1970s and kicked off an era of further text adventure games in the coming years.

As a genre, text adventures are incredibly flexible. While there is a more or less agreed set on standard verbs (cf. Plotkin, 2010), adding any other custom verbs with different effects to a game is possible. A text adventure can be implemented with standard programming languages such as C, C++ (Sutherland, 2014), Python (Johnson, 2018), or the BASIC programming language (Lampton, 1986; Montford, 2005), which used to be typically integrated into the ROM of home computers in the 1980s. A recent example of a simple text adventure written in BASIC is "Tiny Quest" (Derocher, 2024), which fits into the 3.5 kB BASIC memory of the VIC 20 (and therefore easily fits on all other systems that typically have larger memory). On the other hand, there exist dedicated programming languages and systems for text adventures, most notably Inform (Nelson, 1993), The Quill (Yeandle, 1983), and the D42 Adventure System (Lesch & Erbsland, 2014) that offer streamlined and specialized tools tailored to the unique demands of interactive storytelling.

Implementing money systems in text adventures is a challenge for several reasons: First, on a fundamental level, money comes in units, so unlike many unique objects in adventure games, one piece of money is like the other, and you can obtain multiple of them. Second, money is a means to ease trading and exchange of goods by being a joker item that can be bought or sold for any other good in a market. In the context of a text adventure, this challenges the creation of puzzles, which are an intrinsic element of these games. Money obtained in the game could be used to shortcut the need to obtain an item needed in a puzzle, thus breaking puzzle complexity. The versatility of money interactions can also affect playability: the player might spend the money on the wrong items just because it is possible, ending up with an unsolvable game state. While the last two issues require to be solved within the context of the particular setup of a text adventure, we will focus on generically implementing a money system in

Inform6. This system was chosen because it is the programming language that allows the most complexity for implementing a text adventure among the possibilities listed above. Inform 7, a newer version of the Inform language, is quite different from Inform 6. It adopts a natural-language-oriented approach to source code, which sets it apart from established systems. Because Inform 7 has a significantly different syntax and is less widely used than Inform 6, it is outside the scope of this paper.

This paper investigates the topic of money systems in text adventures. In particular, it contributes three parts: The following section presents a discussion on the challenges of integrating money systems as a game mechanic in text adventures. Subsequently, we present an overview of notable text adventure games with money systems. The third section of the paper elaborates on how money systems can be implemented in a text adventure using the programming language Inform 6. The concluding section summarizes the findings and gives an outlook on possible future work.

2. Money as a Game Mechanic

Literature on money as a game mechanic usually understands the topic as players spending real money in (mostly online) games (Wohn, 2014), or interpreting the game as a marketing instrument to advertise virtual goods (Hamari & Lehdonvirta, 2010). Besides this direct link to real money, findings suggest that even simulated gambling games using virtual currency may promote gambling with real money (Armstrong et al., 2018). In addition, in-game currencies that are connected to the real-world economy also pose a threat of being misused for money laundry and concealment of money flows (Cloward & Abarbanel, 2020).

Kinnunen, Alha, and Paavilainen (2016) further suggest that F2P gamers spending real money on their game will need to develop methods similar to those used by gamblers who frame or separate play money from other forms of money, such as money for groceries. Leijnen, Brinkkemper, and Bouwer (2015) discuss games with a money system and procedurally generated goods as a learning game for a general audience, teaching them how banks function within a market-guided economy.

A discussion on currency in fictional works[1] describes challenges regarding naming, appearance, and possibilities of obtaining money in fiction, which also apply to interactive fiction/text adventures. When naming currencies, authors must consider cultural associations to maintain coherence within their worlds and to avoid associations with existing currencies (Athans & Salvatore, 2010). Narrative challenges arise in ensuring the credibility and stability of these money systems, particularly in the face of futuristic technology or magical elements (Gliddon, 2005). Some currencies are inherently valuable within their fictional universes, serving as more than mere mediums of exchange, as seen in works like Frank Herbert's Dune series or Iain M. Banks's Consider Phlebas.

Text adventures, being a form of interactive fiction, face unique challenges related to fictional currencies. Critical questions include: Is the currency name appropriate for the world setting? Does it make sense within the context of advanced technology or magical abilities? As seen in some fictional works where currencies transcend their role as mere exchange mediums, money systems in text adventures are expected to have a similar impact, particularly given the complex nature of their puzzles. It is impractical for players to gather enough in-game money to buy all quest items outright. Instead, some items must be acquired through traditional means, with the money system playing only a partial role in item acquisition.

3. Text Adventures with Money Systems

Colossal Cave Adventure, being the first game in the genre, did not have a dedicated money system, but valuables and treasures that could be discovered in the caves, which could be seen as the predecessor of an in-game currency.

In-game currencies have been used in several text adventures, most notably in games by Infocom. Table 1 gives an overview of some examples: The names of the currencies are typically very diverse: there are Zorkmids in the classic text-based adventure game series Zork (Infocom, 1980,1981,1983) (referred to as "coin" in Zork I), Buckazoids in the interactive fiction games Planetfall (Infocom, 1983) and its sequels, the humorous use of "Flotsam and jetsam" in the text adventure The Hichhiker's Guide to the Galaxy (Infocom, 1984). Players typically

[1] https://list.fandom.com/wiki/List_of_fictional_currencies

obtain money by exploring the game world, discovering treasures, solving puzzles, and completing tasks. The money is then used to purchase goods and services (sometimes via a bribe) and advance the player's character. However, the use of money in these adventures is always limited to specific parts of a puzzle, unlike in, for example, economic simulation games where money is the principal means to purchase all relevant goods and services.

Fallen London (Failbetter Games, 2009) is a bit of a different case: it is a free-to-play text-based open-world RPG played in the web browser. In Fallen London, Echos, Pennies, and Shillings serve as the primary forms of currency in the dark and mysterious Victorian setting. Players can earn these currencies by completing storylines, engaging in trade, and participating in challenges. They are essential for purchasing goods and services and advancing the player's character. Since the game is a multiplayer game, the money also serves as a unit of exchange for trading between players.

Table 1. Text Adventures with Money Systems

Game	In-game currency
Colossal Cave Adventure (1976)	Valuables and treasures
Fallen London (2009)	Echoes, pennies, shillings
Planetfall (1983)	Buckazoids
The Hitchhiker's Guide to the Galaxy (1984)	Flotsam, jetsam
Zork (1980-1982)	Zorkmids

4. Case study: Implementation of a Money System in Inform 6

Inform 6 is a sophisticated system tailored to the creation of narrative-driven text adventure games. It offers a comprehensive suite of tools to facilitate the translation of textual descriptions into virtual worlds. At its core, Inform consists of a library of pre-defined elements and a compiler that allows authors to construct complex textual game environments with relative ease. The foundation of Inform is its library, which includes a parser and a world model. The parser acts as the interface between the player and the game world, interpreting the commands typed and executing the corresponding actions within the virtual environment. At the same time, the world model defines a set of standard rules that govern interactions within the game, such as visibility constraints in the absence of light sources.

Since its establishment in 1993, Inform has become a significant tool for creating interactive fiction in various natural languages. It has developed into a complete software suite, including a compiler and a library, that is essential for designing games of any size. Its versatility extends beyond entertainment, finding applications in commercial game prototyping and academic contexts alike. According to the original Inform 6 page[2], Inform is used in a range of educational settings, from computer science curricula to theoretical architecture seminars. In her blog, Emily Short (2019) lists resources and examples for pedagogical uses of interactive fiction (IF) in an educational setting, covering its application in teaching English, language arts, literature, history, and foreign languages. She also provides specific examples of IF games written in Inform 6, Inform 7, and Twine. Although newer tools and languages have emerged, Inform 6, with its text-based syntax, remains relevant for text adventures due to its robustness, simplicity, and community support.

In the following, we sketch an implementation of a money system for the programming language Inform 6. Inform, being a domain-specific language for text adventures, already supports the implementation of objects that can be discovered and acquired when playing a game. A money system is more intricate because it requires objects (coins) that can be obtained multiple times and that need to be used together in case an object is purchased that costs a multitude of coins (which is usually the case).

While there exist several tutorials for implementing adventure games with Inform, this guide pertaining to money systems that are presented here has been elaborated from scratch - to our knowledge no such resource exists up to now. As a prerequisite, we assume that the reader is already familiar with the basic usage of Inform 6 and the PunyInform library. A recommended tutorial is the

[2] http://www.inform-fiction.org/introduction/index.html

Inform Designer's Manual (Nelson, 2001) and the PunyInform Manual (Berntsson & Ramsberg, 2023).

```
Constant Story      "Monetary System";
Constant Headline   "^How to implement a money system.^";
Constant STATUSLINE_SCORE; Statusline score;
Constant NO_SCORE = 0;

Constant OPTIONAL_LIST_TOGETHER;
Constant OPTIONAL_LANGUAGE_NUMBER;
Constant OPTIONAL_ALLOW_WRITTEN_NUMBERS;
Constant OPTIONAL_FLEXIBLE_INVENTORY;

Constant INITIAL_LOCATION_VALUE = Library;
Include "globals.h";

! routines here

! include PunyInform library
Include "puny.h";

! classes here

! example game code here

! routine that runs at the start of the game
[Initialise;
  print "^^That's how you do it";
];
```

Listing 1. Header section of .inf source file

You start by defining constants such as Story, Headline, etc. All constants should be defined before you include "globals.h".

The "Initialise" routine is a code block that executes certain actions when the game is initialized or started. In this case, it simply prints the message "That's how you do it" to the screen.

As the next step, it is necessary to add the routines that calculate the object's depth and its final destination (Listing 2):

```
! Calculate an object's depth in the containment hierarchy
[ ObjDepth p_obj _i;
while(p_obj) { p_obj = parent(p_obj); _i++; }
  return _i;
];

! final object destination, ensuring objects in the same group are handled
properly
[ ChooseObjectsFinal p_arr p_len _i _j _o _o2 _sg _d _d2 _other_group_pre-
sent;
#Ifdef DEBUG;
    print "*** ChooseObjectsFinal, action is ",(DebugAction) action,",
object count is ", p_len, ": ^";
#Endif;
  ! Iterate over all objects in the array
  for(_i = 0: _i < p_len: _i++) {
    _o = p_arr-->_i;
    if(_o provides same_group) {
      _sg = _o.same_group;
      _d = ObjDepth(_o);
      ! Iterate over the remaining objects in the array
      for(_j = p_len - 1: _j > _i: _j--) {
        _o2 = p_arr-->_j;
        if(_o2 provides same_group) {
          if(_o2.same_group == _sg) {
            _d2 = ObjDepth(_o2);
            ! swap if the other object is shallower in hierarchy
            if( _d2 < _d) {
              _o = _o2;
              p_arr-->_j = p_arr-->_i;
              p_arr-->_i = _o;
              _d = _d2;
            }
            ChooseObjectsFinal_Discard(_j);
            p_len--;
          } else
            _other_group_present = true;
        }
      }
      ! If no other group is present, terminate early
      if(_other_group_present == false)
        return;
      _other_group_present = false;
    }
  }
];
```

Listing 2. Routines

The overall implementation of the adventure game is in a single .inf file. The routines will be added where the comment "! routines here" is placed in Listing1.

The routine "ObjDepth" calculates the depth of an object within its object hierarchy. It starts with the given object "p_obj" and iterates through its parent objects using a while loop. For each parent object it increments a counter "_i". Finally, it returns the value of "_i", which represents the depth of the object within its hierarchy. Essentially, it counts how many levels of parent objects the given object has until it reaches the top parent.

The routine called "ChooseObjectsFinal" sorts objects stored in an array "p_arr" by their group membership and depth. It iterates over each object and checks if it has a property called "same_group". If it does, it compares its depth to other objects in the same group. Objects with lower depths are moved to the front of the array. If there are objects from other groups, it continues processing, otherwise it stops and returns. The routine essentially organizes objects by group and depth.

```
! Generic coin class, used by SilverCoin and GoldCoin
Class Coin
  with
    name ',//',
    parse_name [ _w _n;
      _w = NextWord();
      if(_w == self.name) {
        _w = NextWord();
        _n++;
      }
      if(_w == 'coin')
        _n++;
      else if(_w == 'coins//p') {
        parser_action = ##PluralFound;
        _n++;
      }
      return _n;
    ];


Class SilverCoin
  class Coin,
  with
    same_group 2, ! Group identifier for same types of coins
    name 'silver',
    short_name "silver coin",
    list_together [ _obj _n;
      if(inventory_stage == 1) {
        for(_obj=parser_one: _obj ~= 0: _obj = NextEntry(_obj, parser_two)) _n++;
        print (LanguageNumber) _n, " silver coins";
        if(c_style & NEWLINE_BIT)
          new_line;
        rtrue;
      }
    ];

  Class GoldCoin
  class Coin
  with
    same_group 3, ! Group identifier for same types of coins
    name 'gold',
    short_name "gold coin",
    list_together [ _obj _n;
      if(inventory_stage == 1) {
        for(_obj=parser_one: _obj ~= 0: _obj = NextEntry(_obj, parser_two)) _n++;
        print (LanguageNumber) _n, " gold coins";
        if(c_style & NEWLINE_BIT)
          new_line;
        rtrue;
      }
    ];
```

Listing 3. Classes

The classes will be added where the comment "! classes here" is placed in Listing1.

The "Coin" class defines the behavior and attributes of coins in the game. It contains an attribute called name, which defaults to ",//" (a placeholder). It also contains a method called "parse_name", which is responsible for parsing the name of a coin during gameplay input processing. This method checks the next word in the input and adjusts the parsing based on matches with the name attribute, "coin", or "coins//p" (plural form). Finally, it returns the number of words used during parsing. The "Coin" class thus facilitates accurate recognition and processing of coin-related commands by handling variations in coin names.

The "SilverCoin" and the "GoldCoin" classes extend the functionality of the "Coin" class, specifically for representing silver and gold coins in the game. They introduce attributes such as "same_group", "name" and "short_name" to define coins. They also include a method called "list_together", which handles the inventory listing of silver and gold coins, ensuring accurate identification and labeling in the game environment.

```
Object Library "The Library"
  with
    description "You are in a library."
  has light;

Object -> Table "table"
  with
    name 'table',
  has supporter open enterable;

Object -> -> Box "box"
  with
    name 'box',
    inside_description "It feels so nice, standing in the box.",
  has container open openable enterable;


GoldCoin -> -> -> GoldCoin1;
GoldCoin -> -> -> GoldCoin2;
GoldCoin -> -> -> GoldCoin3;

SilverCoin -> -> -> SilverCoin1;
SilverCoin -> -> -> SilverCoin2;
SilverCoin -> -> -> SilverCoin3;
```

Listing 4. Example game code

Additional game code will be added where the comment "! example game code here" is placed in Listing 1.

The "Library" object represents a location within the game environment that is described as a library. It contains a description that provides information about the environment, stating "You are in a library." Additionally, it is specified to have light, indicating that the location is bright. The "Table" object represents a table in the game environment. It is defined with the name 'table' and specified to be a supporter, indicating that it can hold other objects. It is also open and enterable, suggesting that characters or items can be placed on or inside it during gameplay. The "Box" object is described as a box in the game. It is named "box". The inside of the box is further described with the text "It feels so nice, standing in the box." This object is specified as a container, indicating that it can hold other objects. It is set to be open, openable, and enterable, suggesting that characters or items can be placed inside it during gameplay and that it can be interacted with by opening it.

The provided example of the implementation of a monetary system in Inform 6 defines classes such as "Coin", "SilverCoin", and "GoldCoin", allowing for the creation of various types of currency within the game world. Each coin is associated with its respective class ("GoldCoin" or "SilverCoin") and is uniquely identified by a numerical suffix. These instances represent individual coins that can be interacted with separately within the game. The presented approach enables efficient tracking and management of similar coins within the player's inventory, with clear inventory management features. Players can seamlessly interact with monetary objects, including picking them up, dropping them, and potentially using them for in-game transactions or interactions. Descriptive content for monetary objects is supported, enhancing player immersion and understanding of the game's economic elements.

Although the code example shows proficiency in handling basic monetary systems, it needs to be extended when dealing with more complex economic interactions. Advanced economic features, such as intricate trading mechanisms or dynamic market systems, may require additional implementation beyond the capabilities provided in the code. The debugging and testing tools for the monetary system within the code snippet may be limited, which can complicate the identification and resolution of issues related to monetary interactions.

5. Conclusion

This paper explored strategies for integrating the concept of currency into text adventures without compromising puzzle-solving intricacies. In particular, a challenge arises when puzzles traditionally have a singular solution whereas a currency system introduces a multitude of decision points. Generally, money systems should be introduced with care, even if they do not involve real money. Our literature research in Section 2 suggests that even simulated gambling systems can negatively affect gamers in real life. For game economies that are connected to real-world money, there is the risk of adverse effects on players spending significant money in order to perform well in-game. However, the described effects typically apply to online games, where players employ all kinds of means to outperform each other.

Money systems in interactive fiction games come with distinct challenges. They need to align with the theme and be carefully managed. Players should not gather enough in-game money to purchase all quest items at once. Traditional methods should still be necessary for obtaining several items, with the money system playing a minor role.

The case study in Section 4 shows how such a money system can be implemented in Inform 6. While the overall effort is concise, the implementation steps are intricate due to the complexity and versatility of the Inform programming language. The guide included in this paper thus is intended to serve as an enabler for implementing text adventures with meaningful and game-enhancing money system mechanics. In future work, we expect the implementation of money systems in Inform to become more accessible by providing the necessary steps in the form of a library or being supported by a tool. What remains further open are test strategies for games with money systems. The versatility of money introduces complexity for both players, who may welcome new possibilities, and testers, who will face considerable challenges. Therefore, a future convenient-to-use money system will benefit from an automated testing approach.

Acknowledgments

The work leading to these results has received funding from the Federal Ministry for Climate Action, Environment, Energy, Mobility, Innovation and Technology Austria (BMK), from the HTBLuVA Villach, and its parent association.

About the Authors

Lea Stella Santner is a student of the HTL Informationstechnologie in Villach and an associate student of psychology and informatics at the University of Klagenfurt. Her interests cover Software and Web development, as well as game engineering, virtual worlds, character design, storytelling, and game graphics.

Lea was working with the Smart Grids group at the University of Klagenfurt in July 2023 on the analysis implementation of different text adventure systems. The work involved devising an Italian and German grammar module for the PunyInform library and the evaluation of money systems in interactive fiction games.

LinkedIn: lea-santner-45a50228b

Wilfried Elmenreich is professor of Smart Grids at the Institute of Networked and Embedded Systems at the Alpen-Adria-Universität Klagenfurt, Austria. His research interests include intelligent energy systems, self-organizing systems, and technical applications of swarm intelligence. Wilfried Elmenreich is a member of the Senate at the Alpen-Adria-Universität Klagenfurt, Counselor of the IEEE Student Branch, and is involved in the master program on Game Studies and Engineering. He is the author of several books and has published over 200 articles in the field of networked and embedded systems. Elmenreich researches intelligent energy systems, self-organizing systems, and technical applications of swarm intelligence.

LinkedIn: wilfriedelmenreich
Website: https://mobile.aau.at/~welmenre/

References

Nelson, G. (2001). The Inform Designer's Manual, Fourth Edition.

Crowther, W. (1976). *Adventure* (also known as *Colossal Cave Adventure*) PDP-10 game published via ARPANET.

Johnson P. (2018). Make Your Own Python Text Adventure. Apress.

Sutherland, B. (2014). Text Adventure. In: C++ Game Development Primer. Apress, Berkeley, CA. https://doi.org/10.1007/978-1-4842-0814-4_6

Lampton C. (1986). How to Create Adventure Games. Ed. Franklin Watts; Library Binding Edition

Montford N. (2005). Twisty Little Passages - An Approach to Interactive Fiction. MIT Press.

Plotkin A., Albaugh L. (2010). How To Play Interactive Fiction (An entire strategy guide on a single postcard). People's republic of interactive fiction. http://pr-if.org/doc/play-if-card/

Derocher, R.J. (2024). Tiny Quest. Computer Game. Binary Legends. https://csdb.dk/release/?id=239276

Short, E. (2019). Mailbag: Pedagogical Uses of IF in the Classroom. Blog: Emily Short's Interactive Storytelling. Retrieved from https://emshort.blog/2019/09/10/mailbag-pedagogical-uses-of-if-in-the-classroom/

Nelson G. (1993). Inform. Programming Language. https://ganelson.github.io/inform-website/

Berntsson J. & Ramsberg F. PunyInform. Library for Inform 6. https://github.com/johanberntsson/PunyInform

Yeandle G. (1983). The Quill. Computer Software. Gilsoft.

Lesch, S.& Erbsland T. (2014) D42 Adventure System: Klassische Adventures selbst entwickeln für den Commodore 64/128. BoD – Books on Demand.

Wohn, D. Y. (2014). Spending real money: Purchasing patterns of virtual goods in an online social game. In Proceedings of the SIGCHI Conference on Human Factors in Computing Systems (CHI '14) (pp. 3359–3368). Association for Computing Machinery. https://doi.org/10.1145/2556288.2557074

Hamari, J., & Lehdonvirta, V. (2010). Game design as marketing: How game mechanics create demand for virtual goods. International Journal of Business Science & Applied Management, 5(1), 14–29. https://ssrn.com/abstract=1443907

Armstrong, T., Rockloff, M., Browne, M., et al. (2018). An exploration of how simulated gambling games may promote gambling with money. Journal of Gambling Studies, 34, 1165–1184. https://doi.org/10.1007/s10899-018-9742-6

Cloward, J. G., & Abarbanel, B. L. (2020). In-Game Currencies, Skin Gambling, and the Persistent Threat of Money Laundering in Video Games. UNLV Gaming Law Journal, 10(1), Article 6. Retrieved from https://scholars.law.unlv.edu/glj/vol10/iss1/6

Kinnunen, J., Alha, K., & Paavilainen, J. (2016). Creating play money for free-to-play and gambling games. In Proceedings of the 20th International Academic Mindtrek Conference (AcademicMindtrek '16) (pp. 385–392). Association for Computing Machinery. https://doi.org/10.1145/2994310.2994336

Leijnen, S., Brinkkemper, P., & Bouwer, A. (2015). Generating game mechanics in a model economy: A MoneyMaker Deluxe case study. Paper presented at the 6th Workshop on Procedural Content Generation in Games (PCG 2015), Pacific Grove, United States.

Athans, P., & Salvatore, R. A. (2010). The Guide to Writing Fantasy and Science Fiction. Adams Media.

Gliddon, G. (2005). The Greenwood encyclopedia of science fiction and fantasy, Volume 2. Greenwood.

Infocom. (1980). Zork I [Computer game]. United States: Infocom (Developers: Tim Anderson, Marc Blank, Bruce Daniels, Dave Lebling).

Infocom. (1981). Zork II [Computer game]. United States: Infocom (Developers: Tim Anderson, Marc Blank, Bruce Daniels, Dave Lebling).

Infocom. (1982). Zork III [Computer game]. United States: Infocom (Developers: Tim Anderson, Marc Blank, Bruce Daniels, Dave Lebling).

Infocom. (1984). The Hitchhiker's Guide to the Galaxy [Computer game]. Cambridge, MA: Infocom (Developers: Douglas Adams, Steve Meretzky).

Infocom. (1983). Planetfall [Computer game]. Cambridge, MA: Infocom (Developer: Steve Meretzky).

Failbetter Games. (2009). Fallen London. [Online Game]. Failbetter Games.

Nelson, G. (2001). *The Inform Designer's Manual* (4th ed.). (G. Rees, Ed.). Retrieved from https://www.inform-fiction.org/manual/DM4.pdf

Berntsson, J., & Ramsberg, F. (2023). *PunyInform: An Inform library for writing compact and fast text adventures* (Version 5.3). Retrieved from https://github.com/johanberntsson/PunyInform/wiki/manual

THE SOCIO SPATIAL ECONOMIES OF DARK SOULS, DEATH STRANDING & SUPER MARIO BROS. WONDER

Kevin Mercer

Dark Souls, Death Stranding, and Super Mario Bros. Wonder feature asynchronously shared virtual spaces in which the players' understanding, navigation, or alterations of the in-game architecture are made possible through socio-spatial economies. These game worlds are informed by geographically dispersed, yet virtually close player-controlled inhabitants, each seeking to care for said worlds. Dark Souls features treacherous, labyrinthine environments that are explored incrementally during cycles of the player's life and death. Progress requires venturing beyond the safety of a bonfire checkpoint, into ruins, cathedrals, and hamlets replete with vicious enemies and unseen traps. Death Stranding tasks the player with transporting resources and rebuilding the infrastructure of a post-apocalyptic United States. The gameplay loop sees the protagonist traversing extreme landscapes, seeking natural paths while constructing new paths along the way.Super Mario Bros. Wonder features series of linear play spaces of variable complexity and difficulty. The player may exchange flower coins for standees, deployable checkpoints available to many other asynchronous online players. Players unknown to one another shape these virtual environments, enabling easier, safer, and faster traversal for all. Each of these titles deploys players as bodies in spaces (Lefebvre, 1992) enabling them to infuse said spaces with new meaning through emergent play (Nitsche, 2008). The result is a more utopian and less neoliberal play space.

Keywords: currency, economy, emerging collectivity, knowledge creation, socio-spatiality

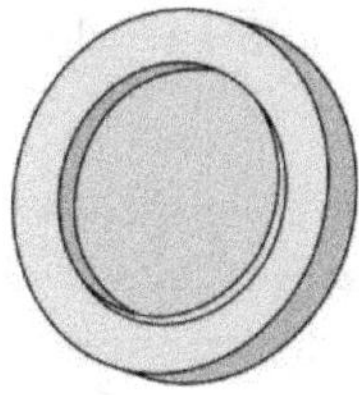

1. Unlikely Kinship: Intertextuality & Cooperative Play

Dark Souls, Death Stranding, and *Super Mario Bros. Wonder* (*SMBW*) each individually stand in stark contrast to one another, bearing few similarities with respect to genre, aesthetics, gameplay mechanics, or other common, defining characteristics of video games. Where these titles overlap, however, is through their atypical cooperative play that does not necessitate synchronous player activity.

Dark Souls, first released in 2011 and developed by FromSoftware under the direction of Hidetaka Miyazaki, is a third-person role playing game set in and around the fictional medieval kingdom of *Lordran*. The player is tasked with ringing two *Bells of Awakening* to lift a curse responsible for the subjugation of the kingdom's undead inhabitants. The player must navigate dangerous, labyrinthine environments, seeking bonfire checkpoints as much-needed sites of respite along their journey. Asynchronous online players can compose messages from lists of nouns, verbs, and qualifiers and leave them in the game world as signposts for others. This sharing of information, and, in many cases, misinformation, affects a given player's creation of knowledge regarding a dangerous play space steeped in imposing, Gothic architecture (Rutten, 2016).

Death Stranding, first released in 2019 and developed by Kojima Productions under the direction of Hideo Kojima, is a third-person, semi-open world action-adventure title set in a post-apocalyptic United States of America. The player embodies *Sam Porter Bridges,* played by Norman Reedus, and is charged with reconnecting the fractured US through various delivery missions and construction projects made possible, in part, by speculative technologies and supernatural powers. Natural features in the landscape, such as rivers, canyons, or sheer cliff faces, must be negotiated by the player to progress through the game world and advance the narrative. *Death Stranding* enables players to use structures built by one another, then award them likes, perhaps the most prevalent social currency in the online world.

Super Mario Bros. Wonder, released in 2023 and developed by Nintendo under the direction of Shiro Mouri, is a two-dimensional action platforming title in which *Mario* must save the *Flower Kingdom* from the clutches of *Bowser* who has fused himself with the *Flower Castle,* merging his body with the game world's architecture. The player clears predominantly linear stages, many featuring ancillary spaces varying from underground, overhead, background, or even hidden zones. Levels are transformed temporarily upon the player's interaction with *wonder flowers*, yielding surprising, dynamic shifts in gameplay.

These titles offer gameplay loops in which the player must engage with virtual landscapes and architecture, learn their layouts and rules for traversal, then ultimately progress through said worlds as they simultaneously improve them. Their gameplay systems offer unique opportunities for asynchronous, online interactions among communities of players which enable individuals to affect their game worlds, activating them as what can be called socio-spatial architects; structural alterations to the game worlds, the conveyance of information, and progression assistance are achieved through player collaboration. Such interactions arise out of necessity as each game's environment poses navigation challenges; among these three titles, examples of unicursal, multicursal, rhizome, and logic mazes must be solved (Nitsche, 177). It should be noted that *Dark Souls* and *SMBW* do support synchronous online play, though such systems will not be covered here as they exceed the scope of this research.

2. In-Game Economies & Social Interactions

The three titles covered here model, at their surfaces, capitalist economies. Performing successfully within the systems of each game rewards the player with capital of varying types (outlined in Table 1). Furthermore, the player, as a participant within each game economy, becomes a consumer. Important junctures in the progression of *Dark Souls* are often predicated on whether the player has enough *souls*, the game's in-game currency, to afford levelling-up various character attributes, a process which becomes exponentially more costly with each new level.

Table 1. In-Game Currencies (Non-Exhaustive)

Game	Currency
Dark Souls	Souls
Death Stranding	Ceramics
	Chemicals
	Chiral Crystals
	Metals
	Resins
	Special Alloys
SMBW	Coins
	Flower Coins
	Wonder Seeds

In-game capital is then exchanged for various goods and services (outlined in Table 2). Crafting useful gear in *Death Stranding* requires stockpiling large quantities of raw materials, then processing them with rapid prototyping equipment. Meeting the platforming challenges of *SMBW* means the player must purchase *badges* that provide unique abilities. Of course, a capitalist economic model is not, by any means, unique to these three games. The post-modern gamer may safely assume that their avatar's identity – its appearance, equipment, and abilities – be defined in part by its consumptive behaviors (Oring, 211). *Dark Souls* sees players consuming what are known as *soul items* in exchange for currency.

Table 2. In-Game Goods & Services (Non-Exhaustive)

Game	Goods & Services
Dark Souls	Healing Items Status Effect Items Ammunition Blacksmithing
Death Stranding	Clothing Exoskeletons Vehicles
SMBW	Standees Badges 1-Up Mushrooms

Where these titles differ from many others, however, is through their optional online gameplay systems composed of asynchronous and abstract cooperation (Hardt & Negri, 294-5). *Lordan*, a fractured United States of America, and *The Flower Kingdom* digitally embody network societies that facilitate encounters among dispersed strangers (Shaviro, 249). In the online encounters described henceforth, players cannot see one another, interact, or communicate directly in real time. They can instead interact with a variety of spatialized remnants evident of other players' traversal through their own versions of the same game worlds.

The dangerous environments of *Dark Souls* are made less so when valuable information is conveyed through shorthand messages situated within its play space. The *Orange Guidance Soapstone* is a tool which allows the player to compose rudimentary messages from finite menus of pre-written words and leave them for other players to find. Game critics Jason Killingsworth and Keza MacDonald, when first experiencing the game in 2011, played it offline. In You Died: The Dark Souls Companion, they share an excerpt from an email chain among several critics attempting to complete and review *Dark Souls* ahead of its official release. On September 29th, 2011, video game critic Mitch Dyer wrote to MacDonald:

> Two hours of exploring later, I've made no forward progress from the stone bridge (up high) bonfire in Blighttown. I've climbed so many ladders. Where. Do. I. Go. (Killingsworth & MacDonald, 56)

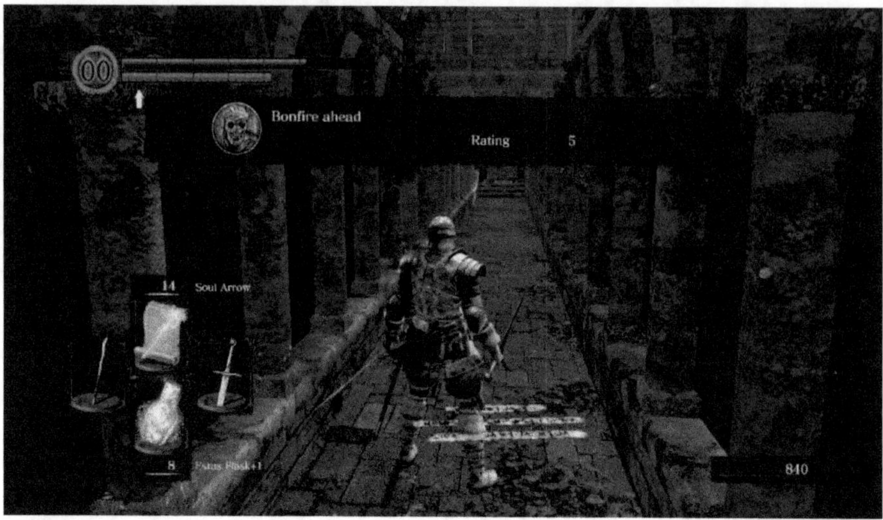

Figure 1. An Orange Guidance Soapstone message indicating a nearby bonfire. Dark Souls Remastered, 2018.

In the absence of the soapstone messaging system, this email chain, dubbed the *Chain of Pain,* highlights the necessity of social interactions and the exchange of information intrinsic to *Dark Souls* (Killingsworth & MacDonald, 49-61). This necessity becomes evident to the player at key locations in *Lordran* where condensations of messages litter the ground. Such instances indicate far more than an active messaging system, they represent diverse bodies gathering around a particular digital, spatial problem, resulting in a temporary, invisible public (Bennet, 100).

Where *Dark Souls* may experience dense pockets of player communication, *Death Stranding* enables user-initiated projects that may be executed by many. Though players will not engage with one another directly, they will contribute raw materials to the construction of architectural components which aid in traversing the harsh game world. The project and its positive effect on the world become the impetus for online, cooperative play (Boltanski & Chiapello, 104-5). One built architectural work, for instance, a bridge, will persist across all collaborators' worlds. Many online players yield more frequent and cost-effective structures than solitary, offline players.

SMBW's Flower Kingdom incorporates a new mechanic to the *Super Mario* franchise through its *standees,* akin to cardboard cutouts, representing player characters. *Standees* are purchased with *flower coins* and may be deployed in levels to serve as checkpoints. A mid-level defeat requires the player to float, in spectral form, to the nearest *standee* for revival rather than restarting the level entirely. A *standee* placed in one player's instance of the game world may also appear in that of another player's, becoming a boon to their progression. In this way, an expenditure of one player's currency results in a social resource useful to many.

3. Socio-Spatial Economies & The Player as Socio-Spatial Architect

The social interactions outlined thus far constitute secondary, socio-spatial economies which subvert the traditional capitalist models of many contemporary video games. These socio-spatial economies form evolve temporary systems and require no traditional capital. In the void left by souls, raw materials, and coins, the dissemination of information through social interactions and cooperation takes hold.

Dark Souls' soapstone messages constitute an online message board, complete with erroneous claims. Players may appraise these messages, parsing their structural and selective information (Hayles, 50-57), then award either a *+1* or *–1* rating. Over time, comments on the spatialized message board are effectively upvoted or downvoted as players assess their validity.

In addition to *Death Stranding's* players' ability to pool building resources, they may also *like* one another's projects, either manually or by interacting with components built or placed by others in the world. Granting *likes* increases players' efficacy as socio-spatial architects by strengthening their *bridge link* statistic, a metric of connectivity between a single player and other players sharing a server. As this statistic increases, so too will a player's threshold for awarding *likes* to others. Furthermore, a stronger *bridge link* results in more incoming crafting resources.

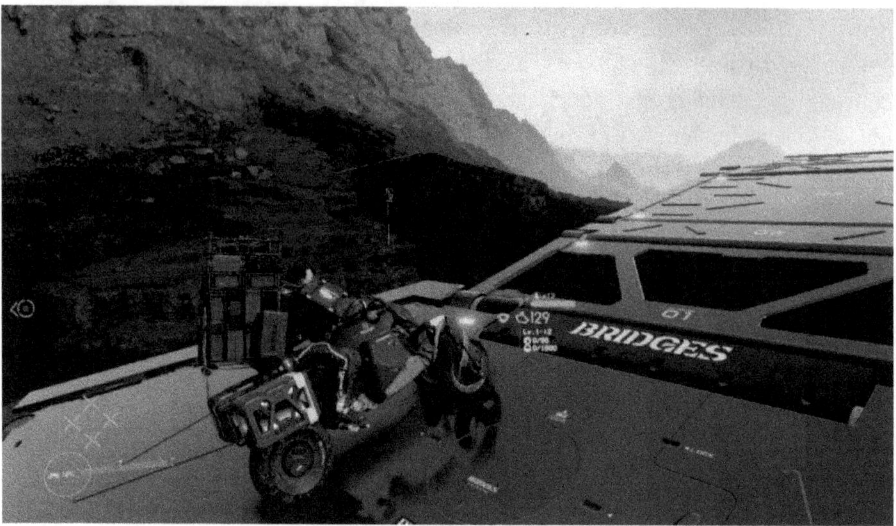

Figure 2. A community-built bridge which has received 129 likes at the time of writing. Death Stranding. 2019.

The *standees* of *SMBW* limit the loss of forward progress for dispersed players. In specific cases, a *standee* may even be situated in space such that it appears to hover impossibly above the ground. Such an instance indicates the presence of a secret, invisible platform, yielding knowledge creation and a platforming possibility within the level (Nitsche, 177).

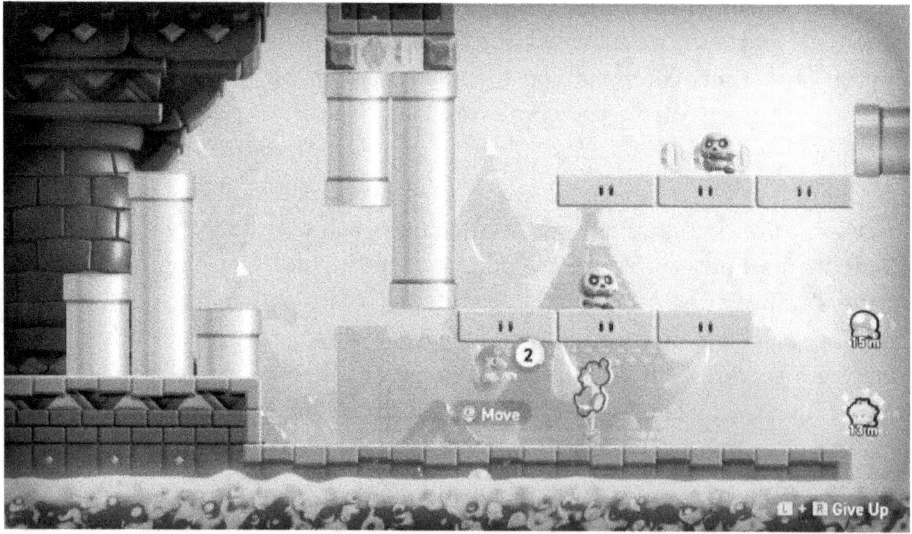

Figure 3. Mario makes his way toward an online player's Standee. Super Mario Bros. Wonder. 2023.

Such online interactions sustain and improve communities that are at once geographically dispersed and digitally concentrated. Temporary, proximal conversations evolve according to players' locations within play spaces, and they are critical to the primary objective of each game: explore, survive, and save the fractured and hostile worlds of *Lordan*, a fictionalized United States of America, and *The Flower Kingdom*. As messages, signposts, bridges, and checkpoints populate these game environments, players assume agency as socio-spatial architects. To engage with each game in a manner most beneficial to the physical improvement of their respective worlds is to participate in the subversion of their traditional capitalist models.

Socio-spatial economies underpin the gameplay goals of *Dark Souls, Death Stranding*, and *Super Mario Bros. Wonder* all the same. It costs nothing to leave a soapstone message, nothing to like a well-placed ladder, and nothing to plant a checkpoint. Playing strictly offline, eschewing these socio-spatial economies, however, means playing incomplete, less rich versions of these games devoid of social dynamics; what remains is a reversion to self-preservation and a denial of the games' emerging collectivities (Dean, 86-7). While the player may forego online interactions, instead investing more deeply in their grind for capital, the sprawling, node-based networks of spatial problems persist (Jones, 76).

About the Author

Kevin Mercer holds a BFA degree from Western Illinois University and an MFA degree from The Pennsylvania State University. Mercer is an artist and game developer. His work focuses on interactive installation, experimental narrative, rurality, and the environment. Mercer currently serves as Assistant Professor of Digital Media Arts & Animation at Southern Illinois University, USA.

Social: @professorspacegames
Website: https://www.kevinrmercer.com

References

Bennett, Jane. *Vibrant Matter: A Political Ecology of Things*. Durham, Duke University Press, 2010, pp. 100, 113–17.

Chiapello, Eve, and Luc Boltanski. *The New Spirit of Capitalism*. Translated by Gregory Elliot, London; New York, Verso, 2005, pp. 104–5.

Dark Souls: Remastered. Directed by Hidetaka Miyazaki, FromSoftware, Bandai Namco, 2018. Microsoft Windows, PlayStation 4/5, Switch, and Xbox One/X/S game.

Dean, Jodi. *Collective Desire and the Pathology of the Individual from the Psychopathologies of Cognitive Capitalism - Part One*. Edited by Warren Neidich and Anne De Boever, Berlin Archive Books, 2013, pp. 69–87.

Death Stranding. Directed by Hideo Kojima, Kojima Productions, Sony Interactive Entertainment, 2019. IOS, Microsoft Windows, PlayStation 4/5, and MacOS game.

Hardt, Michael, and Antonio Negri. *Empire*. Cambridge, Massachusetts, Harvard University Press, 2000, pp. 294–7.

Hayles, N. Katherine. *How We Became Posthuman: Virtual Bodies in Cybernetics, Literature, and Informatics*. University Of Chicago Press, 1999, pp. 50–7.

Jones, Stephen. *A Cultural Systems Approach to Collaboration in Art and Technology: Proceedings of the 5th Conference on Creativity and Cognition*, 12-15 April 2005, Goldsmiths College London. New York, NY, Association for Computing Machinery, 2005, pp. 76–85.

Lefebvre, Henri. *The Production of Space*. 1974. Oxford, Blackwell, 1991, pp. 169-171.

MacDonald, Keza, and Jason Killingsworth. *You Died: The Dark Souls Companion*. Dublin, Ireland, Tune & Fairweather, 2020, pp. 49-61.

Nintendo. "Super Mario Bros. Wonder: Here's a Few Tips for Secret Seekers!" *Nintendo*, Nintendo, 9 Jan. 2024, mario.nintendo.com/news/super-mario-bros-wonder-heres-a-few-tips-for-secret-seekers/.

Nitsche, Michael. *Video Game Spaces: Image, Play, and Structure in 3D Game Worlds*. Cambridge, Mass., Mit Press, 2008, pp. 176–8, 187–97.

Oring, Elliott. *The Arts, Artifacts, and Artifices of Identity. The Journal of American Folklore*, Vol. 107, No. 424, 1994, p. 211.

Rutten, Roel. "Beyond Proximities: The Socio-Spatial Dynamics of Knowledge Creation." *Progress in Human Geography*, vol. 41, no. 2, 10 July 2016, pp. 159–177.

Shaviro, Steven. *Connected, or What It Means to Live in the Network Society*. University of Minnesota Press, 2003, pp. 131–3. *Super Mario Bros. Wonder*. Directed by Shiro Mouri, Nintendo, 2023. Switch game.

THE MEANING OF MONEY MADE VISIBLE IN ANNO 1800

FROM A VIDEO GAME TO A BOARD GAME

Andreas Wieser

This paper focuses on the question which money-centred challenges players are faced with in the video game Anno 1800 and how these issues were transferred to the board game of Anno 1800. Methodically, this paper is based on an analysis of money-focused challenges given to the player in both video and board game. The board game abstains from the use of money and rather focuses on another main resource of the game: workforce. It seems to be a game of non-capitalist tendencies, using the workforce to gain products by processing resources. At second glance, it still consists of and builds on capitalist ideas such as the five working classes featured in the video game and the persisting idea of economic growth and competition between the players. This paper concludes that even if monetary capital is nearly completely removed from a game, it can still be a highly capitalist game using capitalist systems of economic growth and an obvious separation between working classes. Complex capitalist ideas, which normally revolve around money, are therefore still embedded, seemingly without money as its centrepiece.

Keywords: Real-Time-Strategy, Money, Capitalism, Game Metaphors

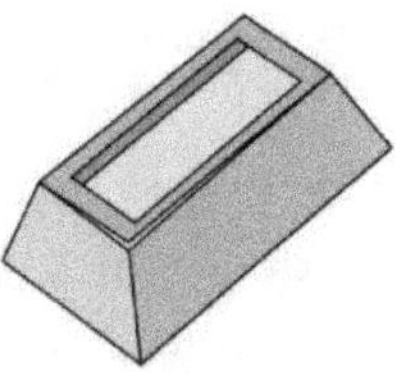

1. Introduction

Imagine that you control a world made up of five classes of population: farmers, labourers, artisans, engineers and investors. Your goal is to build the largest, most productive city possible, fulfil the needs of your population, protect them from external threats and still build a profitable economy.

This is the main objective of Anno 1800, now the seventh title in the Anno series, which differs greatly from its predecessors thanks to its twelve different DLCs and numerous additional decoration packs. This obvious success is due to the strong fan involvement of the so-called Anno Union in the development of the game and the incorporation of feedback from many users during the pre-alpha to the open beta phase of the game: Wishes and ideas about the 19th century and the gameplay of this new Anno title were incorporated by the developers and the game was adapted accordingly (Anno Union 2017).

Ubisoft tried to follow up the success of digital Anno 1800 with a board game. But in an analogue space, the game's many calculations (taxes, classes, growth) cannot be automatized. Accordingly, various aspects had to be reshaped, greatly reduced and in some cases removed entirely. This paper deals with the question of which aspects of production and money have been reshaped in the game and whether capitalist tendencies according to Marx, as clearly recognisable in the video game, have been reduced in the tabletop game. To get to the bottom of this question, both the computer game and the board game are analysed in terms of their respective purpose and the use of money or gold, and these results are compared in the light of theories of capitalism.

It should be emphasised here that this paper is not about the production, marketing, or presentation of video games, but about the representation of money or gold and the associated system in Anno 1800, which is used as an example of the transformation from video to board game.

2. The problem of converting video games into board games

Board games were digitised early on with increasing technical possibilities: The famous boardgame *Carcassonne* was digitised already in 2002 by Koch Media two years after its publishment (Jacob 2018). There are different problems in converting such games: The physical access due to their materiality is lost and must be replaced. A digital game has cinematic possibilities including scenic music and a lot more interactivity than a board game. The handling of problems in this regard has also been pointed out many times: Rogerson/Gibbs/Smith highlight three different games and various reasons for a successful transition from board games to video games in their article "Digital Boardgames: Issues and Tensions" (2015). The main reason lies in the so-called "board game metaphor". According to this concept, a metaphor "utilises well-understood concepts or attributes from one domain to make points or provide insights about another" and "it is a device for seeing something in terms of something else" (Hamilton 2000, 239). Jens Junge, Director of the Institute for Ludology in Berlin, confirms this: "A good game in the digital realm is also easy to transfer if you take the spirit with it" (Siebert/Lütticke 2023).

The challenge in a transition lies in preserving certain metaphors that constitute the game principle and clarifying them where necessary. Different games need different ways of converting from one type to another in order to maintain the game metaphor. Adaptions are needed to keep up playability over time: *Hearthstone* has adopted elements from *Dungeons and Dragons*, such as experience points, level systems, classes, characteristics, etc. (Rogerson/Gibbs/Smith 2015, 6–7). The only important thing for users is that the game itself remains the same: There is an inherent tension in staying true to the boardgame while maximising the affordances of the digital medium (Rogerson/Gibss/Smith 2015, 8).

Thanks to its technological possibilities, the digital medium offers users more entertainment due to its diversity: Minigames can be implemented in games, huge amounts of side quests fascinate the players, cinematic details enhance the immersion. A modern video game is often characterised by its huge computing power, which is reflected in its graphics and gameplay: Attack power and damage, production and costs etc. do not have to be worked out by hand over and over again using many big tables, computing is done in the background and consumers can focus on the game itself. When a video game is converted into a board game, this background work is no longer provided. The complexity of the game must be reduced to make it playable. There are now several examples where this change has been successful: *Frostpunk, Dorfromantik* or Anno 1800.

3. Methodology of video game analysis

A conceptual video game analysis from a historical perspective or with a special focus on historical mechanisms and concepts is still being developed as an independent approach. With the HGP method – a method developed as a part of a horror-games-and-politics analysis based on a historical, source-critical perspective – Eugen Pfister and Arno Görgen enable a consistent approach to analysing video games to ensure a deeper insight into the political themes of video games (Pfister/Görgen 2023). Based on Clara Fernandez-Vara's "Introduction to Video Game Analysis" (2015), they utilise historical source criticism and apply it to video games. The procedure consists of a four-step process:

1. the production analysis, in which the game is examined for its origin and historical context;

2. the product analysis, in which the game is examined for its form and content;

3. the self-explanatory reception analysis;

4. the creation of a myth catalogue.

Pfister and Görgen refer their use of mythologies on Roland Barthes definition of myths: They are discursive elements in different forms: They can be a text, an image, or an object and "with Ian Bogost's concept of procedural rhetoric, one must also consider processes, performative practices, and actions [...]" (Pfister/Görgen 2023). Therefore, a whole concept can be such a myth. A main concept within a game can be interpreted as a metaphor, according to the theory about the game metaphors mentioned above, concerning the transition of a board game to a video game and vice versa.

The advantage of using this method lies within the four steps: it takes in context the production as a historical context. In today's video game development, the future audience takes a huge impact: What does the public expect from the game? Where are niches, needs and possibilities in today's entertainment? By opening the production process to the public –just like Anno 1800 did – gamers become produsers, not by interfering directly but with posting their opinions publicly and openly. As Axel Bruns states: There is a "fluid movement of produsers between roles as leaders, participants, and users of content" (2007, 3).

It is the huge impact from the public, which makes a short production analysis necessary to gain a broad understanding of the reasons, why both Anno 1800 – the video game and Anno 1800 – the board game are similar and/or different as they are. The product analysis is the main aspect of the method described above as it centres the focus on the game itself and not on its surroundings as the production analysis did.

In the following, the individual steps of this video game analysis are described individually and applied to the example of Anno 1800 – first to the video game, then to the board game – in relation to money. This means that the myth catalogue can be reduced to two main myths for this analysis: money and workforce. The reception analysis will not be covered in this paper, as Pfister and Görgen already state its extensive work for little usable output (Pfister/Görgen 2023).

4. Production analysis – The Anno Union and Anno 1800 video game series

According to Pfister and Görgen, production analysis deals with various questions:

> "How big was the team? What was the demographic composition of the team during product development? What was the biographical background of the developers? How has the development process changed over time? What design decisions have arisen here due to structural/external constraints and influences? What conflicts existed during the development process and how were they resolved?" (Pfister/Görgen 2023)

Many of these questions are very difficult to answer; especially with large AAA titles, investigations of this kind are quite extensive, even if they are sometimes made known to the fan community by the developers in interviews or press releases. However, the influence of the Anno Union should be emphasised here as significant for the development of Anno 1800. Fans are collected in this Anno Union and their input is analysed by the Anno Community Team:

> "You are not only at the right place to get all Anno 1800 information and updates to come, we also will actively look out for your input in

> order to use the vast knowledge of our Anno Union member to shape and test our game." (Anno Union 2017)

This enables close contact between the fan community and the developers and influences the game to meet future expectations.

Table 1: Comparison between the last three Anno-titles (Steam Stats) (VG-Insights)

	Anno 2070	**Anno 2205**	**Anno 1800**
Active players (1h peak)	52	58	2032
Active players (24h peak)	96	129	3962
% of positive reviews	60,4	69,8	81,5
Gross revenue in $	11.700.000	7.800.000	6.600.000
Units sold	771.000	315.000	340.000
Avg. play time in h	100,8	72,9	201
Median play time in h	37,2	40,1	81

The revenue and sales of Anno 1800 are not transparent: following its release in April 2019, Ubisoft withdrew the game from the Steam gaming platform due to an agreement with Epic Games and did not make it available on the gaming platform again until 2022. Furthermore, this is only the data from the Steam gaming platform; Ubisoft's own gaming platform Ubisoft Connect and the Epic Games Store are not included. Therefor the Gross revenue and the units sold are heavily distorted.

Nonetheless, this table clearly shows the effects of such a fan-based influence: The positive reviews have increased by more than ten percentage points from the predecessor Anno 2205 to Anno 1800. However, the average playing time in hours as well as the better feedback show the increasing success of the Anno series, which has gone hand in hand with the establishment of the Anno Union and the consideration of user feedback.

5. Product Analysis – The video game

According to Pfister and Görgen, product analysis refers to three important vectors: story, audio-visual aesthetics, and game mechanics (2023). The aim is to include all aspects of a game as comprehensively as possible. In the following, this is reduced to the aspect of money, whereby the game principle of Anno is first explained in general. Then, the significance of money in terms of the game mechanics, as well as the visual preparation and representation, are explained.

5.1 Game principle of Anno – The video game

The previous ANNO titles for the PC were based on a simple system: Players generate building resources such as wood or steel and consumer products such as food or clothing for the population by constructing buildings. By consuming these products, the population generates money, which can then be invested. Some of this income is used to maintain the production buildings, but there is always a surplus that can be used for the military, infrastructure, ships, or ornaments, etc.

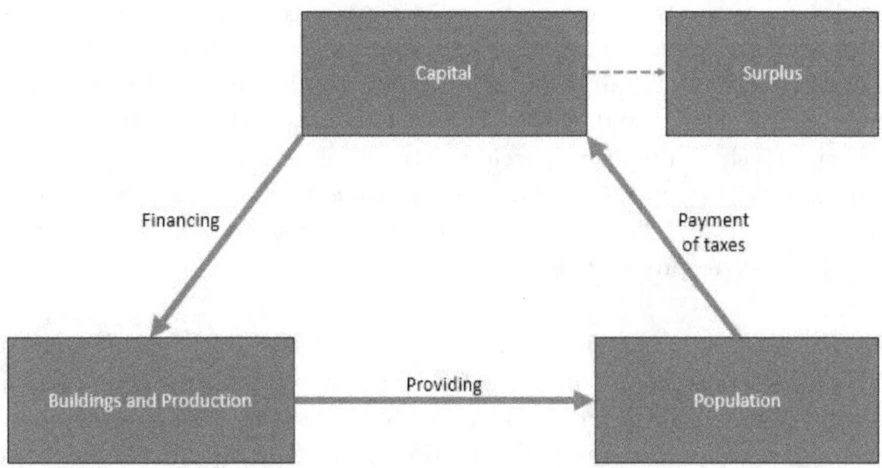

Figure 1. Game Principle - Anno Series

This seemingly simple game principle challenges players: the production chains become increasingly complex as the game progresses and the production of higher-value goods requires a wide variety of resources and several work steps. The population is divided into up to five different classes. Each class requires different goods: while the goods of the lower classes can usually be produced on a single island, the goods of the higher classes require different fertilities and resources. This results in complex economic infrastructures and trade routes, which are particularly susceptible to military attacks from outside and therefore require military escorts. The earlier Anno games were reduced to a single region but were characterised by different climate zones in which different peoples lived and different resources could be cultivated or mined. Anno 2205 featured the colonisation of other regions and eventually the moon, but infrastructure and trade routes were no longer as complex as in the previous parts, much to the chagrin of the fan community. Anno 1800 subsequently also introduced a variety of regions characterised by different climate zones, different populations and different needs: The "Old World", the "New World", "Enbesa" – a clichéd African-influenced land, "Cape Trelawney" – similar to the "Old World" with larger islands, and the Arctic. With the reintroduction of trade routes, this led to corresponding challenges for the players.

Anno 1800 – in contrary to its predecessors – also saw the introduction of labour: Each production building needs a certain number of workers of a certain class to be functional and thus generate maximum output. Increasing production therefore requires a larger neighbourhood consisting of larger residential buildings with space for more workers, who ultimately require a huge supply of products to generate enough money sustaining the economy. This growth needs to be financed: While lower classes such as farmers and labourers generate little income and tend to produce cheap products, the upper classes with the craftsmen, engineers and investors procure more valuable products and more money, which in turn can be reinvested: be it in more efficient and larger productions, be it in the military. Higher-value productions produce higher-value products, but also cost more money to maintain and require more labour than lower-value productions.

The highest class of the population are the investors, who are no longer counted among the labour force: While these have the highest demands of products and generate a lot of money for the players, they are no longer labourers as they are not needed as such in any building. The resources required by investors are largely produced by engineers and craftsmen. Instead, the investors generate influence, a kind of secondary currency, which is used for the construction of large buildings, for particularly large military or trading fleets or the colonisation of new islands.

5.2 Multiple meanings of money in the video game

Money is the main resource for players at the start of the game: Already in the game settings, money becomes relevant to the difficulty of the game in several ways. The amount of starting capital, but also the amount of building maintenance and the costs for a possible building demolition can be set here and directly influence the way the game is played: Do you want to expand your own islands slowly and safely or would you prefer to achieve an economic boom through overproduction and sales? The biggest cost driver for players, however, is the royal tax, which is a special in-game mechanic: This penalises oversized cities that are characterised by a high population. Each class on each island is taxed individually according to its population, so that a higher population also results in higher tax sums. With this knowledge, players can colonise several islands instead of one large one to "save money" (Anno 1800 Wiki). This creates motivation to expand their empire and develop their infrastructure. In addition to a military or economic defeat – whether through the loss of all islands through attacks or by losing all its own shares due to investment of other players– it is possible to lose through bankruptcy by falling into negative balance twice. The first time you are helped by an NPC, the second time the game ends in a defeat screen. This hurdle creates an extrinsic motivation for the player to build up a functioning economy. Anno 1800 introduces the sandbox building feature, in which all costs are cancelled, and players have therefor no problem to sustain the economy anymore. As a result can be concluded: money is a central hurdle and challenge in the game.

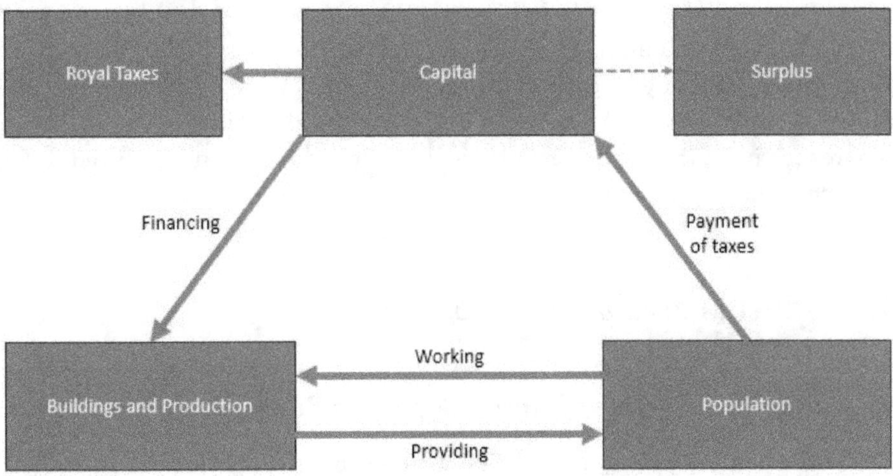

Figure 2. Game Principle Anno 1800 – The Video Game

But how does money appear on the game interface? At the top left, a separate bar shows the population and two other values: the current assets and the balance sheet, which are updated several times per second. This provides players with constant feedback on their own growth and investments. On the other hand, there are detailed production statistics that players can access. Here, players cannot only see how many resources are required and produced, but also how much money is gained from each individual resource per island and in total, or how much is lost through building maintenance.

6. Production analysis – The board game

6.1 Why a board game Anno 1800?

There are already two board games in the ANNO series before Anno 1800: Anno 1503 (Weber 2004) and Anno 1701 – Das Brettspiel (Bruhn 2008). Both were developed by Klaus Teuber at KOSMOS-Verlag but have taken on ever stronger traits of "Settlers of Catan". The latter in particular seems like a strong adaptation of the Settlers mechanics and shows little innovation of its own and is criticised accordingly. It is therefore obvious that Anno 1800 is a new, more international attempt at a board game, especially in the context of the success of the video game. Martin Wallace gave the game its board game adaptation in the KOSMOS publishing house. A striking number of drawings, symbols and thus familiar graphics from the video game were adopted, so that video game players recognise their beloved game. In his analysis of the board game adaptation of the game, Bornschein emphasises that the video game is better than its two predecessors, although he criticises the built-in luck factor (Bornschein 2021). The board games in the Anno series, and therefore also Anno 1800, are based on the respective video games, but are heavily adapted and reduced by the respective game designers.

7. Product analysis – The board game

7.1 The game principle of Anno 1800 – The Board Game

The board game is primarily based on the new labour force feature added to the computer game and the associated buildings. The labour force is divided into the same five classes – farmers, workers, craftsmen and investors – and is required for various productions. These are based on the video game: in the board game, players start with a basic set of buildings and population on their starting island. The labourers are then placed in these buildings to produce resources, which must be used immediately in their own turn to construct a new building or for other actions. The labourers then remain consumed until they are reset by a city festival – the deliberate renunciation of actions in your own turn. Various cards are acquired and played via various actions such as expanding your own production or investing resources in population or exploring new islands to increase your building area. These then count towards victory points at the end, which are called influence points in this game.

In contrast to the video game, the board game does not have as many options for expansion into non-European regions: The starting island is central, which can also be expanded slightly. In addition, "South American islands" can be explored, although nothing specific can be built on them as opposed to the home island, but the productions are already available.

7.2 Little importance of money in the board game

In contrast to the video game, the board game cannot easily represent the maintenance of many buildings operating in parallel, which is why money in the form of maintenance and capital has been completely removed. Instead, a different currency was introduced in the form of gold. With this gold, buildings that have already been used can be used again. This is the only function of a currency. This gold is generated by "selling": It is possible to use the buildings of other players with your own merchant ships. As a reward, they then receive a certain amount of gold, which can be used for their own progress in the game. Gold also plays a role in the scoring at the end of the game, as every three gold points generate one point. This counts very little toward a win in an average game and is essentially negligible. On the other hand, gold can be used to reset some of your workforces without use of the action "city festival". Each class costs a different amount of gold to be reset.

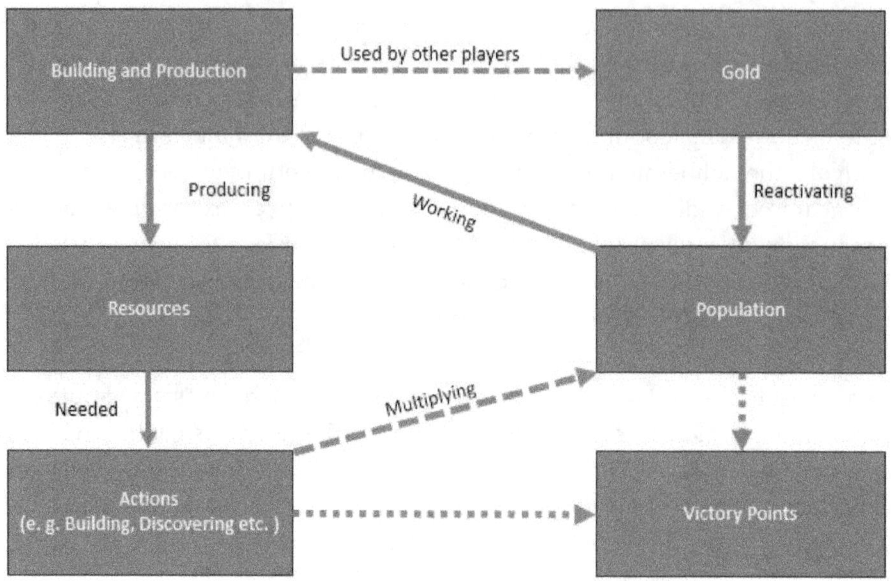

Figure 3. Game Principle Anno 1800 - The board game

How is this currency presented here? Gold is represented as a cardboard tile with gold bars printed on it, the symbol for which was taken from the video game. This makes its use confusing for players who are used to the video game, where the resource "Gold" has a different purpose in typical production chains. The main currency lost its value in comparison to the currency in the video game, as it is not an omnipresent measure of value.

8. Differences between the two analyses

The two production analyses are very different: while the video game is backed by an AAA studio, a board game is usually created by one person or a small team, in this case Martin Wallace. In addition, the fan community was taken into account when creating the video game, which made its success possible.

The most noticeable difference between the video game and the board game is money. While in the video game, money is a game-determining factor, which is also shown to players through statistics, there is no corresponding counterpart in the board game. In the video game, money is part of the game cycle and the inner game principle. Gold in the board game does not play the same role as money in the video game. The mechanics of money influencing the difficulty of the game can no longer be found. This can also be seen in the representation: in the video game, money is omnipresent: from rising construction costs and maintenance to detailed statistics. In the board game, gold is only part of a secondary mechanic, but it is present in its haptic form. Gold is actively interchangeable with workforce as the player can invest it to reuse already used workers. But gold is difficult to gain as it can only be earned by trades of other players. Therefore, the substitute gold only takes on a minor role within the board game, which means that a currency is no longer part of the central game principle.

The metaphor described at the beginning of this paper, which focuses on the concept of money and currency, can therefore no longer be described as central in the transition from video game to board game. Gold as a currency takes on a different function. The main metaphors linking the two games relate to labour and production, both of which are presented through the same visual representation.

9. Theories of Marx and Anno 1800

This small chapter tries to highlight some core elements of capitalism according to Marx and connecting them with the metaphors from Anno 1800.

Finding a satisfying definition of the word capitalism, regarding its history of ideological conflict between the East and the West, is a difficult task. Christine Resch and Heinz Steinert succeeded in explaining the capitalist system as a means of production. There are two types of labour: domestic labour and wage labour. In the 19th century, the latter prevailed over domestic labour, on the one hand through the "heroism" of industrial labour and on the other through the mass consumption of Fordism (2009, 25):

The heroism is based on a two-split-male-society: the mere mortals and the heroic image as an incarnation of heroic ideals and images, which adapts over time to the different cultural and economic circumstances (Hadamitzky 2020, 18–27): "Saints and Heros of humanism, " as men to be remembered for effective work in the development of human society as society existed in Western Europe about the beginning if the nineteenth century" (Comte 1920, vi); "Therefore […] is a notion of working hard towards an improvement of society as a whole […] the work of the individual is placed into a larger scheme and the achievements are important in their relevance for a common greater good, not because of personal success." (Hadamitzky 2020, 37–38).

The Fordism represents – as Harland Prechel pointed out in his paper "Fordism and Post-Fordism" (2017) – "three critical developments in the standardization, fragmentation and specialization of the labor process." Mechanics like this allowed the production to gain a higher output, hence the term mass-production (Prechel 2017, 1).

And with Anno 1800, we are exactly in the period revolving around the ambivalence of labour and weather a worker should be seen as a hero or as a centrepiece working at a conveyor belt resulting in a higher output. Furthermore, they define capitalism through the involvement of everyone in the production process, the achievement of a positive balance and the highest possible output in an industrialized and capitalist-structured society (Resch/Steinert 2009, 24–32). One could argue, the aim of every worker involved in the production processes of an island or even a whole region, does so for the greater good of all the population and not for personal enrichment.

Applied to the video and board game, principles of work and output are clearly recognisable: each worker or group of workers is assigned a direct, measurable output. In the video game, this is visible via statistics, in the board game via directly produced resources.

For Marx,

> "The Reproduction of labour power, which must incessantly be re-incorporated into capital as its means of valorization, which cannot get free from capital, and whose enslavement to capital is only concealed by the variety of individual capitalists to whom it sells itself forms, is in fact a factor in the reproduction of capital itself. Accumulation of capital is therefore multiplication of the proletariat." (Marx 1977, 763–764)

Hence, the capital the player gains, controls and invests is based on the workforce (the proletariat) they develop over the course of the game. According to Jason W. Moore and his influential work "Capitalism in the Web of Life" such a growth goes according to the expansion in the world and according to geographical conditions (2015). This corresponds to the idea of growth, which is addressed in both the video game and the board game. Whereas in the video game, other regions with different climate zones are discovered and colonised, the board game includes new "islands" in the sense of areas that can be connected to your own starting island.

Furthermore, as Moore states, the production of surplus value is not only the proletarianization of labour and the accumulation of capital, but the production of global spaces of appropriation. Anno 1800 – the video game relies on this surplus of production, which can be reinvested, and the accumulation of space for expansion.

Marx already states, if wares are not sold to buy other wares but simply to accumulate money or gold and not to sustain the money cycle, money itself loses its purpose as a trading good (Marx 2020, 118). Gold in the board game is a trading good and used in a kind of cycle, but it is highly limited and not gained and used directly. If someone wants to get a resource another player produces, they use a specific amount of trading points gained by building trade ships. The player providing the resource gets a little reward: one gold. The amount is always the same, independent of the original worth of the resource. The value of gold therefore does not correspond to the actual commodity value or the production value, as a normal determination of value would require. Gold in the board game can thus not be equated with a currency whose goal is to represent the commodity value as such, but at the same time to separate it from the commodity itself (Marx 2020, 75). Gold is therefore no currency per se and lacks the capitalist characteristics money does in the video game.

In addition, the Anno-Concept of investors, who do not work anymore but live on the products and resources produced, is purely capitalistic – if not a critique on capitalism itself. The highest and most influential class of population contributes nothing but the immaterial resource of influence and money to the economy. It simply seems like they do not work and therefore according to the theories of Marx do not generate a valuable output for the imaginary society of Anno 1800. Investors are not that tangible for the players as the other working classes, as they are not depicted as workforce and not directly used for anything but their passive output of influence-points and money. In giving influence and money importance in the game – be it victory points in the board game or the possibility to settle on further islands in the boardgame – investors become the highest goal within the game. Supplying them with all the amenities possible by using other workforces and giant production lines seem like the climax of exploitation of the lower masses and therefore also as a prime example of capitalism itself.

10. Conclusion: What about the game metaphor(s)?

Even though this analysis of the conversion from a video game to a board game started off with the two myths workforce and money, there is also a third very important concept: The production(-chains). Having a look again at the figures concerning the video game all three of those concepts are present and characterize the game. This leads to the conclusion that those are the three game metaphors important for the player to recognize the game. But money as one of those game metaphors and core concepts is not recognizable in the board game. Money takes up a huge part in the video game, is omnipresent and especially vital for the game experience in the early game. The need to strip such an important game mechanic in the board game is inevitable: Computing costs and administrating them for each player would force the introduction of budget-tables and an accessible, haptic currency. Therefore, this core metaphor could not be adapted into the board game. In consequence the board game seems kind of missing something in comparison to the video game. Even though the other two core concepts –production chains and workforce – are recognizable, the game itself changes its shape and focus. But nonetheless it is still capitalistic, it is just shown differently: through workforce and production. Arthur Seldon highlights in "Capitalism" the transition from Fordism to the Domestic System, the Spread of Capitalism and other important mechanics and points out that even in anti-capitalist systems of government, like in socialist or communist states, capitalism is still implemented in its core: The economy, and human nature, revolve around growth and providing an enriched and better surrounding for its own (1990, 48–97). A game that attempts to depict such central capitalist structures of reality as an economic simulation is inherently capitalist. A corresponding board game that does not contain the central mechanics of capitalism, money, must still be capitalist according to Seldon's definition.

Parallel to Pfister's and Tschiggler's case study on Civilisation, Anno 1800 can also be described as a game of constant further and higher development, even if this is made possible less by researchable technologies than by population and supply (2013, 132–133). It is increasing development, increasing efficiency, and the ever-decreasing importance of the lower classes of the population that characterise the game Anno 1800 as capitalistic. This culminates in the class of investors, who are presented and valued as the fifth and highest class of society and no longer belong to the labour force (i.e. the proletariat). They merely serve to generate influence, a special currency in the game which, unlike money, has a much greater significance in the late game. At this point, money is already abundant, as players need a large and stable economy to reach such an advanced game state. Maybe it is this point the board game wants to highlight: the moment money itself is abundant and therefore not necessary anymore as a core concept.

Interestingly, in the board game, the highest class, the investor, fulfils the same role as in the video game: it is only important if the player wants to gain a lot of influence points, i.e., victory points. The investor has no share in production and is therefore the symbol of capitalism itself. The investor is the furthest away from a resource or product and therefore has little to no contribution to the value of the product itself.

As a result, the following can be concluded: Labour power is split into classes according to capitalism and a class society in both games, reinforcing capitalist narratives of upward mobility. The highest class, the investors, are the pinnacle of capitalism in the game, and their name testifies to the importance of money. Expansion, and space are signs of a growing economy and are closely linked to it. This shows that economic growth is central to both games. It can therefore be said that the board game, like the video game, has capitalist tendencies, although gold only slightly replaces money. In terms of the theory of preserved metaphors and myths to enable a transition from video game to board game and vice versa, it is not the currency that has been preserved, but labour power, production, and the associated capitalist constructs as the central element.

About the Author

Andreas Wieser is enrolled in the Master's Programme of Teacher Training for the Secondary Grade in History, Social Studies and Political Education & Latin at the Leopold-Franzens-University in Innsbruck. His main research focus lies within the influences of video games on the perception of historical concepts and culture.

Acknowledgments

Special thanks to my friends, supporters, and fellow players Sabrina Leitner, Markus Saurwein and Luke Tran, who helped and assisted me in many different ways.

Ludography

11 Bit Studios. "Frostpunk", 2018.

Blizzard Entertainment. "Hearthstone: Heros of Warcraft", 2014.

Blue Byte. "Anno 2070", 2011.

Blue Byte. "Anno 2205", 2015.

Gygax, Gary and Dave Arneson. "Dungeons and Dragons", Lake Geneva: Tactical Studies Rules, 1974.

Koch Media. "Carcassonne", 2002.

Kwapiński, Adam. „Frostpunk", Glass Cannon 2022.

Teuber, Klaus. "Anno 1701 – Das Brettspiel", KOSMOS 2007.

Teuber, Klaus. "Anno 1503", KOSMOS 2003.

Toukana Interactive. „Dorfromantik", 2022.

Ubisoft Mainz. "Anno 1800", 2019.

Wallace, Martin. "Anno 1800", KOSMOS 2020.

Wizards of the Coast. "Magic: The Gathering", 1993.

Wrede, Klaus-Jürgen. "Carcassonne", Hans im Glück Verlag 2000.

Zach, Lukas and Michael Palm. "Dorfromantik: Das Brettspiel", Pegasus Spiele 2022.

References

Anno 1800 tutorials. "Making Money – Royal taxes." Accessed February 19, 2024. https://anno1800tutorials.wordpress.com/2020/05/01/anno-1800-making-money-royal-taxes/

Anno 1800 Wiki. "Royal Taxes." Accessed February 19, 2024. https://anno1800.fandom.com/wiki/Royal_Taxes

Anno Union. "Jump abord the Anno Union." Accessed February 19, 2024. https://Anno-union.com/articel-no-2/

Barthes. Roland- "Mythologies", Paris: Les Lettres nouvelles, 1957.

Bornschein, Nick. "Anno 1800." Accessed February 19, 2024. https://www.hall9000.de/html/spiel/anno_1800

Bruhn, Ralph. "Anno 1701." Accessed February 19, 2024. https://www.hall9000.de/html/spiel/anno_1701_das_brettspiel

Bruns, Axel. "Produsage: Twowards a Broader Framework for User-Led Content Creation", *Proceedings Creativity & Cognition 6*, Washington, DC, 2007.

Burke, Kenneth. "Four Master Tropes" *The Kenyon Review* 3, no. 4 (1941): 421–438.

Comte, Auguste: "The New Calendar of Great Men. Biographies of the 559 Worthies of All Ages and Nations", London 1920 [1849].

Fernández-Vará, Clara. "Introduction to Video Game Analysis", New York-London: Routledge, 2015.

Hadamitzky, Christiane. "Heroism in Victorian Periodicals 1850–1900." *Chambers's Journal – Leisure Hour Fraser's Magazine* 15, no. 1, 2020.

Hamilton, Anne. "Metaphor in theory and practice: the influence of metaphors on expectations." *ACM Journal of Computer Documentation* 24, no. 4 (2000): 237–253.

Jacob, Stephan. "Die große Digital-Offensive der Brettspiele." *Teilzeithelden. Magazin für gespielte und erlebte Phantastik*, 10. November 2018. Accessed February 29, 2024. https://www.teilzeithelden.de/2018/11/10/die-grosse-digital-offensive-der-brettspiele/

Marx, Karl. "Capital. A Critique of Political Economy, Vol. 1", New York: Vintage 1977 [1867].

Marx, Karl. "Das Kapital. Der Produktionsprozess des Kapitals", Hamburg: Nikol 2020 [1867].

Moore, James W. "Capitalism in the Web of Life. Ecology and the Accumulation of Capital", London-New York: Verso 2015.

Pfister, Eugen and Arno Görgen. „How to analyse a Video game from a historical, source-critical perspective: The HGP-Method." *Horror – Game – Politics. Die visuelle Rhetorik politischer Mythen in digitalen Horrorspielen* (01.02.2023). https://hgp.hypotheses.org/1754

Pfister, Eugen and Martin Tschiggerl. „Ranke ex machina? Geschichtstheorie in digitalen Spielen" *Geschichte in Wissenschaft und Unterricht* 74, no. 3/4 (2013): 125–139.

Prechel, Harland. „Fordism and Post-Fordism." In: Turner, Bryan S. (Ed.) "The Wiley-Blackwell Encyclopedia of Social Theory", s. l.: John Wiley & Sons 2017, 1–4.

Resch, Christine and Heinz Steinert. "Kapitalismus: Porträt einer Produktionsweise" (Einstiege 19. Grundbegriffe der Sozialphilosophie und Gesellschaftstheorie), Münster: Westfälisches Dampfboot 2009.

Rogerson, Melissa J., Martin Gibbs and Wally Smith (2015). "Digitising Boardgames: Issues and Tensions (Proceedings of DiGRA 2015: Diversity of play: Games – Cultures – Identities), Accessed February 19, 2024. http://www.digra.org/wp-content/uploads/digital-library/66_Rogerson-etal_Digitising-Boardgames.pdf

Seldon, Artur. "Capitalism", Oxford-Cambride: Basil Blackwell 1990.

Siebert, Benjamin and Florian Lütticke. "Fußball, Tetris, Anno1800? Diese 6 Brettspiele sind auch etwas für Gamer." *Welt* (06.10.2023). https://www.welt.de/wirtschaft/webwelt/article247772692/Brettspiele-Fussball-Tetris-Anno-1800-Diese-6-Brettspiele-sind-auch-etwas-fuer-Gamer.html

VG Insights. "Anno 1800 – Steam Stats." Accessed February 19, 2024. https://vginsights.com/game/916440

VG Insights. "Anno 2070 – Steam Stats." Accessed February 19, 2024. https://vginsights.com/game/48240

VG Insights. "Anno 2205 – Steam Stats." Accessed February 19, 2024. https://vginsights.com/game/375910

Weber, Willi. "Anno 1503." Accessed February 19, 2024. https://www.hall9000.de/html/spiel/anno_1503

LIFE IS CHEAP

THE CYCLE OF PROFIT, INVESTMENT AND (SELF)IMPROVEMENT IN ROLEPLAYING GAMES.

Fiona S. Schönberg

Whether it's Septims or Eurodollars, Nuyen, Bottlecaps, some flavor of Galactic Credit or the ever ubiquitous gold and silver pieces – most roleplaying games feature some form of diegetic currency. When observing what these games permit the players to spend that money on a common trend emerges. Even though a wide range of these games feature mechanics to spend money on food, housing, and a number of leisure or luxury items and activities, and even though the accumulation of wealth is presented as an actual diegetic goal in many such games, the vast majority of opportunities to spend money (both in number and quantity) are focused on improving the mechanical efficiency of the player avatar to perform whatever (usually violent and mercenary) work they do to earn money to begin with. This paper will explore the procedural rhetoric of this loop. The loop of all but (mechanically) guaranteed profit, generating money as a diegetic currency of mechanical progression, and specifically how the progression of profit to invest into greater (combat) efficiency in turn leads to greater profits, which closely mirrors capitalist libertarian theories of individual economic progression but eschews the many pitfalls that such theories chafe against outside the realm of gamified fiction.

Keywords: RPGs, In-game Economy, Procedural Rhetoric, Self-Improvement, Investment.

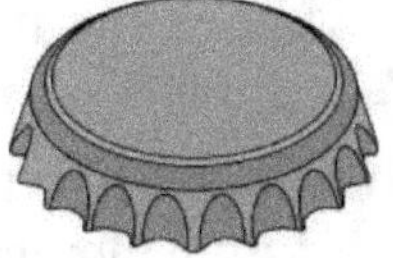

1. Money Makes the World(s) Go Round

Almost every mainstream narrative[1] roleplaying game features some kind of diegetic currency. Diegetic currency can manifest in any number of ways – there's no shortage of permutations of gold coinage, from games such as *The Elder Scrolls* Series to the recent *Baldur's Gate III*. In science-fiction games, there's many different kinds of Galactic Credit, from *Knights of the Old Republic* to *Mass Effect* to *Starfield*, while the cyberpunk genre frequently features fusions of contemporary currency, like *Shadowrun*'s 'Nu-yen' or *Cyberpunk 2077*'s 'Eurodollars'. And some franchises feature entirely different types of money, such as the *Fallout* franchise's bottle-caps.

What might appear at first glance like a fairly arbitrary selection of games across a number of different genres, decades, and, if taking the tabletop variations of some of the mentioned franchises into account, different forms of media, is by no means an exhaustive list of games that exhibit the patterns that this chapter will highlight. This eclectic selection will serve as an illustration of the comprehensiveness of these patterns. In all the games listed above there are three commonalities in how the in-game economies of these fictional worlds function.

Firstly, all of these games heavily feature profit as a motivator for player action. This occurs diegetically – player avatars in games like *Cyberpunk 2077* or the *Shadowrun* games are explicitly mercenaries and *Fallout: New Vegas*' Courier is a mail delivery person. But the factor of profit as motivation also exists on a metadiegetic level. All of the games mentioned are virtually packed with side quests and activities to distract from the (sometimes quite urgent) main stories. And more often than not, the primary motivator that is offered to the player to engage in such side-quests is a financial motivation. While all of these games afford the player some level of agency over the persona that the player avatar presents to the world, along different axis of (gamified) morality, they always afford the player the possibility of putting forward a persona purely driven by financial self-interest disassociated from morality. It is not by accident, then, that

[1] The somewhat loaded 'narrative' term is here used as per Michael Nitsche's and Clara Fernández-Vara's definitions to mean "a form of comprehension that can be triggered and affected by the game world" (Nitsche 2008, p. 52) and as games where emphasis is placed on navigating story problems over navigating mechanical challenges (cf. Fernández-Vara 2015, p. 27ff.) to draw a distinction toward more mechanically focused roleplaying games, such as 'Soulslikes'.

one of the most common 'speech checks' across any number of these games, is a check to demand or extort greater monetary reward for a completed quest.

Secondly, though the extent varies, all of these games, while it may not be central to their flow, include some tacit attempts at what will here be called an 'economic life simulation'. 'Economic life simulation' is here used to mean two things. Although the exact degree varies, these games acknowledge the basic material needs of the player avatar. They feature ways to spend diegetic currency to purchase food, shelter or other forms of living expenses (such as *Knights of the Old Republic* charging the player docking fees whenever they land on a planet). The other constituent aspect of an 'economic life simulation' is that they feature some manner of depictions of diegetic poverty and economic inequality. Beggars are loitering at street corners, and most of the listed games feature some sort of shantytown or economic ghetto, whether that is the dark elf quarter in *Skyrim*'s Windhelm, *Fallout: New Vegas*' Freeside, the lower city *Knights of the Old Republic*'s Taris, the day-laborer's coffin hotels of *Starfield*'s Neon or *Cyberpunk 2077*'s lawless Dogtown.

Thirdly, and drawing upon the first two commonalities, at least as far as the player character is concerned, *life is dirt cheap*. Food is usually largely superfluous, at least from a game mechanical perspective, often functioning as a health item or providing minimal stat boosting effects. In most of these games, the player avatar does not need to eat. They could go from start to finish of the game's story without ever eating once. In games like *Starfield* or *Skyrim*, food provides negligible amounts of healing compared to dedicated healing items. In games like *Cyberpunk 2077*, foodstuffs grant small temporary buffs. But in general, even in the rare case where food is necessary, such as *Fallout: New Vegas'* optional Survival Mode or in *Baldur's Gate III* where food is used as a resource to fuel the resting mechanic, foodstuffs are found in abundance throughout the game world. So the player never actually needs to purchase food. But even if the player is inclined to actually pay for food, because they have neglected to collect some around the game world or because the player wishes to add this element to the simulation, what is available for purchase will only incur minimal costs compared to the amount of money that regularly passes through the player avatar's hands. These diegetic worlds may be full of characters who are starving, but the player avatar never seriously runs that risk.

The same goes for shelter. Shelter and housing in role-playing games are usually a purely aesthetic choice, at most offering minor conveniences like easier access to crafting stations or item storage. In games where the player avatar is regularly required to rest (like *Baldur's Gate 3*) or where they derive mechanical benefits from rest (like *Skyrim* or *Fallout: New Vegas*), the player avatar is usually able to rest in the wilderness, no matter how ostensibly hostile the environment. Where that is not an option, either because the setting does not permit it or because the narrative requires the player avatar to have a roof over their heads, the game will happily provide one free of charge (at least free of charges that occur in gameplay) – be that V's Megabuilding apartment in *Cyberpunk 2077*, the suite in the Lucky 38 gifted to *Fallout: New Vegas'* Courier, the room in the Constellation headquarters gifted to *Starfield*'s player avatar, or the space ships that are swiftly entrusted to the player avatar in *Starfield*, *Mass Effect* or *Knights of the Old Republic*. Some of the games mentioned permit the purchase of additional properties at more significant expense, but those are cosmetic choices. Although these diegetic worlds are full of homeless or precariously housed NPCs, the player avatar never suffers a lack of shelter, and even if they choose to rent a room somewhere (an option present in most Bethesda made entries) that too will carry only negligible expense.

And it bears mention that this phenomenon of depicting diegetic poverty as never quite reaching the main character [2] is almost unique to role playing games. For a very illustrative example, one need not look further than the anime *Cyberpunk: Edgerunners*. David Martinez, the protagonist of the animated television show set in the same franchise and the same diegetic world, inhabits the exact same size and layout of apartment as *Cyberpunk 2077*'s V does, just in a different building. But David is under immense pressure to make money. In a similar (arguably less dire) situation to V, he is constantly struggling to make ends meet. Rent is due week by week and David gets locked out from the apartment repeatedly, due to late payments. He's struggling to put food on the table, even his laundromat gets cut off due to lack of funds.

Meanwhile, V can tarry as much as they (or rather their player) would like. They do not need to eat, and they don't need to worry about payments, their rent will

---

[2] At least as far as the game mechanics are concerned. Some of these games may at times claim the player avatar to be destitute or at least poor, but these financial concerns never begin to impinge on the player's freedom to act mechanically. For a more detailed discussion of this concept of aligning (or decoupling) the (economic) concerns of player and avatar, cf. Schönberg 2023.

never be due.[3] The economic uncertainty and institutionalized poverty so common to the cyberpunk genre, and visible in every narrative and environmental design aspect of *Cyberpunk 2077*, never quite reaches the player avatar.

So what then, do player avatars actually spend their often vast fortunes on?

1.1 Self-made Character-Builds

> It's not about your upbringing! Look, I'm a self-made man. Borrowed a hundred grand from my parents and invested it. In myself. Didn't go spending it all on syncoke and expensive ass, but on implants and training. Gave it all back the second I could. Exactly. It's about self-discipline and ambition. If you're poor, you really have no one to blame but yourself.[4]

To put it simply, if somewhat provocatively, self-improvement.

The majority of currency spent in any one of these games goes toward improving the player avatar's mechanical effectiveness and, by extension, their diegetic effectiveness at whichever violent trade earned them that money to begin with. This increase can happen indirectly – by purchasing newer, better equipment, armor, weapons, ammunition or consumables. But it can also be quite literal – in games like *Cyberpunk 2077* or *Shadowrun,* their respective cyberware and implant systems permit immediate improvement of the player avatar's body, but even a game like *Skyrim* depicts its 'Training' mechanic as a direct and immediate exchange of money for improved ability of the player avatar. Speaking strictly in game design terms, money then becomes a secondary gauge of game progress and character advancement next to the more traditional character levels and

---

[3] Or at least not during play – technically, in the 'Tower' ending introduced in the game's *Phantom Liberty* DLC, V can lose the megabuilding apartment due to missed payments, but that occurs due to a two year coma that happens entirely within cut-scenes, and past the point where any game mechanical interaction occurs. Prior to this ending, not only will the player never be charged rent for the Megabuilding apartment, even the other housing options, ostensibly rented, will never incur a cost beyond the initial first month of rent.

[4] 'Ziggy Q' in *Cyberpunk 2077: Phantom Liberty.*

experience counters.[5] In gameplay, money functions quite similar to experience – both are naturally accumulated through playing the game (after all, whatever the player avatar does tends to turn out quite profitable) and both are expended to shape, customize and advance the player avatar.

Following this function as an alternate gauge of progress and reward, diegetic currency also typically follows a similar pattern to the exponential escalation of experience points. Early investments into equipment and improvement enable intermediate quests, which yield greater rewards, enabling more expensive investments, which in turn allow the completion of the most challenging quests, which yield the highest rewards. 'Vanity purchases' (such as cosmetic items or particularly high-end player housing or vehicles) are usually reserved for purpose in these late game stages, once enough money has been invested into a character-build to meet the challenges of these endgame quests (and indeed, making such vanity purchases too early in the game could quite easily result in a temporary increase in difficulty).[6]

This pattern encapsulates a particular rhetoric, so it is worth asking: What is the procedural rhetoric (that is the systemic 'persuasiveness of rules-based interactions'[7]) of these processes?

Playing the game, what has thus far been called advancement, generates profit – the funds derived from going on quests and selling plunder far exceed the player avatar's operating costs (ammunition, healing items, etc.) This profit is invested into increasing the player avatar's ability and capacity (by purchasing better weaponry or directly improving the avatar's physical capacities) to deal with increasingly difficult or sturdy enemies. Increased ability allows access and

---

[5] Indeed their function is so similar that many games less concerned with presenting a fully logistically realized, non-abstracted diegetic world than the subjects of this paper ('soulslike' games, such as *Elden Ring*) have combined 'experience points' and 'money' into a singular gauge of mechanical progress that can be used both to purchase items from vendors and to improve the player avatar's mechanical statistics.

[6] It is quite conceivable, for example, that a V whose player has decided to invest their first hundred thousand Eurodollars into a luxury care or Corpo Plaza apartment, might find themselves struggling through early midgame quests for lack of cyberware or weapon upgrades, or that a Dragonborn who has rushed into home-ownership before enchanting their armor will have a harder time plundering *Skyrim*'s dungeons.

[7] Cf. Bogost 2007.

accomplishments of greater tasks, which incur greater profit (a late game, high 'Street Cred' gig in *Cyberpunk 2077* can easily pay ten to a hundred times as much as one of the early gigs completed in the prologue). The cycle of increasing profits leading to increasing capacity leading to greater profits continues throughout the game, with cosmetic purchases often relegated to the late game, when no further increase in capacity is necessary to keep generating profit, or when a sufficient surplus has been achieved.

As Bogost would suggest, this pattern contains a rhetorical strategy that teaches and persuades players to adapt to the systems they are faced with while playing the game. This rhetorical strategy mirrors advice given by LinkedIn co-founder Reid Hoffman and Village Global co-founder Ben Casnocha in their self-help book *The Startup of You*, in which the following pieces of career advice appear:

> Whether you want to learn a new skill or simply be better at the job you were hired to do, it's now your job to train and invest in yourself. (p. 12)
>
> [Most people] focus, in short, on hard assets instead of soft assets. This is a mistake. [...] as much as you can, prioritize plans that offer the best chance at learning [...] Not only will you make more money in the long run, but your career journey will be more fulfilling. Ask yourself, "Which plan will grow my soft assets the fastest?" (p. 51)

Or to translate back into video game parlance – rather than focusing on the accumulation (and unproductive usage) of hard assets (that is to say, money), they advise a focus on soft assets, which they define as "knowledge and information in your brain [...] skills you've mastered; your reputation and personal brand; your strengths" (ibid. p. 30). Instead of focusing on the accumulation of wealth for frivolous purposes [8], focus on developing the abilities of your avatar to get ahead in your career/game progression.

Sound advice in any of the games that are being discussed here, and not out of place among any of their loading screen tips. It is perhaps not without reason that hustle and gamer culture share even the parlance of 'grinding'. These games

[8] Keeping in mind that, as previously discussed, for the most part everyday expenses of food and shelter are frivolous purchases, or at least unnecessary purchases of little value to the mechanical advancement.

mechanically reward continuous investment with ever greater financial incentive. But beyond simply implicitly replicating this rhetoric in a diegetic space, there is a key difference.

The narrative of hustle and grind is challenged in public discourse. Foregoing monetary compensation in favor of growing 'soft assets', sacrificing personal comforts in favor of career advancement along an axis of meritocracy intrinsically linked to personal ability, where increased personal capacity is inevitably rewarded, tends to face a number of criticisms. [9]

But in the confines of the diegetic worlds that are being discussed here, none of those criticisms apply. Flesh and blood people have to worry about maintaining themselves, physically and mentally, regardless of their individual willingness to advance. Food, shelter and rest are basic necessities that require a certain amount of funds, and the false dichotomy of either self-improvement or wastefulness is easily questioned, when there is no disposable income to begin with and the available funds are spend toward basic survival. On the other hand, player avatars, as detailed previously, do not have to worry about meeting their basic needs – all, or most of their income is disposable, so investment into becoming more efficient at pursuing gainful activity is an easy choice, since the only alternatives are leisure spending, rather than basic survival. Much in the same vein, player avatars never risk burnout – on the contrary, the things that they make money with, tend to be the very things that are fun for the player (i.e. gameplay).

Player avatars also take little to no risk in their investments. All the uncertainty of shifting job market demands investment risks, of cost and the potential for failure, are largely eschewed by the games. The nature of the gameplay loop mandates that the avatar's mechanical (if perhaps not their narrative) [10] career is

---

[9] This discourse at large is of limited relevance for this paper, which mainly aims to highlight the peculiarities of certain games in this discourse, but anyone interested in further reading on the contemporary political contention may confer Schor 2020, Dooner 2021, Ravenelle 2019.

[10] Once again, it bears remembering that this entire argument is made exclusively on the level of formal elements. On a narrative level, a character like *Cyberpunk 2077*'s V might be

always in demand – just as it guarantees a steady supply of not just gainful but profitable employment, which will be carefully balanced to provide a beatable challenge to any who invest enough to keep up with the expected curve of character improvement. At worst, a player might invest into the wrong thing, purchase the wrong item and be set back some amount of effort but there are likely to be more opportunities to make money. In the absence of any real cost of living, should a player spend too aggressively, running out of funds only spells a temporary inability to invest further, rather than existential threat of bankruptcy. On top of that, unlike in an uncertain and quickly changing job market, there is rarely ever uncertainty in a game. Learning a new skill, investing in personal infrastructure or similar strategies may very well not produce the desired career advancement or advantage, but in a video game, the player can gauge the exact mechanical effects that an investment will provide, displayed in cold hard math that is accessible to and understood by the player.

It is also worth noting that all the player avatars discussed in this paper earn their keep, either directly or indirectly, doing what is essentially violent mercenary work. This is not to reheat the well-treaded violent video game debates of yore – for the purposes of this observation, what is important is this: violence, certainly the way that roleplaying games portray it, is an intimate act of clear and immediate competition.

Committing acts of violence is an externalization of the sum total of the player's merit, their planning capability and understanding of the game's mechanics as well as the game statistics of their avatar, pitted against a challenge. There is little in the way of external factors, left to chance or fully outside the players' awareness that affect the outcome of a violent altercation. Overcoming these challenges – challenges that, depending on selected difficulty and similar choices within the player's control may be more or less stacked in the avatar's favor, but will always remain guaranteed to be theoretically manageable – is designed to

---

broke, or struggle to make ends meet, particularly at the beginning of the game, but so long as that narrative status is not reflected in the ludic framework, it can only ever affect the player's decisions on a basis of voluntary buy-in – the player has to decide to make this diegetic poverty their own concern, for the game does not.

impart a feeling of power and personal achievement to the player, while aspects of design that aid the player are deliberately obfuscated.[11]

In short, the way that a roleplaying game player's avatar turns a profit is immediately, intrinsically and obviously tied to their personal merit and ability. As far as the procedural rhetoric imparts, there is no (mechanical) privilege – player avatars succeed (and inevitably, with the sliding scale of increasing difficulty and investment) progressively achieve greater wealth on the basis of their own personal capacity. Equally, the investments that the player makes into improving the character, directly and immediately improve the avatar's capacity.

At least in the worlds of these games – worlds that very much do contain and display poverty – meritocracy is real. And since the accumulation of resources, much like experience points, is tied to the mechanics of progression, as far as the player avatar is concerned, as far as the player can mechanically experience, poverty is not only not that bad – representing little more than a temporary inability to spent, rather than an existential threat – it is a choice, brought about only by a refusal to play the game (and incur inevitable profit), or by 'living well beyond their current means' (by making frivolous and unnecessary vanity purchases too early).

The procedural rhetoric speaks, and it speaks with the voice of Ayn Rand.

That is not to imply that this is what these games are *about*. On the contrary, their narratives and designs often paint a very different picture. Even the quote that stands as epigraph to this section of the paper, taken in context, is clearly meant to be satirical. It is espoused by a comic relief character, at a party for the ultra-wealthy, a haven of utterly decadent luxury in the middle of the game's worst slum. The character that speaks it, both in this scene and in the segments of his TV show in the game, is meant to come off as detached and oblivious at best and callous at worst. And yet the quote itself is not an inaccurate description of the path that V takes through the story of *Cyberpunk 2077,* from quite literally initially taking on debt[12] to purchase new cyberware for an oncoming job, to riding the

[11] For a more detailed overview of the design concepts that are here only alluded to, cf. Upton 2015, p. 95 – 114.

[12] Though once again a debt that exists only narratively, and while it can be repaid if the player so chooses, it will never be collected or in any way impede upon the player's mechanical freedom, if they are inclined to leave it be.

cycle of investment, (self)improvement and growing profits to the very top of Night City.

1.2 Brass Tax / Conclusion

So what is to be taken away from this observation?

A game world that features rampant poverty and economic inequality, with mechanical processes that all but guarantee that characters in this game world can rise from this poverty to the heights of wealth, by the sweat of their brow, their merit, their willingness to grind alone, is not an ideology free space. This is not to imply the intentional inclusion of this ideology (often in conflict with what the narrative means to imply), far from it. Rather, this paper means to imply that ideas about the hustle and grind, the merits of personal entrepreneurship and success on merit alone are deeply ingrained into the conventions of roleplaying game design. Perhaps as deeply as Mark Fisher suggested, they are ingrained in all of popular discourse. [13]

But in games at least, they are by no means a necessity.

For an example of what could be, one need not look any further than *Disco Elysium*. Protagonist Harry duBois has a very different relationship with money than the avatars discussed in this paper. Money in *Disco Elysium* is almost exclusively collected through distractions from the main objective rather than by exercising the core gameplay loop of investigation. Shelter costs money and losing access to proper shelter has not just narrative implications but leads to a non-standard game over. It seriously infringes upon the player's mechanical freedom. The mechanical benefits that can be purchased are not investments, quite the opposite – they are temporary benefits, all directly linked to Harry duBois' self-destructive vices.

So the procedural rhetoric observed throughout this paper is by no means necessary to make a successful or critically acclaimed roleplaying game. But it *is* common practice.

---

[13] Cf. Fisher 2009.

Ian Bogost ended his 2007 book with a warning:

> We must recognize the persuasive and expressive power of procedurality. Processes influence us. They seed changes in our attitudes, which in turn, and over time, change our culture. As players of videogames and other computational artifacts, we should recognize procedural rhetoric as a new way to interrogate our world, to comment on it, to disrupt and challenge it. As creators and players of videogames, we must be conscious of the procedural claims we make, why we make them, and what kind of social fabric we hope to cultivate through the processes we unleash on the world. (p. 340)

And at the conclusion of this paper, I would like to join this plea – to scholars, but also to fellow makers of games – to take great care to not simply include game mechanics and systems to satisfy genre conventions or habit, but to carefully examine what the mechanics of a game are actually saying – and to question if that aligns with how we want our games to speak.

About the Author

Fiona S. Schönberg is a novelist, narrative designer, script writer and researcher from Germany. She holds a Bachelor of Arts in Film and English Literature and Culture, as well as an MA in Media-Dramaturgy from the Johannes Gutenberg University of Mainz, and is currently writing her PhD in Media Studies as an associate researcher of Regensburg University's Digital Area Studies Lab. Her research focus lies in digital and analogue narratology and particularly in the narrative spaces that careful examination and curation of game rules can open up.

Bluesky: @ohthehumanities.bsky.social

References

Baldur's Gate III. [Videogame]. 2023. Larian Studios.
Bogost, I. (2007). Persuasive Games – The Expressive Power of Videogames. The MIT Press.
Cyberpunk 2077. [Videogame]. 2020. CD Project Red.
Disco Elysium. [Videogame]. 2019. ZA/UM.

Dooner, C. (2021). Tired as F*ck – Burnout at the Hands of Diet, Self-Help, and Hustle Culture. Harper Collins.
Elden Ring. [Videogame]. 2022. FromSoftware Inc.
Fallout: New Vegas. [Videogame]. 2010. Obsidian Entertainment.
Fernández-Vara, C. (2015). Introduction to Game Analysis. Routledge.
Fisher, M. (2009). Capitalist Realism – Is There No Alternative? Zero Books.
Hoffman, R. & Canocha, B. (2012). The Startup of You – Adapt to the Future, Invest in Yourself, and Transform your Career. Random House, Inc.
Mass Effect. [Videogame]. 2007. BioWare.
Nitsche, M. (2008). Video Game Spaces. The MIT Press.
Ravenell, A. J. (2019). Hustle and Gig – Struggling and Surviving in the Sharing Economy. University of California Press.
Schor, J. B. (2020). After the Gig – How the Sharing Economy got Hijacked and how to Win it Back. University of California Press.
Schönberg, F. S. (2023) All Work and No Play - Economic Alienation and Design Imposed Bleed in Neo Cab. In N. Koenig, N. Denk, A. Pfeiffer, T. Wernbacher, S. Wimmer (Eds.): Freedom | Oppression | Games & Play 2023, p. 311-322).
Starfield. [Videogame]. 2023. Bethesda Game Studios.
Star Wars: Knights of the Old Republic [Videogame]. 2003. BioWare.
The Elder Scrolls V: Skyrim [Videogame]. 2011. Bethesda Game Studios.
Upton, B. (2015) The Aesthetic of Play. The MIT Press.

FROM FLAME TO FAME.

WOMEN PLAYER CARDS IN EA'S FC24 AND THEIR JOURNEY TO ACCEPTANCE

Michaela Wawra, Alexander Pfeiffer

The inclusion of women player cards in EA's FC24 Ultimate Team (FUT) represents a significant shift in sports video gaming, marking the first time female footballers have been integrated into this popular mode. This study explores the community's evolving perceptions of this inclusion through a qualitative content and sentiment analysis of two key Reddit threads. The first thread, analyzed prior to the game's release, captures initial skepticism and concerns, particularly around realism and the impact on FUT's competitive integrity. The second thread, from the near endgame phase, reveals how these perceptions have shifted, with many players eventually embracing the diversity and new dynamics brought by female players. Despite the positive reception, challenges such as card saturation and ongoing debates about the balance between realism and fantasy remain. The study highlights the educational impact of including women in FUT, contributing to greater awareness of women's football. The findings suggest that while the inclusion has been polarizing, it has also catalyzed important discussions about gender inclusivity in sports video games, setting the stage for further research and broader acceptance in the gaming community.

Keywords: EA Sports FC24. FIFA Ultimate Team (FUT), Loot Boxes, Women Player Cards, Gaming Community Sentiment

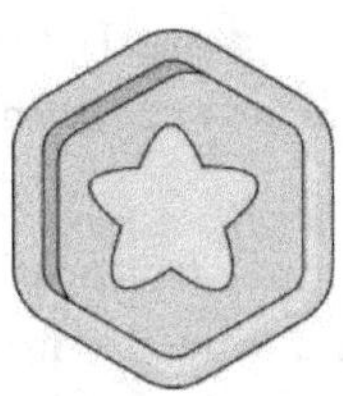

1. Introduction

Since its inception in FIFA 09, Ultimate Team (commonly referred to as FUT) has evolved into one of the most popular and financially lucrative game modes in EA Sports' association football video games. [1] Designed to allow players to build and manage their dream teams, FUT combines elements of strategy, skill, and chance, offering a dynamic experience that has captivated millions of players worldwide [2]. Player cards, representing real-life footballers, are central to this mode and are obtained through packs that players can purchase or earn within the game. These packs function as loot boxes, a feature introduced initially in free-to-play mobile games where players could access the game for free but were incentivized to purchase these randomized packs. This system has become a significant revenue source for game developers. However, the reliance on randomization and the potential for gambling-like behavior have sparked considerable debate, with concerns about the risk of gaming disorder [3, 4,14].

A loot box is a virtual item within a video game that contains a randomized selection of other virtual items, which can be utilized by players once the loot box is unlocked. These items, often termed "loot," may enhance the player's in-game experience or increase their chances of success. Loot boxes can be obtained either through gameplay achievements or by purchasing them through microtransactions. The process of obtaining items from loot boxes is likened to gambling mechanisms, such as slot machines or scratch lotteries, because the outcome is random and does not depend on player skill. This randomization, coupled with the potential need to purchase multiple loot boxes to obtain a desired item, has raised concerns about the predatory nature of loot boxes, particularly given their accessibility to minors [14, 15, 4, 16, 19].

For instance, players in FIFA's Ultimate Team mode can use real-world money to buy 'player packs,' which include a randomly selected group of footballers.

Loot boxes in FUT function similarly to traditional trading cards, where players buy packs without knowing what specific items they will receive. These packs can include player cards, consumables, and other in-game items that can enhance the performance of a team. The player cards evolve over time, as more and more special edition cards are being release [5]. The value of the contents varies widely, with some packs containing rare and highly sought-after players while others might offer less desirable items, often referred to as "fodder" [6] by the community.

The randomness of these packs is what drives both the excitement and the controversy surrounding FUT. Players can spend in-game currency (earned through gameplay) or real money to purchase these packs, leading to concerns about the potential for players, especially younger ones, to spend excessively in pursuit of rare cards [7]

This business model proved so successful that it was later adopted by major developers in pay-to-play games, leading to increased revenue. In fact, Electronic Arts (EA) became the first major game developer to introduce loot boxes with the launch of FIFA Ultimate Team (FUT), a new online-only game mode, in FIFA 09 [14].

Ultimate Team's reliance on loot boxes has been both a driver of its success and a source of significant criticism. The thrill of opening packs and the possibility of acquiring a top-tier player like Lionel Messi or Kylian Mbappé can be incredibly appealing. Hand in hand with building your very own squad you relate to, combining strategic decision, tactics and players you adore in real life. However, this system has also been criticized for fostering a "pay-to-win" environment, where players who spend more money on packs have a better chance of building stronger teams. This issue is compounded by the fact that the contents of packs are random, leading to frustration when players spend money only to receive low-value cards. As already mentioned, we identified player types in regard to their behavior when it comes to loot boxes and spending FIAT money to purchase them, instead of relying only on cards achieved through gameplay. Those playertypes include [4]:

Esports Players/Streamers: These players often have predefined budgets and require top-tier squads for competitive play, using loot boxes strategically to maintain their edge.

Self-Budgeted Players: Players in this category carefully manage their spending, often sticking to a budget and making calculated decisions about when to invest in loot boxes.

High Division Aspirants: These players aim for high competitive rankings and may occasionally overspend on loot boxes in pursuit of the perfect team, sometimes realizing too late that skill, not just team composition, determines success.

Pressure-Driven Purchasers: These players are often influenced by external factors, such as social media or peer pressure, leading them to make spontaneous purchases that can exceed their budget.

Road to Glory Players: Proud of their ability to succeed without spending money, these players focus on earning rewards through gameplay alone, often achieving high levels of success without financial investment.

The introduction of women players into FUT with the release of EA Sports FC 24 marked a significant shift in the mode's history. Not only did it represent a departure from the FIFA branding after EA's split from the governing football body, but it also introduced a new level of inclusivity by allowing female footballers to be part of mixed-gender teams. [8] This was a bold move by EA, reflecting broader societal changes towards gender equality in sports, but it also sparked intense debate within the gaming community. A reason why EA has been focusing on reducing toxic behaviour within the game. [9]

Initially, the inclusion of women was met with skepticism, with many players expressing concerns that it would detract from the realism of the game. Some feared that high-rated female players would upset the balance of FUT, particularly in a mode already criticized for its reliance on randomization and the influence of loot boxes. We would like to introduce a particularly insightful sentence from the pre-release Reddit thread in our analysis here, as it effectively encapsulates the core issue at the heart of the debate surrounding the inclusion of women in FC24: *"I'm really hoping they keep it separate as it just isn't realistic… Men and women will never play in the same teams professionally, so why muddy the waters?"* This sentiment was echoed by others who were wary of the impact on the game's competitive integrity and the already contentious economy driven by loot boxes. [10]

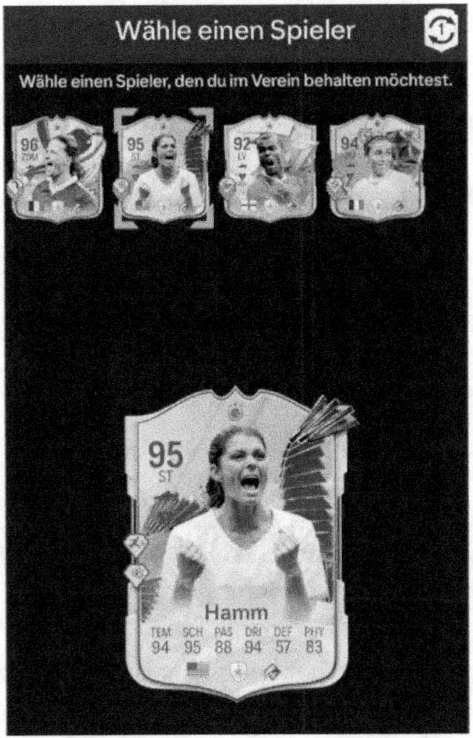

Figure 1. Mia Ham (TOTY-ICON edition) - a member of Alexander Pfeiffer's FC24 Squad. Female and Male Icons in one pack, the player can decide, whom to pick.

However, as players spent more time with the game, sentiments began to shift. Many who were initially resistant to the inclusion of women came to appreciate the diversity and new dynamics they brought to FUT. The realization that FUT had long embraced fantasy elements, such as the use of Icons (retired legendary players) or "Future Stars" (young promising players with stats they might have in the future on the real world's pitches), helped ease some of the initial concerns.

Over time, this shift in sentiment was further supported by content created by popular YouTube influencers within the FIFA community. Influencers like Mike LaBelle, with 310,000 followers [11] and Zelonius, with 40,900 followers [12], began producing videos that embraced the use of female player cards. These videos showcased the competitive viability and unique attributes of female players, helping to normalize their inclusion in the game. However, it remains unclear whether these influencers were driven purely by a genuine belief in the value of these cards, a desire to generate views and likes, or if they were potentially incentivized by EA as part of affiliate marketing efforts.

Moreover, the inclusion of women has also had a positive impact beyond the virtual pitch, increasing awareness of women's football among players who might not have followed it otherwise. This educational aspect has helped bridge the gap between virtual gaming and real-world sports, fostering a new generation of fans for women's football. As one commenter reflected, *"I think it's equally good for women's football too. Brought a lot of attention to the players."* [13]

2. Related Research – Loot box controversy and gaming community reaction

The implementation of loot boxes in top-tier games, particularly after the 2017 release of Star Wars: Battlefront II by Electronic Arts, sparked global debate. This controversy highlighted concerns over the ethics of monetization practices in games, a discussion that continues today [14]. This shows it is not the first time EA is under critic by the gaming community.

The controversy surrounding loot boxes intensified due to consumer backlash, particularly on social media platforms like Reddit. Electronic Arts (EA) faced significant criticism for its heavy reliance on microtransactions, culminating in widespread outrage during the beta testing of Star Wars: Battlefront II. The backlash was so severe that EA was forced to remove the microtransaction system just before the game's official release. EA's initial attempts to defend its practices on Reddit were met with overwhelming negativity, resulting in the most downvoted comment in the site's history. This consumer resistance movement not only damaged EA's reputation but also led to a significant loss in stock value. This incident also ignited calls for greater regulation of the video game industry, particularly concerning microtransactions and loot boxes [17].

The gaming community's reaction, especially on platforms like Reddit, has proven to be a crucial factor in shaping the industry's approach to loot boxes. Developers now recognize the importance of engaging directly with customer communities and maintaining transparency to build consumer confidence. Proactive measures, such as revealing the odds of loot boxes before any backlash occurs, are seen as vital to maintaining good relationships with players. The case of Battlefront II demonstrated that empathy and accountability are essential in customer relations, as opposed to the dismissive attitudes previously displayed by some developers [17].

The game FIFA has been used as example and even been researched in many recent studies [18, 14, 15, 4, 5]. Especially [4] has focused on the game FIFA ultimate team, where the author explores the relationship between loot box spending in FIFA Ultimate Team (FUT) and gaming disorder, identifying employment status and reward sensitivity as key predictors of spending behavior.

The results of a content and sentiment analysis of two significant Reddit threads are now examined: one from before the release of EA FC24 and the other from the late-stage, or endgame, phase of the game. These threads provide first insights into how players' perceptions of women in FUT have evolved over time, from initial resistance to a more nuanced acceptance. By analyzing these discussions, we aim to explore the impact of this landmark change on the Ultimate Team community and what it signifies for the future of sports video games.

3. Methods

Our study employs a qualitative content and sentiment analysis of two key Reddit threads to explore community reactions to the inclusion of women in EA's FC24 Ultimate Team. The first thread, posted prior to the game's release, captures the initial skepticism and concerns surrounding the introduction of female players. The second thread, from the near endgame phase, provides insights into how player sentiments evolved after engaging with the game over an extended period.

The analysis involved systematically reviewing comments within these threads to identify recurring themes, such as realism, gender inclusivity, and the impact of loot boxes on the game's economy. Sentiment analysis, aligned with the methods discussed by [23], was conducted to gauge the overall tone of the community's responses, categorizing them as positive, negative, or mixed. By manually coding sentiments, as recommended in qualitative sentiment analysis, we ensured that the nuances of player opinions were captured, allowing for a detailed understanding of the factors driving their perspectives.

Direct quotes from the threads were used to illustrate these themes and sentiments, providing a richer, more contextualized view of the community's evolving attitudes towards the inclusion of women in FUT. This approach allowed us to comprehensively explore the complex and varied reactions within the gaming community.

3.1 Self-Criticism and Limitations

While this study offers first insights into community reactions, it is important to acknowledge its limitations. The analysis of only two Reddit threads serves as a preliminary exploration rather than a comprehensive study. This approach provides a first look into the topic, acting as an indicator of broader trends and as a nudge for further research. The findings should be interpreted with caution, as the sample is limited to specific discussions within a particular online community. Future research could benefit from a more extensive data set, incorporating a wider range of social media platforms, forums, and player demographics to achieve a more representative understanding of player sentiment.

4. Results of the Content and Sentiment Analysis of Two Reddit Threads

The inclusion of women players in EA's FC24 Ultimate Team (FUT) marked a groundbreaking shift in sports video games, sparking significant debate about gender inclusion and gameplay dynamics. Early player reactions, as captured in Reddit discussions, reflected skepticism about the impact on realism, with many concerned about the integration of female players into a traditionally male-dominated mode. However, as players engaged with the game, sentiments began to shift, revealing an evolving acceptance of women in FUT.

In FC24, women occupy significant positions in the top 10 rankings based on "gold cards" (best type of the basic card set, without taking special edition cards into account. Learn more about different type of cards here [20]) with Alexia Putellas tied for second place alongside Kylian Mbappé, both boasting an overall rating of 91. Despite women comprising less than one-tenth of the player base (1,501 women to 16,169 men), they are prominently represented among the highest-rated cards. Notably, female players like Wendie Renard and Mapi Leon lead in defensive ratings, underscoring their competitive viability in FUT [21].

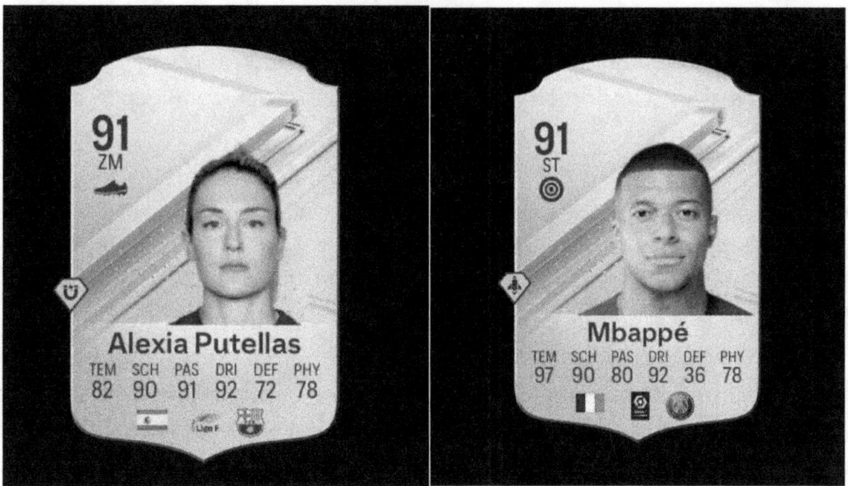

Figure 2 - Gold Cards Putellas and Mbappé in comparison

4.1 Initial Reactions: The Pre-Release Thread

The first thread, titled "Are mixed (Male & Female) Teams confirmed for FUT in EAFC24?" [10], set the stage for a heated discussion about the potential impact of including women in FUT. The original poster expressed a common sentiment at the time: *"I'm really hoping they keep it separate as it just isn't realistic... Men and women will never play in the same teams professionally, so why muddy the waters?"* This post immediately drew a flood of responses, many of which reflected deep concerns about the direction EA was taking with its popular Ultimate Team mode.

One of the most vocal criticisms was the perceived loss of realism. A commenter argued, *"So tired of people using shapeshifters and icons to justify this. It's simply not the same."* They were frustrated that female players, particularly those with high ratings from day one, would make the game less realistic, likening the situation to worsening weather: *"Realism isn't black and white. The game doesn't need to be 100% realistic currently for people to be against it becoming more unrealistic."* This comment captures the fear that FUT would become more of a fantasy game, straying further from its roots as a football simulation.

Another player dismissed the idea that FUT was already unrealistic enough to justify the inclusion of women. "I mean, you can't really call much of UT realistic anyway considering you have Icons like stated and then shapeshifter cards and ridiculous cards for very average players," they noted, highlighting the perceived inconsistency in arguments that supported the inclusion based on existing fantasy elements like shapeshifter cards, which allow players to perform in positions they wouldn't typically play, such as a goalkeeper becoming a striker.

Despite these concerns, some players saw the inclusion of women as an inevitable evolution of the game, albeit not without potential drawbacks. *"Only 4% of players used women's teams in kick-off a single time,"* one commenter pointed out, questioning whether catering to a small minority justified the potential disruption to the game's balance and realism. Another commenter went further, arguing that if women were to be included, their ratings should be significantly lower to reflect what they perceived as the realistic gap in skill: *"If they're included, but they're all rated below 74, fair enough. But any more and we may as well add Spider-Man while we're at it."*

The thread also included more extreme views. One particularly strong reaction came from a commenter who stated, "I have no problem with adding women into FUT only if they'd have realistic ratings - below 20 for base cards and below 35 for icon women cards. That's it. No way Marta or Kerr are better than Mbappe, CR7, Son, Haaland, etc." This comment reflects a deeply entrenched belief in the superiority of male footballers, with the suggestion that even top female players should be rated far lower than their male counterparts. This can be seen as toxic behaviour and highlight one of the extremes, of the discussion in regard to female FUT cards.

4.2 Evolved Perspectives: The Near-Endgame Thread

Nearly a year later, the community had spent considerable time in the game and had the opportunity to engage with the mixed-gender teams. The thread titled "I assume we can now finally all admit women have been a positive addition to this game?" [13] captures the evolved sentiments of the community as the game approached its endgame phase. This threat has more than 400 comments and has therefore been chosen to represent the status quo of the discussion.

4.3 Positive Receptions and Cultural Impact

A significant number of players expressed that their initial skepticism had transformed into appreciation. One player admitted, *"I was a massive hater. Can't lie, love the girls now. Bompastor made this game fun for me."* This comment highlights a broader trend among players who, after spending time with female players in the game, came to appreciate their contribution to the gameplay experience. Another player shared a similar story, saying they had packed Gold Putellas early in the game and quickly realized that the inclusion of women was beneficial, particularly for raising awareness of women's football: *"I think it's equally good for women's football too. Brought a lot of attention to the players."*

The educational impact of including women in FUT was another recurring theme. Many players admitted that they were previously unfamiliar with female footballers but had come to know and appreciate them through the game. *"I only knew about Putellas, now I feel like I know all the women from top teams,"* one commenter noted, reflecting how the game served as a gateway for many to discover and follow women's football, thereby expanding the sport's fan base. This finding can be perceived important for the "game-based learning" community and highlights the point from Konstantin Mitgutsch, who almost ten years ago started to speak about the learning transfer from games to real world context (see [22]).

4.4 Challenges and Frustrations: Card Economy and Gameplay Mechanics

Despite the positive reception from many, significant challenges and frustrations persisted, particularly concerning the game's economy and the saturation of cards. The term "fodder" was frequently used to describe how some players viewed the majority of female cards—valuable primarily as material for SBCs (Squad Building Challenges) rather than as key members of their teams. *"Never had an issue, more fodder,"* one player remarked, indicating that they didn't see these cards adding substantial value to their gameplay experience.

The issue of card saturation, exacerbated by the inclusion of women, was a common point of contention. *"Card saturation is too high, except for that I have never had a problem with women in the game,"* one player commented. They acknowledged the positive aspects of inclusion but were concerned that the sheer number of cards had diluted the excitement of opening packs. Another player expressed frustration with the game's RNG, particularly when receiving female players they didn't want: *"Will I pay to open a pack and a what? Will I go on weekend league and hope to win POTW or something and it's a woman POTW? I don't understand that."*

Skepticism about the motivations behind these changes also lingered. Some players felt that EA's decision to include women was driven more by a desire to complicate the card economy than by any genuine effort to enhance the game. *"Let's be very honest and real with yourselves—EA only added them to make it harder to pack better players,"* one commenter stated, reflecting a broader distrust of EA's intentions.

4.5 Realism vs. Fantasy: Ongoing Debate

The tension between realism and fantasy in FUT continued to be a divisive issue. For many players, FUT has traditionally been a male-dominated space, and the inclusion of women challenged their expectations of what a "realistic" football simulation should look like. As one commenter expressed, *"I like to play a realistic XI, which would be 11 men,"* reflecting the discomfort some players felt with the idea of mixed-gender teams.

A substantial part of the debate centers on the physical attributes of female players compared to their male counterparts, particularly in key positions like goalkeeper and center-back. Many players questioned the competitive viability of female goalkeepers, noting differences in height and physical presence. Comments like *"It feels unrealistic when a 5'4'' female goalkeeper can stop shots just as effectively as a 6'5'' male goalkeeper"* highlighted concerns about how these attributes translate into gameplay. Similarly, the physicality of female defenders—especially their ability to win aerial duels against taller male players—was frequently cited as an area where realism seemed to be compromised.

In FC24, the introduction of detailed player attributes such as strength, heading accuracy, and jumping has further intensified these discussions. Some players argued that high ratings in these attributes for female players seemed inconsistent with their real-world performances. For instance, the ability of female players to out-muscle or out-jump male players in certain scenarios was seen as unrealistic by some, leading to frustrations about the game's mechanics.

4.6 Hostility and Exclusionary Attitudes

Unfortunately, some reactions remained deeply hostile and exclusionary. *"We don't want women in FUT because we just want to play with hairy sweaty dudes, that's all. Women SUCK at football,"* one commenter declared, dismissing any notion of inclusivity. This comment, laden with derogatory language, reflects the extreme end of resistance within the community, where the inclusion of women is seen not just as unnecessary but as an affront to the game's male-centric identity.

However, more balanced views also emerged, with players recognizing that the inclusion of women, while controversial, had brought positive changes to the game. *"If you don't like it, then don't buy, don't play,"* one commenter suggested, also emphasizing that the changes were inevitable and that the community would adapt, particularly if women proved to be competitively viable.

4.7 Cynicism and Resignation

Cynicism toward EA's motives **were** also prevalent, with some players feeling that the company was more interested in complicating the game's economy than in genuinely improving it. *"EA have really turned the game into shit,"* one commenter remarked, expressing frustration over various changes to the game, including the inclusion of women. Despite their harsh criticism, there was an ironic resignation in their comment: *"This for me is definitely end of an era. (Proceeds to buy it.) No but really, let's fuck EA."* This captures a sentiment where, despite their dissatisfaction, players continue to engage with the game, possibly due to a lack of alternatives or a deep-rooted attachment to the franchise. The German term to explain it would be "Hassliebe".

5. Conclusion

The inclusion of women in EA's FC24 Ultimate Team has catalyzed a significant and multifaceted discussion within the gaming community, reflecting a wide spectrum of opinions on the balance between realism, fantasy, and inclusivity. Initially met with substantial skepticism and concern about diluting the realism of the game, many players feared that integrating female players would undermine the authenticity of FUT. The pre-release discourse was marked by apprehension, with critics questioning whether this move catered to a small minority at the expense of the broader player base.

However, as players engaged with the game over the year, sentiments evolved. While some maintained their original concerns, others came to appreciate the diversity and new dynamics that female players brought to FUT. The game's educational impact, particularly in raising awareness of women's football and expanding the fan base, has been a significant positive outcome. Many players who were initially unfamiliar with female footballers found themselves learning about and enjoying these players, leading to a broader cultural impact beyond the game.

Despite the positive developments, challenges remain. The issue of card saturation and the impact on the game's economy, as well as ongoing debates about the balance between realism and fantasy, continue to generate mixed reactions. Some players still express frustration with how the inclusion of women has affected pack openings and gameplay dynamics, while others see it as a refreshing change in a game that had become increasingly repetitive.

Hostility and exclusionary attitudes, though present, have been countered by more inclusive perspectives that advocate for embracing the evolving nature of FUT. As the game continues to develop, the community's feedback will be crucial in shaping future iterations of Ultimate Team. The overall trend suggests that while the inclusion of women has been a polarizing issue, it has also been a catalyst for change, encouraging a broader discussion about the future of gaming and the importance of inclusivity in virtual sports. This ongoing dialogue will undoubtedly influence how EA approaches similar decisions in future releases, balancing innovation with the diverse expectations of its player base.

To build on the findings of this research, it is suggested that, in addition to repeating the study with a larger, more quantitative dataset, interviews be conducted with players across various levels of professionalism, ranging from casual gamers to competitive Esports players. These interviews would provide valuable insights into how the inclusion of women in FC24 Ultimate Team has impacted their gameplay experiences and perceptions.

By engaging directly with this diverse group, future research can explore the broader implications of gender inclusivity in sports video games and validate the initial trends observed in our study. This approach would help deepen our understanding of how these changes are being received across the player spectrum, from those who engage with the game casually to those who compete at the highest levels.

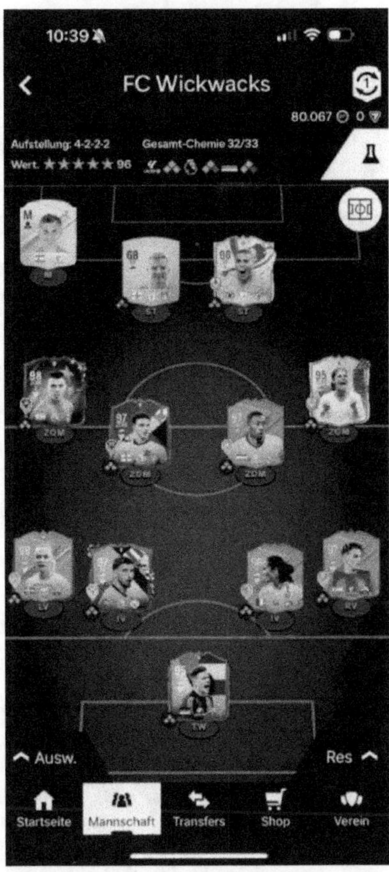

Figure 3 - Endgame Squad from Alexander Pfeiffer, total money spent for lootboxes - 50 €. Two female player cards are in the final team

6. Personal Reflection from the Authors

Reflecting on our exploration of how women player cards in EA's FC24 have transitioned from a source of controversy to a celebrated feature, we'd like to share some personal insights into why this topic is particularly meaningful to us.

Michaela Wawra is currently pursuing her doctorate at the Vienna University of Economics and Business, where her research is centered on the intricate world of loot boxes in video games. Her work delves into the complex dynamics of virtual economies and examines how in-game purchases, like loot boxes, influence player behavior and game design. For Michaela, this topic is more than just an academic inquiry; it's a critical analysis of how modern gaming intersects with economic principles, often blurring the lines between entertainment and gambling.

Alexander Pfeiffer, on the other hand, approaches this topic from a lifelong passion for EA's football games. Having been an avid player since the early days of the franchise, Alexander has witnessed the series' evolution firsthand, from straightforward gameplay mechanics to the sophisticated, economy-driven systems that define today's Ultimate Team mode. This extensive experience has given him unique insights into how these changes have shaped the player experience over the years.

In 2023, we co-authored a paper that introduced a player type model within FIFA, categorizing players based on their engagement with loot boxes. This work laid the foundation for our decision to explore the perception of female player cards in FC24. We recognized a gap in the academic discourse, with little attention given to how these new additions were being received by the gaming community. This realization fueled our passion to pioneer this research, hoping to inspire other scholars and game studies enthusiasts to further investigate this evolving aspect of sports video games.

About the Authors

MICHAELA has a master's degrees in Business Administration and is in a prae-doc position at University for Continuing Education Krems in Austria. Her research focuses on game studies especially on loot boxes and their economical impact. Since 2023 she is a doctoral candidate at the Vienna University of Economics and Business.

LinkedIn: michaela-wawra-39708723a

ALEXANDER PFEIFFER, a Max Kade Fellowship recipient, focused on the impact of blockchain technologies on game-based education at MIT's Education Arcade. He has returned to Austria, where he leads the emerging technologies experiences lab at the University for Continuing Education Krems. He co-founded tech start-ups Picapipe GmbH and B & P Emerging Technologies Consultancy Lab. Dr. Pfeiffer holds a doctorate and a social and economic sciences degree from theVienna University of Economics and Business, a Master ofArts from University of Krems, and an Executive MBA from Alaska Pacific

University. He is also Ph.D candidate at the University of Malta in the field of AI.

Website: https://www.alexpfeiffer.at/

AI Disclaimer

The authors fully embrace the exciting possibilities offered by Artificial Intelligence, particularly tools like [GPT-4, Teams Version]. While such tools are invaluable for tasks like qualitative content analysis, translation, and other helpful endeavors, it's important to remember that the true magic (and occasional missteps) happens under human oversight. So, while the AI might assist in structuring ideas or untangling complex sentences, the responsibility for any content quirks, structural hiccups, or clarity confusions rests squarely on our human shoulders. In short, if something's gone awry, blame the humans, not the helpful AI—it's only doing its best to follow our sometimes unclear instructions!

References

[1] eSports.com, 2024. Knapp 7,5 Milliarden: EA macht Rekordumsatz dank FIFA 23. Available at: https://www.esports.com/de/knapp-75-milliarden-ea-macht-rekordumsatz-dank-fifa-23-413727 [Accessed 19 August 2024]

[2] PC Games, 2024. EA Sports FC 24: Spielerzahlen nach Woche 1. Available at: https://www.pcgames.de/EA-Sports-FC-24-Spiel-74640/News/Spielerzahlen-nach-Woche-1-1430952/ [Accessed 19 August 2024]

[3] Pfeiffer, A. & Sedlecky, G., 2020. An Introduction to Gambling inthe Context of Game Studies. Mixed Reality and Games: Theoretical and Practical Approaches in Game Studies and Education, pp.transcript Verlag, pp. 281-296; https://doi.org/10.1515/9783839453292-026

[4] Lemmens, J. S., 2022. Play or pay to win: Loot boxes and gamingdisorder in FIFA ultimate team. Telematics and Informatics Reports8, p. 100023; https://doi.org/10.1016/j.teler.2022.100023.

[5] Wawra, M- & Pfeiffer, A. (2023). The Freedom of Choice Subtitle: A Preliminary Analysis of Lootboxes in EA FIFA Ultimate Team and the Introduction of a Player Type Model. In FREEDOM | OPPRESSION | GAMES & PLAY, University of Krems Press

[6] FIFPlay, 2024. SBC Fodder. Available at: https://www.fifplay.com/encyclopedia/sbc-fodder/ [Accessed 19 August 2024].

[7] Meschik, M., 2018. "Loot Boxes" – Über die Verwandschaft von Videospiel und Glücksspiel. medienimpulse, Jg. 56, Nr. 1, pp.1-20.

[8] ORF, 2024. FIFA: Was bedeutet SBC-Fodder? Available at: https://oe3.orf.at/stories/3036440/ [Accessed 19 August 2024].

[9] play3.de, 2023. EA Sports FC 24: Darum sind erstmals Frauen in Ultimate Team dabei. Available at: https://www.play3.de/2023/07/19/ea-sports-fc-24-darum-sind-erstmals-frauen-in-ultimate-team-dabei/ [Accessed 19 August 2024].

[10] Reddit, 2024. Are mixed male/female teams confirmed for FUT in EA Sports FC? Available at: https://www.reddit.com/r/EASportsFC/comments/14wl18r/are_mixed_male_female_teams_confirmed_for_fut_in/ [Accessed 19 August 2024].

[11] YouTube, 2024. EA Sports FC 24 Official Reveal Trailer. Available at: https://www.youtube.com/watch?v=9IxTVnZ7s2I [Accessed 19 August 2024].

[12] YouTube, 2024. EA Sports FC 24 Ultimate Team Trailer. Available at: https://www.youtube.com/watch?v=yvW47dhlA5Y [Accessed 19 August 2024].

[13] Reddit, 2024. I assume we can now finally all admit women have no place in FUT? Available at: https://www.reddit.com/r/EASportsFC/comments/1cviq3t/i_assume_we_can_now_finally_all_admit_women_have/?rdt=62499 [Accessed 19 August 2024].

[14] Baeck, J. & Claeys, I., 2021. Restitution of money spent on loot boxes in video games? Computer Law & Security Review, 41, p.105566. Available at: https://doi.org/10.1016/j.clsr.2021.105566.

[15] King, D. L. & Delfabbro, P. H., 2018. Video Game Monetization (e.g., 'Loot Boxes'): a Blueprint for Practical Social Responsibility Measures. International Journal of Mental Health and Addiction, 17, pp.166–179. Available at: https://doi.org/10.1007/s11469-018-0009-3.

[16] Zendle, D., Meyer, R., Cairns, P., Waters, S. & Ballou, N., 2020. The prevalence of loot boxes in mobile and desktop games. Addiction, 115, pp.1768–1772. Available at: https://doi.org/10.1111/add.14973.

[17] McCaffrey, M., 2019. The macro problem of microtransactions: The self-regulatory challenges of video game loot boxes. Business Horizons, 62(4), pp.483-495. Available at: https://doi.org/10.1016/j.bushor.2019.03.001.

[18] Adam, M., Roethke, K. & Benlian, A., 2021. Gamblified digital product offerings: An experimental study of loot box menu designs. Electronic Markets, 32, pp.971–986. Available at: https://doi.org/10.1007/s12525-021-00477-0.

[19] Brooks, G. A. & Clark, L., 2019. Associations between loot box use, problematic gaming and gambling, and gambling-related cognitions. Addictive Behaviors, 96, pp.26-34. Available at: https://doi.org/10.1016/j.addbeh.2019.04.009.

[20] eSports.com, 2024. FIFA FUT Karten Glossary. Available at: https://www.esports.com/de/glossary-fifa/fifa-fut-karten [Accessed 19 August 2024].

[21] Sports of the Day, 2024. FC 24 FUT Equality: What EA Makes Women Better At and What It Doesn't. Available at: https://www.sportsoftheday.com/fc-24-fut-equality-what-ea-makes-women-better-at-and-what-it-doesnt/ [Accessed 19 August 2024].

[22] YouTube, 2024. EA Sports FC 24 - Women in FUT Trailer. Available at: https://www.youtube.com/watch?v=oIl7orT98OI [Accessed 19 August 2024].

[23] Kirilenko, A. P., Wang, L., & Stepchenkova, S. O. (2022). Sentiment Analysis. In R. Egger (Ed.), Applied Data Science in Tourism: Interdisciplinary Approaches, Methodologies, and Applications (pp. 363-374). Springer International Publishing.

III. DARK PATTERNS IN AND BEYOND GAMES

PLAY TO PROSPER

TEACHING FINANCIAL LITERACY THROUGH GAMES

Sonja Gabriel

In an age where finances, currencies, money and credit are also shaped by digitalization, the teaching of financial literacy has become increasingly important in recent years, not only in terms of financial knowledge, but also increasingly in terms of application skills, attitudes and behavior. From primary school to adulthood, different approaches are being pursued to strengthen financial literacy. Financial literacy has found its way into the curriculum in many countries. Games (both analogue and digital) have become an important part of these approaches. After a basic clarification of the underlying terms, this paper explains which aspects of financial literacy are considered important at which age group and why games have been an integral part of teaching money-related knowledge and skills for many decades. Finally, the potential of digital games in the area of financial literacy will be discussed and three examples of financial literacy games will be analyzed in terms of how far they can be used to help strengthen financial literacy.

Keywords: financial literacy, serious games, education, experiential learning

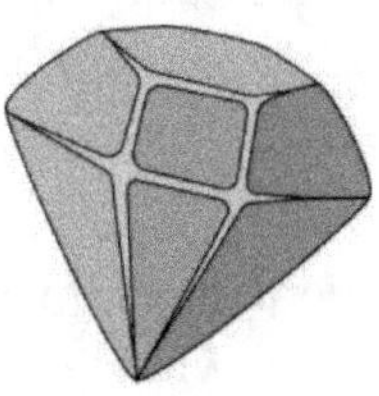

1. Financial Literacy

Before talking about the role digital games can play when it comes to teaching financial literacy, it is useful to have a closer look at the term of financial literacy. As per Cude (2022) financial literacy was first used in literature in the USA at the end of the 1990s / beginning of 2000s and has soon gained popularity since then. The OECD uses the following definition:

> a combination of financial awareness, knowledge, skills, attitudes and behaviours necessary to make sound financial decisions and ultimately achieve individual financial well-being. (OECD 2024, p. 6)

According to this definition, it can be stated that financial literacy is the ability to understand and use financial skills, including personal financial management, budgeting, and investing. It involves a broad range of financial knowledge and skills necessary to manage financial resources effectively throughout one's lifetime. This involves being aware of important financial concepts, having a grasp of financial products and services, and being able to apply financial knowledge and skills to a variety of real-life situations. Financial literacy involves the attitudes and behaviors necessary for sound financial decision-making. This includes the motivation and confidence to seek information and advice about participating in financial activities, as well as the ability to manage emotional and psychological factors that influence financial decision-making. Developing financial literacy is crucial for protecting oneself from financial fraud, preparing for emergencies, and achieving financial goals.

When looking closer at the components of financial literacy, Cude (2022) defines and explains four different ones: knowledge, numeracy, attitudes and behaviors and confidence (or self-efficacy). When it comes to which knowledge people should have when being financially literate, experts include different kind of knowledge, also depending on the age of the person in question and comprises areas like money and transactions, managing finances, knowing about risk and reward and which financial products there are for adolescents whereas for adults it also often includes debts, financial planning, wealth accumulation as well as pensions (Cude 2022). The concept of numeracy is also discussed in literature if it is a cognitive ability that supports financial literacy or actually is part of financial literacy. In the International Survey of Adult Financial Literacy (OECD/INFE 2020) the concept of financial attitude was introduced by assessing it on the basis of the spending and saving preferences of participants. Other researchers have included spending behavior and connected it to financial literacy (Cude 2022). Finally, the component of confidence is taken into account in some definitions as well. Confidence (self-efficacy) refers to the concept of agency, in how far individuals believe that they can succeed in given tasks or are able to cope with challenges they encounter in life (with regard to financial decisions).

As we can see, a definition of financial literacy is neither easy nor consistent. However, with the continuing use of digital devices and digitalization in general, there need to be some additional factors included. Digital financial literacy refers to the set of skills and knowledge that enable individuals to understand and effectively use digital financial services and technologies (Lyons & Kass-Hanny 2021). It encompasses a broad range of competencies, including the ability to access, manage, and use digital financial tools such as online banking, mobile payment apps, digital wallets, and cryptocurrency platforms. Digital financial literacy involves understanding the risks and benefits associated with digital financial transactions, protecting personal financial information, and making informed decisions about digital financial products and services. Koskelainen et al. (2023) suggest that the digital innovations in the financial sector need to be addressed in research as well as in financial education.

While traditional financial literacy focuses on fundamental financial concepts such as saving, investing, budgeting, and borrowing, digital financial literacy builds on these basics by integrating the digital dimension. The key difference between digital financial literacy and traditional financial literacy lies in the focus on technology. Traditional financial literacy is concerned with the principles of managing money and understanding financial systems, products, and services. In contrast, digital financial literacy adds the layer of navigating these principles through digital means, requiring skills such as navigating online financial interfaces, understanding digital security measures, and staying informed about evolving digital financial trends and regulations.

2. Financial Literacy Education

In the beginning, experts assumed that it was enough if financial knowledge in the general audience was strengthened to achieve financial well-being (Drever & Else-Quest 2022). However, financial knowledge, while foundational to understanding how to manage money, save, invest, and budget, is not solely sufficient for achieving financial well-being as it does not only involve theoretical understanding but also practical application, emotional discipline, and adaptive behavior especially with the focus on changing financial landscapes and personal circumstances. Firstly, without the skills to apply financial knowledge effectively in daily life, individuals may struggle to make informed decisions that align with their long-term financial goals. Practical financial skills encompass budgeting, managing debt, and investing wisely, which require more than just knowledge – they require action. Moreover, emotional discipline plays a critical role in financial well-being. Financial decisions are often influenced by emotions and psychological biases, such as impulse spending or the fear of financial loss (Panos & Wilson 2020). Knowledge alone does not equip individuals to navigate these emotional challenges; it requires psychological resilience and discipline to make choices that benefit long-term financial health over short-term gratification. Additionally, the dynamic nature of the financial world, with its evolving markets, emerging financial products (especially with regard to changes due to digitalization), and changing regulations, demands adaptability and continuous learning. Financial knowledge might become outdated, making it essential for individuals to stay informed and adaptable to new financial tools and environments, particularly in the realm of digital finance. Finally, financial well-being is also intertwined with external factors such as economic conditions, social safety nets, and access to financial services. These elements can significantly impact an individual's financial situation, irrespective of their financial knowledge. Therefore, while financial knowledge is crucial, achieving financial well-being requires a broader set of skills, emotional intelligence, and an adaptive mindset to navigate the complexities of personal finance in a continuously evolving world.

Schools all over the world – from preschool over elementary and middle school to high school – have already included some kind of financial literacy education in their curricula. In 2012, financial literacy assessment was even included in PISA testing. A cross-country analysis, however, shows that only some countries' results show a positive correlation between the kind of financial education and the students' financial literacy scores (Salas-Velasco et al 2020). The way of integrating financial literacy education in formal education depends on the type of school.

In the realm of primary education, enhancing financial literacy effectively involves a holistic approach that weaves financial concepts seamlessly into the curriculum, making use of interactive learning tools and incorporating real-life financial experiences. This method entails the integration of basic financial principles such as savings, budgeting, and the understanding of currency into existing subjects, thereby contextualizing financial knowledge in a manner that resonates with students' everyday lives (Amagir et al. 2017). To complement this, engaging students through digital simulations, educational games, and applications that simulate financial scenarios provides a hands-on learning experience, promoting active participation and deeper understanding of financial decision-making. Further enriching this educational landscape, the introduction of practical financial activities, such as classroom economies or mock entrepreneurial projects, bridges the gap between theoretical knowledge and its application, fostering a comprehensive, experiential learning environment where students can explore and grasp the complexities of financial literacy from an early age. Especially when it comes to younger children (elementary and middle school), Drever & Else-Quest (2022) stress the importance of parents serving as role models for the children and thus should be integrated into the financial education approach as well.

In lower secondary school, advancing financial literacy calls for a nuanced strategy that deepens students' understanding of financial concepts through curriculum integration, advanced interactive learning tools, and enriched real-life financial engagements. At this educational level, financial education can be expanded within the curriculum to include more sophisticated topics such as personal finance management, investment basics, and understanding credit. Utilizing technology-driven learning platforms and simulations becomes increasingly important, as these tools offer more complex scenarios that challenge students to apply their knowledge in diverse financial contexts, enhancing their analytical and decision-making skills. Moreover, the introduction of real-world financial projects, such as stock market simulations, budgeting for hypothetical life events, or exploring the fundamentals of entrepreneurship, allows students to engage with financial concepts in a deeply practical manner.

At the higher secondary level, fortifying financial literacy necessitates an advanced, integrative approach that not only consolidates students' foundational knowledge but also exposes them to more complex financial instruments, markets, and decision-making processes. The curriculum at this stage should incorporate in-depth studies of financial concepts, including investment strategies, risk management, international finance, and the implications of global economic trends. Leveraging sophisticated interactive learning tools, such as high-fidelity simulations of stock exchanges, cryptocurrency markets, and personal finance management software, can significantly enhance students' ability to analyze and interpret financial data, fostering a more nuanced understanding of the financial landscape.

Additionally, facilitating real-life financial experiences through internships, investment clubs, or participation in national and international financial competitions enables students to apply theoretical knowledge in real-world settings, promoting practical skills such as strategic planning, critical analysis, and ethical financial decision-making.

3. Using games for financial literacy education

The integration of gaming methodologies into educational frameworks is increasingly recognized as a powerful tool for improving learning outcomes across a wide range of disciplines (Tsai & Tsai 2020, Lampropoulos 2023), including financial literacy (Lengyel 2020). This approach goes beyond traditional didactic teaching methods by incorporating interactive and experiential elements that stimulate cognitive engagement and facilitate the internalization of complex concepts. In the context of financial education, the use of games - from digital platforms to physical board games - is a versatile and effective medium for teaching financial knowledge and skills. By simulating economic transactions, financial planning and resource management in a controlled yet realistic environment, games offer a unique blend of entertainment and education, fostering an immersive learning experience (Platz et al. 2021). Such an innovative educational strategy not only appeals to learners' curiosity and competitive spirit, but also promotes a holistic understanding of financial principles through practical application, critical analysis and decision-making in a simulated financial environment.

3.1 Experiential learning

Kolb's Learning Cycle, conceptualized in 1984, represents a seminal framework within experiential learning theory (an approach which dates back to Aristotle), positing that learning is a process whereby knowledge is created through the transformation of experience. This model delineates four distinct stages that constitute the learning cycle, each stage representing a critical dimension of the learning process. These stages are: Concrete Experience, Reflective Observation, Abstract Conceptualization, and Active Experimentation.

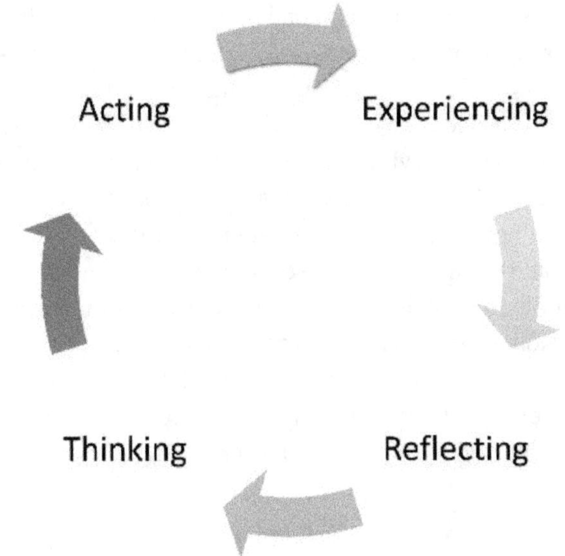

Figure 1. Kolb's Learning Cycle

Concrete experience involves direct engagement with the learning environment, where the learner actively experiences an activity or event thus emphasizing the importance of immersion in concrete, practical experiences as a precursor to learning. Reflective observation involves the learner reflecting on the experience, considering its meaning and looking at it from different perspectives. During this stage, learners analyze their experiences, identify inconsistencies between experience and understanding, and draw insights from their observations. The next stage, thinking, requires the learner to synthesize the reflections and observations into new ideas or concepts, formulating theories or models that capture the essence of their insights. This stage represents the cognitive process of conceptualizing experience by integrating new knowledge into existing cognitive frameworks. Active experimentation involves putting these newly formed concepts and theories into practice by testing them in new situations. This stage completes the cycle as the learner actively experiments with their ideas, leading to new concrete experiences and subsequent cycles of learning.

The integration of Kolb's Learning Cycle with game-based learning, which includes both digital and analogue games, offers a dynamic approach to education that accommodates different learning modes and enhances understanding through engagement and interaction. This combined methodology emphasizes the value of immersive experiences where learners actively participate in game environments by stepping into the magic circle (Huizinga 1981), allowing for direct exploration and application of concepts.

Reflection on these experiences is crucial – which means leaving the magic circle and stepping back, allowing learners to analyze their choices and outcomes, gaining insights that deepen their understanding of the subject matter. The abstraction of these reflections into broader principles facilitates the formation of new concepts and theories, which learners can then test and apply in subsequent games or new contexts. This cyclical learning process, underpinned by active experimentation, not only fosters deeper cognitive connections, but also promotes adaptability and problem-solving skills. Game-based learning, in its digital and analogue forms, provides a rich and varied platform for implementing Kolb's experiential learning cycle, making education a more engaging, effective and inclusive process (Ahn 2008). This approach emphasizes the importance of a holistic learning experience that combines theory with practice, reflection with action, preparing learners for complex real-world challenges.

3.2 Non-digital games

The board game Monopoly, one of the most iconic and enduring games in history, dates back to the early 20th century, when it was rooted in the principles of economic theory and designed as a critique of land ownership and monopoly (Pilon 2015). Its predecessor, The Landlord's Game, was invented by Elizabeth Magie in 1903 with the explicit intention of illustrating the negative aspects of concentrating land in private monopolies. Over time, Monopoly evolved from Magie's educational tool into a commercial product that gained widespread popularity. This evolution transformed it into a medium through which basic financial literacy concepts – such as money management, negotiation and strategic planning – could be taught informally. By engaging players in transactions involving the purchase, rental and trading of real estate, Monopoly provides a rudimentary simulation of real-world economic competition and capitalism. Despite its primary intention as entertainment, the game inadvertently serves as an early introduction to the principles of financial literacy, offering insights into the dynamics of economic leverage, investment risk and the importance of financial decision-making, thereby embedding basic financial lessons in the context of play.

Role plays and simple simulations have spread among educators worldwide to teach learners from primary school up to university personal finance concepts (Sardone 2012, 2019, Batty et al. 2020). Financial institutions started to provide educators with role plays, analogue simulations or board games to strengthen financial literacy [1].

3.3 Digital games

As Kalmi & Sihvonen (2022) state, gamified approaches like role-playing games, have already been used quite frequently in financial literacy interventions as they allow learners to put on different roles and experiment in a safe environment. Dating back to as early as the 1980s and the 1990s, edutainment games were quite popular by combining typical school subjects like math or history with the motivational factor of digital games. Although these early games did not necessarily focus exclusively on financial literacy, they laid the basis for educational game design principles and their pedagogical approach. Especially computer-based simulation games were likely to be used to teach business concepts, sales and marketing (Nightingale 2019). As financial markets evolved and personal finance management became increasingly complex in the late 20th century, there was a recognized need for better financial education. This presented an opportunity for developers to address this gap through digital games.

In the 2000s, the internet became ubiquitous and gaming technology advanced, leading to the emergence of specialized games that focus on financial literacy. These games simulate real-world financial situations, such as budgeting, investing, and debt management. For example, players may be put in scenarios where they manage virtual money, make decisions about spending versus saving, or navigate the complexities of investing in stocks. Some games incorporate role-playing elements, allowing players to simulate running a virtual business, managing finances, or strategizing to achieve financial goals [2].

Financial institutions have recognized the importance of financial literacy as a public good and a means of fostering future customers. As a result, they have begun to sponsor or collaborate on the development of financial education games. These games aim to improve financial literacy and promote responsible

---

[1] Examples for analogue games provided by financial institutions are: The budgeting money game by Barclays (https://barclayslifeskills.com/help-others/lessons/the-budget-game/)

[2] For example, Hubro Education (https://hubro.education) provides simulations on business contexts and also one on investment and finance.

financial behavior. For instance, banks, credit unions, or investment firms may have partnered with developers to create games that teach budgeting, saving, or the basics of credit[3]. With the prevalence of mobile and smartphones and advancements in browser technology, financial literacy games have become more accessible to a wider audience[4].

Maynard et al. (2012) suggested five research and evaluation questions to find out if the financial entertainment approach leads to strengthening financial literacy. These questions deal with the engagement of players as well as the promotion of financial knowledge and self-efficacy. Furthermore, the game should find a way to get the players active with their real-world finances and promote ongoing positive financial behavior. Finally, it is necessary to have a look at the realization of the positive outcomes in real life.

3.4 Digital financial literacy games

When designing digital games to further financial literacy, several factors are important to bear in mind to ensure the games can be used for teaching and are engaging at the same time: As Thomas (2024) states the objective of the financial game must be clearly defined, and the mechanics, rules, and goals must adhere to the objectives to ensure the game is effective and delivers the desired outcome. Another important point Thomas mentions is the balance between fun and learning – financial knowledge should be taught but there should also be interaction as well as immersion. When it comes to using games in school contexts, age appropriateness is also essential. Incorporating real-life financial scenarios which are related to players' every-day-life make learning experiences practical and relatable. Other factures address meaningful feedback, alignment with learning objectives and providing collaboration among players as well as competition.

If and in how far these game-design elements are integrated in digital games might differ from game to game. Thus, the last section is going to have a closer

---

[3] Examples therefore are the Financial Literacy Challenge by Bank of America (https://www.finlitchallenge.com/), The European Money Quiz by the European Banking Federation (https://www.ebf.eu/priorities/financial-education/european-money-quiz/) or Hit the Road by MyCreditUnion (https://mycreditunion.gov/financial-resources/hit-road-financial-adventure).

[4] For an example look at https://www.playmoneyrace.com/

look at three games that have been designed to strengthen financial literacy in children/teenagers. The games were chosen as examples for a great number of games that deal with financial literacy. The following criteria were important: The games are intended to be used in classroom settings and should thus be put in a didactic setting. The target group is teenagers and they use different settings and game-design approaches. Moreover, the games needed to be still available to play them.

Moneymaster (designed by 10Monkeys in 2018[5]) is a digital role-playing game that immerses players in various financial management scenarios. Players make decisions and receive feedback on them. The game is designed for 13 to 17-year-olds and can be played in segments, with a total duration of approximately 45 to 60 minutes. Success in the game depends on the player's ability to master financial modules, gain experience, and increase their monetary reserves. The game is accompanied by a comprehensive suite of lesson materials, which offer educators fully structured lesson modules to enhance the gaming experience. Additionally, the game is available in both Finnish and Swedish. The *Moneymaster* mobile game was developed and implemented through a collaboration between Nordea, the Finnish Foundation for Share Promotion, and Economy and Youth (TAT). By depicting situations that are taken from life of the target group (for example taking on a job because the game character would like to go on holidays like all the friends) it is rather engaging for young people. The game is rather linear – there are not so many instances when players can decide which option to take. The choices to be taken are, however, meaningful and not obvious (for example earning more money and working more hours or earning less and enjoying some free time). There are also some ethic choices to be taken (like telling your boss that you are afraid some guests might leave without asking even if your character is in love with one of the guests). Players can see their progress in form of money they own and experience points. The game is easy to play by clicking the dialogue options the player wants to choose but it is very much to read and might get boring for students. Information is given in form of dialogues which can be clicked away quite easily without any consequences for the gameplay. For this game it is really essential that the contents of the chapters are discussed in lessons in order to have a transfer of knowledge, but it definitely is a good way of making adolescents aware of different money issues.

[5] https://taloussankari.com/?localeId=en_gb

Financial Football (developed by Epic Games in 2018[6]) is presented as a digital educational tool designed to complement the classroom curriculum through the provision of engaging lesson modules. These modules have been designed to fit into existing educational frameworks, providing a structured approach to financial education. Aimed at a wide range of students of different ages, the game and its accompanying lesson modules are designed to teach basic financial concepts such as saving, spending, budgeting and the prudent use of credit in preparation for playing the game. The curriculum is divided into three distinct age groups: Rookie (11-14), Pro (14-18) and Hall of Fame (18+), ensuring content is relevant and appropriate for each stage of development. The game design includes a feature that allows students to email their game results directly to their teachers, facilitating the tracking and assessment of learning outcomes. Each lesson module contains several key components designed to enhance the learning experience. An overview introduces the core concepts, giving teachers and students a preliminary understanding of the module's content. This is followed by clearly defined teaching aims and objectives that outline the expected learning outcomes. The Teaching Notes section is the main content of each module, providing comprehensive material for teaching the concepts, which can be used as provided or modified by teachers according to their pedagogical preferences. In addition, the modules encourage the application of acquired knowledge through discussion of practical examples and an Activity section designed for either group engagement or individual assessment of learning. The instructional materials for *Financial Football* are designed to be user-friendly. They include pre- and post-tests for students and lesson plans with scripted instructions and resource links to aid research activities. These materials are structured to assist educators, even those with limited financial literacy expertise. To enhance engagement, activities such as creating a movie trailer about identity theft are also included. The educational program includes PDF lessons as the primary educational component. The game is a motivational tool to encourage engagement with the content, but educators must provide additional reinforcement to ensure comprehension. The game's questions should not include content from all lessons to maintain its flexibility as a teaching tool. The football-themed game is engaging, but its educational content is primarily metaphorical. The 'Getting Game-Ready' section makes connections, but the game mainly focuses on recall, classification, and identification through

[6] https://www.financialfootball.com/

true/false and multiple-choice questions. This limits critical thinking opportunities.

Night of the Living Debt (iOS App for the iPad developed by Learning Games Lab in 2016) is a digital game that simulates real-world financial management in a post-apocalyptic scenario dominated by zombies. The game's primary objective is to maintain and enhance players' credit rating while ensuring they have sufficient funds to meet various financial obligations, such as rent, healthcare emergencies, and payments towards credit cards, automobile loans, and student debts. At the beginning of the game, players receive a starting financial package consisting of $1,000 in savings, a credit card limit of $750, and a debt of $400. Additionally, they start with a baseline credit score of 600, which can be influenced by their financial decisions throughout the game, such as making timely payments and strategically using credit facilities. The gameplay mechanics focus on progressing from an initial state of destitution, living in a shack without a vehicle, to achieving financial stability and acquiring better housing and transportation. This progression is facilitated through strategic activities such as scavenging for resources to sell and managing finances to improve one's living conditions. The game integrates educational components into the gameplay by introducing financial products such as student loans and insurance, which directly impact the players' financial health and capabilities. The game consists of 10 rounds and presents players with periodic financial obligations, teaching them how to manage regular bill payments within a given timeframe. Failure to meet these obligations or opting for high-interest payday loans can have a negative impact on the player's credit score. On the other hand, judicious financial management and savings can accrue interest, contributing to overall financial growth. There are teacher resources provided which include talking points as well as ideas for how to use the app. The students interact with scenarios that show how financial decisions affect their credit scores immediately. The game highlights the consequences of missed payments and the benefits of consistent, timely financial behaviors. Additionally, it addresses the advantages and disadvantages of using sub-prime lenders and payday loans, presenting these options within the context of their long-term financial repercussions. Repeated gameplay helps students understand the importance of good credit for achieving financial stability and accessing better living conditions and transportation options. However, the game's replay value is limited, and once the educational objectives are internalized, motivation to continue playing may diminish. This highlights the challenge of balancing educational content with sustained engagement in educational gaming.

4. Conclusion

In the current era, marked by rapid digital transformation, the integration of games into education offers an interesting approach to strengthening financial literacy in various age groups. With regard to experiential learning and their immersive nature, games can motivate learners to engage with the topic in more detail or provide a start for further discussion. As the few examples of digital games presented have shown, various aspects of financial literacy can be covered – from basic budgeting to complex decision making – thus making games a good material to be used in a didactic setting. However, when using games for financial literacy, teachers or trainers need to be aware that the games can only cover certain aspects of the extensive competencies included in financial literacy. Moreover, to make sure transfer from the game to real-world-action takes place, there need to be measures taken like discussing the experience made in the game. Games can help to tackle the topic and to raise interest, but they are only one piece of the mosaic among many on the path towards financially literate adults.

About the Author

Sonja Gabriel works as a professor for media didactics and media education at the KPH Vienna/Krems, where she is active in the education and training of teachers. Her research focus is on digital game-based learning, gamification and the use of (serious) games for teaching and learning, for teaching values as well as on the pedagogical potential of digital games in school and out-of-school settings. In addition, she participates in national and international projects dealing with topics related to teaching and learning with digital media, generative artificial intelligence, information literacy and game design approaches in education.

LinkedIn: sonja-gabriel-48116041
Website: https://kphvie.ac.at/pro/sonja-gabriel/home.html

References

Ahn, J-H. (2008). Application of the Experiential Learning Cycle in Learning from a Business Simulation Game. E-Learning and Digital Media 5/2 (pp. 146-156).

Amagir, A., Groot, W. & Wilschut, A. (2017). A review of financial-literacy education programs for children and adolescents. Citizenship, Social and Economics Education 17/1 (pp. 56-80).

Batty, M., Collins J. M., O'Rourke, C. & Odders-White, E. (2020). Experiential financial education: A field study of my classroom economy in elementary schools. Economics of Education Review 78.

Cude, B. J. (2022). Defining Financial Literacy. In G. Nicolini & B. J. Cude (Eds.), The Routledge Handbook of Financial Literacy. Routledge (pp. 5-17).

Drever, A. I. & Else-Quest, N. M. (2022). Financial Literacy among Children. Supporting the achievement of financial well-being in adulthood. In G. Nicolini & B. J. Cude (Eds.), The Routledge Handbook of Financial Literacy. Routledge (pp. 18-30).

Huizinga, J. (1981). Homo Ludens. Vom Ursprung der Kultur im Spiel. Rowohlt.

Kalmi, P. & Sihvonen, T. (2022). Education or Entertainment? On the potential of games in financial education. In G. Nicolini & B. J. Cude (Eds.), The Routledge Handbook of Financial Literacy. Routledge (pp. 259-273).

Kolb, D. A. (1984). Experiential learning: Experience as the source of learning and development. Prentice-Hall.

Koskelainen, T., Kalmi, P., Scornavacca, E. & Vartiainen, T. (2023). Financial literacy in the digital age – A research agenda. The Journal of Consumer Affairs 57/1 (pp. 507-528).

Lampropoulos, G. (2023). Educational benefits of digital game-based learning: K-12 teachers' perspectives and attitudes. Advances in Mobile Learning Educational Research 3/2 https://doi.org/10.25082/AMLER.2023.02.008

Lengyel, P. S. (2020). Can the Game-Based Learning Come? Virtual Classroom in Higher Education of 21st Century. International Journal of Emerging Technologies in Learning 15 (pp. 112-126).

Lyons, A. C. & Kass-Hanna, J. (2021). A methodological overview to defining and measuring "digital" financial literacy. Financial Planning Review 4/2. https://doi.org/10.1002/cfp2.1113

Maynard, N. W., Mehta, P., Parker, J., & Steinberg, J. (2012). Can games build financial capability? Financial entertainment: A research overview (RAND Corporation Working Paper WR- 963- SSA). www.rand.org/pubs/ working_ papers/ WR963.html/

Nightingale, J. (2019). Using a Simulation Game to Teach the Concept of ERP. In A. Al-Masri & K. Curran (Eds.) Smart Technologies and Innovation for a Sustainable Future. Advances in Science, Technology & Innovation (pp. 457-463) Springer

Organisation for Economic Co- operation and Development. (2020). OECD/ INFE 2020 International Survey of Adult Financial Literacy. www.oecd.org/ financial/ education/ oecd- infe- 2020- internationalsurvey-of- adult- financial- literacy.pdf

OECD (2024). Recommendation of the Council on Financial Literacy, OECD/LEGAL/0461

Panos, G. A. & Wilson, J. O. S. (2020). Financial literacy and responsible finance in the FinTech era: capabilities and challenges. The European Journal of Finance 26/4-5 (pp. 297-301).

Pilon, M. (2015). The secret history of Monopoly: the capitalist board game's leftwing origins. https://www.theguardian.com/lifeandstyle/2015/apr/11/secret-history-monopoly-capitalist-game-leftwing-origins

Platz, L., Jüttler, M. & Schumann, S. (2021). Game-Based Learning in Economics Education at Upper Secondary Level: The Impact of Game Mechanics and Reflection on Students' Financial Literacy. In C. Aprea & D. Ifenthaler (Eds.) Game-based Learning Across the Disciplines. Advances in Game-Based Learning (pp. 25-42) Springer.

Salas-Velasco, M., Moreno-Herrero, D. & Sanchez-Campillo, J. (2020). Teaching financial education in schools and students' financial literacy: A cross-country analysis with PISA data. International Journal of Finance & Economics 26/3 (pp. 4077-4103).

Sardone N. (2012). Exploring Personal Finance Concepts Through Simulation Role Play. https://ssrn.com/abstract=1984970

Sardone, N. B. (2019). Gaming Economics in the Middle School Classroom. The Clearing House: A Journal of Educational Strategies, Issues and Ideas 92/4-5 (pp. 163-173).

Thomas, N. M. (2024). Game On: The Power of Gamification in improving Financial Literacy. https://www.marketexpress.in/2024/05/game-on-the-power-of-gamification-in-improving-financial-literacy.html

MONETIZING MINORS

CHILDREN SPENDING MONEY ON GAMING CONTENT – AND HOW TO PREVENT INDUSTRY FROM KEEPING IT!

Ralph J. Moeller

In-game purchases have become a major part of the gaming industry's income. Underage kids buy loot boxes, in-game currency and other content, sometimes for considerable amounts of money, sometimes with, but more often without their parent's consent. Later, with the damage done, said families face crisis and anger. In many cases, filing for a refund is not even considered.

The purpose of this paper is to take a look at the methods publishers use to get people to spend money, later to be followed by the means and possibilities consumers have to get this money back. There are multiple institutions all over Europe whose purpose is to strengthen consumer's rights and, if necessary, enforce them against the industry. It is not acceptable letting an ever-growing industry just get away with it, to let them take money from underaged children and teenagers.

Keywords: Underage monetization, Loot boxes, Play store, Dark Patterns, Legal Action

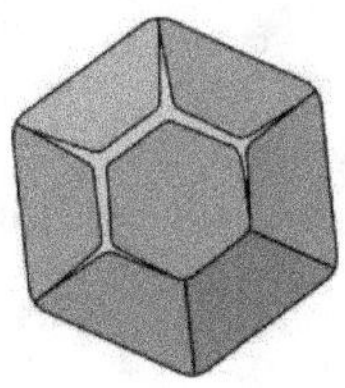

1. Making Money

The gaming industry is in a permanent state of flux. In the early days of home gaming on consoles and PCs, games were sold as boxed products through retail and wholesale channels. Back then, data was mostly transferable from producers to consumers using storage media like cartridges, (floppy) disks[1] or, later, CDs. Due to the low production cost CDs (and later, DVDs) became the media of choice for next-gen consoles like the Sony PlayStation as well as for PCs.

The rise of the internet brought a major change to the whole system as broadband and fibre channels enable producers to deliver the product directly to the consumer without the tolerated-but-not-endorsed necessity of retailers. Thus, *Direct Sales* emerged as a new distribution model.

This instantly proved very profitable for producers, who were now able to make much larger profits by eliminating the direct market distribution. Furthermore, the next innovation was already at the doorstep: Online gaming became very popular amongst gamers all over the world, even more so as several publishers started a new distribution model: Free To Play.

But, *is* Free-To-Play *really* for free?

2. Free To Play

By definition, "Free To Play" means that you do not have to pay for playing the game you are playing or, in a more refined definition, for the entertainment you are provided with.

Free-to-play concepts come in several shapes and colors.

---

[1] Due to its physical appearance early disks (with the 5¼" disk being the most wide-spread format) diskettes were referred to as "floppy" disks. The later 3½" disk with its sturdy outer shell was commonly only referred to as "disk".

First, there are games that really ARE free to play. It is not within the scope of this paper to provide a list of such "free-for-real" titles, but you can find plenty of good and fine games on the internet that really live up to the definition.

You might find that most of these games that are 100% free of charge are either hobby or enthusiast products, art projects or vintage games made publicly available for the community by their creators or producers.

On the other hand, there are those games that are marketed as being Free-To-Play but make you spend money on them nonetheless [2]. Often to be found in the online RPG genre, these games first provide a pleasing gaming experience for the players to get hooked. All too often, said games will try to get the players to spend money on in-game content. There are multiple methods to get consumers to buy content, be it intended item shortage or avoidance of less enjoyable parts of their games like the ever-present *grinding*. We shall get back to this later.

3. In-Game Stores

The mere fact that a game is not free but actually has a rather steep initial sales price (normally ranging from EUR 60,- to 80,- for a AAA title) and is marketed as a premium product does not keep producers from trying to make the extra buck by adding in-game purchase options to such titles.

Electronic Arts, for example, has mastered this to perfection within some of their sports titles.

Games are business. Big Business. For example, take a product like EA Sports FC (formally known as FIFA Soccer). EA does not release numbers to the public, but analysts assume the revenue for FIFA Soccer 2030 to exceed USD 100M [3].

These numbers do not result from game sales alone. EA's (FIFA) Soccer, along with its sibling brands *NHL Hockey* and *NBA Live*, contain game modes allowing gamers/users all over the world to participate in online gaming leagues. To

[2] Ask yourself: If a game is *free*, why even make the effort to actually *market* it in the first place?

[3] See statista.com for further information

participate the gamer/user is urged to create an in-game playing team to use in those online leagues. To form a team, the gamer needs in-game characters. Those in-game characters are personas of real-life players like Kylian M'Bappé (a world famous French soccer player) or Connor McDavid (captain of the Edmonton Oilers and MVP in the 2024 Stanley Cup finals). Those in-game characters have to be acquired to use within the game, at sometimes exorbitant extra cost.

To give an impression of how the EA in-game purchase system works I shall refer to NHL Hockey as I have some first-hand experience with the game and its in-game store[4]: First, one can not just buy an in-game player directly from the store. Rather, you have to buy "HUT packs", being more or less an electronic pendant to the infamous trading card pack.

A HUT pack contains several surprise player and/or item cards (for an overview see nhlhutbuilder.com). The players and items you receive by buying packs are later used to strengthen / power up your Hockey Ultimate Team – and you need a HUT team to be able to participate in online leagues. Bottom line: To play online (successfully) you have to invest.

To make things more interesting, every single "card" (keep in mind: we are referring to non-physical content!) is of a certain rarity. The better the card (better meaning higher player skills), the more valuable it becomes as highly skilled players can form a better team. Therefore, better skills pave the road to success in HUT / FUT. To make things even more interesting, there are multiple versions of so-called HUT packs.

Of course, better cards have a much higher rarity than average or below average cards. If you look at the NHL pack statistics available online, you will find that packs are sold firsthand with some kind of guarantee to contain a certain amount of rare and super-rare cards (this is normally indicated by the card color, being bronze, silver and gold for rarest).

Take the "Premium Players Pack" for example: Advertised to contain *10 ITEMS, ALL GOLD PLAYERS, AT LEAST 2 80+ OVR PLAYERS* by EA, you are therefore promised that you get 10 "Gold" items and 2 players with a rating of 80/100.

---

[4] According to multiple video sources available online, the mechanics for (FIFA) Soccer and NBA Live are pretty much identical to those used in NHL

According to nhlhutbuilder.com' statistics, buying this pack results in a probability of 2.6% that you will receive one (!) player with a rating of 86/100 or better. And all this for a price of 450 EA Points.

Wait a minute. EA points? Another interesting aspect in the world of in-game purchases is the fact that items are generally not directly sold for real money, but for currencies created for and valuable only within one certain game. This, of course, helps publishers obfuscate actual in-game item cost[5]. 450P (points) – how much is that in real money? At the time this paper was written, 250 Points cost $2,49 which results in 450P equaling to approx. $4,50. That means that you spend short of five bucks for ten (!) player items you can use in NHL 24.

Consider this: A hockey team normally consists of at least 25-30 players (four lines, three goalies, trainer, extras) and, as many HUT gamers will confirm, with players maxing out at 80/100 participation in the higher leagues is no fun as these characters are sometimes unable to hit the proverbial barn from 30 feet away. So you start buying additional packs, hoping for better players. A feat that *may* turn out expensive in the end.

EA's aesthetics for their Ultimate Team systems are a digital recreation of a collector's experience when buying actual, physical sports card packs. Take the presentation of a pack opening: Cool animations, lights and sound effects[6] In fact, the only differences to real life are(i)) in e-sports in-game stores packs come in different "flavors" (i.e. content probability, see above) and (ii) real-life cards do not lose all their usability (and value) at the end of a season.

EA simply created a system using aesthetics and mechanics that gamers and collectors both respond to. Their continued success proves that the formula works, as the keep electronic content to gamers world-wide. For a lot of money.

---

[5] For a deeper understanding of in-game currencies see egdf.eu: In-game currencies (2023)

[6] On YouTube there are whole channels dedicated to "pack openings" – and interestingly enough, those YouTubers always receive the really rare stuff. In all honesty and without sleight of hands, of course!

4. Minors affected

Now, this could all be considered fine and well, if the game consumers' community only consisted of adults with a regular income and the intellectual and legal abilities to spend their money the way they saw fit, fully understanding the consequences of their monetary actions.

But – and this will not be too much of a surprise – not all gamers are adults. Games like the EA sports titles hold a high percentage of players who are 17 years or younger (according to *statista.com* in 2019 17% of EA Sports players were under 18 years old [7]).

All players are by default able to use EA's in-game stores to buy additional content for their games. And they do. Sometimes spendings sum up to figures high enough to exceed an average credit card's monthly limit. For example, the Austrian Association of Consumer Affairs (*Verein für Konsumentenschutz*) reports the case of a 13-year-old kid spending more than EUR 4.000,- over a period of two months on FIFA soccer in-game content [8] using their mother's credit card.

This is not an isolated case. Many games try to get minors to spend their (or rather their parent's or grandparent's) money. Konsument.at also reports the case of a father whose kid bought in-game content for the game *Brawl-Star* amounting to EUR 1.086,73.

In-game purchases are part of a large multimedia infrastructure consisting of hard- and software services including shopping opportunities and payment. For payment, consumers are normally encouraged to store one or multiple methods, normally credit card data or bank account information, to enable instant withdrawal. This makes your in-game shopping experience a rather streamlined experience. Click "buy", confirm, and you are done.

Now, if your kid owns a gaming console, desire to play online is imminent. However, the two game consoles dominating the market, namely Microsoft's Xbox and Sony's PlayStation, can only be used for online playing if the gamer has a paid membership for the platform's online service. To pay for those the

---

[7] See Statista.com (2022-11-28): Distribution of EA gaming audiences in 2019

[8] Konsument.at: Zahlen für den Sieg.

service urge players to purchase said services instantly online by linking a credit card as payment method to the player's account[9].

As minors do not usually have their own credit cards, parents come into play as only a parent can provide the necessary credit card. And they will, as all too often kids will start nagging at their parent's nerves until they are allowed online play. And thus, the kid's platform profile contains valid payment means for any content available.

In the author's own experience, parents often do not consider the consequences of a credit card linked to their kid's gaming profile. In my own family I have experienced first-hand a financial loss of approx. EUR 800,- for in-game items purchased using a grandparent's credit card linked to a gaming account.

5. Dark patterns

To get people to spend money on their product, the industry does not only rely on product quality and consumer confidence. Rather, influential methods are used to impact on the consumer's decision-making process, some even on a subconscious level. Those methods are often referred to as *dark patterns*[10]. Their goal is simple: *Close the deal!*

This is a short summary of methods often seen in real-life use:

Decision-influencing GUI-design: "BUY NOW" button is prominently placed, highlighted and colored, the "no thanks" button is hardly visible

Limited offers: Timers are running out. In EAs NHL on multiple occasions throughout the season, limited packs with fancy names are offered *for a limited time only*. Some contain player cards not available anywhere else (consider the

---

[9] Alternatives like pre-paid cards exist, but the platform will always urge you to pay on-line, on the fly

[10] See Beuc.eu: "Dark Patterns" and the EU Consumer Law Acquis

Movember[11] packs in which EA sells cards with stars with moustaches, or the Playoff Cards released during the Stanley Cup Playoffs), others have higher odds of getting good players, often for an enormous price.

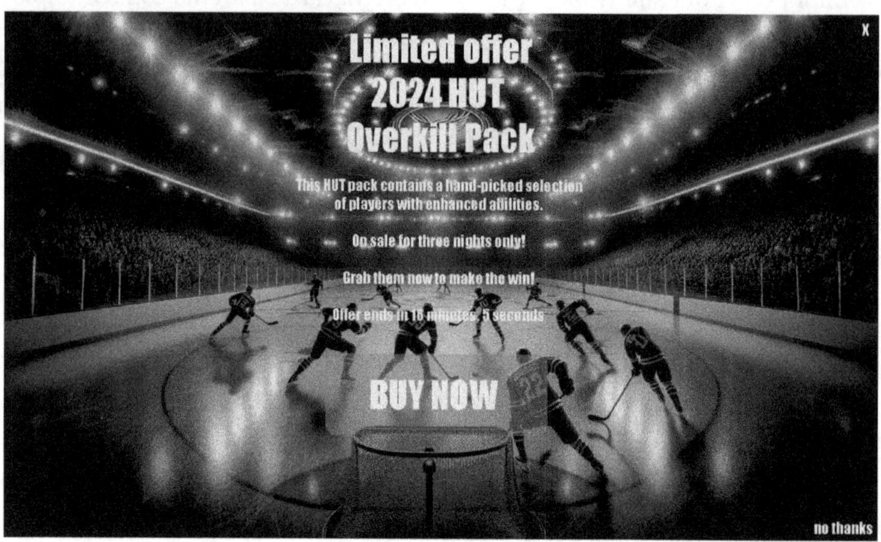

Figure 1. BUY NOW and Limited Offers (Not an actual screenshot!)

The principle of so-called "sunk cost fallacy": If a person has already invested a considerable amount of time and/or money into a product, their readiness to keep on investing will increase due to the desire to back the investment already taken; think along the lines of "I already spent 100 bucks, another 10 won't matter much". Feel free to multiply both figures by a random factor *X*, the principle remains the same.

Survivorship bias: Many games use rankings and championships to make player success visible to the world. Losers are invisible.

Gambler's fallacy: Players consider their history of purchases to have an influence on future transactions ("I have invested so much, it simply has to pay off one day"). This is a mindset often seen in gambling. While mathematically proven

[11] The "Movember" movement was created to raise awareness of male health issues like prostate cancer or depression and by this make people consider health checks and raise general awareness. Every November, stars grow moustaches as a visible symbol for the movement.

incorrect, it is still a common behavior pattern resulting in a major issue people are often affected by.

Confirm-shaming: Also considered as *group pressure,* often seen within younger peer groups. A person not participating in a group event is subject to shame and guilt. When said group event necessitates purchase of certain products like in-game objects ("only players of level 30 and above can participate"), said pressure results in revenue for the game publisher.

Not to be tempted is *hard* even if you are an "experienced adult" gamer, let alone a minor with less experience in online gaming. One is susceptible to dark patterns and before you know it, your money is gone.

6. Get a refund - if you can

Purchasing electronic content legally is nothing but a contract established between a buyer (you) and a seller (the publisher or store provider). Thus, certain rules and regulations apply. These being online transactions of non-physical products, there are some differences to transactions applying to physical objects (this is a mere technicality and will not be discussed further in this paper).

It all comes down to the fact that the object of this discussion is a financial transaction.

In Austria, consumer law is applicable as a means of regulation for financial transactions between private persons (not companies!) and vendors / sellers: Consumers between 7 and 14 years of age only have limited freedom of action [12]. This means that consumers of that age can only become part of business transactions of limited financial value and impact; for example buy snacks, soft drinks or a movie ticket.

Minors between 14 and 18 years of age can conduct business transactions of higher amounts/values and have full control over their income, but only if those transactions do not have a major influence on their financial situation. The so-

---

[12] For a general overview see oesterreich.gv.at: Allgemeines zum Vertragsabschluss durch Kinder und Jugendliche

called "major influence" is a rather vague definition, but the core of it is that, if an underage teen, for example, buys a luxury watch without the parent's consent, the purchasing contract is likely to be invalid and the child is entitled for a refund [13]. For a cheap fashion or sports watch, this might not be the case as it is not of substantial value and the purchase will probably not have a major impact on the minor's financial situation.

Now, if a minor spends excessive amounts of money, thereby exceeding what is often referred to as *pocket money* [14] on digital content, such transactions are likely to be considered invalid/illegal and therefore reversible.

This is where the problem starts as one cannot just walk into an online in-game store and demand a refund as one would do in the case of your average high street store. This makes getting a refund much harder to come by for said cases.

Take the one case I described earlier in this paper: The kid spending more than 4.000,- on FIFA in-game content. Taking into account what we have just heard, this transaction should normally be reverted by EA (actually by Sony, as the purchases were done using their PlayStation store).

The kid's mother actually *did* get her money back, but not before she – backed by the Austrian Association of Consumer Information – filed for a refund [15]. In the first place before giving in, Sony argued that the mother missed out on creating multiple accounts – one for herself as parent and guardian, another for her child – thereby forfeiting control over her kid's financial transactions.

The mother argued that no such information was presented to her when setting up the console for the kid to play, also there was no budget maintenance available to prevent transactions exceeding certain limits. This argumentation was found to be the stronger one and Sony had to refund €4.068,71.

---

[13] See for example Arbeiterkammer.at: Musterbriefe / Kaufvertrag von Minderjährigen

[14] a term often used in discussions involving the subject – although being a bit vague one gets a sense of the meaning behind it

[15] A description of this case can be found at Konsument.at

This case ended well for the consumer, but that's not always the case. There are no statistics available on how many people just give up when faced with the obstacles that publishers put in the way of a refund.

In a case I supervised myself I can report of the frustrations caused by the producers. In my family, one family member (the grandma) complained to me about a "credit card fraud" or "hack" when a considerable amount of money was discovered having been transferred from her account for unknown purposes.

As I am the go-to computer guy within our family, she asked for help and I quickly found out that this was no fraud, no "hack", but rather a series of "Google Play Store" transactions amounting to roughly €500,- over a span of 2 days for products yet unknown.

It turned out that one kid from the family had asked their grandma's permission to enter a credit card into a Google account "for age verification" and connect the Google account to the game account. A rather creative explanation in my opinion, but (sadly) it worked.

With these facts we logged into the grandma's Google Play Account (which she had not had any knowledge about) to check the order history and found this:

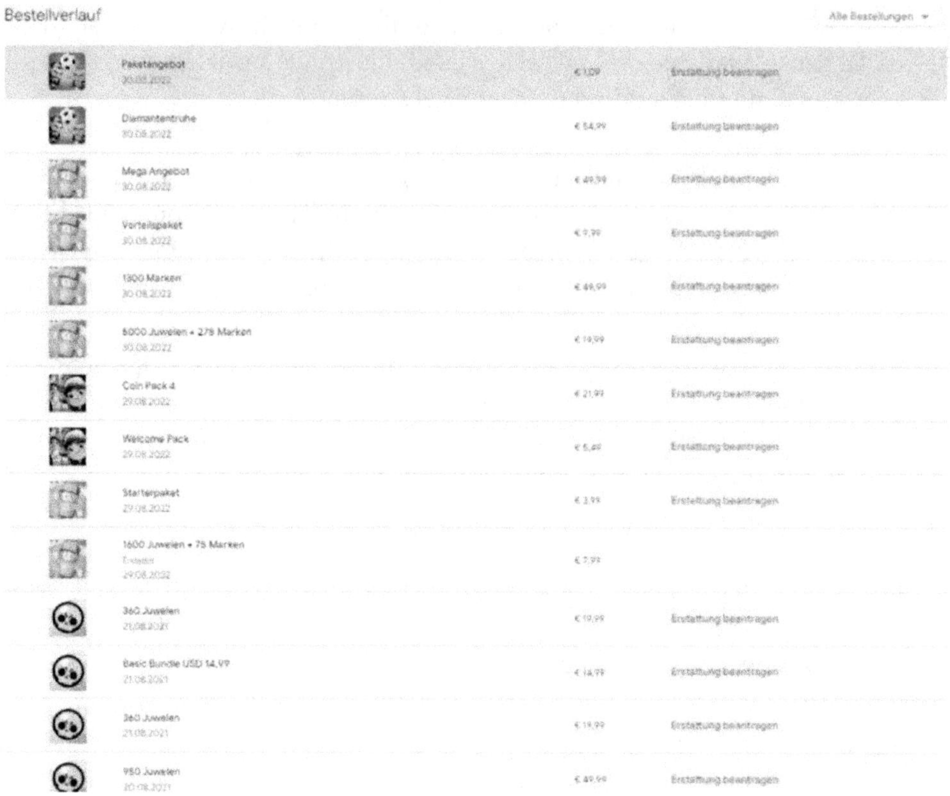

Bestellverlauf

Alle Bestellungen

Paketangebot 30.08.2022	€ 1,09	Erstattung beantragen
Diamantentruhe 30.08.2022	€ 54,99	Erstattung beantragen
Mega Angebot 30.08.2022	€ 49,99	Erstattung beantragen
Vorteilspaket 30.08.2022	€ 9,99	Erstattung beantragen
1300 Marken 30.08.2022	€ 49,99	Erstattung beantragen
6000 Juwelen + 278 Marken 30.08.2022	€ 19,99	Erstattung beantragen
Coin Pack 4 29.08.2022	€ 21,99	Erstattung beantragen
Welcome Pack 29.08.2022	€ 5,49	Erstattung beantragen
Starterpaket 29.08.2022	€ 3,99	Erstattung beantragen
1600 Juwelen + 75 Marken Erstattet 29.08.2022	€ 7,99	
360 Juwelen 21.08.2021	€ 19,99	Erstattung beantragen
Basic Bundle USD 14,99 21.08.2021	€ 14,99	Erstattung beantragen
360 Juwelen 21.08.2021	€ 19,99	Erstattung beantragen
950 Juwelen 20.08.2021	€ 49,99	Erstattung beantragen

Figure 2. Google Play Store after the shopping tour

Next step – talk to the kid. After some fruitless discussions (hackers, no idea, aliens) the kid admitted the age verification trick enabling the purchases. Case solved.

Next step. Get the money back. At the time of the transactions the kid's age was 12, and by this consumer laws and regulations became applicable: Spending €500,- on loot boxes and jewels, gold or other junk for online games is in no way in line with the definition of an underage kid spending some pocket money.

Now, if one tries to file a complaint within the Google Play Store to get a refund, the process works pretty much as follows:

- You have to create a case for every single transaction by clicking through multiple screens within the store

- You can even select "was purchased by a family member without my consent" as a reason for filing the complaint!

- Then, your cases are sent "for review"

- After 24 hours, we received a mail message for every single case stating:

> We received your inquiry over €xxx for [enter name of the junk your kid threw money at here]. However, we have to decline your inquiry as the purchase was not made in accordance with our guidelines. We understand that this can be frustrating and apologize for any inconvenience. *And so on.*

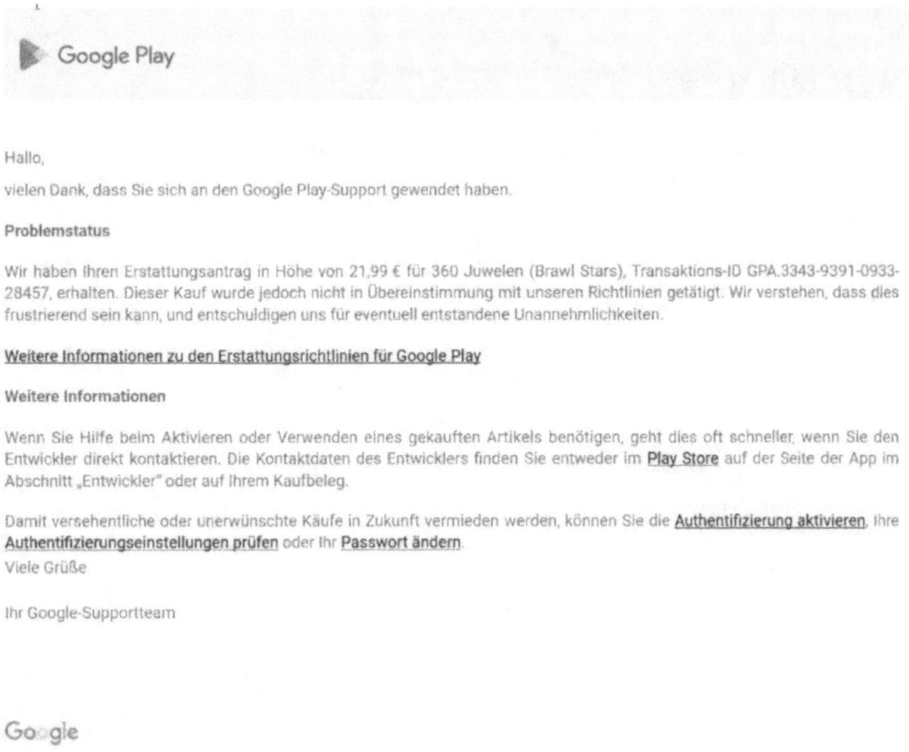

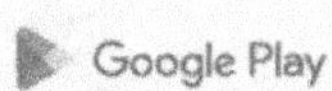

Hallo,

vielen Dank, dass Sie sich an den Google Play-Support gewendet haben.

Problemstatus

Wir haben Ihren Erstattungsantrag in Höhe von 21,99 € für 360 Juwelen (Brawl Stars), Transaktions-ID GPA.3343-9391-0933-28457, erhalten. Dieser Kauf wurde jedoch nicht in Übereinstimmung mit unseren Richtlinien getätigt. Wir verstehen, dass dies frustrierend sein kann, und entschuldigen uns für eventuell entstandene Unannehmlichkeiten.

Weitere Informationen zu den Erstattungsrichtlinien für Google Play

Weitere Informationen

Wenn Sie Hilfe beim Aktivieren oder Verwenden eines gekauften Artikels benötigen, geht dies oft schneller, wenn Sie den Entwickler direkt kontaktieren. Die Kontaktdaten des Entwicklers finden Sie entweder im Play Store auf der Seite der App im Abschnitt „Entwickler" oder auf Ihrem Kaufbeleg.

Damit versehentliche oder unerwünschte Käufe in Zukunft vermieden werden, können Sie die Authentifizierung aktivieren, Ihre Authentifizierungseinstellungen prüfen oder Ihr Passwort ändern.
Viele Grüße

Ihr Google-Supportteam

Google

Figure 3. Automated Message from Google Play

I find this reaction interesting for multiple reasons. First, the option to select "purchased by family member without my consent" indicates that these cases are a regularity. Second, the statement "purchase was not made in accordance with our guidelines" is, if any, an argument FOR a refund, not against it, as a purchase not made in accordance with any applicable guidelines is normally invalid.

However, any contact with an actual person was suppressed by Google; in our case, the only thing possible was "to get in touch with the publisher of the software".

We also contacted publisher Epic Games as some transactions affected their game FortNite, whose reactions were similar. We received a mail asking us to provide

- The Transaction-IDs for every single transaction, which would be found on an invoice from a company named "Xsolla"

- The in-game username / display name

- The mail address linked to the gamer profile

If we would kindly provide that, things would move forward.

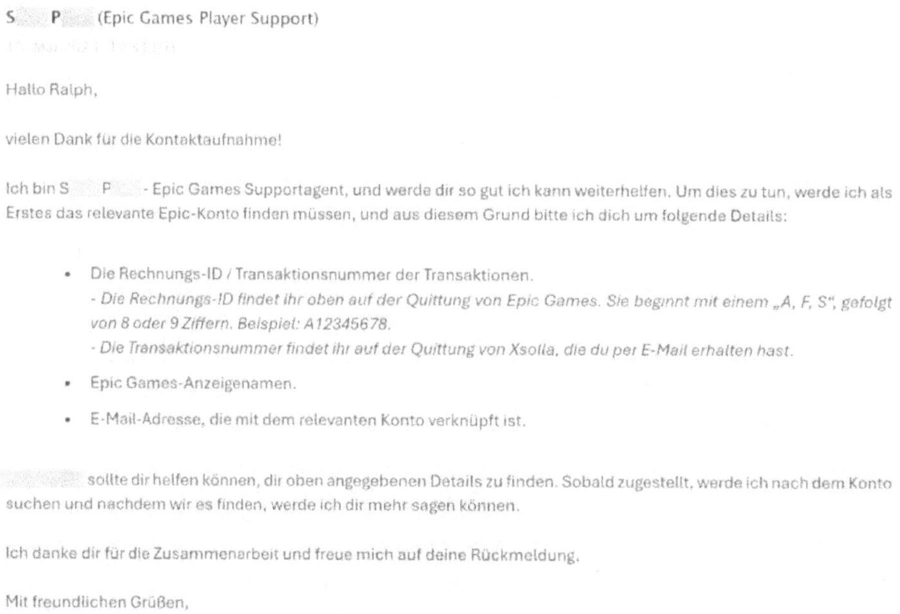

S P (Epic Games Player Support)

Hallo Ralph,

vielen Dank für die Kontaktaufnahme!

Ich bin S P - Epic Games Supportagent, und werde dir so gut ich kann weiterhelfen. Um dies zu tun, werde ich als Erstes das relevante Epic-Konto finden müssen, und aus diesem Grund bitte ich dich um folgende Details:

- Die Rechnungs-ID / Transaktionsnummer der Transaktionen.
  - Die Rechnungs-ID findet ihr oben auf der Quittung von Epic Games. Sie beginnt mit einem „A, F, S", gefolgt von 8 oder 9 Ziffern. Beispiel: A12345678.
  - Die Transaktionsnummer findet ihr auf der Quittung von Xsolla, die du per E-Mail erhalten hast.
- Epic Games-Anzeigenamen.
- E-Mail-Adresse, die mit dem relevanten Konto verknüpft ist.

sollte dir helfen können, dir oben angegebenen Details zu finden. Sobald zugestellt, werde ich nach dem Konto suchen und nachdem wir es finden, werde ich dir mehr sagen können.

Ich danke dir für die Zusammenarbeit und freue mich auf deine Rückmeldung.

Mit freundlichen Grüßen,

Figure 4. Mail from Epic

This seems reasonable at first, and more user-friendly than Google's reaction. But once you consider that it is not possible to even get in touch with Epic without providing the account data (you need to be logged into the account to file a complaint) this seems much less reasonable, but rather just another nag to keep consumers from filing their complaints.

I argue that these obstacles set in place by the publishers are nothing but further means for preventing refunds at any cost. This is yet another Dark Pattern, just like those discussed earlier.

It is not unlikely that many consumers, facing those obstacles, simply give up; even more so as your average consumer is overwhelmed by the data they need to provide just to see their rights enforced. But this is not necessary! There are institutions who provide help, all over Europe (see list below).

7. Keep on trying!

The purpose of this paper is to encourage you to, if your kid did fall for the temptations of the digital world and thereby spending your money, enforce your consumer rights! The last word is not spoken after the transaction is closed. Consumer rights associations all over Europe are trying to help and get publishers to prevent cases like the ones discussed above. But they need to know about such cases.

Just giving up only backs the industry's position. Children are tempted, sometimes pressed, to buy gaming content. Aside from morality, there is a legal aspect that backs the consumer's position against the industry. Therefore, it must be said that just letting the industry keep the money and forget about it is not an option.

> The line must be drawn here!
>
> *Jean-Luc Picard*

8. Acknowledgments

A big Thank You to my family giving consent to discussing our case within this paper.

9. About the Author

Ralph J. Moeller is the CEO of two independent software/service vendors and has been working in IT as a consultant, software developer and trainer since 1991. He is married and lives in Vienna/Austria.

His big interest in games led to a postgraduate study program in Game Studies which he finished in 2016, to be followed by a further degree in Game-based Media and Education. He is very interested in Transmedia Storytelling.

In his free time he plays the piano and electric guitar. He also is a vivid collector of books, comics, musical instruments and vinyl records. He has way too little space for all of his stuff.

Facebook: RJMoeller
Website: www.ant.at

References

Egdf.eu / Pekka, Jari: https://www.egdf.eu/documentation/7-balanced-protection-of-vulnerable-players/consumer-protection/in-game-currencies-2023/

Statista.com (2024-03-04): EA top grossing mobile games 2023 https://www.statista.com/statistics/1208392/top-global-electronic-arts-app-revenue-google-play/#:~:text=From%20January%20to%20August%202023,revenues%20in%20the%20measured%20period.

Statista.com (2022-11-28): Distribution of EA gaming audiences in 2019: https://www.statista.com/statistics/1283980/ea-player-base-age-group/

Nhlhutbuilder.com: https://nhlhutbuilder.com/hut-packs.php

Beuc.eu: "DARK PATTERNS" AND THE EU CONSUMER LAW ACQUIS Recommendations for better enforcement and reform (7.2.2022) https://www.beuc.eu/sites/default/files/publications/beuc-x-2022-013_dark_patters_paper.pdf

Oesterreich.gv.at: Contract closure by Children and Minors (Allgemeines zum Vertragsabschluss durch Kinder und Jugendliche (Geschäftsfähigkeit)) https://www.oesterreich.gv.at/themen/gesetze_und_recht/gerichtsorganisation_der_justiz/zivilrecht/8/Seite.1740317.html

Konsument.at: Sony Playstation: 4000€ für FIFA-21-Spieler ausgegeben https://konsument.at/sony-playstation-4000-eu-fuer-fifa-21-spieler-ausgegeben/65318

Sigl, Rainer: Kinder und Videospiele https://www.derstandard.at/story/3000000209724/kinder-und-videospiele-gamer-vater-sein-ist-schwer

List of consumer rights institutions and organizations

Europäisches Verbraucherzentrum Österreich: *https://europakonsument.at*
Europäisches Verbraucherzentrum Deutschland: *https://evz.de*
Verein für Konsumenteninformation: *https://vki.at*
European Consumer Organisation: *https://beuc.eu*

Disclaimer

Images and screenshots were created solely by the author.

The ice rink image background for the "dark pattern" sample was created using Microsoft AI image generator. (https://designer.microsoft.com/image-creator)

KOPFGELD

DARK PLAY IN AN AI BASED INDIVIDUALIZED MONEY GAME

Margarete Jahrmann, Thomas Brandstetter,
Stefan Glasauer

The exemplary low interaction game KOPFGELD, developed in 2023 by Margarete Jahrmann and Stefan Glasauer and first exhibited in a show on the topic of cash at Re:Publica Berlin (RP23.-) defines the price of a player's face by using the latest developments in AI image generation and face recognition systems.

In a theoretical framework we reflect KOPFGELD as a radical art game on "non-consensual play" by AI systems with human entities. In playful settings actual face recognition directly capitalizes biometric data. The emerging AI systems use human play with AI for training of their own systems and turn interaction and attention into cash. Using methods of playful artistic research (LUDIC method), the artistic low interaction game KOPFGELD furthers the understanding of non-consensual play and so-called "dark patterns of game design". Situating the installation in the context of idle/low interactions and the artistic tradition of "dark play", we show how actual games, exemplified by a mobile racing game, provide a dark mirror in which we can see glimpses of a future of pervasive gamification driven by non-human players: "you are being played".

Keywords: art, non-consensual play, dark patterns of game design, AI, low interaction games

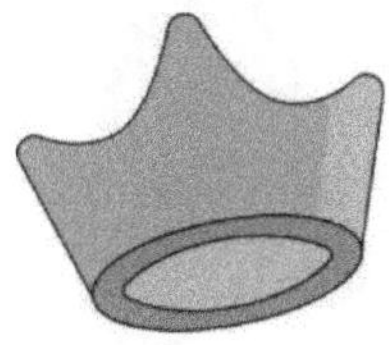

1. Introduction

This article is less a game studies analysis of existing video games than a proposal inspired by experimental games and artistic research on how to deal with the highly topical issue of translating (personal) data into cash within game situations. Based on a current phenomenology of play as inquiry (play as opposed to game), we analyze the relationship between exploitation, control and play in low interaction games with colonial non-consensual unilateral game mechanics or, in short, in capitalist cultural rules of the game.

We introduce our own experimental art game, KOPFGELD, which is part of a larger endeavor to use methods from neurosciences and artificial intelligence for critical play projects. We describe KOPFGELD in detail, building on the institutional, theoretical, and practical background of our artistic research projects "Neuromatic Game Art" and "The Psycholudic Approach". Our art game is then situated in the wider context of non-consensual play (Trammell 2023). We argue that KOPFGELD opens activist proposals for emancipation from technological control, data capital and money through an essential feature of play: the irony of the irony of irony (Strouhal & Geringer 2023). We hope that this will serve as a starting point to draw attention to the often involuntary or unconsidered disclosure of data in games and especially in the playful use of social media and facial recognition technologies as well as in the increasingly ubiquitous artificial intelligence. We then take a close look at incremental/idle/low interaction games and their relationship to surveillance capitalism (Zuboff 2018). This provides us with a framework for understanding how players are capitalized by game companies without their knowledge or explicit consent. If that is not ironic! Finally, we point towards an escape hole: Do nothing in games to escape capitalization.

2. KOPFGELD

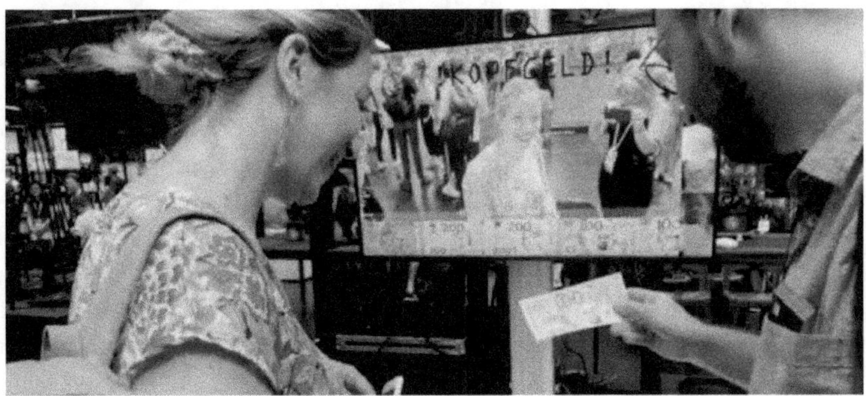

Figure 1. KOPFGELD. Ludic Eigenface Currency Converter Game, Jahrmann& Glasauer, 2023

In 2023 we developed and exhibited the interpassive game KOPFGELD (a term that translates as bounty or head-money) at Re:Publica Berlin, as an outcome of the artistic research projects "Neuromatic Game Art" and "The Psycholudic Approach", both located at the Experimental Game Cultures Department, University of Applied Arts Vienna [1]. In this minimal game installation, we played with the latest developments in AI image to image generation and face recognition systems. By looking into a camera, the players agree (=dark pattern) that their face is used as input for a closed AI system. Each face is monetarized by the AI: a „game score" is attributed. It is higher the more similar the player's face is to the average face of all former players. Within three days, the game system captured and locally stored over 800 faces of visitors of the international Re:Publica Conference players at Kreuzberghalle Berlin.

---

[1] The institutional, theoretical, and practical background of KOPFGELD is artistic research. Over a period of three years, from 2020to 2023 as part of the FWF funded project *Neuromatic Game Art: Critical Play with Neurointerfaces* we undertook a series of experiments. Its focus was on making a research processes publicly visible and to show how any artistic player can appropriate medical or scientific devices or methods as means of expression. Our original idea shifted over the course of the research. We embraced emerging developments in Artificial Intelligence in relation to the personal data collected and given by many players on "free will" to achieve a state of personal optimization and flow. See https://neuromatic.uni-ak.ac.at and https://psycholudic.uni-ak.ac.at.

From all locally saved faces an artificial face is generated which looks like the actual player but does not actually exist in reality. The new face is composed of "Eigenfaces" — and serves as basis for a Geldschein (banknote) design. We used the generative AI Stable Diffusion for an individualized Geldschein look, including the original cam-shot. By looking longer into the installation camera so that more pictures are taken, the player can bias the image database and thereby increase their score. The player's action in the game is reduced to looking into the camera. If a face looks as "average" as possible a high-score is achieved – or the AI system is as much trained as possible by the player. The face is then used as input to the image-to-image ("img2img") mode of Stable Diffusion with the additional text prompt to generate a banknote. Thus, as a direct reward, money is generated – a unique individual money design. This graphic design of a fictional money is then combined with the player's real face-shot (=Kopfgeld) and printed as artefact in the form of valueless "individualized" AI money. The art piece is pure worthless cash.

In our example of a very low interaction game, monetarizing human face data, the person thinks he/she/they is playing: many of our visitors stayed desperately in front of the camera for a prolonged time, trying to get a high-score, and if that occasionally did not happen, left frustrated. But only a non-human actor plays: A combinatorial system configuration of AI and face recognition plays with the human — in an emotionally touching experimental system on personal data, AI, and a cashless world in crisis. KOPFGELD provides a dark mirror in which we can see glimpses of a future of pervasive gamification driven by non-human players: You are being played.

Kopfgeld translates as "head-money". So, in the art game discussed, Kopfgeld is a sum paid for capturing someone´s face. We, the casual players, are paying with our data in front of all the face capture and recognition systems used in everyday life. This playful practice can be compared to the concept of the capitalization of social representation as introduced by Michel de Certau (1984) in "The practice of everyday life". Certau described how we are all measured with our social behavior in modern societies. Today, 2024, in the play of everyday life, in front of cash machines everywhere or on the street for social credit system tokens (in China), the biometric info is taken all the time. Not the worktime, but our face or in general, personal data are our capital. Often it is given away freely or taken without consent. Ironically, in the KOPFGELD game, the player gets some sort of individualized art money – as opposed to the actual world, where we get nothing. AI will not make the artist or creative work obsolete; it only means that creative work can take different forms, such that artists can focus more on conceptualization. Similarly, this might be the chance to rethink the systems of creative economy we live in. Why do we need to accumulate capital? Why isn't it better to make a flow of merits that fluctuates all the time? What if money lost value, the more that you held? KOPFGELD asks all these questions through a playful experience. And like all money, Kopfgeld money is play money.

In a sense, the experimental game installation KOPFGELD can be said to follow a dark pattern: players do not have to give their consent to play the game. If they step in front of the camera, maybe guided by curiosity, they are immediately and without being asked whisked into a game. In a supposed blatant breach of privacy as well as personality rights[2], the game takes their image and processes it. And then, in a very literal sense, the game monetarizes them: it transforms their image into a banknote. This banknote is then handed back to the player. This is a game mechanic of *the irony of the irony of irony (Strouhal, 2023)* – we do nothing to win, nothing to play, nothing to earn money – but in a *non-consensual play* our bodily data is playfully and involuntarily taken from us.

2.1 Theory of an experimental art game on non-consensual play

Aaron Trammell (2023) argues that game studies must look at the phenomenon of non-consensual play. While for traditional definitions of "game", the voluntariness of participating in the magic circle of play is central, Trammell argues that for African Americans, non-consensual play has since long been a lived experience. Citing examples from slavery, he shows that play is a power relationship: persons can become objects of the play of others. This is corroborated by the experience of persons of color, but also women and other groups, who participate in online video games: many of them can tell of instances in which they became part of play experiences that were not consensual. For Trammell, it is vital to acknowledge that such phenomena are not exceptions to the rules, but that a power dynamic is present in all games. Even in the most harmless game, someone will take up the role of the enforcer of rules, subjugating others to their vision of how the game should work. By making those fundamental power relationships visible, Trammell also discards the notion that play is necessarily fun. Play, he argues, can produce many affects: pleasure, which is not necessarily the same as fun, but also grief or pain. And perhaps, he

[2] In the artistic research game KOPFGELD, visitors are informed in the usual way of a disclaimer, put on display in the installation, that their images are taken for artistic purposes.

suggests, deliberately making games that produce painful experiences may be a way to illuminate those power relationships and thereby help to change them: "repairing play courts resistance by promising more than mere fun - it flirts with difficult and undesirable feelings - thus it is decidedly against the capture of our attention, bodies and money within its aesthetic." (Trammell 2023, p. 54).

Interestingly, the idea that play is a power relationship has already been discussed in the field of game design under the moniker of "dark patterns". In an influential paper, José Zagal and others have started by acknowledging that despite what game design textbooks say about "player-centered" design, game designers do not always have the players' best interests at heart. They identify several "patterns", that is, recurring design decisions, which are intentionally used by designers to create negative experiences for the player. Among those are temporal patterns, where players are "cheated" out of their time, monetary patterns, where players are deceived into spending more money than expected or planned, and social capital-based patterns where players' social standing and status are being risked.

There are two important points about those dark patterns: First, they exploit the players, usually to further profit of the game company by making the game more addictive, incentivize the players to spend money, etc. Under this aspect, they are a clear manifestation of a power relationship in the sense of Trammell. Secondly, they "happen without consent" (Zagal et al. 2013). While the players usually entered the game voluntarily, they are unable to change the gameplay itself - e.g. they can't just skip certain annoying parts or not do unpleasurable tasks if they want to keep playing. While this, of course, is not as violent a relationship as those put forward by Trammell, it nevertheless constitutes a power relationship that is not reciprocal and in which not all participants are on an equal footing.

However, in our own experimental game designs the question remains: Can doing nothing contain the potential for some kind of resistive play? Where do we find this kind of play? The answer is given in an analysis of Low Interaction Games.

3. Incremental/idle/low interaction games and surveillance capitalism –do nothing in order to escape!

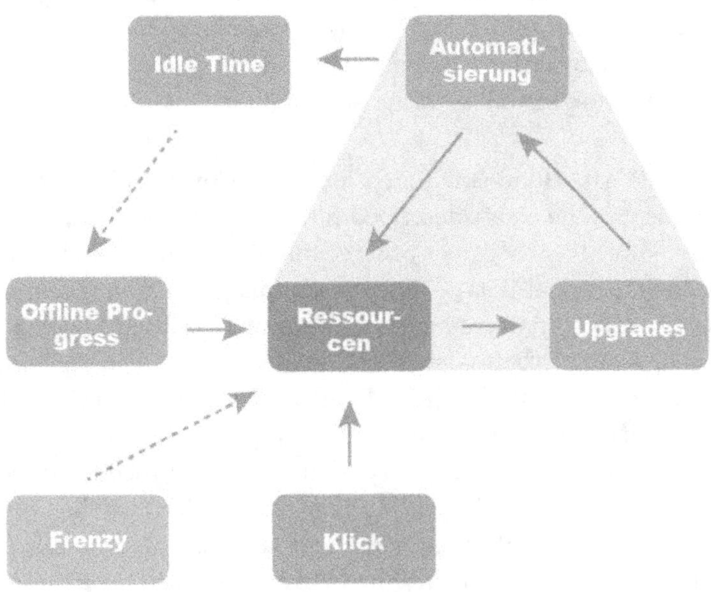

Figure 2. Resource cycle of low-interaction games, Larissa Wild 2019, p. 29.

To analyze the potential of Low Interaction Games as tools to escape monetarization, we need to touch the border of games, the dark side of games and of play motivation. Presently, we see the rise of concepts of the joy of delegated play as expressed by Sonja Fizek (2018). The game studies scholar Fizek speaks very clearly about "Self-playing Games: Rethinking the State of Digital Play". This study gives us deeper insights about the concept of play itself, given the special conditions of contemporary computer and online systems or AI in play.

Building on her profound studies on idle games, the artist and emerging game designer Larissa Wild expands Fizek´s concepts and notices the increasingly present passivity in games as "a mirror of the world as we know it". She stated at a *Ludic Method Soiree*[3] in 2022: "The new genre of Low-Interaction Games challenges the definition of games, their limits and their rules. Low-Interaction Games take away an integral part of games and thus propose a new range of definitions. They develop a new type of relationship with the player – almost a dominant one – and are still widely enjoyed and played by thousands. Through analyzing Low-Interaction Games we can find and compare patterns in other game genres as well as in our society."

This statement on the dominant dimension of such low interaction games sounds like a precedent of the above-described reflections on non-consensual play. We all know why free-to-play games are free but not without cost: because players pay with their personal data — but mostly this game is non-consensual, and players can hardly stop. Incremental games, games with little gameplay action and automated game progress, such as Cookie Clicker (Julien Thiennot, 2013) or the social idle game COW CLICKER by game theorist and designer Ian Bogost (2010) are particularly vivid examples of such game-mechanics. Bogost's game quoted Cookie Clicker, took it up in a playful way and turned it around. In doing so, he applied the aforementioned art game strategy "irony of the irony of irony" in the sense of Ernst Strouhal (2023) as a resistant political practice in experimental game production. In Cow Clicker, a cow had to be clicked on every 6 hours. Click progress or specially designed cows could be shared on the social network Facebook, which contributed to the success of the game.

The game Cookie Clicker, itself ironically designed, is about cookie production using a simple click mechanic. Wrath cookies are a special type of currency within the game. Clicking on such a wrath cookie halves the targeted cookie production for 30 minutes to an hour. However, there is a minimal chance that cookie production will increase 666 times over a limited period of time. Automation increases during the game until the so-called Grandmapocalypse, a black-humored surreal critique of capitalism. Cookie Clicker is a kind of idle game, where cookie production starts in assembly line work until the game plays itself. However, players are not rationalized away, but rather pay with what could be called a sedated presence. Referring to the master thesis of my former student Larissa Wild (2021), I would like to use her concept of Low-Interaction

---

[3] Ludic method soirées are a lectures series format with international speakers, defining strategies of artistic play. It is hosted and initialized by Margarete Jahrmann at the Experimental Game Cultures Department, University of Applied Arts Vienna. https://www.dieangewandte.at/aktuell/aktuell_detail?artikel_id=1644244159247

Game (LIG for short) as an umbrella term to summarize games with few, reduced or limited player interactions, such as idle, incremental and clicker games. In Wild's model (Wild 2021, pp. 11), the term LIG is presented as a new prevalent form of game. As in this article we are mainly interested in understanding money and players as capital, the capitalist aspect of LIGs is essential. Although the player's action is reduced to a minimum, it is repeated an infinite number of times, so, for example, a button must be pressed thousands of times to obtain in-game currency or points.

3.1 Art Games escape vs Asphalt 9: Legends

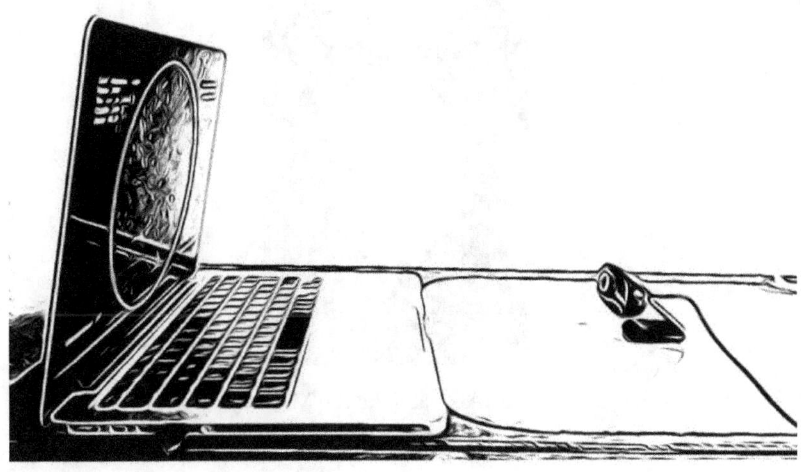

Jahrmann & Glasauer, autodemon, 2017

Figure 3. Autodemon Self Playing Game, Jahrmann & Glasauer, 2017

Many low-interaction games ironically quote other games, are self-deprecating and use storytelling elements. Brecht's method of breaking the fourth wall, for example, is used to actively address players. This shows that developers of low-interaction games often cross the blurred line between game and performance, which can lead to their games not being seen as real games. This is precisely why many LIGs are artistic games that focus on message and content and pay little attention to distribution and marketing restrictions. The game "Every day the same dream" by Molleindustria (2009) is a prominent example of this, as is "Autodemon" (2017), developed by Margarete Jahrmann and Stefan Glasauer. In the latter, an optical flow analysis of what happens on the screen using a webcam is converted back into inputs, which leads to the game playing itself.

Absurdly, games are extremely successful as incremental games precisely because of the minimal possible game action - even though it is obvious that payment is made via the advertising that is played and confirmed via clicks. The "click", however, is intimately tied to the physical. It can only be made by the person themselves, who places their finger on the keyboard or game pad. In a sense, the click is a form of biometric data capture of a player's action in connection with capital and consumption or future consumption. An extreme example of this is TAMAGO: Shake the Million (Peter Weiss, 2009): You win if you tap the egg on the screen a million times or shake the cell phone a thousand times.

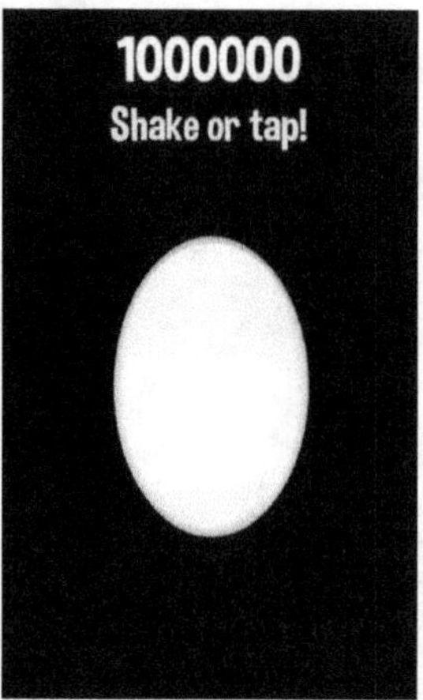

Figure 4. Screenshot TAMAGO: Shake the Million, Peter Weiss, 2009.

These meaningless and alienated forms of play coincide with early capitalist thinking in the sense of Karl Marx's labor theory of value, according to which a commodity is worth as much as the labor time "coagulated" in it. The worker must reduce alienated monotonous labor to a single activity stripped of its meaning. (see Marx, Das Kapital, page 4). Today, in her reflections on the capitalization of big data, Shoshanna Zuboff (2019) speaks of a reversal of labor and capital to mere being through the involuntary and often unconsented capitalization of the individual's data. Consent to data harvesting is often hidden in dubious, too long to read forms of consent. Above all, it is a non-consensual game that is being played here. As Shoshana Zuboff says:

> „Surveillance capitalism has succeeded through its aggressive declaration. (...) These 21st century conquistadors are not asking for permission. They go ahead and paper over the scorched earth with false legitimizing practices. Instead of cynically mediated monarchical

edicts, they offer cynically mediated service agreements whose terms are equally vague and incomprehensible." (Zuboff 2019, p. 2. In: Wiener Stadtgespräch. Shoshanna Zuboff im Gespräch mit Armin Thurnher. FALTER: Nr. 46/2019).

Analogue to this general mark on forms of consent, in games, the supposedly voluntary player becomes an involuntary worker who is not even aware of her exploitation through surveillance capitalism. This is because payment is made using in-game currency - which, as an absurd parallel currency with no purchasing power in the real world, is pure fiction, i.e. pure but not hard cash, albeit of high value in the game. This is noticeable, for example, in the racing game Asphalt 9: Legends (GameLoft Barcelona, 2018).

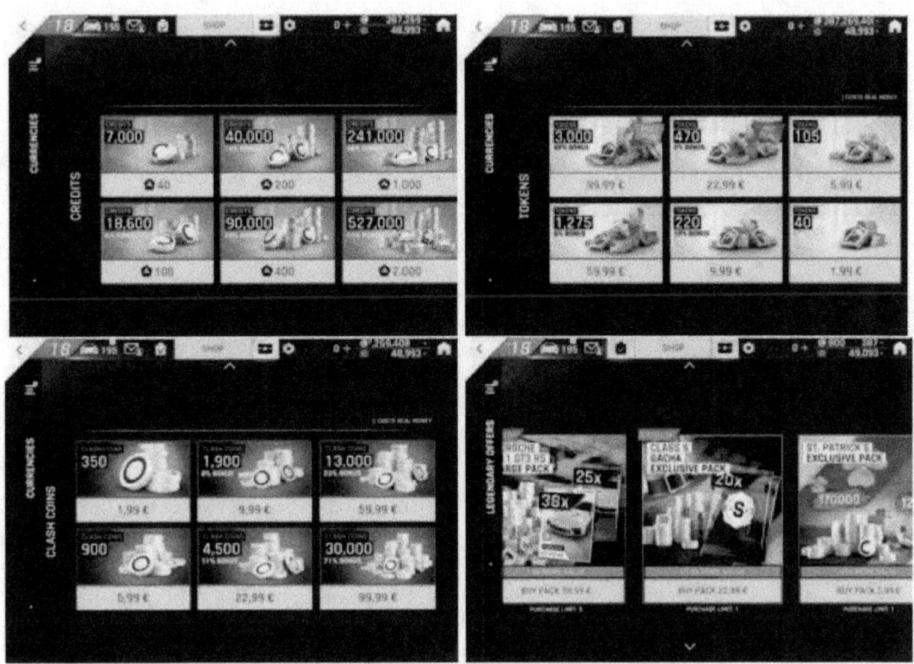

Figure 5. Credits, Tokens, Clash Coins, Legendary Offers in Asphalt 9. Screenshots from March 2024.

The racing game Asphalt 9: Legends is officially a racing simulation game. However, when observed critically, it becomes obvious that it also introduces and conditions the players to monetary systems. The developer company Gameloft of the Vivendi Group makes a good profit out of this. But why do you need money in a racing game at all? As Zuboff writes, everything should remain hidden in a cloud, in a cloudy appearance, in the interests of the profit-making companies. Because the same applies to the monetization of games: value generation should remain opaque. Three years after the launch of the game, the headline applies:

> „Asphalt 9: Legends Has Surpassed $100 Million in Consumer Spend Since its 2018 Launch." Donny Kristianto, data.ai Blog. August 2021.

How are such enormous profits generated in a free-to-play racing game and how are players capitalized? In Asphalt 9, players are introduced to a complex system of different currencies, which are linked to real currency at critical moments. In the game display, there is a separate tab for currencies. First, blueprints for cars must be collected. I can obtain these by completing races or by purchasing them in exchange for in-game currency via so-called multicard packs, which are a type of loot box. I have the option of purchasing these packs in the in-game store. They contain blueprints for cars, either to acquire cars or to upgrade them, but they may not be usable if the cars they contain have already been upgraded to the maximum possible. Cars are never awarded directly in races as featured rewards, but tokens are awarded that can be exchanged for multicard packs. Or real money can be used to buy blueprints in time-limited offers.

In the following self-experiment, let's take our current score from March 2024 as an example. We are holders of an astronomical total of 387,099,392 credits (yes, we are talking about a player who, despite this number, can fill an academically quite successful position). Credits are earned by driving and winning races and fulfilling certain conditions (such as completing a certain number of jumps, time, obstacles). Credits are needed to improve the vehicles. Credits cannot be acquired with real money, but only via the game or the in-game currency of tokens. 527,000 Credits cost 2000 tokens, which is the best offer. Tokens can be bought by real money, see below. To improve cars, i.e., to increase your chances of winning, you need to earn upgrade cards, which are activated using coins. There are also trade coins. This is where trading with and in the game begins. Superfluous items can be converted into trade coins and then traded for blueprints or upgrade cards. And so on and so forth. The system of value creation is constantly changing and is constantly adapted to user behavior - in other words, to their disadvantage and to the benefit of the game company.

On the day of the self-experiment, we hold 48,868 Asphalt Tokens, which were generated via events and daily game participation and winnings. Tokens and cash coins can also be purchased with real money, for us with Euros. 3000 tokens cost exactly 99.99 euros on March 17, 2024. [4] This is the best offer, if you buy fewer tokens, you will get a worse price. In our club, we know from our club chairman that this is his minimum monthly investment. In addition, there is the investment of a lot of lifetime: when asked personally, we receive the answer from the club chairman that they play more than five hours a day. When checking our own screen time on the tablet, we spend two to three hours a day in Asphalt 9 in a self-experiment. Playing time is added to the time during which we must consume advertisements. A Legend Pass frees you from consuming advertising, which costs about 10 euros per month. This makes it increasingly obscure how value relationships are created and how lifetime coagulates into capital.

This game shows idle game and self-play aspects. If no game is played or no money is spent - which is even worse than not playing – certain in-game currencies are automatically traded from time to time to the disadvantage of the capital-accumulating players. This applies to special in-game currencies from racing game events. If the in-game currency is not spent for blueprints within the event time window, the system automatically converts it at a very poor rate. Thus, inactive trading with in-game currency is penalized. In the spirit of classic predator capitalism, this can be said of Asphalt 9: If you buy a lot, you get everything particularly cheaply, and if you have a lot, you play a lot. Daily presence in the game is particularly rewarded. Or even doing nothing while watching the advertisements and confirming this by clicking.

Summing up the self-experiment on monetarization and capitalization of lifetime and player data it can be said that here an extremely high investment of lifetime is required in order to generate capital. This capital is necessary for being able to play. It is hard to withstand the social pressure of a racing game in which other players can also purchase minimally faster vehicles for standard money. This pressure is intensified by the clubs in which the game is played. The only escape is doing nothing- while touching the ad screen – **do nothing to escape!**

---

[4] Note that the above-mentioned in-game credits would require 48.964,- Euros to buy via buying tokens for real money. A black market of trading in-game credits to other players is, however, not possible: neither credits, not tokens, nor blueprints or cars can be given to other players.

As consequence we investigate in the Psycho-Ludic Approach[5] artistic research project play motivation and develop optional mechanics. Doing nothing is an optional mechanics, facing capitalist monetarization of games.

4. Finale: Do Nothing games towards the Psycho-Ludic Approach

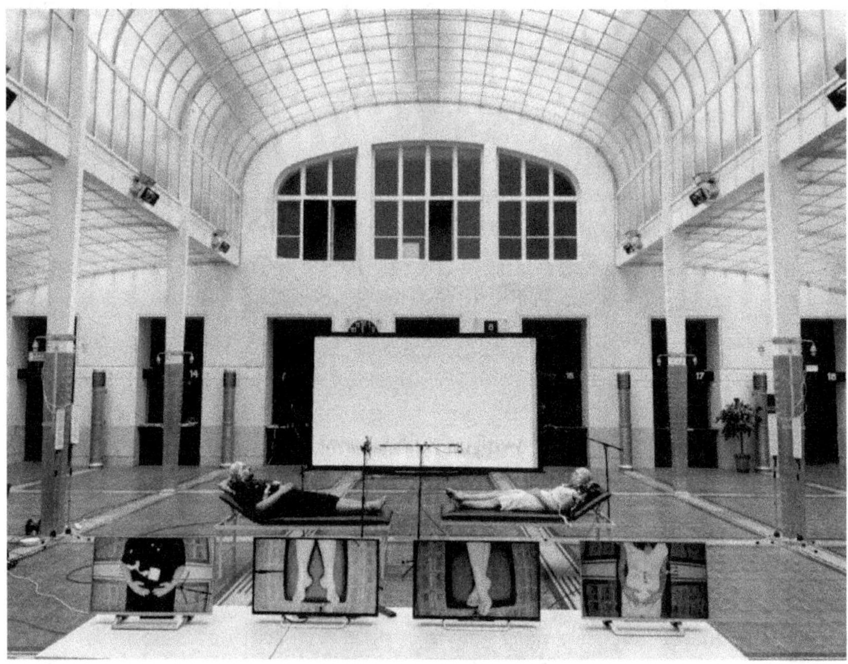

Figure 6. artefacts of mico-performativity, Aleksic, Jahrmann and Glasauer, Otto-Wagner PSKVienna 2022.

[5] The Psycho-Ludic Approach: Exploring play for a viable future (AR 787), is our newly launched artistic research project, supported by the Austrian Science Fund FWF under the program PEEK. The project claims, that the strategies, now leading to failure, are reflected in games and their mechanics: it's all about winning, accruing possessions, conquering new levels. Using methods of artistic research, experimental psychology, and neuroscience in a combination that we term the PSYCHO-LUDIC APPROACH, we will investigate alternative motivations for game-playing, how we can learn from these about possible future forms of society, and whether, by using new game mechanisms in experimental, playful contexts we may unlock better means of mediating reflection, thoughts, and action, creating a powerful, transdisciplinary basis for ecologically respectful ways of living.

A radical do-nothing game was performed by Zarko Aleksic, Margarete Jahrmann, and Stefan Glasauer under the title "artefacts of micro-performativity" at the AIL Vienna in 2022. It was a play that capitalized doing nothing, under the title "Zero Action in the Savings Bank", which dealt with the synchronization of brain signals of two performers in the cashier's hall of the Otto Wagner Postsparkasse in Vienna. In this metaphorical work, there was no money transaction in the cashier's hall, only the flow of thoughts between the two performers, who rested on examination tables and were filmed by surveillance cameras. Brain waves measured via neuro-interfaces appeared live on a large screen like stock market prices. The absurd game setting made it possible to vividly demonstrate that test subjects are also generators of data. In playfully taking research out of the laboratory and into the public sphere, in a form of self-empowerment, the capitalist productive play imperative is broken.

This neuro-game used idle game principles of minimal action. They demonstrate how the increasingly available neuro-interfaces can be used as vehicles of a new form of passive play. Such a ludic approach critically addresses via performances the non-consensual play by technological systems with human entities that directly capitalize biometric data.

5. Conclusion

Intrinsic forms of motivation, such as curiosity, creative work, participation, and emotional flow could replace profit-oriented game mechanics, enhance emphatic bonding, and foster a positive exchange with the environment.

Juxtaposed with the concept of non-consensual play and dark patterns, KOPFGELD raises a lot of interesting issues. Obviously, the players are being played, that is, they are an object of the game and not a reciprocal partner when they enter the relationship. However, before the player even realizes what has happened, the game is already over and they are presented with a product: an, albeit false, banknote. Is it a parody of payment? Or is it real payment (after all, it is an artwork)? If the players accept the banknote, has the game really ended, or can the players be considered to continue to play the game if they take the banknote, as it is a game token?

Whatever the case, the players are not obliged to take the note, and if they take it, they may keep it or destroy it, or swap it or give it away, or do whatever else they want. The important thing is that there are no rules governing the handling of the note, and if there were, there is no power to enforce rules. In this way, the banknotes constitute hybrid objects that undermine and subvert the power relationship encoded into the installation.

On the one hand, they exhibit the dark pattern encoded in the installation by making fun of monetarization. On the other hand, the proliferating notes, printed on cheap thermo-paper, are objects that carry the potential of other forms of play in them - new games with new rules, games that bring together the people that have been tricked into the game to invent new ways of interacting, new ways of playing and maybe even new ways of exchanging values. In this way, the banknotes provide a way to transform a power relationship governed by dark patterns into one of consent and experimental gameplay.

About the Authors

Margarete Jahrmann, is a ludic artist and artistic researcher, full university professor and since 2021 head of the Department EXPERIMENTAL GAME CULTURES at the University of Applied Arts Vienna. She leads since 2023 the artistic research projects "The Psycholudic Approach" and 2020-2023 "Neuromatic Game Art: critical play with neurointerfaces", both funded by the Austria Science Fund FWF in the frame of the artistic research program PEEK. As artist Jahrmann creates artworks dealing with play as creative principle. She developed a practice based ludic method as artistic research strategy, questioning the principles of player motivation and play dynamics for viable futures.

Thomas Brandstetter is a philosopher, historian, and games researcher. He has worked at Universities in Austria, Switzerland, and Germany in the fields of media studies and history of science. His main research interest are analogue games, their design, and their potential for critical play. He teaches at the Department EXPERIMENTAL GAME CULTURES at the University of Applied Arts Vienna.

Stefan Glasauer is full professor for Computational Neuroscience, teaching and working at Brandenburg University of Technology Cottbus-Senftenberg, Germany. He is interested in general principles of brain function underlying perception, action, and sensorimotor control. In his scientific practice, he uses various methods ranging from behavioural experiments and psychophysics, over neurophysiological methods such as eye and motion tracking and brain signal recording using EEG, to mathematical methods from computational and theoretical neuroscience. Besides science, he participates in art-science conferences and events and is project partner in Jahrmann's artistic research projects "The Psycholudic Approach" and "Neuromatic Game Art".

Websites:
https://experimentalgamecultures.uni-ak.ac.at, https://neuromatic.uni-ak.ac.at, https://psycholudic.uni-ak.ac.at/, https://www.margaretejahrmann.net

Acknowledgements

Funded in part by Austrian Science Fund FWF-PEEK AR 787 (doi: 10.55776/AR787).

References

Certeau, M. (1984). The Practice of Everyday Life. University of California Press, Berkeley.

Fizek, S. (2018). Interpassivity and the joy of delegated play in idle games. Transactions of the Digital Games Research Association, 3(3), 137-163. [6]. https://doi.org/10.26503/todigra.v3i3.81

Fizek, S. (2017). Self-playing Games: Rethinking the State of Digital Play. In: Proceedings of The Philosophy of Computer Games Conference, Kraków.

Marx, K. (1967). Das Kapital. Kritik der politischen Ökonomie. Erster Band. Marx-Engels-Werke Band 23. Berlin: Dietz-Verlag.

Strouhal, E., Geringer, C (2023). Die Phantome des Ingenieur Berdach. Ellmauer. Edition Konturen, Wien.

Trammell A. (2023). Repairing Play. A Black Phenomenology. MIT Press, Massachusetts/ London, England.

Wild, L. (2021). LOW-INTERACTION GAMES. Wie geringe Interaktivität Spiele, Spielmechanik und Motivationsdesign prägt. Kategorien und Muster für Low-Interaction Games. Master Thesis ZHdK Zurich

Zagal, J. P., Bjork, S., Lewis, C. (2013): "Dark Pattern in the Design of Games," Foundations of Digital Games Conference, FDG 2013, May 14-17, Chania, Greece (available online at http://www.fdg2013.org/program/papers/paper06_zagal_etal.pdf)

Zimmerman, E. (2012). Jerked around by the magic circle-clearing the air ten years later. Gamasutra - The Art & Business of Making Games.

https://www.gamedeveloper.com/design/jerked-around-by-the-magic-circle---clearing-the-air-ten-years-later

Zuboff, S. (2019). The Age of Surveillance Capitalism: The Fight for a Human Future at the New Frontier of Power. PublicAffairs, Boston.

Games

Artefacts of mico-performativity, Aleksic, Jahrmann and Glasauer, (2022), do-nothing game.

Asphalt 9 Legend, Gameloft Barcelona (2018), platform game.

Autodemon, Jahrmann & Glasauer, (2017), self-playing game.

Cookie Clicker, Julien Thiennot (Orteil), (2013), browser game.

Cow Clicker, Ian Bogost, (2010), facebook game.

Every day the same dream, Molleindustria, (2009), online game.

KOPFGELD, Jahrmann & Glasauer, (2023), Ludic currency converter game.

TAMAGO: Shake the Million, Peter Weiss (2013), mobile game.

IV. OPPORTUNITIES FOR THE GAMING INDUSTRY

GENERATIVE AI IN VIDEO GAME PRODUCTION

MORE CONTENT DOES NOT (NECESSARILY) MEAN MORE MONEY

Benjamin Hanussek, Yaraslau Kot

This paper explores the integration of generative artificial intelligence in video game production and its implications for game studios. Through an exploratory blend of literature review, expert survey, and analysis, we investigate the potential benefits and challenges associated with the adoption of AI in various aspects of game development. Despite the promise of AI to generate more content and streamline workflows, our findings suggest that the correlation between AI implementation and increased revenue for game studios is not straightforward. While AI can enhance efficiency and scale operations, it also presents challenges such as job displacement and concerns regarding the quality of AI-generated content. Ultimately, we argue that successful integration of AI in game development requires a strategic approach that prioritizes enhancing production capabilities and quality control over mere cost-cutting measures.

Keywords: game studies, game production, artificial intelligence, generative ai, games industry

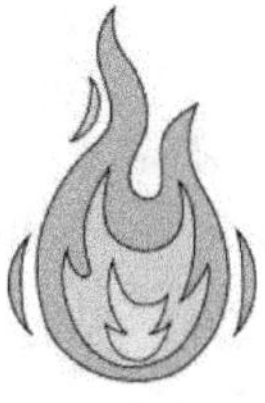

1. Introduction

Generative AI has emerged as a transformative technology with the potential to revolutionize various industries, including video game production. Ferrari and McKelvey speak in these regards of "hyperproduction" (2023), a circular dynamic in the production of AI-generated media, blurring the line between inputs and outputs in contrast to traditional linear production processes. In recent years, advancements in AI, particularly in natural language processing and computer vision, have enabled the development of systems capable of generating text, images, and other content. Within the realm of video games, this technology holds promise for creating vast and immersive virtual worlds, populated with rich narratives and diverse characters, as easy as rubbing a magic lamp and making a wish. Yet, the integration of generative AI in video game production raises several questions and challenges. While AI-driven tools can facilitate the creation of more content and streamline production workflows (i.e., concept and asset creation, testing etc.), there are concerns regarding the quality and originality of AI-generated assets (Xia et al. 2020, p. 508; Wang et al. 2023). Moreover, debate surrounding legal infringements (Melhart et al. 2024, p. 81), the potential impact of AI on job displacement (Neufeind 2018; Carras 2024) within the games industry and its resulting implications for studio revenue remains inconclusive.

In this paper we aim to explore especially the latter, the resulting implications for game studios' sustainable revenue streams which has become a dire issue in the global games industry since recent years leading to unprecedented waves of layoffs at game studios of all sizes (Schreier 2021; Park 2024). It seems that by automating repetitive tasks and streamlining production processes, generative AI allows developers to operate within tighter budgets while delivering diverse and engaging content at a rapid pace by offering new tools and techniques for game development (Porokh 2023).

There are numerous areas within game production, encompassing the entirety of the process involved in creating and shipping a video game, that delve into the utilization and challenges of generative AI (Fraser et al 2018; Pfau et al. 2020; Melhart et al. 2024). However, in this paper, we aim to exclusively focus on visual and textual content generation and its potential to assist game studios in expanding the margin between production costs and sales.

Our research question is whether game studios could increase their revenue by utilizing generative AI to enhance their content output. In this paper, we explore this question by initially defining three content areas: in-game graphics, in-game text. We then present the findings of a literature review conducted to gather information on how these content areas are already influenced by the use of generative AI. To contrast these insights, we compare the outcomes of an expert survey conducted in September 2023 conducted with four games industry professionals, providing industrial perspectives into the current and future use of AI in game production. Lastly, we engage in a discussion and draw conclusions based on our findings.

2. Content Areas in Game Production

In this section we define the domain of game production and our two key content areas within the realm of game production: in-game graphics and in-game text. These content areas serve as focal points for our investigation.

Video game production encompasses the entire process of conceptualizing, designing, developing, marketing, testing and releasing a video game (Sotamaa & Švelch 2021, pp. 8-9). It involves a multidisciplinary team which collaborates in a production cycle that typically begins with creating a concept, followed by planning, prototyping, and iterative development. During and after the production process the game is marketed to ensure a profitable launch and drive engagement. Before (and often after) being launched to the market the game undergoes quality assurance, where post-launch support and updates may continue based on player feedback.

2.1 In-Game Text

In-game text refers to the written or textual elements integrated within a video game environment, encompassing a wide range of content such as dialogues, character interactions, narrative sequences, user interface (UI) text, tutorial messages, subtitles, quest logs and other (Mauger 2016). These textual components play a crucial role in conveying information, storytelling, character development, and guiding player actions and decisions throughout the gameplay experience. In-game text serves as a means of communication between the game's design and players, facilitating any significant form of immersion, comprehension of game mechanics, and engagement with the game world (Egenfeldt-Nielsen et al. 2019, p. 205), thus significantly establishing the game's atmosphere, setting the tone, and enhancing the overall narrative coherence and player experience.

AI-powered natural language processing (NLP) algorithms are increasingly used to generate dynamic dialogue options for non-player characters (NPC) (see Figure 1), providing players with more and contextually relevant interactions. AI-driven text generation models, such as language models trained on large corpora of text data, are utilized to create procedural narrative elements, generate quest descriptions, and dynamically adapt in-game text based on player actions or choices, thereby increasing the variability and replayability of the game (Karpouzis & Tsatiris 2021). Moreover, AI-based translation tools are already used for partial and full-scale localizations of games into multiple languages (Al-Bathineh & Alawneh 2021).

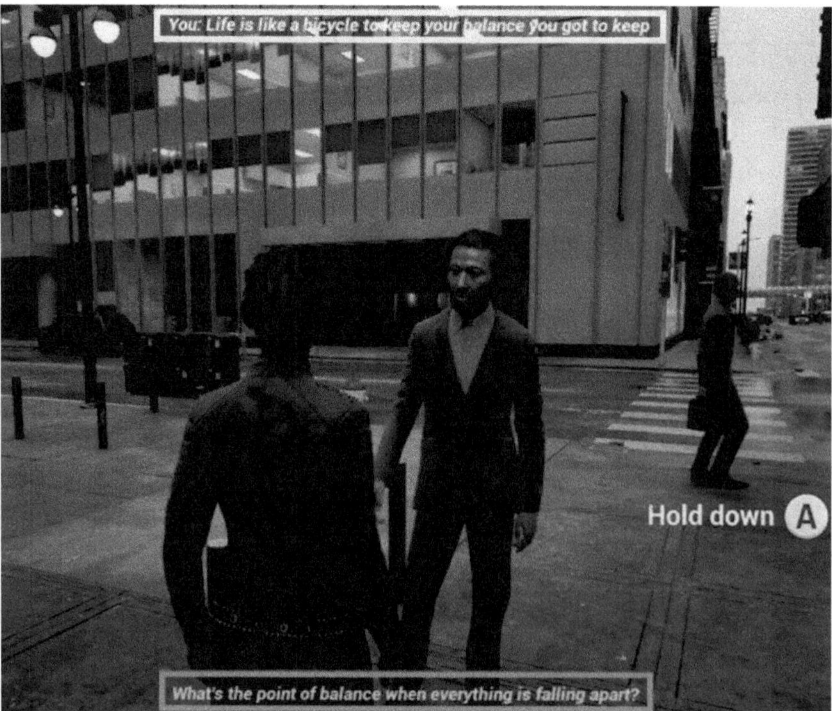

Figure 1. Receiving real-time AI dialogue responses from NPCs (red) to user input (yellow). Screenshot taken from "Talking to Smart AI NPCs in Unreal Engine 5" (TmarTn2 2023)

2.2 In-Game Graphics

In-game graphics refer to the visual elements and assets that constitute the visual representation of a video game environment, including characters, objects, landscapes, textures, animations, special effects, and UI. These graphics are generated (in 2D) and/or rendered (in 3D) by the game engine to create interactive virtual worlds for players to explore and interact with. In-game graphics are the foundation of any *video* game through displaying game states, defining the aesthetic style, atmosphere, and overall visual fidelity of a game, influencing player perception, engagement, and enjoyment (Arsenault et al. 2013). In-game graphics complement gameplay mechanics, convey narrative elements, provide visual feedback, and optimize performance across different gaming platforms and hardware configurations.

AI-driven techniques, such as machine learning algorithms and neural networks, are already employed for tasks such as texture synthesis, character animation, and environment generation. Generative adversarial networks (GANs) are utilized to generate high-quality textures (see Figure 2), landscapes, and character models, enabling developers to produce realistic and detailed graphics with reduced manual effort (Cao et al. 2023). AI-based algorithms are used for image upscaling and denoising, enhancing the visual quality of in-game graphics while optimizing performance and memory usage (Hossain et al. 2023). AI-powered tools for procedural content generation (i.e., Houdini) enable the automatic creation of extensive game environments, populated with diverse landscapes, structures, and other elements.

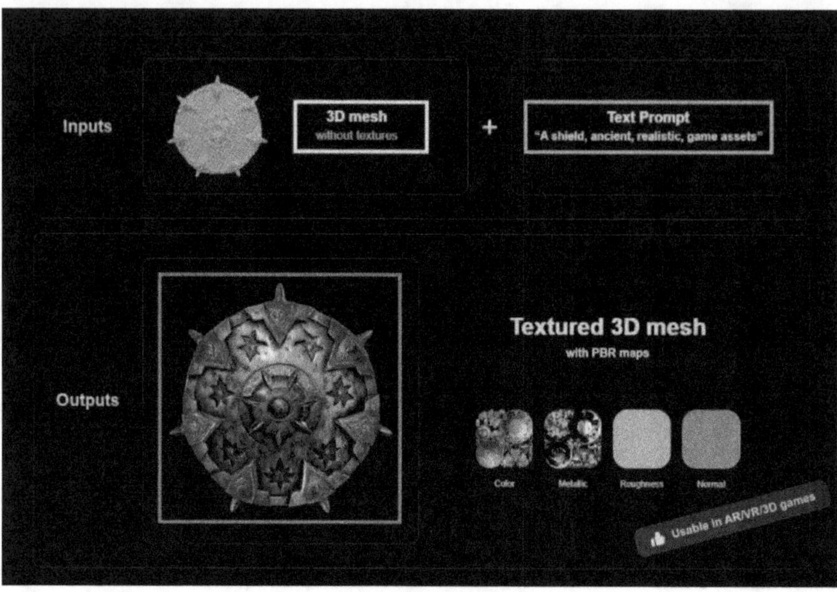

Figure 2. AI generated texture output (red) based on 3D mesh (yellow) and text prompt (orange) input. Screenshot taken from "meshy.ai/features/text-to-texture" (2024)

In this section, we outlined the field of game production and discussed two content areas within its production processes that are and will be increasingly affected by generative AI. These areas are integral to game design and gameplay experience, and serve as scope for our investigation. In the next section, we focus exclusively on the application of AI in text-to-text and text-to-image generation within these content areas of game production.

3. Literature Review

In this section, we review existing literature surrounding the application of generative AI in our two key content areas of game production: in-game text and in-game graphics. By analysing both academic publications and industry news, we aim to identify prevalent tendencies and emerging trends pertaining to the usability, quality but also general opinion on the integration of AI-driven technologies in content generation processes.

3.1 Academic Publications

Currently, academic publications in this field are scarce, primarily exploratory and focus both on generative text-to-text and text-to-image approaches for in-game content but also ethical concerns. Those that have been selected for this section, are considered to be representative for trends in research and provide valuable indications and insights into the topic. Yet, we suggest to approach these findings with caution due to the limited availability of data.

Experimental research on text-to-text generative AI can be considered as the most active field in academic research on AI-generated content for video games; exemplified by a remarkable graduate project at the University of Twente, where the aim was to explore affective text generation in in-game dialogues. Focusing on the video game *Fallout 4* (Bethesda 2015), Kalbiyev developed a generative language model to produce affective dialogue and compared it against human-written text to assess its accuracy in conveying emotions (2022). The process involved selecting, extracting, and pre-processing the *Fallout 4* dialogue dataset, followed by fine-tuning the Generative Pre-trained Transformer (GPT) 2 language model. Human evaluation revealed that the model-generated responses performed poorly compared to human-written ones across various metrics, indicating unsuccessful expression of emotions. The findings underscored the need for further research to address limitations in model performance and evaluation methodology. By refining these aspects, it is argued that future studies can enhance the quality and effectiveness of affective text generation in video games.

In another project, Ashby and his colleague introduce a novel framework for procedurally generating quests and NPC dialogue in role-playing games (RPGs), aiming to enhance player engagement and satisfaction through co-creative narrative experiences (2023). By leveraging a combination of hand-crafted knowledge bases and large-scale language models, the framework generates quests grounded in in-game context and accompanied by fluent, unique dialogue. Human evaluation confirms the framework's ability to produce quests comparable to hand-crafted ones in terms of fluency, coherence, novelty, and creativity, while enhancing player experience through greater dynamism. The paper envisions future extensions where all NPC speech is generated via automated means, allowing for fully co-creative game environments. The framework's compatibility with narrative tools aims to deepen immersion and satisfaction for players, fostering increased agency within the game narrative and facilitating emotional resonance with NPCs. As a proof-of-concept, the framework demonstrates comparable results to hand-crafted quests in *World of Warcraft* (Blizzard 2004), with player preference for generated quests when matching knowledge graph nodes to player input.

Research on text-to-image generation for video games is an emerging field and in a paper on automatically generated animation Khatri focuses on keyframing, a popular animation method that involves generating animation at specific points and letting the computer create transition frames between them (2021). Precise control over animation parameters like position, rotation, and scale is crucial, often achieved by placing keys at the beginning and end of desired paths within frames. Real-time animation allows for the simulation of physical properties and the creation of dynamic, immersive experiences within virtual environments. As technology advances, more powerful real-time complex animation systems driven by simulations are anticipated to emerge, potentially leading to automated animation processes dominated by artificial intelligence. According to Khatri the future of animation with AI holds promises for increased efficiency, automation of routine tasks, and innovative storytelling techniques, shaping the landscape of the animation industry.

At a more advanced industrial front, a team of researchers at Nvidia has published their work on TexFusion (Texture Diffusion), a novel method for synthesizing textures for 3D geometries using large-scale text-guided image diffusion models, offering a contrast to previous approaches. Unlike methods relying on slow and fragile optimization processes, TexFusion utilizes a new 3D-consistent AI generation technique specifically tailored for texture synthesis. By leveraging latent diffusion models and applying a neural colour field optimization, TexFusion efficiently produces diverse, high-quality, and globally coherent textures without relying on ground truth 3D textures for training. While TexFusion represents a significant advancement, limitations include non-real-time texture generation and potential sharpness issues, suggesting avenues for future research to explore.

Although not strictly within the scope of our paper, ethical considerations represent a significant trend in academic research on AI-generated content for video games, making it important to address here. Neglecting player ethics can lead to community backlash, ultimately impacting sales through boycotts and review bombing.

Melhart and his colleagues explore the ethical implications of integrating artificial intelligence (AI) in video games, addressing concerns that have not been extensively discussed in the gaming context (2023). Through the lens of the "affective game loop", which encompasses emotion expression, elicitation, sensing, detection, prediction, and reaction, the authors analyse the ethical challenges AI faces in game development (p. 79). They identify key areas of concern, such as the manipulation of player emotions, privacy trade-offs, transparency issues, and ownership of data and models during adaptation phases. The paper provides a structured overview of ethical dimensions within the affective loop, covering aspects of elicitation, sensing, detection, and adaptation. Recommendations are made for integrating ethics into AI and game research and innovation, emphasizing the need for collaboration between industry stakeholders, policymakers, and researchers. Affective computing researchers are highlighted as crucial contributors to this dialogue, given their multidisciplinary expertise in sensor technology, AI, and psychology. The paper concludes by advocating for increased ethical awareness and action to ensure the mutual benefit of players and their gaming experiences.

Academic literature in the games industry demonstrates a growing interest in the development of generative text and graphics for video games but also ethical frameworks that guide their development. It is worth noting that high costs, difficulty of designing and executing experiments regarding AI in video games remain core reasons for the prevalent scarcity of comprehensive research in this field.

3.2 News Articles

Industry news articles on the use of generative AI are plentiful and exhibit generally a mixed opinion with a negative tendency towards consequences associated with unsupervised use in in-game text and graphics. They also address the implications for writers and artists employed within the industry. The selected articles discussed below highlight prevailing trends in game production.

In 2023 Ubisoft officially announced a new AI tool called Ghostwriter, aiming to streamline the process of writing NPC dialogue in its games (Barth 2023). The tool is designed to assist scriptwriters by generating a first draft of ambient NPC phrases and sounds, thereby alleviating some of their workload while allowing for creative control. Ubisoft emphasizes that Ghostwriter is not intended to replace human writers but rather to complement their efforts. However, Verbrugge from Press-Start points out that concerns arise regarding the potential implications for the role of scriptwriters and voice actors in the industry (2023). Despite Ubisoft's assurance that the tool is meant to enhance rather than replace human creativity, the introduction of automated models like Ghostwriter raises questions about the future of narrative creation in video games.

Blizzard Entertainment has reportedly developed an AI-powered image generator called Blizzard Diffusion to create concept artwork for new game characters, outfits, and environments, aiming to streamline the game development process. Williams from Gamehub highlights that, while the tool may be praised for its potential to enhance creativity and save time, concerns arise regarding potential job losses and the reliance on AI for creative inspiration (2023). Blizzard's cautious approach and emphasis on using AI as a time-saving tool rather than a replacement for human creativity reflect the delicate balance between innovation and job security in the games industry.

A rather peculiar case in which modders abused text-to-image generative AI happened in the game *Fortnite* (Epic Games 2017). Nelson from Decrypt reports that following player complaints, Epic Games is actively removing racist AI-generated images uploaded by users to *Fortnite* (2024). The game's feature allowing users to create and share maps has led to the dissemination of offensive content, including maps titled "Arab Zonewars" and "Nigerian Zonewars," featuring crude depictions perpetuating stereotypes like Middle Eastern men holding bombs and Black men eating fried chicken. Although many offending islands have been removed and creators penalized, Epic Games emphasizes that discriminatory content violates island creator rules, with perpetrators facing potential permanent bans. The company's human moderation team reviews content before publication, but Epic Games is updating its island creator rules and moderation training to better address violations. Meanwhile, as generative AI becomes popular, platforms like Epic Games Store permit AI-generated content submissions, despite concerns about offensive material circulating online.

In another controversial case, the use of AI in public communications became present. Walker from Kotaku writes that shortly after the launch of *Lord of the Rings: Gollum*, its developer Daedalic appeared to issue an apology on social media for the extremely negative reception of the game (2023). However, the apology raised eyebrows as it misspelled the game's title and contained vacuous statements. Subsequently, it was revealed that the apology was not crafted by Daedalic but by their new parent company, Nacon. Strikingly, two undisclosed developers from Daedelic informed the German media outlet Game Two that the apology was generated by ChatGPT.

An article from CNN summarises the general situation as somewhere between gold rush, new democratization of the industry and a creative mess in which Cairns states that generative AI is poised to revolutionize the games industry by transforming NPCs and open-world gameplay (2023). AI tools like Ghostwriter and ChatGPT are already enhancing NPC dialogue promising more realistic and engaging gaming experiences. However, challenges remain, such as maintaining control over narrative. Generative AI holds potential for user-generated content, empowering players to customize their experiences and facilitating game development by automating repetitive tasks. While concerns about job displacement and ethical implications persist, she points towards industry experts that anticipate generative AI to become an essential tool for game design, ultimately leading to higher-quality and more "immersive" gaming experiences in the future.

The selected sample of articles highlight contemporary AI-related cases in the games industry, revealing a mixed sentiment towards the seemingly inevitable changes brought about by AI technology. The articles emphasize the importance of maintaining human control over AI to prevent abuse, community backlash, job loss and uphold quality standards in the industry. Despite the potential benefits of AI in enhancing gaming experiences and streamlining development processes, there is a sceptical attitude towards its implementation to ensure that it complements human creativity and expertise rather than replacing it entirely.

Conclusively, based on our literature review, which has examined a small yet representative sample, we contend that academic research on the topic remains in its infancy but shows cautious optimism regarding the potential of AI generated content as far as ethical frameworks provide guidelines. News articles underscore a somewhat chaotic and problematic aspect of integrating generative AI into production processes. Additionally, it is noteworthy that we struggled to find articles or publications specifically addressing the potential for revenue increase, suggesting that the utilization of generative AI at this stage is primarily exploratory and centred on demonstrating its efficacy in production. Articles purporting financial growth through AI largely remain vague and speculative (Mochizuki & Zhang 2023).

4. Expert Survey

In addition to our literature review, we have conducted an expert survey with four industry professionals to provide first-hand insights and perspectives on the topic. These interviews serve as invaluable supplements to our research, offering nuanced understandings and real-world applications of the topics discussed. By engaging directly with experts in the field, we gain access to their hands-on experience, enabling us to consider latest trends and challenges from the perspective of practitioners.

Aimed to explore various facets of AI integration within the gaming sector, this expert survey has been designed and evaluated in concordance with guidelines and recommendations from Steenbergen and Marks (2007). The data, gathered September 2023, including participants' current professional roles, seniority, and company size, was utilized exclusively for this research paper and has been anonymized. The participants consist of colleagues and acquaintances of the authors and were asked to fill out a survey on Google Forms which took each participant on average around 20 minutes (Access survey here: https://forms.gle/bdKxnnrzo5YwTkBu8). The survey delves into potential job displacement due to AI, strategies for professionals to adapt to AI integration, and the prospects of AI in regards to revenue generation for game developers. Experts shared insights on the challenges and opportunities associated with implementing AI in game development processes, emphasizing its current and future applications in streamlining production pipelines. In the following the responses of each expert have been condensed to essential statements and insights. All participants consented to the sharing of the survey's general results but explicitly requested that their responses cannot not be directly quoted in this publication.

4.1 Expert A

A founder and executive with over six years of industry experience, primarily working for a small company with 1-50 employees. They believe that AI will lead to job displacement in the games industry, particularly affecting roles in writing, art, and design, with a specific emphasis on concept art. They envision AI contributing to increased revenue generation for game developers through lower production costs resulting from reduced payrolls and shorter production cycles. However, they caution that implementing AI for revenue enhancement may face challenges such as community backlash and legal uncertainties. Currently, their company uses AI in selected areas of concept art. Looking ahead, Expert A anticipates significant changes in game production within the next 5-10 years, including the potential for prompt-to-game level AI, which they believe could transform the industry drastically. Their advice for aspiring game developers and industry professionals interested in leveraging AI is to be patient and wait for developments. They acknowledge the intersection of AI and the games industry as both terrifying and inevitable, highlighting the disruptive nature of technological change.

4.2 Expert B

A mid-level game designer with 3-5 years of industry experience, primarily working for a large company with over 501 employees. They believe AI will lead to job displacement in roles such as copywriting and translation. To prepare for AI integration, they recommend professionals in the games industry to educate themselves about AI's functionality and legal implications. They envision AI contributing to increased revenue generation by saving time and money on certain tasks. However, they caution that implementing AI for revenue enhancement may pose challenges related to copyright issues. Currently, AI is not used in their game development processes. In the next 5-10 years, they anticipate significant societal resistance to AI replacing human roles in game production.

4.3 Expert C

A senior-level position tech designer with over six years of industry experience, primarily working for a small company with 1-50 employees. They foresee AI leading to job displacement in the games industry, citing examples such as Nvidia Audio2Face replacing facial animators and voice deepfakes reducing costs for voice actors. To prepare for AI integration, they recommend professionals broaden their skill set as narrow specialization may become obsolete. They anticipate AI contributing to increased revenue generation by reducing costs in asset creation and quality assurance. However, they caution game developers about legal uncertainties surrounding the use of AI models like deepfakes, which could lead to potential lawsuits. Currently, their company utilizes AI to reduce the number of animators and employs deepfake technology for generating voiceovers to test actors' voices in-game before recording. In the next 5-10 years, they believe AI will significantly impact game production, potentially leading to increased industry layoffs akin to the impact of internal combustion engines on the horse industry. Their advice for aspiring game developers and industry professionals interested in leveraging AI is to learn how to work with open-source solutions, emphasizing the availability of AI models like those released by OpenAI.

4.4 Expert D

a mid-level Game Designer with 3-5 years of industry experience, primarily working for a large company with over 501 employees. They anticipate AI leading to potential job displacement in concept art disciplines and analytics roles within the games industry. To prepare for AI integration, they suggest practicing with AI tools and even training personal machine learning models. They envision AI contributing to increased revenue generation by reducing work hours and improving operational efficiency through accurate forecast analytics systems. However, they caution that AI implementations for revenue enhancement should be approached cautiously, preferably on low-risk, low-budget projects. Currently, AI is used in their game development processes for generating item descriptions and even for conceptualizing in-game events, though with mixed results. Looking ahead, they foresee AI significantly impacting art disciplines and potentially affecting screenwriters and copywriters. Their advice for aspiring game developers and industry professionals interested in leveraging AI is to treat it as a tool to enhance effectiveness rather than relying on it to perform tasks autonomously.

The survey responses collectively highlight concerns about job displacement and the potential impact of AI integration in the games industry. Respondents emphasize the importance of preparing for AI integration by understanding its workings and legal implications. While recognizing AI's potential for reducing costs and streamlining production processes, respondents also express concerns about legal risks, community backlash, and the need for cautious implementation strategies. It's important to note that these insights are based on a small and subjective sample size, comprising only a few experts with varying levels of experience and perspectives within the industry. Therefore, while these responses provide valuable insights into individual opinions and experiences, they may not fully represent the broader spectrum of perspectives within the games industry. Thus, caution should be exercised when deducing from and generalising these finding.

5. Discussion

The synthesis of survey data and the literature review offers insights into the potential impacts and challenges associated with AI integration in current and future game production processes. While survey responses highlight cutting costs but also concerns about job displacement, the literature review sheds light on emerging research in AI-driven content generation and surrounding controversies. Academic publications demonstrate a growing interest in affective and procedural text generation, AI-driven textures and animations. However, the limited availability of comprehensive research indicates a nascent stage in academic exploration. Industry news articles provide real-world cases of AI content in game production, ranging from NPC dialogue generation to concept artwork creation. These cases illustrate concerns regarding job displacement, quality standards, and ethical implications. While AI tools like Ghostwriter and Blizzard Diffusion offer promising opportunities for streamlining production processes, there is a palpable apprehension about the potential loss of human creativity and quality control.

Most of the data presented contains a noticeable undercurrent of concerns regarding the need for increased investment in reviewing processes and quality assurance to avoid questionable content in published text and graphics. While AI can expedite content generation, ensuring the accuracy, coherence, and overall quality of AI-generated assets remains a critical challenge. Human oversight and intervention are indispensable in identifying and rectifying errors, maintaining consistency, and upholding creative vision and integrity. Consequently, the integration of AI necessitates a parallel investment in robust and up-scaled QA mechanisms to mitigate the risk of subpar or erroneous content making its way into final game products.

Thus, potential financial gains from AI-driven efficiency improvements may not necessarily translate into substantial revenue increases for game developers at this stage. While streamlining content generation through AI automation can yield cost savings connected to time saved by reducing manual and repetitive tasks, these gains may be offset by the additional expenses incurred in reviewing, QA, and testing processes but also direct losses through player boycott. As such, the net financial impact of AI integration on overall revenue remains uncertain and may even result in a zero-sum game scenario or worse. Developers must carefully weigh the anticipated benefits against the associated costs and risks to determine the viability of AI adoption within their production pipelines.

6. Conclusion

Our investigation into the integration of generative AI in game development reveals a landscape ripe with opportunities and pitfalls. While the potential benefits of AI-driven content generation are evident in streamlining production processes and enabling larger projects, our findings underscore the importance of cautious consideration and strategic implementation. It is imperative for game studios to recognize the dual nature of AI integration: while it can enhance efficiency and the scale of creative output, it also necessitates increased investment in reviewing processes and quality assurance. Studios should consider developing robust QA mechanisms to ensure the accuracy, coherence, consistency and overall quality of AI-generated content that finds itself into a published video game, thus guaranteeing positive player experiences and studio integrity on the market. Moreover, reasonable ethical discussion must find its way into early planning stages of AI generated content process implementation to reduce the risk of reputation damaging and sales affecting community backlash. By considering players' ethical preferences and upholding quality standards studios can build trust with players and stakeholders, subsequently mitigating risks of negative consequences associated with AI generated content integration. Therefore, arriving at a preliminary answer to our research question: Studios could benefit financially from a reasonable integration of generative AI in their production, however, more content does not necessarily mean more money.

Acknowledgments

We extend our gratitude to the FROG team for providing us with the opportunity to share our findings. Additionally, we thank the independent Belarusian community centre Robim Razam in Warsaw for granting us the chance to present and discuss our research. Lastly, we are deeply thankful to the experts who generously dedicated their time to participate in our survey.

About the Author

Benjamin Hanussek works as LQA Specialist at Wargaming while maintaining a role as research advisor and coordinator for educational game development projects at the Polish-Japanese Academy of Information Technology. Additionally, he collaborates with the Austrian Cultural Forum in Warsaw in organising game studies related events.

Dr. Yaraslau Kot acts currently as researcher at the University of Gdansk and counsel of the law firm Rymary Zdort Maruta in Warsaw. He specialises in video game law and history, advised game studios such as The Farm 51 and games industry conferences like GIC Poznan. He is a former Regional Coordinator for Eastern Europe of the International Game Developers Association (IGDA), and founder of the Belarusian Game Developers Association (BelGameDev).

References

Al-Batineh, M. & Alawneh, R. (2022) Current trends in localizing video games into Arabic: localization levels and gamers' preferences. Perspectives, 30:2, (pp. 323-342). https://doi.org/10.1080/0907676X.2021.1926520

Arsenault, D., Coté, P., Larochelle, A., & Lebel, S. (2013). Graphical technologies, innovation and aesthetics in the video game industry: A case study of the shift from 2D to 3D graphics in the 1990s. GAME: The Italian Journal of Game Studies, 1:2 (pp. 79-89).

Ashby, T., Webb, B., Knapp, G., Searle, J., & Fulda, N. (2023). Personalized quest and dialogue generation in role-playing games: A knowledge graph-and language model-based approach. In Proceedings of the 2023 CHI Conference on Human Factors in Computing Systems (pp. 1-20). https://doi.org/10.1145/3544548.3581441

Barth, R. (2023). The Convergence of AI and Creativity: Introducing Ghostwriter. https://news.ubisoft.com/en-us/article/7Cm07zbBGy4Xml6WgYi25d/the-convergence-of-ai-and-creativity-introducing-ghostwriter

Bethesda (2015). Fallout 4. Bethesda Softworks.

Blizzard Entertainment. (2004). World of Warcraft. Activision Blizzard [Vivendi].

Cairns, R. (2023). 'Video games are in for quite a trip': How generative AI could radically reshape gaming. https://edition.cnn.com/world/generative-ai-video-games-spc-intl-hnk/index.html

Cao, T., Kreis, K., Fidler, S., Sharp, N. & Yin, K. (2023). TexFusion: Synthesizing 3D Textures with Text-Guided Image Diffusion Models. In Proceedings of the International Conference on Computer Vision (pp. 4169-4181).

Carras, C. (2024). Which entertainment jobs are most likely to be disrupted by AI? New study has answers. https://www.latimes.com/entertainment-arts/business/story/2024-01-30/ai-artificial-intelligence-impact-report-entertainment-industry

Epic Games (2017). Fortnite. Epic Games/Gearbox Publishing.

Egenfeldt-Nielsen, S., Smith, J. & Tosca, S. (2019). Understanding Video Games: The Essential Introduction. Routledge.

Ferrari, F. & McKelvey, F. (2023). Hyperproduction: a social theory of deep generative models, Distinktion: Journal of Social Theory, 24:2 (pp. 338-360). https://doi.org/10.1080/1600910X.2022.2137546

Fraser, J., Papaioannou, I. & Lemon, O. (2018). Spoken Conversational AI in Video Games: Emotional Dialogue Management Increases User Engagement. In Proceedings of the 18th International Conference on Intelligent Virtual Agents (pp. 179–184). https://doi.org/10.1145/3267851.3267896

Healy, A. & Ó Riain, S. (2018). How to escape the low learning trap in a runaway labour market. In (Eds.) Neufeind M., O'Reilly, J. & Ranft, F., Work in the Digital Age (pp. 345-356). Rowman & Littlefield.

Hossain, S., Hossain, S. & Karim, B. (2023)Training StyleGAN2 on BWW-Texture Dataset: Generating Textures Through Transfer Learning. In Proceedings of the International

Conference on Information and Communication Technology for Sustainable Development (pp. 341-345). https://doi.org/10.1109/ICICT4SD59951.2023.10303468.

Kalbiyev, A. (2022) Affective dialogue generation for video games. https://essay.utwente.nl/89325/

Karpouzis, K., Tsatiris, G. (2022). AI in (and for) Games. In Tsihrintzis, G., Virvou, M. & Jain, L. (Eds.) Advances in Machine Learning/Deep Learning-based Technologies. Learning and Analytics in Intelligent Systems, 23. https://doi.org/10.1007/978-3-030-76794-5_3

Khatri, P. (2021). The future of automatically generated animation with AI. In (Eds.) Chaudhary, V., Sharma, M., Sharma, P. , Agarwal, D. Deep Learning in Gaming and Animations (pp. 19-36). CRC Press.

Mauger, V. (2016). Interface. In Wolf, M. & Perron, B. The Routledge Companion to Video Game Studies. Routledge.

Melhart, D., Togelius, J., Mikkelsen, B., Holmgård C. & Yannakakis, G. (2024). The Ethics of AI in Games. Transactions on Affective Computing, 15:9 (pp. 79-92). https://doi.org/10.1109/TAFFC.2023.3276425

Mochizuki, T., Zhang, J. (2023).AI Is Rewriting the Rules of $200 Billion Games Industry. https://www.bloomberg.com/news/articles/2023-07-25/ai-is-rewriting-the-rules-of-200-billion-games-industry

Nelson, J. (2024). 'Fortnite' Fail: Epic Games Scrambles to Remove Racist AI-Generated Images. https://decrypt.co/215146/fortnite-fail-epic-games-scrambles-remove-racist-ai-generated-images

Park, G. (2024). Layoffs are tearing through the game industry. This year could be worse. Video games can't be this big, this expensive — in this volatile an industry — and remain a sustainable business. https://www.washingtonpost.com/entertainment/video-games/2024/02/15/game-industry-layoffs/

Pfau, J., Smeddinck, J. & Malaka, R.. 2020. The Case for Usable AI: What Industry Professionals Make of Academic AI in Video Games. In Extended Abstracts of the 2020 Annual Symposium on Computer-Human Interaction in Play (pp. 330-334). https://doi.org/10.1145/3383668.3419905

Porokh, A. (2023). How Will AI Disrupt Video Game Industry in 2024?. https://kevurugames.com/blog/how-ai-is-disrupting-the-video-game-industry/

Schreier, J. (2021). Press Reset: Ruin and recovery in the video game industry. Hachette UK.

Sotamaa, O., & Svelch, J. (2021). Game Production Studies . Amsterdam University Press.

Steenbergen, M. & Marks, G. (2007), Evaluating expert judgments. European Journal of Political Research, 46 (pp. 347-366). https://doi.org/10.1111/j.1475-6765.2006.00694.x

Verbrugge, K (2023). Ubisoft's Making An AI To Help Write Game Dialogue: Tom Clancy's Ghost Writer. https://press-start.com.au/news/2023/03/22/ubisofts-making-an-ai-to-help-write-game-dialogue/

Walker, J. (2023). Report Claims Lord Of The Rings: Gollum Publisher Used AI To Write Apology: This accompanies allegations of crunch and difficult working conditions at developer Daedalic. https://kotaku.com/lord-of-the-rings-gollum-daedalic-nacon-chatgpt-apology-1850911747

Wang, Y., Pan, Y., Yan, M., Su Z. & Luan, T. (2023). A Survey on ChatGPT: AI–Generated Contents, Challenges, and Solutions. Open Journal of the Computer Society, 4 (pp. 280-302, 2023, https://doi.org/10.1109/OJCS.2023.3300321

Williams, L. (2023). Blizzard has reportedly trained an AI generator for concept art: New internal tools are reportedly allowing Blizzard to generate concept artwork using AI. https://www.gameshub.com/news/news/blizzard-entertainment-ai-concept-art-may-2023-2617179/

Xia, B., Ye, X. & Abuassba, A. (2020). Recent Research on AI in Games. In Proceedings of the International Wireless Communications and Mobile Computing 2020 (pp. 505-510). https://doi.org/10.1109/IWCMC48107.2020.9148327

EXPLORING ACCESSIBILITY ENHANCEMENT IN PRINTABLE BOARD GAMES THROUGH 3D PRINTING WITH A HEIST BOARD GAME CASE STUDY

Ahmad Kalatiani, Magdalena M. Strobl,
Wilfried Elmenreich

In recent years, 3D printing has emerged as a technology that has the potential to transform various industries. It enables the creation of three-dimensional objects by layering materials based on a digital design. This process has gained widespread attention due to its versatility, efficiency, and possibilities for customization and prototyping. One of these areas in which 3D printing can be transformational is the development of Indie board games or so-called printables. A beneficial aspect 3D printing provides is the ability to add accessibility for visually impaired people into board games by designing game elements that provide haptic feedback. As a case study, we designed a heist board game involving a generated game map assembled using 3D-printed elements that snap together so that an accidental moving of one part does not affect the board. The figures and game elements are also designed as 3D prints so that they can be identified by touch as well as by their visual design. The game also involves cards with a cut edge to signal their orientation and a QR code that enables a mobile app to read the card's content to the player. Producing the game is, however, significantly longer than a standard (2D) printable game since the 3D elements require significant time for printing. The printing time of all elements in full size amounts to 100 hours on a Prusa i3 printer. Thus, the usage of 3D-print technology for producing games is expected to be limited to prototypes or special applications.

Keywords: Accessibility, Tabletop games, Inclusive design, 3D-Printing, Heist board game

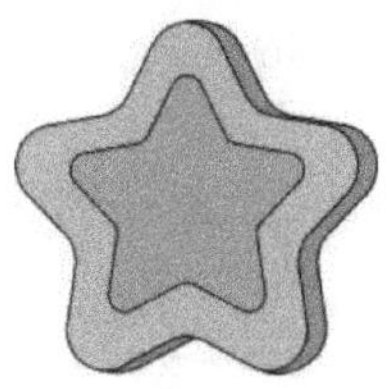

1. Introduction

In recent years, there has been a growing recognition of the importance of accessibility in gaming, particularly within the realm of tabletop games. While much attention has been devoted to enhancing accessibility in video games, the needs of visually impaired individuals to enjoy tabletop gaming experiences have often been overlooked. This gap in research underscores the necessity of exploring and addressing the accessibility challenges faced by visually impaired players within the tabletop gaming community. Additionally, advancements in 3D printing technology present an opportunity to create accessible board games with elements identifiable by touch and sight, offering a versatile and efficient process compared to traditional Print & Play games on platforms like BoardGameGeek. Despite the potential benefits, the extended production times associated with 3D-printed games present a significant obstacle to mass production viability. Even moderately small games can demand printing times of up to 100 hours on a typical hobby 3D printer, rendering large-scale production impractical. In addition to the time spent, economic costs for printer hardware, energy consumption, and printing material have to be considered. Consequently, it's unlikely that mass production by publishers and industry-level printers will be supplanted. However, 3D printing opens avenues for niche markets, facilitating the creation of individualized games and, as demonstrated in the accompanying case study, supporting the development of self-printable games with accessibility features.

This paper aims to contribute to the discussion on creating more accessible games, specifically for people with visual impairments, through the utilization of 3D printing technology. As a case study, we present the development of a printable board game prototype designed to be accessible to visually impaired individuals. The paper begins by reviewing existing research in this field, highlighting the need for accessible board and card games. Subsequently, we outline the processes involved in the development, including finding a game idea, designing the game outline and elaborating solutions to make the 2D and 3D parts of the game accessible for all players. The final design also involves an assistant app that helps with game setup and a text-to-speech feature for reading the cards. At the end, we provide a link to access the complete game and ruleset, offering insights into the practical implementation of accessible gaming through 3D printing technology.

2. Related Work

Even though board games enjoy great popularity, several scholars have noticed that research primarily focuses on accessibility in video games (Tomé et al., 2019; Bolesnikov, Kang, & Girourad, 2022). However, this does not diminish the necessity and demand for accessible tabletop games. Tabletop games include "board games, dice games, and card games" (Bhaduri, Tovar, & Kane, 2017, p. 52). One of the most prominent issues in these games concerning accessibility is how players need to rely on visual information to make them playable for visually impaired people (Johnson & Kane, 2020, p. 1). This leads to the majority of tabletop games not being accessible. As Johnson and Kane mention, they "often rely on printed text and visual distinctions such as colors, text, visual textures, and symbols" (2020, p. 1). Another aspect that the authors noticed was the effect of social and competitive aspects concerning playing board games. The authors argue that in non-cooperative games, blind and visually impaired people will need or want to ask other players for help (Johnson & Kane, 2020, p. 1). Since the majority of competitive board games rely on secret information and strategies, requiring help from rival players can make it nearly impossible to have a fair competition. Therefore, cooperative gameplay can offer more fun elements to the players.

Bolesnikov, Kang, and Girourad research in their article "Understanding Tabletop Games Accessibility: Exploring Board and Card Gaming Experiences of People who are Blind and Low Vision" from 2022 what elements are included in inaccessible games. During their study, the authors noticed that due to an inaccessible rulebook, players reached out for sighted assistance as physical game instructions do not include Braille (Bolesnikov, Kang, & Girourad, 2022, p. 5). However, participants of the study also used online manuals (Bolesnikov, Kang, & Girourad, 2022, p. 5). Yet, these often include several accessibility issues such as the inclusion of images (Bolesnikov, Kang, & Girourad, 2022, p. 5).

Another problem is the implementation of inaccessible game content. According to Bolesnikov, Kang, and Girourard (2022), the resulting physical effort of reading texts due to their smaller text size, led to players abandoning the game (p. 5). In addition, making the communication of information dependent on color also led to difficulties in distinguishing elements (Bolesnikov, Kang, & Girourad, 2022, p. 6). While touch being a suitable substitute for blind and visually impaired people, according to the authors' study, several issues can arise in this area, for example, not using physically distinct pieces, or a lack of tactile features (Bolesnikov, Kang, & Girourad, 2022, pp. 6-7).

Johnson and Kane also add the lack of knowledge of the position of pieces and the information on cards to accessibility problems in tabletop games (Johnson & Kane, 2020, p. 7). For example, the board game Monopoly (Hasbro 2023) consists of one board with different fields of color to differentiate between various districts, 2D printed cards and money, and 3D player figures. It does not include any tactile components on the board for people with visual impairment to distinguish between the single fields. While the 3D figures are distinguishable through having different forms, the player can too easily move the pieces on accident due to no restrictions being on the board itself. The same issue applies to the hotels that can be placed on the fields. The information on the cards is also not available to people with visual impairment. The affected player would need to rely and trust on others to read out the written text truthfully. Additionally, while color is included for each district, people with color blindness would not be able to distinguish between them without relying on the text. Monopoly also includes game currency that is only differentiated by the text and color of the 2D printed paper. It would have been beneficial to design the bank notes in different sizes depending on their value. The same issues are also included with the board game Catan - Das Spiel (Teuber 2015). While the board itself is somewhat accessible due to puzzle tiles restricting the movements of the single fields, the 3D pieces can still move freely on the board and a differentiation between what resource each provides is only available through color. Affected people can also not distinguish between the various card types, the numbers on the coins on the board, and the 3D pieces of each player which rely on color. Compared to Monopoly, it is also more difficult to depend on another player due to information such as what resources are in one's hand and what type of development cards one draws, should be concealed from others. All these issues noticed in analog games lead to either player being reliant on others (Johnson & Kane, 2020, p. 7), the abandonment of games (Johnson & Kane, 2020, p. 8), both of which have also been noticed by Bolesnikov, Kang, and Girourad (2022, p. 5), and an unfair gameplay (Johnson & Kane, 2020, p. 8).

Through 3D printing, this problem could partially be diminished by providing a more tactile experience for players. For example, Bhaduri, Tovar, and Kane (2017) researched that most 3D printable artifacts are items for existing games, while rarely providing and distributing original games (p. 53). To be more precise, he considered 3D-printed objects as a means to "improve the accessibility of existing games for people with vision impairments, including 3D-printed Braille dice and tactile overlays for game pieces" (p. 53),

For this reason, we designed a printable tabletop game that uses 3D printing to enhance playability for visually impaired people. Tomé et al. provide a guideline on how to create accessible board games in their paper "Let's Play Together: Adaptation Guidelines of Board Games for Players with Visual Impairment" (2019), which was then expanded and compared with Bolesnikov, Kang, and Girourad's work that centers on the accessibility of mechanics and aesthetics in tabletop games (2022). One aspect Tomé et al. highlight is the usage of tactile feedback. According to the authors, using texture and shapes can help in spatial orienting, and learning and memorizing patterns (Tomé et al., 2019, p. 8). Essential in this case is also the implementation of distinct characteristics for different components so players can distinguish between various items (Tomé et al., 2019, p. 8). Another important aspect is to use fixed components (Tomé et al., 2019, p. 8). This helps to prevent accidental moving (Tomé et al., 2019, p. 8). Various methods are suggested, such as Velcro, magnets, or pegs (Tomé et al., 2019, p. 8). However, when talking to the University's Disability Representative Mark Wassermann, magnets were not recommended due to the fine-tuning necessary of the magnets' strengths to enable the easy movement of items while ensuring stability for components to not fall over easily. (Mark Wassermann, personal meeting, November 7, 2022) The last aspect to add tactile feedback is to use Braille. According to Tomé et al. (2019), this inclusion helps to provide information and to discern different items (p. 8). However, more space is required to communicate information (Tomé et al., 2019, pp. 8-9). Another drawback to this method would be that visually impaired people do not often learn Braille nowadays and rather learn to distinguish between Roman characters as stated by Mark Wassermann (Mark Wassermann, personal meeting, November 7, 2022). This observation is supported by Bolesnikov, Kang, and Girourad (2022, p. 13). For that reason, alternatives need to be applied.

Another aspect that is important to consider is color and contrast. As stated by Tomé et al., highly contrasted colors need to be used to make items easily distinguishable (2019, p. 9). Additionally, due to different varieties of color blindness, one should use more colorblind-friendly palettes so that everyone is able to discern between the colors (Tomé et al., 2019, p. 9). This is crucial information to consider when designing a board game. However, in the end, the most important aspect is that color is not used to convey meaning (Tomé et al., 2019).

After color, the design of information for better communication is necessary to examine. This entails the inclusion of large size fonts, concise text with the eventual usage of keywords, and the incorporation of iconography (Tomé et al.,

2019, pp. 9-10). However, the authors also note that enlarging the font is not possible due to space restrictions (Tomé et al., 2019, p. 9). For that reason, modifying components, text, or even restricting them, might be necessary (Tomé et al., 2019, p. 9).

An essential part of a board game to evaluate is the game rules and with that the rulebook. Without being able to communicate these instructions, playing the game will be impossible for visually impaired people. Tomé et al. highlight that many rulebooks make use of images that contain information that cannot be translated via a screen reader (2019, p. 10). For that reason, the authors suggest adding descriptions or including audio and video as alternatives (Tomé et al., 2019, p. 10). Bolesnikov, Kang, and Girourad further recommend providing text that is simple to understand so players can focus their energy on the main aspects of the game (2022, p. 14).

Essential developments in digital technology are helpful to communicate information to visually impaired people. Tomé et al. state that there are various possibilities such as QR code, Radio Frequency Identification, and Near Field Communication (2019, p. 10). These systems make it possible for game elements "to be identified and described using sound," and "identifying changes in game state [...] and communicating these" (Tomé et al., 2019, p. 10). This leads to providing constant feedback during the game (Tomé et al., 2019, p. 10).

Bolesnikov, Kang, and Girourad also highlight the importance of "encourag[ing] autonomy in games," (2022, p. 14). They argue that visually impaired people should not be dependent on sighted assistance (Bolesnikov, Kang, & Girourad, 2022, p. 14). This argument includes all the previous aspects already mentioned as these elements ensure the accessibility of a board game but is important to point out again.

3. Game Design

After deciding to create a printable game based on 3D printing with accessibility in the foreground, we created one mind-map each for two different game ideas to decide what we want to develop. First, we identified which elements are essential for designing a game. These would be "Type," "Mechanics," "Game Time" or playtime, "Genre," "Board," "Number of Players," and "Winning Condition." The result of one mind-map was a cozy game with around 45-60 min playtime that should be able to be played between 1, 2, or 4 players. The design decisions also led to both a competitive and cooperative mode, with the players using action points and tokens to play the game. Due to the printable element, players should be able to play on one board with tiles together and/or separately on individual boards. The win condition should consist of a number of reached victory points. However, after some iterations, the competitive mode was canceled due to being less fun for visually impaired people for the various reasons mentioned above, and the cozy genre was changed because of our choice of theme.

The game's theme was decided to be a heist game where players try to rob a bank vault while avoiding robot guards. The main goal is to make a successful heist, and escape the bank, while cooperating and helping eac

Subsequently, we discussed which elements should be included and what the game should look like in terms of these categories. In the end, we decided on a cooperative game that could last between a short and long game length, depending on each round. The cards and turn-based movements were included for the mechanics from one mind map as well as the tokens from the other. At first, the board would have been one single tray with singular tiles slotted into it, with the winning condition being to reach a specific destination and kill an opponent there. However, after the first prototype was made in the tabletop simulator (Berserk Games 2015), the game was adapted and improved as the play experience was neither satisfying nor exciting. The mechanics needed a more unpredictable element that engages the players. For this reason, dice were included. Even though we liked the decided-upon win condition, we added a more challenging one in which the players must reach an end destination. This means that there are four goals in total: getting keys, reaching destination 1, defeating the opponents, and reaching destination 2.

4. Card Design

The event cards, skill cards, and guard randomizers are distinguished both by the color and by the symbol on the back of the card. A significant color difference has been used to ensure that people with specific color blindness can still differentiate between these. The symbols also establish a high contrast with the back, and due to the black and white coloration, they are easily distinguishable. It was decided to add a colorful background to provide a more aesthetically pleasing style rather than just a black-and-white theme and symbols (see Figure 1). More difficult was the design choice for the front side of the event cards. Due to the already established meaning of colors - red signals danger, while green is associated with a more positive meaning - it was impossible to create a set of cards without losing the aesthetical element for people with, specifically, the red-green blindness. Nevertheless, these cards are still understandable without depicting the right coloration due to the text. They only add a more aesthetically pleasing design. However, after some feedback, adding more contrast to the colors would help to distinguish the cards more easily if wanted.

To add more tactile components, the right top corner is cut off to signal the front of the card. This is helpful for people with visual impairments, as the cut-off corner always has to be on the top right side so that it is turned in the correct direction. This feedback was provided by Mr. Wassermann (Mark Wassermann, personal meeting, November 7, 2022). Additionally, a QR code has been added in the bottom right corner on all cards so that the specific game app can read the provided text out loud. This is helpful for people with low vision. The codes are always placed in the same place to facilitate scanning.

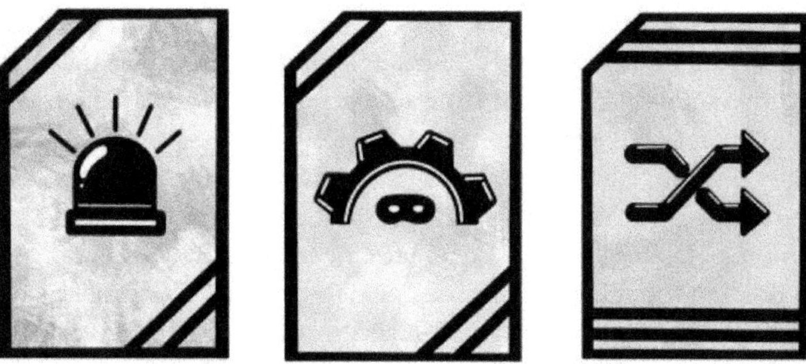

Figure 1. Event, Skill, and Guard Randomizer Cards - Back Design

5. Token Design

Due to efficiency problems concerning 3D printing, a 2D design and print were necessary for various tokens. Instead of 3D-printed weapons, players are able to print out 2D designs of both the lethal and non-lethal weapons. As the guards are robots, an object that looks similar to Tasers was designed to signal the effect of electricity on technology. One difference that distinguishes them from each other is the triangle form at one end of this element. This form is inspired by literature on the aesthetics of game art. According to Solarski (2013), triangles are associated with "aggression, masculinity, [and] force" (n.p). For this reason, due to the connection to more physical energy, lethal weapons have a triangular edge that indicates a more aggressive method of attack. This form is also helpful in identifying each type of weapon for visually impaired people. It ensures that they can feel the differences between both forms while still keeping a similar design (as seen in Figure 2).

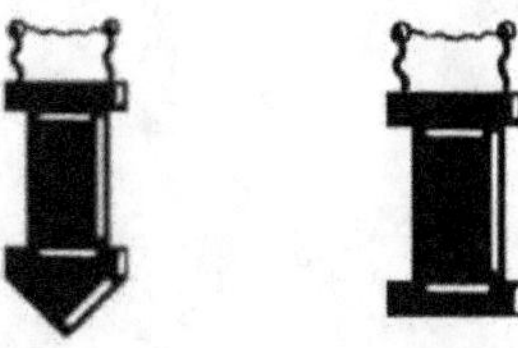

Figure 2. Lethal and Non-Lethal Weapon Design

6. 3D-Printed Parts

The game models are designed to provide a good game feel while being accessible and recognizable for different groups with visual impairments. As the game is intended to be highly replayable, the game board consists of 16 tiles, representing different rooms, each printed separately. The individual pieces include their name written in 3D on top of them, which allows for an easy reading of their label by touch. To keep the game as time and cost effective as possible, the tiles are designed in a way to require a minimum amount of material for printing, while they still maintain and offer the feeling of a board game. To achieve this goal, each tile is printed in an L-shape to only include the two necessary sides for each room, which are then connected with notches on the top left corner to form the entire game board. These parts are designed to fit perfectly together like a puzzle to allow the players an easy setup of any board that is given to them through board randomizer cards or the application. There are also special slots on the tiles designed to attach walls.

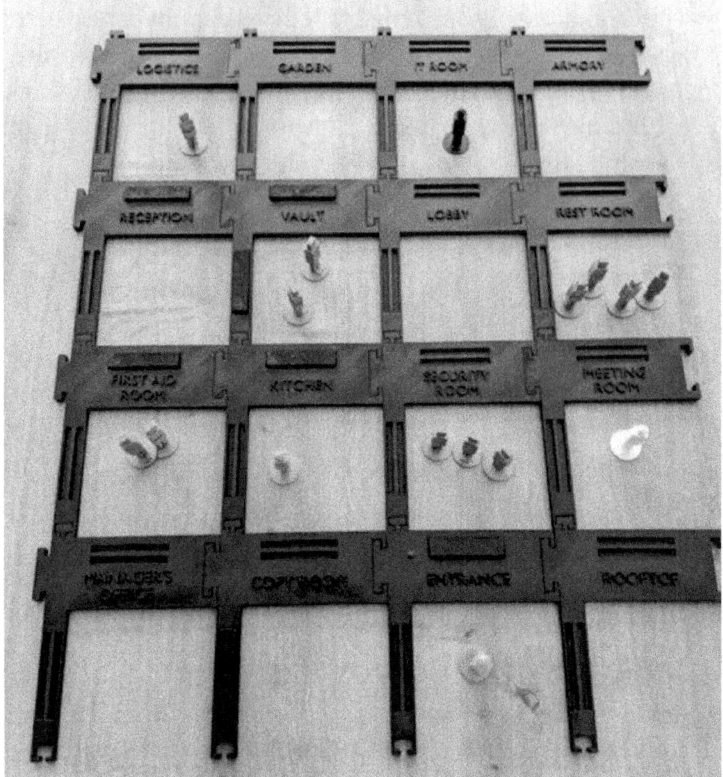

Figure 3. Game board consisting of L-shaped connectable tiles

The game uses three figure types: players, enemy robots, and hacked robots. To distinguish all these in the models, different shapes of heads are used. The player pieces have round heads. To add more contrast, a marking that helps to identify the player's number was added on the front side of their bodies, which is also feelable by touch. Compared to these figures, the enemy robots use a square head. The hacked robots have the same shape as the enemy robots, but they have a pointy part on their head.

Figure 4 shows three player pieces and two robot guards as 3D-printed figures. The circles visible on the enemy robots are used as tactile counters for cases where they are t disabled due to events in the game. By putting the figure to its side and rotating it every round, the player can keep track of how many rounds the robot is turned off for and when it should be reactivated and join back the game.

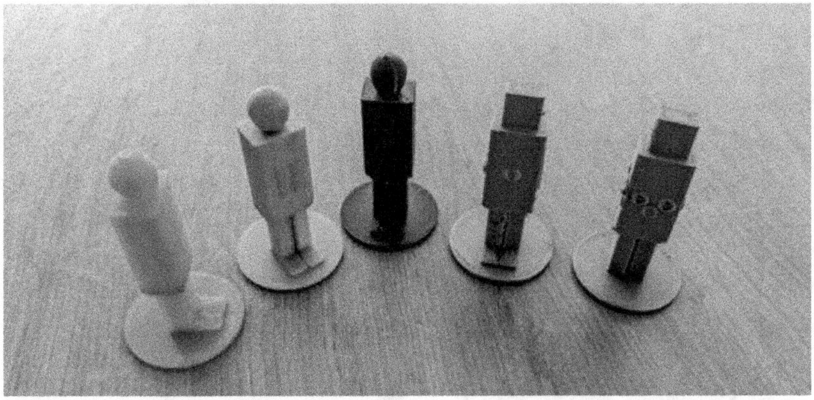

Figure 4. 3D-printed figures with embossed markings

7. Assistant Application

An assistant application was developed to support visually impaired players well through its voice reader function, while also enhancing the game for all players. This app was designed using Flutter Framework (Google 2017) and is targeted for Android devices. The built-in narrator system included in Android devices is utilized to talk and communicate with the users. To support all types of players, well-contrasted colors between background and foreground have been taken into consideration. Using the free applications offered by W3Schools (Refsnes Data AS 1998) and Webaim (Utah State University 1999), the contrast of colors has been checked and confirmed to offer clear visibility also for color-blind people.

With all that in mind, the application includes three parts: QR Reader, Board Randomizer, and Guard Randomizer. The QR Reader is the part designed specifically for visually impaired players. This feature is used to read the cards out loud. For this to work, a QR code is printed on every card used in the game. By scanning the QR codes using the application, the cards' content will be read out to the player due to the voice reader function. The board randomizer takes advantage of the app to provide a better experience for every player while offering an accessible system for the visually impaired. Similarly, the guard randomizer provides variability by generating different scenarios for randomizing guards. The guards and keycards are randomly placed in the game, following placement rules implemented in the app. A narrator is also available to read the setup out loud for players to follow. The same settings as the board randomizer are available for the narrator in this section.

8. Gameplay Example

For better understanding of how the game plays, this section includes one scenario of gameplay. In the following image, the green player is 2 moves away from reaching the Vault, which is the first goal of the game. However, the player is stuck between 2 active guards and due to the rules of the game, is not easily capable of moving out of the room. To move out, they either have to defeat the guards using their available ammunition and throwing the required die or escape by throwing the needed die for that.

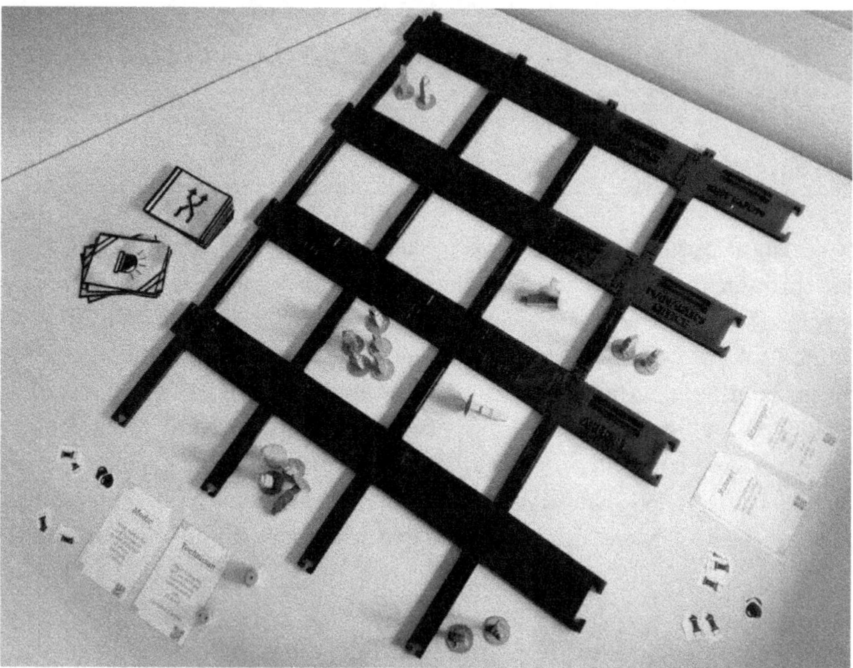

Figure 5. A gameplay scenario from a 2-player game

The blue player, however, is capable of moving due to the single guard present in their room being inactive, but due to the positioning of the walls in this randomly generated scenario, the player does not have a direct and quick path to the Vault and can only move thereby passing through the same room as the green player. Having the Runner skill card makes this easier for them.

The situation shows a relatively easy scenario where players have a few actions in front of them. With good cooperation and smart use of their available skill cards, players are able to get to the Vault and continue forward with their goals.

That being said, with the random event cards in the game, everything can change at any moment for the players, making the situation tough and more challenging.

9. Conclusion

This paper's main contribution is elaborating a method to design and develop a printable board game prototype designed to be accessible to visually impaired individuals. Using 3D printing technology and carefully designed 2D elements, we have addressed the need for accessible board and card games for people with visual impairments in the example of a heist board game. Our considerations highlight the importance of inclusive game design, including large-size fonts, concise text, iconography, and alternative formats like audio and video descriptions. As we have shown in the case study, these things can be well addressed in a homebrew board game, given the availability of a 3D printer and a hybrid game design using an assistant app. The prototype game is a heist game where players aim to rob a bank vault while avoiding guards. While the main goal is to make a successful heist, there is also competition between players to make the most revenue. Thus, the money aspect leads to competitiveness in an otherwise cooperative setting in the game. Overall, this paper offers practical insights for implementing accessible gaming through 3D printing technology, By looking into the accuracy and time and financial resources required for a 3D accessible game, this paper provides a valuable contribution to the field using widely available technology.

The resources of the complete game, including rulebook, 2D and 3D models, assistant app, and sources, are available at https://github.com/farhadk100/3D_board_assistant under a Public domain license.

10. Acknowledgments

We are grateful to Mark Wassermann, Disability Representative of the University of Klagenfurt, for the valuable feedback and insights on the inclusive design of game elements for visually impaired individuals. Mr. Wassermann's expertise has greatly contributed to enhancing accessibility in gaming experiences.

About the Authors

Ahmad Kalatiani is a graduate of the master program Game Studies and Engineering at the Alpen-Adria-Universität Klagenfurt, Austria. His research interests are in fields of modern technologies such as Virtual Reality and 3D-Printers and their innovative use cases in development of new software and games. Ahmad Kalatiani is a software engineer at the Alpen-Adria-Universität Klagenfurt.

LinkedIn: ahmad-kalatiani-51960274

Magdalena M. Strobl is a student assistant of the Game Studies and Engineering program at the Alpen-Adria Universität Klagenfurt, Austria. She has nearly completed her masters degrees in the aforementioned program as well as in English and American Studies. Magdalena M. Strobl is also a representative of Team Klagenfurt for Austria's Young Americanists (AYA). Her last conference presentation with the title "'But Somewhere Along the Way, I Started Changing': Death Stranding's Road Towards Mindfulness and Environmental Awareness Through the Act of Walking" connected her research interests of ecocriticism and game studies.

Wilfried Elmenreich is professor of Smart Grids at the Institute of Networked and Embedded Systems at the Alpen-Adria-Universität Klagenfurt, Austria. His research interests include intelligent energy systems, self-organizing systems, and technical applications of swarm intelligence. Wilfried Elmenreich is a member of the Senate at the Alpen-Adria-Universität Klagenfurt, Counselor of the IEEE Student Branch, and is involved in the master program on Game Studies and Engineering. He is the author of several books and has published over 200 articles in the field of networked and embedded systems. Elmenreich researches intelligent energy systems, self-organizing systems, and technical applications of swarm intelligence.

Social: https://www.linkedin.com/in/wilfriedelmenreich/
Website: https://mobile.aau.at/~welmenre/

11. References

Berserk Games. (2015). Tabletop Simulator. Florida, United States: Berserk Games.

BoardGameGeek. (n.d.). Print & Play. Retrieved May 15, 2023, from https://boardgamegeek.com/boardgamecategory/1120/print-play.

Bolesnikov, Adrian, Kang Jin, & Audrey Girouard. (2022). Understanding Tabletop Games Accessibility: Exploring Board and Card Gaming Experiences of People who are Blind and Low Vision. In TEI '22: Sixteenth International Conference on Tangible, Embedded, and Embodied Interaction (pp. 1-17). https://doi.org/10.1145/3490149.3501327.

Google LLC. (2017). Flutter Framework. California, United States: Google LLC.

Hasbro. 2023. Monopoly. Pawtucket, RI: Hasbro.

Johnson, Gabrielle M., & Shaun K. Kane. (2020). Game Changer: Accessible Audio and Tactile Guidance for Board and Card Games. In W4A '20: Proceedings of the 17th International Web for All Conference (pp. 1-12). https://doi.org/10.1145/3371300.3383347.

Refsnes Data AS. (1998). W3Schools. Rogaland, Norway: Refsnes Data AS.

Solarski, Chris. (2013). The Aesthetics of Game Art and Game Design. Last modified January 30, 2013. Retrieved May 20, 2023, from https://www.gamedeveloper.com/design/the-aesthetics-of-game-art-and-game-design.

Teuber, Klaus. 2015. Catan - Das Spiel. Stuttgart: Franckh-Kosmos.

Tomé Filho, da Rocha Frederico, Kapralos Bill, Mirza-Babaei Pejman, & Glaudiney Moreira Mendonça Junior. (2019). Let's Play Together: Adaptation Guidelines of Board Games for Players with Visual Impairment. In CHI '19: Proceedings of the 2019 CHI Conference on Human Factors in Computing Systems (pp. 1-15). https://doi.org/10.1145/3290605.3300861.

Utah State University. 1999. Webaim. Utah, United States: Utah State University.

PROTOTYPING DIVERSITY SENSITIVE GAME DESIGN

AGILE SOFTWARE DEVELOPMENT AS A SIMULATION GAME WITH SCRUM (SCRUMSIMPLAN)

Linda Rustemeier

The following exposé would like to introduce the online simulation game ScrumSimPlan , developing a game concept with the aim of understanding and use of the scrum framework. Primarily it is useful for computer science students, but also for everyone interested as a project management tool. The concept follows diversity-sensitive guidelines to make it accessible and inclusive for all participants. The focus is a user-centered approach for the implementation, which includes a constant exchange of ideas with Scrum experts and users. Teams of minimum three player online simulate the scrum roles, like the scrum master, product owner and developers. One after the other in four rounds. Within one day, the entire scrum process is simulated, a facilitator accompanies the process and the game supplements with typical scenarios, such as the execution of a priority estimation. In addition, the players must overcome common obstacles that occur when applying scrum and agile methods. With the help of gamification elements, the motivation to learn the scrum process is to be increased, which saves not only time, but also money for companies the students or one will work for in the future.

Keywords: Serious Game, simulations game, diversity, inclusion, agile project management, scrum guide

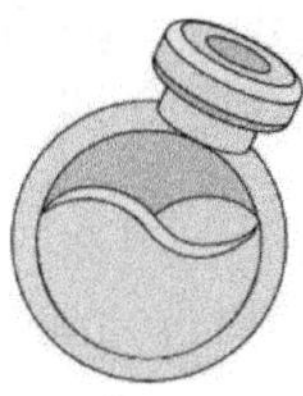

1. Challenges

A big challenge in higher education is that teaching at universities, especially in relation to soft science and the humanities, in general is said to be theoretical. Unlike universities of applied sciences, there is a gap between theory and practice. Above that, another challenge is that there are different knowledge levels and responsibilities between students. Some students are already employees during their study time, too, some worked already in needed areas, and some did not at all. Companies are often happy when their new employees bring work experience. Because when companies hire new employees, they need a lot of training time for the onboarding process. One could also argue that poor onboarding leads to offboarding, especially during times of heavy shortage of skilled workers. New employees need experiences and learning time to achieve good working results, so the time until there will be acceptable results is a time when experienced coworkers are less involved in the daily business. Universities could fill this potential lack by using simulation games at an early stage.

Agility refers to how well a company can adapt to important trends such as globalization, digitalization and demographic change. According to the "Agile Performer Index" [1] by business consulting company goetzpartners and NEOMA Business School, a company's agility is primarily reflected in areas such as overall strategy, organizational structure, market and competitive intelligence, IT infrastructure and data management, leadership and error culture, employee development and recruitment and, finally, working methods.

Regarding the Indexes results economic journalist Kerstin Dämon writes in a German economic magazine *Wirtschaftswoche* about New Work and working agile in 2017: "The more agile a company is overall, the greater its economic success. Accordingly, the most agile companies in an industry are on average 2.7 times more successful than their competitors with rigid structures" (Dämon,2017).

Next to modern strategies, like agility, there is the agenda of new work and diversity (Rath, 2023). Studies say the more diverse teams who work together,

---

[1] Agile Performer Index
https://www.goetzpartners.com/uploads/tx_gp/2017_goetzpartners_Agile_Performer_Index.pdf

the more successful the results are. Diversity is not the only a need, but it is also the inclusion of employees with impairments. Therefore, the used working tools must be inclusive, too. Another challenge that is not always part of the study or job training. If one wants to create simulation games, games as well as representation in games must be inclusive therefore accessible and diverse.

2. Why are simulation games effective for universities?

The term serious game was coined by the German American educationalist Clark C. Abt: "We are dealing here with serious games in the sense that these games pursue an explicit and carefully thought-out educational purpose and are not primarily intended for entertainment" (Abt 1970, p. 26). Simulation games are serious games and give players the opportunity to develop holistic thinking and an understanding of systems. They convey complex structures, processes and interrelationships that enable players to act independently. Another advantage of simulation games is that they can simulate longer processes in a shorter period. They also promote the learning process and strengthen social skills such as teamwork, cooperation, dialog skills, willingness to compromise and sensitivity to communication. Overall, simulation games contribute to the development of soft skills as they help players to make decisions that are more confident and improve their decision-making skills in a risk-free environment. With an "active learning approach", simulation games promote sustainable problem solving, the acquisition of knowledge and create a positive learning environment (Ivens, Kaiser 2021; Petrik 2017).

3. What is scrum?

The economy's most used project management framework is agile and called *scrum.* [2] Scrum is about developing a vision and a media product, originally from software development, companies install scrum as a project management tool. Ken Schwaber and Jeff Sutherland wrote *The Scrum Guide*, which serves as its manifest or agile guideline, in the early 1990s. The successful application of scrum depends on people becoming better at deploying five values:

---

[2] Digital.ai: Digital.ai. 15th State of Agile Report (2021): Agile adoption accelerates across the enterprise. https://info.digital.ai/rs/981-LQX-968/images/SOA15.pdf.

Commitment, Focus, Openness, Respect and Courage (Schwaber, Sutherland 2020). The scrum events include next to a vision, also epics, user stories, sprints, a product and sprint backlog, sprint planning, daily scrum meetings, sprint reviews and the retrospective. "Scrum is a lightweight framework that helps people, teams, and organizations generate value through adaptive solutions to complex problems. The Scrum framework is purposely imperfect because various processes, techniques, and methods can be employed within the framework." (Schwaber, Sutherland 2020)

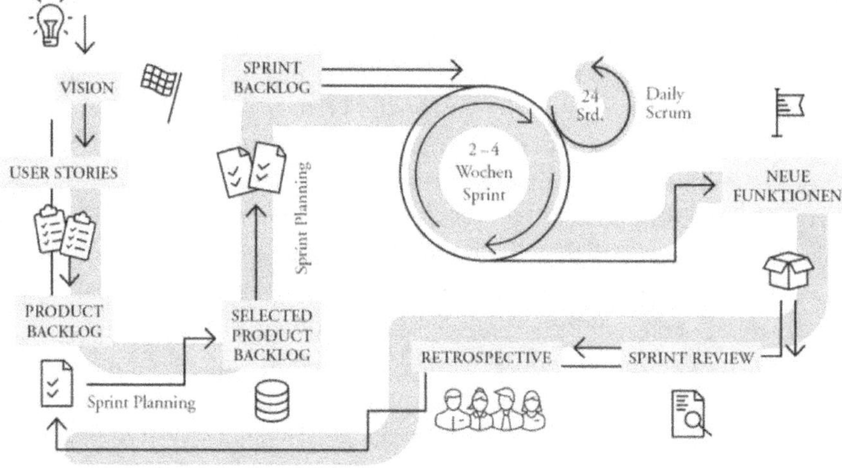

Figure 1. Exemplary representation of a scrum sprint (Abé 2023; Source Agile Heroes)

In addition, writing user stories is essential in scrum that identify roles, needs and functions. For user stories there are several definitions: "User stories are development tasks that are often formulated as "customer type + requirement + purpose". Summary: A user story is an informal, general explanation of a software feature written from the end user's perspective. Its purpose is to show what value a software feature has for a customer." Rehkopf, M. (>n.d.<)

Another definition highlights the urge of shortness in a user story also in opposition to an epic:

> "A user story or user narrative is a short description (story) of what a user wants. User stories are used in the development of products or software within Agile frameworks, including Scrum. A user story consists of a few sentences describing what the user of the product wants or needs to do. It is usually not very detailed and should fit on

> a sticky note. Through the user story, the user influences the development of a system or product and ultimately also its functionality." (Bondarenko 2022)

The importance of a clear user story in this process cannot be underestimated especially for executing developers. It is important to describe the individual user story in one sentence; otherwise, it soon will be like a bigger epic or milestones that contain smaller user stories. e.g.:
"As a [type of user], I want [an action] so that [a benefit/a value]".
A user story consists of three parts, first the form description e.g. "As [role], I want [functionality] so that I can [reason]", then secondly the story will discuss the details, which will be defined and is done during backlog grooming or sprint planning. Finally, yet importantly it must be tested if the user narrative is complete, and the details need to be determined. The last part names the acceptance criteria and the Definition of Done.
Once one asks what the characteristics of a good user story are, an answer is the INVEST-Method by Bill Wake named: Independent implemented functions, freedom of Negotiability, Valuable as a benefit for a stakeholder, Estimable for the capacity required for a user story, Small as shorter than a sprint (otherwise they can be epics)
and the final one Testable as stakeholders and the product owner know the exact content of the user story and know which content will be evaluated in tests, which is formulated as mentioned in the acceptance criteria and the Definition of Done (Bondarenko 2022).

Scrum is suitable for simulation games because it can simulate the process of agile project management in diverse teams in a secure environment without any real consequences. This not only saves time and costs for companies but also helps in gaining competencies at universities. Students receive training in knowledge transfer and practical experience at universities. This helps prevent disappointment in work results or errors in project management before delivering an important service to the customer or company. It can increase the working level, competences, and results. Further research testing the economic opinions in a scrum simulation results and success could evolve specific data. Nevertheless, the shortage will force skilled workers force German or European or global industries and employers to win every skilled employee they possibly can find as well as to think diverse or inclusive to integrate each employee, whether one has an impairment or not.

> "An important point in agile software development is people first.

> Moreover, user stories focus on the end users. They provide context for the development team and their work without using technical language. Once a team has read a user story, they know why they are developing something and what value they are creating." (Rehkopf<n.d.>)

This development and furthermore since the shortage of skilled workers will eventually be positive on inclusive workplaces and accessible tools. The next chapter will be about an experience report on how to use scrum for making authoring tools more accessible.

4. Inclusive design for authoring systems via scrum

In 2020 Voß-Nakkour et. al described how a team of interdisciplinary experts combining informatics and humanities coworkers reflected the authoring system LernBar (to create elearning courses). Many of the workers from the humanities were getting to know scrum and accessibility in scrum for the first time, it was also the initial contact via a LernBar Sprint. The process of making an authoring tool digital accessible backwards instead of from the start, is clearly way more difficult than building an accessibility tool from the beginning. This process happened together with people with an impairment. Through a blind computer scientist's experience as an expert for visual impairments, it was possible to identify difficulties. Getting to know the process of scrum and identifying challenges of software developments and user experiences. The interdisciplinarity of the process of writing user stories and sprint team developments and more helped essentially to gain inclusion for the developers and reflection for a successful implementation of an inclusive authoring tool.

However, what do universities have to do with this? Changing demands on future participants in a more and more digital labor market are a reality. The emerged concept of New Work holds a diversity of content (Foelsing & Schmitz, 2021). A definition of new work (Hofmann et al., 2019):

> "networking of people, flexibilization of work locations, times and content [,] [...] agile, self-organized iterative and highly customer-oriented working principles. [...] [W]ithdrawal from hierarchy to a coaching, lateral and supportive understanding of leadership. But how do these requirements fit with the university practices often en-

> countered? Does traditional knowledge transfer in the form of a lecture support the competency goals mentioned in the examples above? Probably not." (Morisse 2021)

This is a debate by Karsten Morisse, a professor of computer science at the University of Osnabrück, at the *University:Future Festivals 2021* of the German innovation center for digitalization of universities *Hochschulforum Digitalisierung*. He holds the opinion that the didactic e-learning method of inverted classrooms can be one answer to these challenges, too. The reasons are that this kind of teaching allows more flexibility for educators as well as students. With the help of learning management systems or authoring tools there are ways to reach the students before, in between or after the seminar which allows a more sustained effective way of teaching (Dziuban et al. 2018). One can go further with the help of serious games, in detail, simulation games during a blended seminar.

5. Benefits and costs or money and games

Simulation via prototyping as a fictional scenario and a method is way more benefitting than testing a real scenario with real stakeholders. As already mentioned, there are no real consequences, it is a safe space for errors and allows its users getting better. Moreover, it is a multimedia learning process: It could be more sustainable than a single training of a soon forgotten content, unless there is an application to implement learned knowledge (Mayer 2009). Because a sprint will mostly take longer than a seminar time there is a time saving through a time-lapse scenario, so one will have less time and more trying possibilities of the scrum essential roles. Therefore, one has more time to prioritize and to focus on different architectures of scenarios, variables, or agile developments, since there is the mentioned university gap between theoretical and practical experience. This could lead to self-motivation, perseverance and self-regulation competence and others, but must be scientifically proven as well.

6. Case Study: A Diversity Sensible Game Design for Agile Project Management in Gaming

Universities in general are learning spaces where mixed teams are working together. During seminars, especially in seminars with simulation of working processes, students are learning without pressure of working in the industry. They are also able to think about a potential leadership role in role-plays. For a learning scenario like a role-play (e.g. pen and paper), one needs a game world, a scenario, a character development and rules (Schell 2008) which make sense for the individual learning setting. One can develop this concept in a culturally diverse sense. There are several guidelines or tests such as "The Bechdel-Walace-Test". The idea originates from a conversation Alison Bechdel had with Liz Wallace and led to a sequel in her 1985 comic "Dykes to Watch Out For" and asks three central questions to media: Does the media production at least "1) have at least two women in it, who 2) talk to each other, about 3) something other than a man." (Bechdel-Wallace 1985). According to Wikipedia some younger versions would also ask as a fourth question if these women even do have a name. Another idea is to adapt this questionnaire to the game world.

The Input of diversity aspects are for example reading and reflecting the *Game Accessible Guidelines* (GAG, Full list and separated in Basic, Intermediate, Advanced Guideline aspects) and what the concept *Critical Game Design* (Flanagan 2009). In *Critical Play* a game designer called Mary Flanagan examines alternative games. Inclusion is a subject - Diversity Guidelines *Diversity Guide* (by e.g. game – Verband der deutschen Games-Branche e.V.). Mateen, Rustemeier et al. (2023), also describe accessible game decisions (e.g. color contrasts, subtitles, control etc.) from a technical point of view in *Game Accessibility: conception of an accessible Serious Games* (in German).

In addition, the role of a facilitator who will accompany a simulation game cannot be underestimated. While accompanying a facilitator can correct or indicate helpful or false information to the games or students. If one questions what a facilitation in terms of diversity the answer could be an ethical facilitation:

> "ethical facilitation is to behave as ethically as possible given the circumstances. Related to game simulations, it means to have the right intention, for the right reasons with the right kind of preparation (a facilitator has to prepare on what he or she thinks is necessary and achievable given the situation). [...] According to Hughes interpretation of the Nicomachean Ethics (Achterbergh & Vriens, 2009; Hughes, 2013), being ethical is about three components of moral behavior: 1. Moral virtue, meaning doing the right things for the right reasons. 2. Practical wisdom, meaning using multiple situated perspectives and one's own experience (which means to have a feel for the given situation in context) to judge the given ethical challenge. 3. Skill, meaning having the capability to act as a professional and to act likewise to the best of one's abilities."

Ethical Facilitation during a developing phase can also mean, that the critical role of distance to a stakeholder position is reflected together. One could ask, if the position of a client is more king than to stick to sense making developing and how to deal with critical challenges from the stakeholders. Working agile means also, that scrum is not alike another scrum as one learns practical scrum differently in companies and how to reflect the benefits in a seminar from this dealing with scrum as a tool (thinking out of the box). Also developing rules, scenarios, challenges, characters, structures and subjects for a game need to be seen and discussed critical together.

Ethics are abstract, involving a complex process of considering various viewpoints, making it challenging to define the ethical concepts explored in this work. It is only in hindsight that we can determine whether a decision or action was ethical when viewed from different perspectives (Achterbergh & Vriens, 2009; Hughes, 2013). Applied to facilitation, this suggests that facilitators must cultivate their own moral integrity through self-reflection on their choices and discussions with stakeholders in their environment. By doing this, facilitators can develop practical wisdom that enhances their expertise over time by providing relevant contextual information (de Wijse-van Heeswijk 2021). The next chapter will lead not only to facilitation practice, but also about such an attempt of ethical, diverse-sensible intersectional facilitation.

7. Blended Learning Seminar and Evaluation

In the blended learning seminar "Principles of IT project management" (1CP) at the Goethe University Frankfurt computer science students often have the first contact with scrum at an early point of their bachelor studies. The focus of the seminar by Prof. Detlef Krömker with the assistant help of Linda Rustemeier is on the classic (traditional) project management methods and agile approach of scrum. Other project management methods e.g. waterfall, are only presented in an overview. The course is practice-oriented with the help of a part time analogue simulation game including diversity and digital accessibility aspects. It is a blended learning seminar held in person and in preparation for the learning management system *Moodle, Microsoft Office, Excel* as well as *PowerPoint* and analog methods. As the educator of the seminar as well as an expert of scrum, Professor Krömker' function during the simulation is also being a helpful facilitator.

For all participants, the event begins with a kick-off on a set block date. The first full-day session took place in November 2022, followed by two sessions for each of the two groups (1 and 2) where students played a simulation game on scrum. Before one joins the seminar, it is the mandatory requirement that first the Manifesto for Agile Software Development: http://agilemanifesto.org/ and secondly The 2020 Scrum Guide by Ken Schwaber and Jeff Sutherland: https://scrumguides.org/ are read. First, they ask open questions, they show their experiences with reading the scrum guides, and it is about getting to know roles and teamwork. After that, students learn the principles of scrum via a game. The evaluations since 2022 shows that the students who took part saw the blended learning seminar *Principles of IT project management* as successful. Three groups of 24 students completed the evaluation form. The first group 1 winter semester 22_23 - N= 10 (21.11.2022) and a second group 2 in the summer semester of 2023 had 6 participants (N= 6, date 30.06.2023) and the last Group 3: summer semester 23/2 - N= 8 (11.07.2023). The students' citations of the blended seminar were insightful and helpful. [3]

[3] Student results: "Keep the kick-off event a bit shorter (less focus on traditional project development for example), maybe a bit less history, maybe more preparation time for everyone than just the project owners to get into the role play faster, room equipment, allocate more time for planning the 1st sprint - stricter schedule especially for the first appointment, more appointments, get together at the end?, best technical equipment, possibly a little more (pre-)structuring, separate teams more, more guidance, more precise information, let everyone write user stories in their entirety and then get individual feedback on them, maybe somehow include money/budget in the planning game. Then one working day would be a scarce resource, fellow students sometimes are very inexperienced / different experience levels, take into account the abilities of the students, make people more aware that they not only have personal responsibility here, but their openness also has a strong influence on the smooth running of the simulations. "Pulling every word out of your nose" has no value, making lectures better on the first day. Fun (3), interaction (3), practical/practical relevance/future topic (3), small group size (3), Super topic/form business game concept (3), Intuitive content/knowledge transfer, active participation, feedback from the lecturer, this course leads e.g. to good communication between members of a company, and how to behave properly as a manager, gives a good insight into the topic of scrum, practice-oriented, application-oriented, teaching method business game, teamwork, block seminar (intense learning), well structured, descriptive, business game ensures good understanding through own application of the learned

After all the students evaluated the blended seminar mostly positive and are willing to continue with indications or pointing out important improvements. The resumé also led to the question, when something works semi analogue, will the adapted concept also work out in an accessible digital simulation game concept as well? This question and the will of improving the current status quo led this concept to the digital prototype of ScrumSimPlan.

8. Idea and Evaluation of a digital prototype of ScrumSimPlan

In a selected colloquium for game design theses, enabling students to implement diversity-conscious game design in educational game prototypes included creating the game world, the game scenario, avatars, and rules. In the sense of "Constructive Alignment", a meaningful didactic use of educational games in teaching should be justified, planned & thus promoted as a teaching concept. This is a test for a possible workflow. The aim is to get into the prototyping of educational game design quickly. In this way, improving ideas that do not work at an early stage using the feedback method during prototyping is effective. Several theses were written, but the focus will be on the last Master Thesis *"Development and usability optimization of a serious game in university teaching for the teaching of Scrum"* (Ahmed, 2023).

The idea of a scrum-prototype has the following game design decisions: The world of this game is a restaurant, the scenario is the central kitchen, the rules are that each player has read *The Scrum Guide* before and plays three different roles (Scrum Master/Product Owner/Developer) first round corresponds to three sprints, they built their own character design through an avatar. This will simulate the typical scrum characters and stakeholders. A facilitator, in this case the educator, is leading the seminar and will tell students when to change

---

content, the topics are of great relevance for aspiring software developers, friendly atmosphere, through the role play, the content is clarified and it is easier to remember or imagine, for beginners a very good introduction to scrum, business game is great to consolidate, fun, relatively practical, compactly summarized and playful, very practically designed, interactive, several appointments"(Evaluation via online tool EvaSys as a blended seminar 2022-23, upon request)

something. The game's aim is not to win, but to learn what scrum is and how to use it as an effective tool in the first place.

9. Different versions of prototypes

There are several prototype versions, which lead from a process of first seeing the general usability priority to game design decisions and finally to a more playful design. The document below shows the first version, followed by further developments.

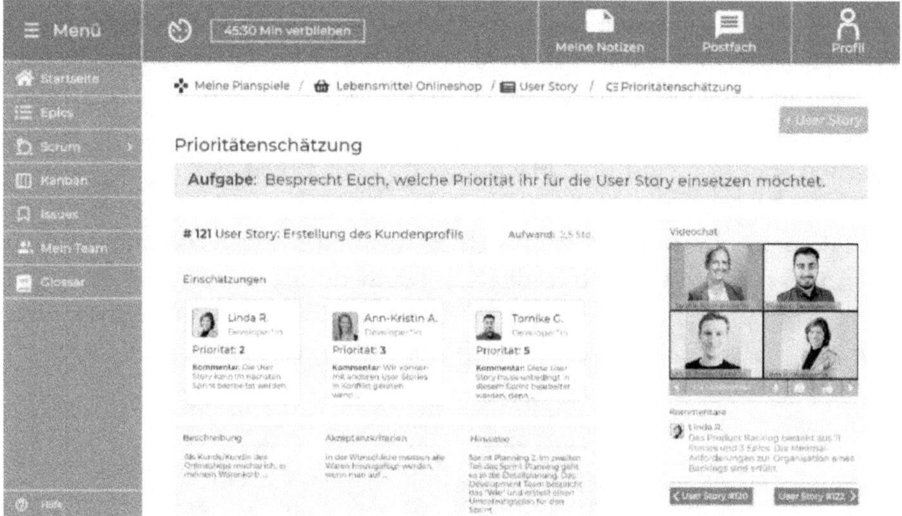

Figure 2. The priority estimation. The figure shows the priorities assigned to the user stories: This was one of the first prototypes made with Adobe XD in 2021. (Source: own image by Tornike Giorgashvili)

The very first prototype is showing a clear structured priority estimation for an old idea of an online grocery shop. During the colloquium, a master student made the next prototypes. First, they must solves quizzes, fill in gaps and get to know the team roles and the own required skills for being in an eventually successful scrum team via avatars.

The focused scenario is scrum in a restaurant/kitchen game world. That is why the user stories focus recipes as well as epics as menus. As already said the scrum events include next to visions and user stories the actual sprints, with a product and sprint backlog, sprint planning, daily scrum meetings, sprint reviews and the sprint retrospective. The prototype set starts with a landing intro or welcome page as well as a participation test. The requirements for scrum as well as ScrumSimPlan are one must read and talk about *The Scrum Guide* ahead of the game to understand the basics. Users must fill out a quiz afterwards which references to the user manual to progress.

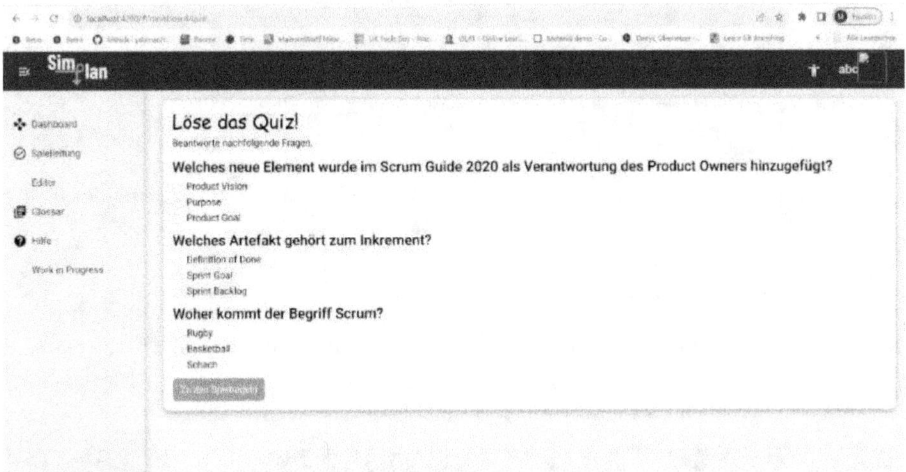

Figure 3. Solve the quiz. It is meant to be a participation pretest asking in a multiple-choice- questions "Which new element was added as a responsibility since 2020 for the product owner? Which artefact belongs to the increment?; where does the term scrum come from?". The quiz is followed by game rules and learning goals.

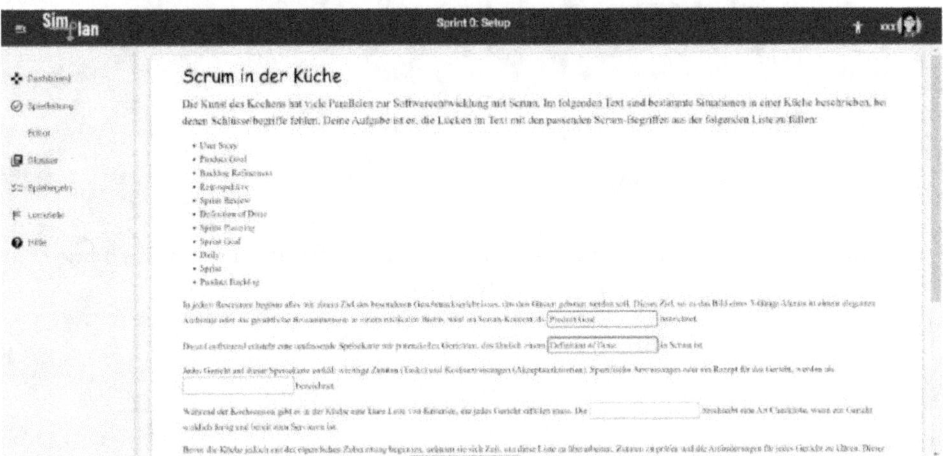

Figure 4. Gap quiz - Fill out the gaps to show you know scrum vocabulary (Accessibility all Colors must be checked by a Color Contrast Analyzer)

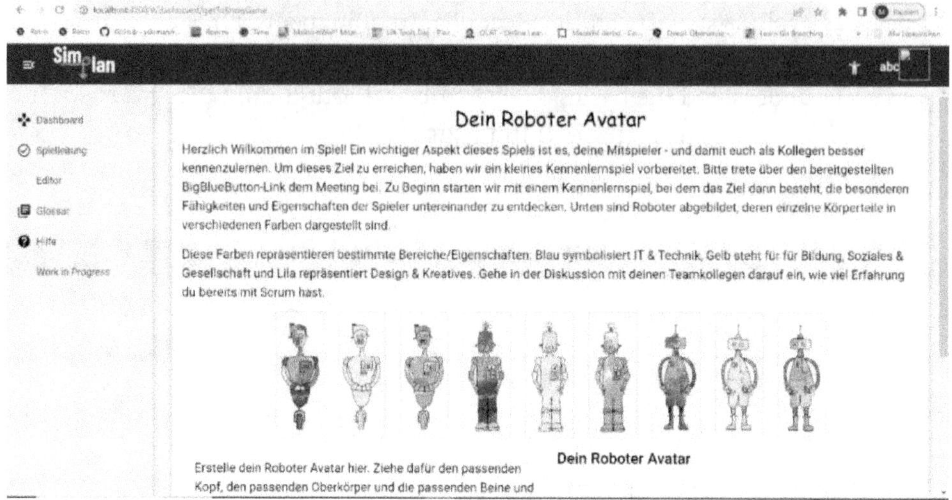

Figure 5. Build your own avatar and describe yourself and yourself to the team

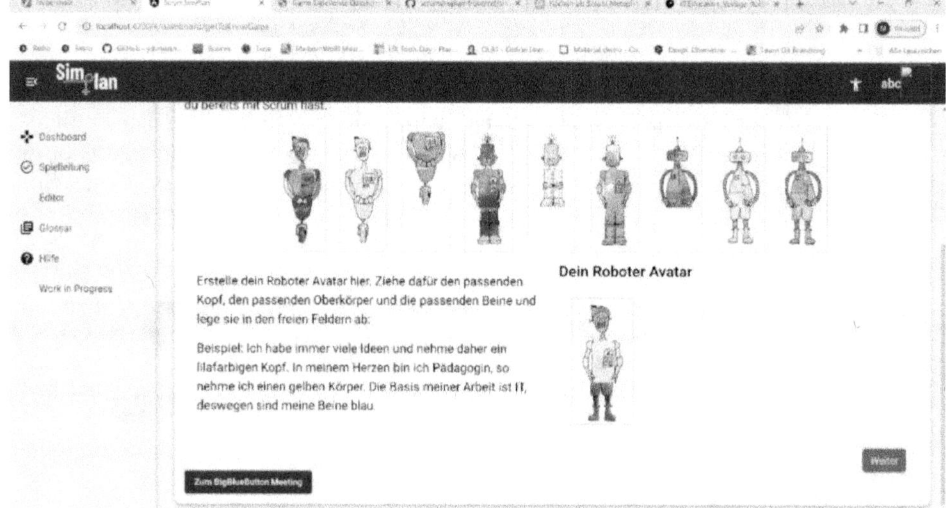

Figure 6. Get to know the scrum roles - Build your own avatar and describe yourself to the team

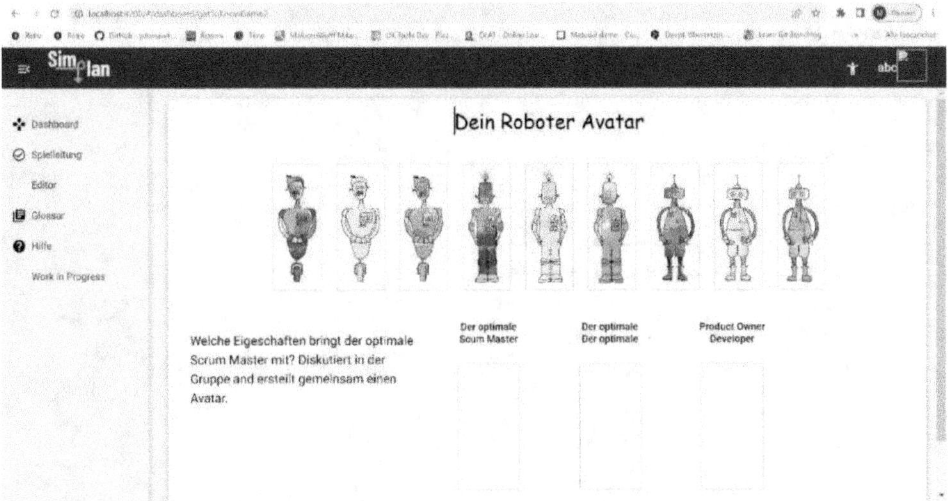

Figure 7. Get to know the roles of scrum. Describe what the central protagonist scrum roles (scrum master, product owner, developer) need to have idealistic via drag and drop

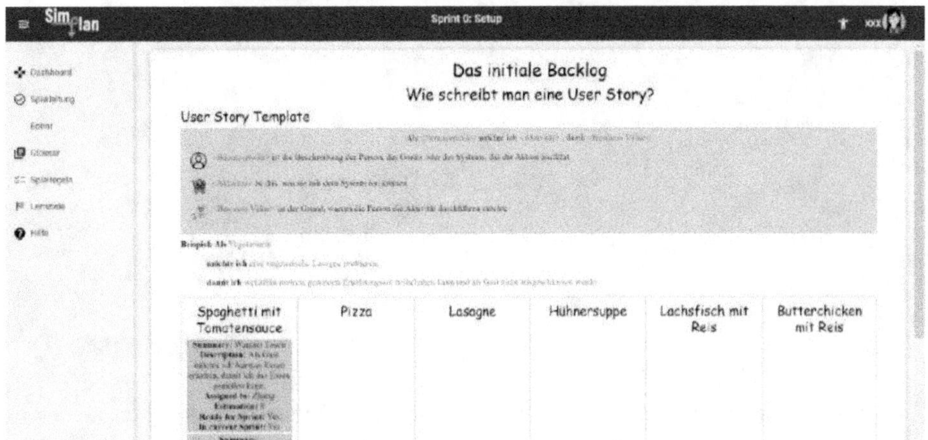

Fig. 8. Content presentation of the initial backlog – how to write a user story regarding writing a recipe

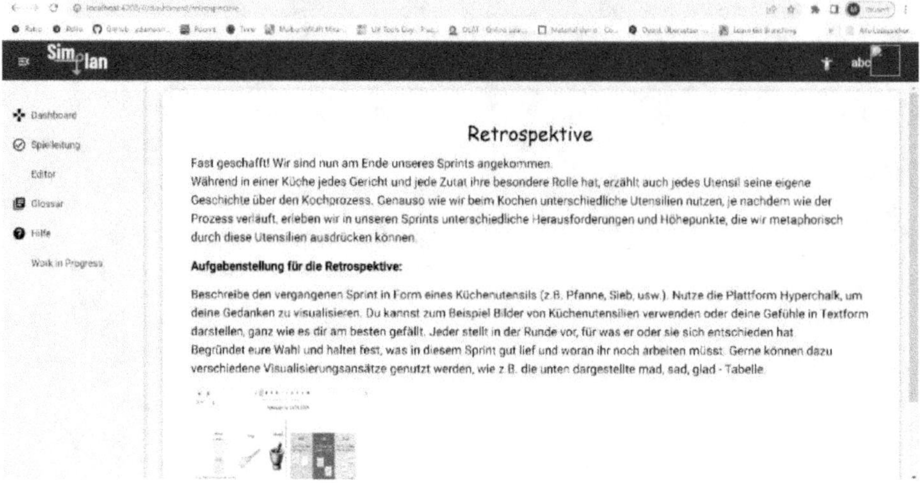

Figure 9. Retrospective process

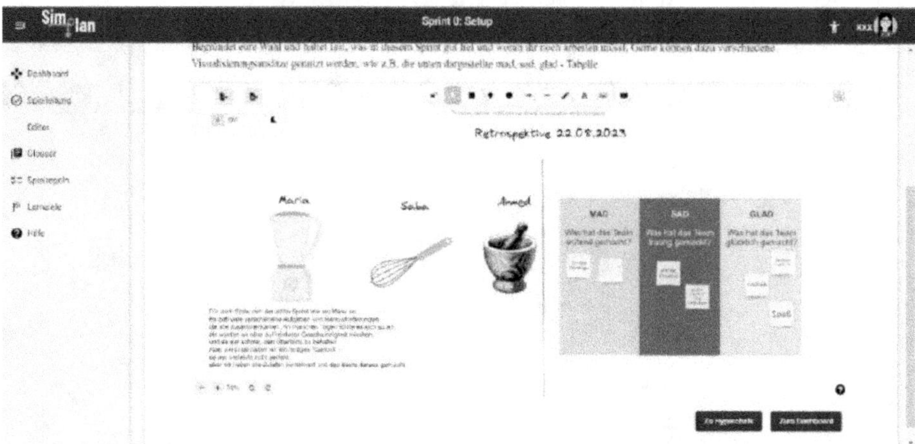

Figure 10. Excerpt from a fictitious retrospective via the open educational resource tool Hyperchalk.

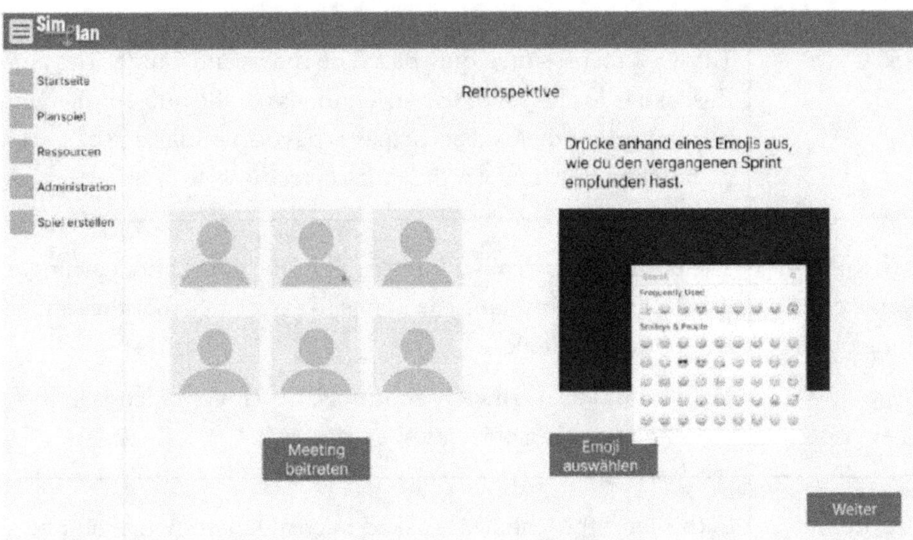

Figure 11. Retrospective process

According to Jakob Nielsen, a usability expert, around 85% of an application's usability problems can be identified with just five testers (Nielsen, 1993). He recommends not carrying out extensive usability tests, because it would be a waste of resources and time. Nielsen's research has shown that after the first five testers, the number of problems discovered decreases sharply. Further users interviewed brought fewer new findings, as most of the problems were repetitive. For this reason, only five people were used as testers in a remote usability test. That is why five interview partners saw and evaluated these prototypes of the simulation game at an early stage of development, utilizing the qualitative interview and the thinking aloud method to test the prototype. Showing prototypes early can save money, time, and effort, as it allows for the elimination of bad or unsuccessful ideas based on potential customers' feedback. The interviewees had to accomplish the following tasks:

Table 1. Qualitative Questionnaire Interview Tasks

Task 1: Introduction to the game	In this task, the participants should get to know the ScrumSimPlan game scenario. The aim is to check the clarity and comprehensibility of the game scenario. They should empathize with the virtual world of the game and assess whether the introduction is clear and understandable.

Task 2: Quiz	This task focuses on a quiz based on the Scrum Guide. The aim of this task is to check the user-friendliness of the quiz implementation. It is important that the participants have an initial sense of achievement when they answer the quiz correctly.
Task 3: Rules of the game and learning objectives	The participants deal with the rules of the game and learning objectives of ScrumSimPlan. The aim is to assess whether these are clear and understandable. They should also critically scrutinize the choice of icons in the game rules and learning objectives.
Task 4: Robot avatar familiarization game	In this task, the testers are asked to create their own avatar by selecting the head, the head, stomach and legs of a robot to create their own avatar. The different colors and the different representations of the body parts of the robots represent character traits and personality traits. The selection is made by drag & drop. The participants should now create their own robot. The aim here is to check the user-friendliness of the drag & drop function and to reflect on why certain body parts were selected. Normally, in the game, the game leader would moderate the introductory game and after a given time, team members should present their robot avatar with reasons. In a live game environment, all players would gather in a video chat via video conference tool "Big-Blue-Button".
Task 5: Creating an optimal Scrum Master, Product Owner and Developer	In the previous context, the next step in the live game is for all players to work out in a joint discussion which characteristics the ideal Scrum Master, Product Owner or even Developer should have. For the remote usability test, the aim is to identify the ideal characteristics for Scrum Master, Product Owner and Developer and to address the ease of use for implementation.
Task 6: Complete a gap text	In this task, participants are asked to fill in a gap text as they would at school. The missing words are to be taken from a given list. The context in which the Scrum terms are missing is the game scenario

	of the kitchen, i.e. the participants have to interpret the terms in the kitchen environment.
Task 7: Designing a user story	The testers should design a user story based on the given user story template for one of the dishes. This exercise aims to check the clarity and applicability of our template. It should be noted that the game does not yet have the possibility to record user stories. For this reason, the task aims to show to what extent the user story template can be used as a tool for formulating a user story.
Task 8: Reflection on the sprint	In this task, the testers should put themselves in the role of the players and imagine that they have completed a sprint. They should now reflect on this in retrospect. The white board tool "Hyperchalk", should be used for this purpose. The testers should now add a fictitious kitchen utensil there, which reflects the emotional situation during the fictitious past sprint.
Task 9: Final Question	The final question was for all participants to evaluate the prototype based on their experience by discussing whether the scenario in the kitchen was chosen sensibly; offering suggestions for improvement and justifying which soft skills were promoted by the game. The kitchen was chosen sensibly, offer suggestions for improvement and justify which soft skills were promoted by the game, and finally talk about whether the game added value for you and improved your understanding of Scrum. The purpose of these tasks is to review various aspects of ScrumSimPlan in terms of usability and to identify potential challenges.

Some of the five participants were criticizing game design decisions like the layout, in general or the size of the fonts or colors of icons. Moreover, they missed "back"- buttons, while they would have liked to change decisions. They liked being in a creative process via a kitchen scenario, also because it is familiar. In addition, the interviewees perceived the online whiteboard "Hyperchalk" as productive and entertaining. During the final question, all participants briefly shared their impressions of the game. They agreed that the cooking metaphor was an apt analogy to the Scrum framework. Even someone who had no prior knowledge found the retrospective helpful and could imagine applying it in different areas of life. Everyone appreciated the playful nature and praised the structure of the game. One participant emphasized that the game helped to make the theory of Scrum more tangible and thus contributed to a better understanding. The interviewees mentioned an easy accessibility of the learning objectives and game rules via the left sidebar as positively, which increases user-friendliness. When asked about the soft skills promoted, everyone mentioned teamwork and self-reflection through the getting-to-know-you game and the retrospective. Some also emphasized that the game also promotes conflict resolution and communication. Overall, the game was rated positively by the participants, although some interviewees made minor suggestions for improving usability in order to optimize the gaming experience. After the answers to the tasks, the final task was to fill out the User Experience Questionnaire (UEQ)[4]. This document lists the items and their order for all the available languages of the UEQ.

Table 2. User Experience Questionnaire (UEQ)

Negative Game Experience Items	Scale	Positive Game Experience Items
obstructive	o o o o o o o	supportive
complicated	o o o o o o o	easy
inefficient	o o o o o o o	efficient
confusing	o o o o o o o	clear
boring	o o o o o o o	exciting
not interesting	o o o o o o o	interesting
conventional	o o o o o o o	inventive
usual	o o o o o o o	leading edge

The free version of the *easyFeedback*- tool, shows only the individual and overall results views as a graph displaying the mean values of all five respondents. The graph shows bipolar terms on both axes, which represent the average rating of

[4] UEQ. https://www.ueq-online.org/

the aspects in the "ScrumSimPlan" game. The results of the UEQ were then evaluated using an Excel file provided, which visualizes the results of the various categories such as attractiveness and effectiveness in a bar chart. The mean values of the six different attributes are calculated from -3 to +3, whereby ratings below -1 are considered negative, between -1 and +1 as neutral and above +1 as positive. Furthermore, calculating the variance and standard deviation for each item to identify any possible deviations. The table shows that the standard deviation of the items is not particularly high, with item 19 having the highest deviation with a standard deviation of 2.3. This item deals with controllability and has a mean value of 1.6.

UEQ Scales (Mean and Variance)		
Attraktivität	↑ 1,967	0,38
Durchschaubarkeit	↑ 2,200	0,39
Effizienz	↑ 1,750	0,16
Steuerbarkeit	↑ 1,600	0,33
Stimulation	↑ 1,900	0,71
Originalität	↑ 2,250	0,16

Figure 14. Average values for the individual categories' attraction, transparency, efficiency, controllability, stimulation and originality.

The evaluation of the online planning game ScrumSimPlan was positive for all six categories of items with a mean value between 1.6 and 2.25. The evaluation of the UEQ shows that users overall rated the game well. The results of the remote usability tests and the UEQ questionnaire provide insights into the strengths and weaknesses of the online planning game "ScrumSimPlan", positive reception of the introduction and the quiz, but also identified usability problems such as the lack of a link to the Scrum Guide and the font size being too small. Enthusiasm was reported for robot avatar task, but difficulties in using it. The interviewees identified confusion about the meaning of the colors and problems with the missing back button. Positive ratings in the User Experience Questionnaire (UEQ) overall, but areas for improvement such as linking in the quiz, adjusting font size, optimizing the drag-and-drop system and adding back buttons were identified. It was perceived overall positively, but usability challenges should be addressed to optimize the player experience.

The game received positive feedback as well as suggestions from the participants concerning usability improvements. Participants found the structure and instructions in the game to be clear and understandable. Those without prior

knowledge expressed a desire for a link to the Scrum Guide. The avatar selection provided ample room for interpretation and fostered creativity, with the aspect of originality receiving high marks. However, they identified controllability as an area in need of improvement, and they recommended enlarging buttons and integrating options that are more accessible. Overall, the interviewees deemed the game attractive and clear, eliciting excitement and interest from participants. Seeing the efficiency of the game as well balanced. The game promoted future skills such as creativity, communication and critical thinking. The results of the remote usability test and the UEQ questionnaire revealed opportunities for optimizing user-friendliness.
In the evaluation of the online simulation game "ScrumSimPlan", the focus is on efficiency and effectiveness. The aim of the remote usability test is to check the game scenario, analyze user experiences and identify potential weaknesses. Positive feedback and constructive feedback provide a good basis for the further development of the game. Suggestions for improvement emphasize the importance of accessibility and user-friendliness. Future versions should focus on events and artifacts of the Scrum framework. The game has already delivered important learning objectives, but it needs further improvements to ensure an optimal user experience. Examples for improvement of usability problems were like larger buttons and larger fonts for digital accessibility.

The drag and drop fields in the get-to-know the participants game should be corrected. Still the question is, if drag and drop is accessible at all. Also game elements like sprint review and backlog refinement must be added to the game. Progress bars in percentage form and time boxes will increase the playfulness and competition will. After a full game implementation, using learning analytics to monitor learning success and identify any potential weaknesses among users is eventually useful.

10. Conclusion and Outlook

Time is money, one says. But one could also say *scrum is money*. Well on boarded employees can save money for an employer, by dealing with effective project management right from the beginning. The scrum framework works for simulation and new work – in a developing process made by students in a colloquium, planning a further development. Students, who become employees, will learn cheaper, easier and sustainable via multimedia game simulation – they will be more experienced and therefore it could be easier to integrate in the labor market with fewer gaps. This needs further scientific confirmation. Through the game, they could get a better understanding early on and better working results. The question of how to integrate the *ScrumSimPlan* simulation game effectively into university teaching is still unanswered. Possibilities for this include integrating the game into courses or classes that deal with topics such as Scrum, project management or agile software development. This also raises questions about the integration of *ScrumSimPlan* into examinations or the assessment of learning success. It would be interesting to explore how to utilize *ScrumSimPlan* to assess students' performance, enhancing their understanding of agile methods, bolstering their practical project management skills, and fostering future skills.

Simulation gaming can be a safe space, because students can make mistakes and reflect with few or less consequences in the real world or in a company. The idea of learning the agile project method scrum is to develop ideas for complex problems at student phase at university and later on, too. The blended learning method is well chosen, because it is more sustainable to learn in a synchronous and asynchronous way with the help of online and offline tools. Especially reviewing the working processes together is a relatively effective learning process especially for students in an early stage. Also having experienced diverse options, opinions and worshiping them is a gift for young adults. Diversity is not just a buzzword but must be lived and experienced as well as tested in a real situation to understand the benefits. A diverse, sensible agile game design for project management by also making it accessible: This could help employees and employers create a better and inclusive working environment. One should further explore the integration of ScrumSimPlan into university teaching to enhance the preparation of students for the job market.

Acknowledgments

Thanks to Prof. Dr. Detlef Krömker, Maria Ahmed, Eike Henrich (as well as the other students of the colloquium, blended seminar and of the evaluation) and Tornike Giorgashvili for your work and support.

About the Author

Linda Rustemeier is an eLearning expert and research assistant at Goethe University Frankfurt. She is doing her doctorate on diversity-sensitive learning games/serious games, game labs and game didactics. After several years at the

Innovation Center for Technology-Supported Learning at Goethe University Frankfurt, she joined the Institute for Didactics (of Mathematics and) Computer Science in May 2024 in the LeseKI:DS and GameLab project.

LinkedIn: linda-rustemeier-7b27bbbb
ORCID: https://orcid.org/0000-0002-5826-4557
Website: https://www.uni-frankfurt.de/122764309/Team

References

Abé, M. (2023). Sprint Retro: Was ist eine Sprint Retrospektive? https://www.agile-heroes.com/de/magazine/was-ist-eine-sprint-retrospektive/ (03.11.2023)

Abt, C. C. (1970): Serious Games. Viking, New York.

Achterbergh J., Vriens D. J. (2009). Organizations: social systems conducting experiments Routledge (406 pages): illustrations (2nd rev. ed.).

Ahmed, M. (2023). Development and usability optimization of a serious game in university teaching for the teaching of Scrum. Goethe University, Frankfurt. (Unpublished Master Thesis)

Arn, C. (2017). Agile Hochschuldidaktik (2.). Beltz Juventa Weinheim.

Astheimer, A.-K. (2021). „Erlernen des Scrum-Prozesses anhand eines Online-Planspiels". Goethe University Frankfurt (Unpublished Master Thesis).

Bergmann, F. (2004). Neue Arbeit, Neue Kultur. Arbor Verlag.

Bernhofer, A., & Wieland, E. (2018). Unterrichtsmodelle des Flipped Classroom für die Sing- und Musizierpraxis im Musikunterricht. In J. Buchner, C. F. Freisleben-Teutscher, J. Haag, & E. Rauscher (Eds.), Inverted Classroom—Vielfältiges Lernen (pp. 29–38). ikon Verlagsgesellschaft.

Bechdel, A., Wallace, L.: The Bechdel-Wallace Test. https://www.themarysue.com/bechdel-wallace-test-please-alison-bechdel/, 26.02.2024 and Bechdel-(Walace) Test.https://de.wikipedia.org/wiki/Bechdel-Test#cite_note-1 (24.10.2023)

Blötz, U.; Gust, M.; Klabbers, J.; Mandl, H.; Geier, B.; Hense, J. (2015). "Grundzüge einer Planspiel-Didaktik". In: Hrsg. von Ulrich Blötz. Planspiele und Serious Games in der beruflichen Bildung. Auswahl, Konzepte, Lernarrangements, Erfahrungen - Aktueller Katalog für Planspiele und Serious Games. Bielefeld. W. Bertelsmann Verlag GmbH & Co. KG, 2015, S. 13–70. isbn: 978-3-7639-1168-4 (eBook).

Bondarenko, A. (2022). How to Write a Good User Story: with Examples & Templates. https://stormotion.io/blog/how-to-write-a-good-user-story-with-examples-templates. (03.12.2023)

Bundeszentrale für politische Bildung. https://www.bpb.de/lernen/angebote/planspiele/266136/nachteile-und-vorteile-der-methode-planspiel/. (31.08.2023)

Calmano, C.; Serhani, K.; Herschbach, E. (2021). "ScrumSimPlan – Umsetzung eines Onlineplanspiel-Konzepts in einem SCRUM-Team". Goethe-University, Frankfurt (Unpublished Master Thesis)

Dämon, K. (2017). Agiles Arbeiten Wer nicht aufpasst, dem fliegt das Projekt um die Ohren (02. Juli 2017) in Wirtschaftswoche: https://www.wiwo.de/erfolg/management/agiles-arbeiten-wer-nicht-aufpasst-dem-fliegt-das-projekt-um-die-ohren/19988386.html (20.08.2023)

de Wijse-van Heeswijk, M. (2021). Ethics and the Simulation Facilitator: Taking your Professional Role Seriously. Simulation & Gaming, 52(3), 312-332. https://doi.org/10.1177/10468781211015707 (05.10.2023)

Digital.ai. 15th State of Agile Report 2021, Agile adoption accelerates across the enterprise. url. https://info.digital.ai/rs/981-LQX-968/images/SOA15.pdf (21.09.2023)

Dziuban, C., Graham, C.R., Moskal, P.D. et al. (2018). Blended learning: the new normal and emerging technologies. Int J Educ Technol High Educ 15, 3. https://doi.org/10.1186/s41239-017-0087-5 (06.10.2023)

Flanagan, M. (2009). Critical Play: Radical Game Design.The MIT Press.

FROG (2023). Rustemeier, L. Presentation video "Diversity-sensitive agile software development": https://www.youtube.com/watch?v=cKNvqIgSB9M. ; „FROG – Future and Reality of Gaming 2023" was funded by the Austrian Federal Chancellery (Sektion VI – Families and Youth) and was organized by the Center for Applied Game Studies (University for Continuing Education Krems). (05.02.2024)

Geurts J. L. A., Caluwé L. o. d., Stoppelenburg A. (2000). Changing organisations with gaming/simulations. 's-Gravenhage Amersfoort. Elsevier bedrijfsinformatie ;Twynstra Gudde.

Henrich, E. (2023). „Serious Games an Hochschulen – Entwicklung eines Planspiels und Bewertung des Einsatzes", Bachelorthesis, Frankfurt am Main: Goethe University, Frankfurt (Unpublished Master Thesis).

Hofmann, J., Piele, A., & Piele, C. (2019). New Work—Best Practices und Zukunftsmodelle. Fraunhofer-Institut für Arbeitswirtschaft und Organisation IAO.

Hughes G. J. (2013). The Routledge Guidebook to Aristotle's Nicomachean Ethics: Routledge.

Ivens, S; Kaiser, K. (2021). „Digitalisierung in Studium und Lehre gemeinsam gestalten. Innovative Formate, Strategien und Netzwerke" (Wiesbaden: Springer Fachmedien Wiesbaden), S.535, S544-545 DOI 10.1007/978-3-658-32849-8.

Kriz, W. "Planspiele als Trainingsmethode in der Hochschuldidaktik: Zur Funktion der Planspielleitung". In: Hrsg. von Maria Meßner, Michael Schedelik und Tim Engartner. Handbuch Planspiele in der sozialwissenschaftlichen Hochschullehre. Wochenschau Verlag, 2018, S. 43–56. ISBN: 978-3-7344-0644-7.

Lauzen, M. M. (2014): It's a Man's (Celluloid) World. On-Screen Representations of Female Characters in the Top 100 Films of 2014. (womenintvfilm.sdsu.edu PDF). (23.09.2023)

Mayer, R. E. (2009). Multimedia Learning (2nd ed.). New York: Cambridge University Press.

Morisse, K. (2022). Inverted Classroom trifft Scrum: https://hochschulforumdigitalisierung.de/de/blog/icm-scrum. (20.07.2023)

Nielsen, J. (1993). "Usability Engineering". Boston: Acad. Press.

Nielsen, J. (1994). 10 Usability Heuristics for User Interface Design. [Online]: https://www.nngroup.com/articles/ten-usability-heuristics/. (30.10.2023)

Nijher, S. S. (2022). "ScrumSimPlan als Educational Game gestalten ". Goethe University, Frankfurt (Unpublished Master thesis)

Olbert, S. et al. goetzpartners (2017). Agilität als Wettbewerbsvorteil- Der Agile Performer Index, online https://www.goetzpartners.com/uploads/tx_gp/2017_goetzpartners_Agile_Performer_Index.pdf. (21.08.2023)

Osmani, B.; Rosenberg,D. „ScrumSimPlan - Umsetzung eines Onlineplanspiel-Konzepts in einem SCRUM-Team. Darstellung von Verlauf, Evaluation und technischer Entwicklungs-Infrastruktur für ein erfolgreiches SCRUM-Projekt". Goethe-University Frankfurt (Unpublished Master Thesis).

Petrik, A; S. Rappenglück (2017). Handbuch Planspiele in der politischen Bildung. Verlag: Schwalbach/Ts.: Wochenschau Verlag, S. 155-156.

Schell, J. (2020) Die Kunst des Game Design: Bessere Games konzipieren. Mitp Verlag.

Schwaber, K.; Sutherland, J. (2020). Der Scrum Guide. Der gültige Leitfaden für Scrum: Die Spielregeln. Nov. 2020. url: https://scrumguides.org/docs/scrumguide/v2020/2020-Scrum-Guide-German.pdf (09. 09. 2023). Und Schwaber, K.; Sutherland, J. (2023). Scrum Guides. 2023. url: https://scrumguides.org (09.09.2023).

Stingeder, K. H. (2011). Critical Play: Radical Game Design by Mary Flanagan. Medienimpulse, 49(4). https://doi.org/10.21243/mi-04-11-25 (15.10.2023)

Rath, G. (2023). Diversity und New Work. In: Meister, J., Hörmeyer, M. (eds) Vielfalt in der öffentlichen Verwaltung. Springer Gabler, Wiesbaden. https://doi.org/10.1007/978-3-658-41702-4_13 (22.09.2023)

Rauschenberger, M.; Schrepp, M. & Thomaschewski, J.. (2013). User Experience mit Fragebögen messen – Durchführung und Auswertung am Beispiel des UEQ and https://user-experience-methods.com/05_evaluate/usability-test.html (05.11.2023).

Rehkopf, M. (>n.d.<) User Storys mit Beispielen und Vorlage. https://www.atlassian.com/de/agile/project-management/user-stories (30.11.2023)

Rustemeier, L.; Astheimer, A.-K.: Giorgashvili, T.; Voß-Nakkour, S. (2022). Experience Scrum! Agile Softwareentwicklung durchspielen. In: Alf, Tobias; Hahn, Simon; Zürn, Birgit; Trautwein, Friedrich (Hg.): Planspiele - Erkenntnisse aus Praxis und Forschung:

Rückblick auf den Deutschen Planspielpreis und das Europäische Planspielforum 2021: Norderstedt. Books on Demand (ZMS-Schriftenreihe), S. 47-61. ISBN 978-3-7568-3700-7.

Rustemeier L. Voß-Nakkour S., Mateen S., Hossain I. (2021) Creation and Future Development Process of a Serious Game. Raising Awareness of (Visual) Impairments. In: Fletcher B., Ma M., Göbel S., Baalsrud Hauge J., Marsh T. (eds) Serious Games. JCSG 2021. Lecture Notes in Computer Science, vol 12945. Springer, Cham. https://doi.org/10.1007/978-3-030-88272-3_10.

Mateen, S., Rustemeier, L., Voß-Nakkour, S., Grimminger, S., (2023). Game Accessibility: Konzeption eines barrierearmen Serious Games. DOI: https://doi.org/10.21248/gups.69163. In Voß-Nakkour, S., Rustemeier, L., Möhring, M. M., Deitmer, A., Grimminger, S. (Hrsg.) (2023). Digitale Barrierefreiheit in der Bildung weiter denken. Innovative Impulse aus Praxis, Technik und Didaktik. Universitätsbibliothek Johann Christian Senckenberg.

Voß-Nakkour, S.; Sacher, P.; Weiß, D.; Gattinger, T. (2020): LernBar 4.6. Barrierearme, für Learning Analytics optimierte Web Based Trainings. DELFI 2020 – Die 18. Fachtagung Bildungstechnologien der Gesellschaft für Informatik e.V.. Bonn: Gesellschaft für Informatik e.V., ISBN: 978-3-88579-702-9. pp. 383-384. Online. 14.-18. September 2020

Voß-Nakkour, S., Rustemeier, L., Möhring, M. M., Deitmer, A., Grimminger, S. (Hrsg.) (2023). Digitale Barrierefreiheit in der Bildung weiter denken. Innovative Impulse aus Praxis, Technik und Didaktik. Universitätsbibliothek Johann Christian Senckenberg.

Wake, B. (2017). INVEST in Good Stories, and SMART Tasks. https://xp123.com/invest-in-good-stories-and-smart-tasks/. (22.08.2023)

W.A. IJsselsteijn,de Kort, Y. A. W., & Poels, K. (2013). The Game Experience Questionnaire. Technische Universiteit Eindhoven.

THE MANY LUDONARRATIVE PROFESSIONS OF A LUDIFIED AND NARRATIFIED FUTURE SOCIETY

Pratama Wirya Atmaja, Sugiarto, Hendra Maulana, Dhian Satria Yudha Kartika, Yisti Vita Via

The uses of games have increasingly become ubiquitous, a phenomenon termed "cultural ludification." Simultaneously, we are witnessing the steady rise of the metaverse and "narratification" in various fields. Together, these trends show that our society is undergoing "ludonarratification" that may culminate in every activity becoming an "informative narrative game" or ING. Thus, game-related expertise and professions may eventually become essential, but in what ways? We answer this question by first defining INGs and how their multiverse and governance structure may "ludonarratify" a future society. We then review principles from various fields, including systems science and transdisciplinary projects, to theorize how current game-related professions, from developers to professional players, may evolve considerably to serve the multiverse. Additionally, we theorize new roles to handle the multiverse's metagame-based middle-level governance and meta-metagame-based top governance. We close this paper by outlining directions for future research, including AI's possible roles in the ludonarratified society.

Keywords: Ludification, narratification, informative narrative games, game-related professions

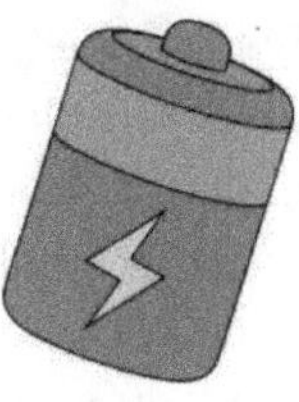

1. Introduction

"As a medium, games are peerless" will hardly be a controversial statement in the 21st century. Games are, after all, capable of so many things: providing virtual worlds to freely explore (Ekdahl & Ravn, 2022), presenting highly engaging narratives (Ip, 2011), challenging the player with complex problems (Denisova et al., 2020), sharpening sensorimotor faculties (Toth et al., 2021), and even invoking noble emotions such as eudaimonia (Daneels et al., 2021). This exceptional versatility birthed the game industry (Wijman, 2021), a behemoth supported by millions of loyal consumers (Zendle et al., 2023), headline-grabbing esports tournaments (Funk et al., 2018), state-of-the-art gaming technology (Reer et al., 2022)... and of course professionals from various disciplines.

These brave pillars of the game industry fit into one of the following categories. The first, game developers, is the liveliest, comprising content designers (Potanin & Davies, 2011), game assets creatives (Zyda, 2022), programmers (Liming & Vilorio, 2011), and various supporting roles. Meanwhile, the second category of professionals develops not the end products but their platforms or infrastructure, including game devices and game engines (Toftedahl & Engström, 2019). Even more indirectly related to game production, the next category is nevertheless essential: game journalists (G. P. Perreault & Perreault, 2021), game scholars (Klabbers, 2018; Stenros & Kultima, 2018), and other cultural and evaluative roles. Lastly, esports athletes exemplify emerging professional game operators (Larsen, 2022).

Due to games' inherent cross-disciplinarity (Klabbers, 2018), each category may vary considerably practice-wise. For example, there are many ways for game developers to integrate the creative and the technical (Keogh & Hardwick, 2023). Although it has led to a myriad of problems unseen in traditional software development (Politowski et al., 2021), it has also prevented the industry from being one boring monolith. Indeed, it is a colorful collection of global and local cultures (Keogh, 2021), which include ecosystems for independent and smaller game production (Parker et al., 2018), oftentimes a champion of non-mainstream gaming tastes (M. F. Perreault et al., 2022).

Still, this landscape is steadily changing. Eschewing pure hedonism, serious games have become widespread in education (Cole et al., 2023), medical treatments (Hooker & Karnes, 2022), and other fields (Laamarti et al., 2014). Similarly, people increasingly turn mundane activities gameful, i.e., gamification

(Krath et al., 2021). In short, games and their components are becoming more ubiquitous, something that has been termed "cultural ludification" (Karhulahti, 2015). The phenomenon's plausibility owes to the fact that games are a subtype of "rituals": rule- and goal-specific sequences of interpersonal actions that form the basis of society (Gazzard & Peacock, 2011). Furthermore, running parallel with this mass ludification is the "narratification" of everyday events, as seen in journalism (van Krieken & Sanders, 2021), science communication (Raile et al., 2022), and others. Both trends have coalesced into the concept of a metaverse, an all-encompassing, virtual, and "ludonarrative" reality (Dwivedi et al., 2022).

What may game-related professions look like in a hypothetical future that has undergone full "ludonarratification"? To illuminate this problem space, we theorize the answers to these more concrete questions: (1) what societal changes facilitate ludonarratification, (2) what new ludonarrative professions will emerge alongside the societal changes, and (3) what old game-related professions will remain relevant, and what evolutions will they undergo. Due to the vast problem space, we support our theorization with a cross-disciplinary and explorative literature review (Berry, 2011; Breslin & Gatrell, 2023).

2. From Current Society to A Fully Ludonarratified One

To answer our first question, we will first describe *informative narrative games* (INGs), the kind most capable of ludonarratification. Afterward, we propose the required societal changes for INGs to ludonarratify not only our daily activities but also the whole social reality. We base these changes on our proposal of a three-dimensional model of ludonarratification, as seen in Figure 1.

2.1 The Right Game for a Ludonarratified Society

Not all games are equal. For example, although games intersect with rituals, only pretense or role-playing games significantly feel ritual-like (Harviainen & Lieberoth, 2012). Thus, we will theorize the basic ludonarrative aspects of games before describing why and how INGs optimize these aspects.

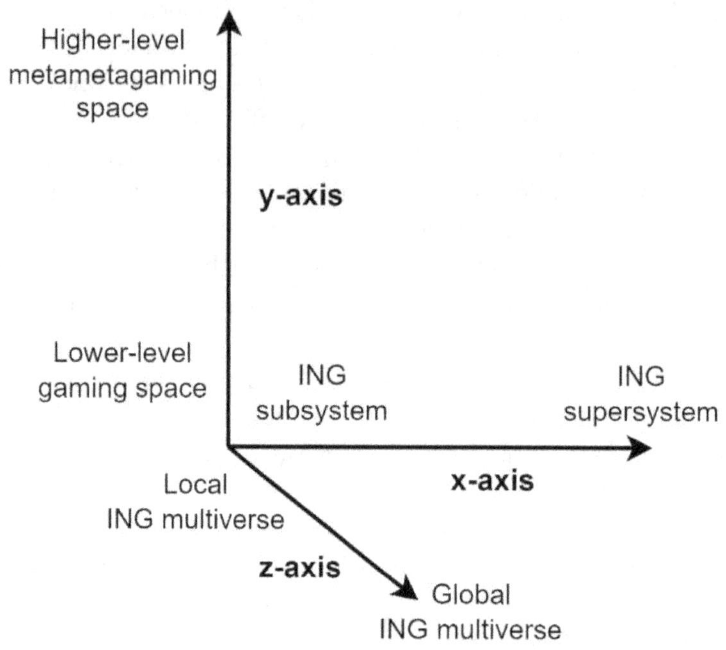

Figure 1. A three-dimensional model of ludonarratification

We base the aspects on our "information, narrative, and interactivity" model (Atmaja & Sugiarto, 2022), which explains how games or similar media, such as interactive digital narratives (IDNs), mediate our relationship with reality by accommodating our cognitive, affective, and sensorimotor learning domains (Dettmer, 2005). First, every game represents or simulates a part of reality through its mechanics (Wardaszko, 2018); this is the "information" aspect. However, not all game mechanics are deeply rooted in reality; many only crudely imitate natural or social processes. Likewise, every game inherently tells a story, yet many do so only implicitly, limiting the story's affective impact (Cardona-Rivera et al., 2023). Lastly, although we cannot have a game without user interfaces (UIs) and presentation assets, these interactivity components do not always align with the player's sensorimotor needs (Abtahi et al., 2022).

We call a game that balances and optimizes all three aspects an ING. It achieves so by first modeling the world's systemic complexity as its mechanics. Such a complex system comprises dynamically interacting entities (Ding et al., 2018), which exhibit intricate patterns like non-linearity, multicausality, emergence, and indetermination (Knoller et al., 2021). How closely the model must resemble the actual system depends on the cognitive needs of the player (Simons, 2008). For example, policymakers may only want to understand the system in a general sense (Sterman, 2018), thus requiring the system to undergo a significant "complexity reduction" (Wardaszko, 2018).

An ING's narrative aspect delivers the system model to the player through storytelling methods regarding the whole story and individual events (Ip, 2011). These methods aim to not only create an engaging experience but also cultivate complex emotions, such as eudaimonia and those toward the climate crisis (Daneels et al., 2021; Pihkala, 2022). Meanwhile, the interactivity aspect delivers multimodal presentation assets and user interfaces to accommodate and sharpen the player's sensorimotor faculty (Toth et al., 2021), especially in dealing with the system's bewildering complexity. To that end, the delivery pays attention to the appropriate "fidelity"; for example, depending on the gaming context, realistic visuals may or may not motivate the player (Lukosch et al., 2018).

2.2 The X-Axis: ING Systems, Supersystems, and Universe

We will now explain how INGs can ludonarratify social fabric, starting from Figure 1's x-axis. Our physical, biological, and social realities are a vast hierarchy of subsystems, systems, and supersystems (Wu, 2013). INGs of the hypothetical future capture this complexity by forming an intricate "universe" of ludonarrative systems, encompassing everything from individual micro-activities to planet-level aggregate processes and beyond.

The phenomenon of "game supersystems," where a group of games nests inside and feeds into a much larger game (Hemmingsen, 2023), is not new. Such "supergames" include contemporary megagames, typically employed by tens to hundreds of players to simulate a complex issue (Johansson et al., 2023). What separates the future ING universe from megagames, besides their massive difference in size, is their subsystems: the latter's subgames are often uninteresting or insufficient by themselves, which contrasts with individual INGs, each of which already possesses high-quality information, narrative, and interactivity aspects. In this regard, the ING universe intersects conceptually with transmedia storytelling, which comprises stand-alone media that form a complex narrative mosaic within a storyworld (Moloney & Unger, 2014). Today's metaverse also aims for this organic complexity by uniting "subuniverses" with distinct purposes and identities under one banner (Yang, 2023).

2.3 The Z-Axis: A Multiverse of INGs

An unfortunate fact will persist: thoroughly comprehending complexity is impossible (Dörner & Funke, 2017). No matter how big of a technological leap the ludonarratified future makes, its INGs can never perfectly simulate reality. Any simulation can only interpret the actual system from a specific perspective (Wardaszko, 2018); consequently, ludonarratification may have to involve multiple ING universes, each employing a different "framing" of reality (Nygren et al., 2022).

Figure 1's z-axis represents this ludonarrative "multiverse". Besides representing complex reality more accurately than any single ING universe can, its parallel universes accommodate the diverse needs of players and leave no one marginalized, something envisioned by multiperspectivity and polyvocality (Hanna, 2022). To that end, some universes vary slightly, i.e., they possess variants of essentially the same INGs, while others diverge quite radically. These differences can manifest at various systemic levels: top-level supersystems, atomic INGs, and even ING aspects. Regarding the information aspect, approaching the same complex issue from multiple viewpoints yields models of the issue's possible spatiotemporal states (Steegen et al., 2016). Likewise, the same model of reality can be told through contesting narrative framings, each serving a specific interest by emphasizing some elements of the model and de-emphasizing others (Baker, 2019).

2.4 The Y-Axis: Hierarchical Gaming Spaces

Even a multitude of planet-scale games cannot guarantee stable ludonarratification. People's ludonarrative aspirations ebb and flow, requiring their gaming arrangements to continuously evolve. The essential mechanism of this evolution, shown in Figure 1's y-axis, is metagaming (Boluk & LeMieux, 2017). Through activities like information sharing and strategizing (Kahila et al., 2023), players negotiate the game's rules or their ways of playing, often according to criteria that are not (directly) related to the game (Hemmingsen, 2023), such as sportsmanship and viewership.

Technically, a "meta-ING" is a form of ING with information, narrative, and interactivity aspects. More specifically, it is a *multiversal supersystem* of INGs from different universes. This way, the meta-ING provides common ground on which its multi-universe subsystems interact productively amidst the tension among them. Metagaming as a means of peacemaking or harmonization has its roots in fields beyond games, including game theory and its extension, drama theory (Bryant, 2021), both of which recognize the emotional and conflict-laden interactions between a metagame's actors, in contrast to more logical ones between a game's players (Klein, 2000). Additionally, policy studies researchers have theorized contesting systems, such as multi-universe INGs, as an "ecology of games" in search of a governing metagame (Berardo & Lubell, 2019).

Yet, this governance function does not stop at the metagaming level. A "meta-meta-ING" goes further by mobilizing efforts for a more fundamental problem: "what game to play" instead of "how to play the game" (Neller, 2019). For this purpose, its subsystems are meta-INGs (Boluk & LeMieux, 2017), encompassing a much larger multiversal space than any single meta-ING can. As a whole, the hierarchy of gaming, metagaming, and meta-metagaming helps establish a democratic yet orderly society (Pies et al., 2010), in which the flow of change traverses smoothly between micro, meso, and macro levels (Dopfer et al., 2004).

3. Ludonarrative Professions in the Future

For our second and third questions, we will theorize categories of future professions supporting INGs and their three-dimensional mechanism of ludonarratification. Following the introduction section, we will start with development-related professions and end with operational ones.

3.1 ING Content Creators

Professions in this category align with current game developers, with two main differences. First, due to aiming for ludonarratification, the work of ING content creators encompasses every facet of life; thus, their artistic scope far exceeds that of current game developers anywhere (Keogh, 2021), including those specializing in non-mainstream games (M. F. Perreault et al., 2022). Second, ING content creators are also significantly more specialized. Depending on one's expertise and interests, one can handle specific ING artifacts: an atomic ING, one of its aspects, an aspect of a supersystem, the whole supersystem, etc., effectively blurring the line between "major" and "indie" creators (Parker et al., 2018). One may also focus on one or several production methods, such as original creation, recombination, and modification, the last one legitimizing the practice of modding (Pereira & Bernardes, 2022). Regardless of their career choice, an ING content creator has little worry about whether their works can interact usefully with other artifacts. Thanks to the ING multiverse's organic complexity, we can more or less "plug and play" the artifacts: an atomic ING plugging into a supersystem, its information module staying intact while connecting to a new narrative module, and many other possibilities.

The skill sets of such extraordinarily versatile creators expand upon current development expertise for games and IDNs: ideation, rules design, narrative writing, virtual space planning, interactivity design, etc. (Koenitz et al., 2021; Liming & Vilorio, 2011; Zyda, 2022). Primarily, this expansion aims to correct two weaknesses: (1) lack of formalization, and (2) lack of artistic richness. The first prohibits INGs and their aspects from straightforwardly interacting, while the second severely limits ludonarratification's scope. Current game developers are torn between formalization for efficiency and artistic freedom for quality (Berg Marklund et al., 2019), a problem stemming from the tension between engineering and humanities approaches to game development (Engström et al., 2018). The first weakness's remedy is solidifying systems thinking and a systems-minded vocabulary as a foundation for inter-creator communication and collaboration (Atmaja & Sugiarto, 2022). Indeed, systems modeling increasingly crosses boundaries between disciplines (Cabot & Vallecillo, 2022), helping their vocabularies, practices, and orders of worth converge (Tharchen et al., 2020). One existing example of an ING-related system model concerns *data storytelling*, an intersection between data science, narratology, and HCI that delivers raw data as a narrative through interactive means (El Outa et al., 2022). Such models can help current development-related professions transition into ING aspect specialists: the mechanic designer handling the information aspect's systemic rules, graphic artists contributing assets to the interactivity aspect, etc.

Meanwhile, overcoming the second weakness requires content creators to fully embrace complexity in their artistic endeavors. It entails comprehending and working transdisciplinarily, a requirement for solving complex issues (Lehtonen et al., 2018). The development model of contemporary serious games and IDNs illustrates such transdisciplinary teamwork (Agusdinata & Lukosch, 2019; Atmaja & Sugiarto, 2022). A subject expert, such as a climate scientist, collaborates with a game developer, an HCI expert, a narrative author, an educator, a cognitive scientist, and other professionals to assemble a serious game or IDN on a complex issue for a specific audience with specific learning needs. Within the co-creation process, the actors gather and apply various state-of-the-art principles such as *predictive processing*, which posits that the human brain seeks to minimize "prediction errors" in our sensory perception, thinking, and actions, including during game-playing (Deterding et al., 2022).

3.2 ING Infrastructure Builders

This category concerns the massive IT infrastructure on which the vast array of ING contents runs. We will discuss parts of the infrastructure directly related to INGs, including software and hardware for ING operation and standards for interactions between INGs.

Game engines constitute the main software for game content execution (Toftedahl & Engström, 2019). Traditionally built in-house, publicly available general-purpose engines such as Unity and Unreal have rapidly risen to prominence. Their power and versatility are such that they have found uses beyond games, such as for agent-based simulations (Marín-Lora et al., 2020), construction projects (Ezzeddine & García de Soto, 2021), and the metaverse (Jungherr & Schlarb, 2022); thus, it is easy to imagine such engines in the service of future ludonarratification. Besides these engines, special-purpose ones are available for developers who wish to speed up their production processes (Toftedahl & Engström, 2019). Popular special-purpose game engines include RPG Maker for the role-playing genre and Twine for HTML-style narrative games (Toftedahl & Engström, 2019), while Mozilla Hubs and various others represent engines specifically for the metaverse (Cheng et al., 2022). Additionally, some specialized engines like uAdventure run on top of general-purpose ones like Unity (Pérez-Colado et al., 2019).

Engines for INGs may work similarly. First, some future infrastructure builders handle the general engine for the ING multiverse's entities, rules, and other basic systemic components. Then, other builders stack, on top of this bottommost layer, additional engines for specific ING aspects, whose interactions follow a specific architecture akin to the data storytelling one (El Outa et al., 2022). Another layer hosts even more specialized engines for specific genres, particularly complexity-minded ones such as social simulation games (Johnson-Bey et al., 2022).

On the hardware side, most devices with which to ludonarratify our daily lives may be ubiquitous (K. Li et al., 2023). These devices, distributed strategically around us, can attune to our needs to dynamically and seamlessly deliver ING experiences (Lyytinen & Yoo, 2002). They can also work in unison while maintaining some independence from each other, meaning each can undergo modifications without disrupting the others (Friedewald & Raabe, 2011), which is a sign of organic complexity. Functionally, some of these devices may mirror current gaming machines by hosting ING engines (Cai et al., 2022); some others will act as UIs; and the rest will consist of IoT devices, including those capable of physical manipulation, such as for construction work and object fabrication (Ezzeddine & García de Soto, 2021; Turakhia et al., 2022).

Besides extended reality (XR) devices for the metaverse (Reer et al., 2022), many innovative UIs have become available. Tangible artifacts-enhanced UIs significantly expand the game's sensorimotor appeal (Echeverri & Wei, 2023). Playful wearables support hybrid interactions while improving the user's appearance (Buruk et al., 2021). At the forefront of technological sophistication, brain-computer interfaces allow for more intimate player-game relationships (Zioga et al., 2018). In the ludonarratified future, all these UIs and many more jointly accommodate the holy grail: "holistically embodied interaction," where the UI and the user's sensorimotor faculty become one (Höök et al., 2021).

Overall, this immense variety of software and hardware invites ING infrastructure builders to specialize and collaborate in ways we have never seen. However, similar to the metaverse (T. Li et al., 2023; Yang, 2023), this collaboration will depend on system interoperability standards, which will be the critical glue between INGs of the same systemic level, between INGs and their supersystem, and, most importantly, between cross-universe INGs. Due to this requirement, establishing and maintaining the standards will be a multiversal effort between infrastructure builders and other stakeholders.

3.3 ING Operators

Similar to ING content creators, this class of profession enables a wide variety of operational specializations, e.g., operators that exclusively play in classrooms to support in-class game-based learning (Baalsrud Hauge et al., 2021). An ING operator may also specialize in specific combinations of information, narrative, and interactivity, e.g., an operator specializing in the pair of a complex world model and colorful UIs, such as in sustainability games for the general public (Johansson et al., 2023).

A dedicated ING operator is armed with knowledge and skills related to INGs, their operation, and their infrastructure. These components align with current esports competencies: physical, sensorimotor, strategic-cognitive, mental-emotional, social, metagaming, UI-related, game content-related, and game system-related (Larsen, 2022; Nagorsky & Wiemeyer, 2020). Yet, how do ING operators compare with current esports players in terms of these competencies? Firstly, they both possess general and specific knowledge and skills related to their media and their specialties. An example of general knowledge concerns INGs' three aspects, which are to ING operators what game objects, game rules, and UIs are to esports players (Larsen, 2022). Where they differ is in the expected level of their competencies. While esports athletes cultivate idiosyncratic mastery of a game, which can be "patched out" at the whim of the game's developer (Kokkinakis et al., 2021), the relationship between an ING and its operators is much more systematic and scientific, thus much more stable. While esports athletes hunt for the most accurate and precise mouse (Conroy et al., 2022), ING operators ponder how to synergize their entire body with the UI (Höök et al., 2021). While esports athletes are content with discovering, implementing, and propagating winning strategies for their audience's amusement (Kokkinakis et al., 2021), ING operators juggle many operational goals and constraints, some clashing with each other, to keep their ludonarratified society running.

Due to the complexity of their knowledge and skill set, ING operators must undergo formal learning and rigorous training. In contrast, current esports athletes develop their know-how mostly informally out of preference or necessity (Meng-Lewis et al., 2022). Although education and disciplined training for esports athletes, such as through scholastic programs (Williams, 2020), have gained traction, they are still far from being systematic (Chang et al., 2024); at best, current scholastic esports serves as a "trojan horse" for traditional subjects like STEM (Steinkuehler et al., 2023). For esports athletes to reach the caliber of ING operators, their career development must evolve into a self-sufficient field worthy of structured support from health organizations, the government, and other pillars of society (Hong, 2023). The result of this legitimacy will be a sustainable operational ecosystem centering around professionals with excellent work-life balance and long-term motivations, i.e., beyond simply loving the game (Bányai et al., 2020; Nyström et al., 2022).

3.4 Meta-ING Facilitators

As previously discussed, a dedicated facilitator of a meta-ING is tasked with harmonizing its multi-universe subgames, particularly those with conflicting goals. For this reason, their most crucial role resembles the "peace mediator" in a *Diplomacy*-like game (Mattlin, 2018), striving to keep the subgames' operators from taking their disputes "out of the game" into the real world. Additionally, the facilitator wears the hat of the mere "mediator" at other times to help broker agreements between orthogonal, instead of opposite, INGs like "community service" and "physical exercise."

Metagaming is already an established part of the gaming culture (Boluk & LeMieux, 2017). Although every gaming activity involves metagaming of some sort, its most advanced form is seen in esports. First, players compete, discover new strategies, and propagate them through various channels (Thaicharoen et al., 2023) in immediate and long-term contexts (Donaldson, 2016). Second, event organizers alter the game as part of their events, such as by enforcing new tournament rules. Third, spectators, commentators, and journalists steer the metagame indirectly through their appreciation of spectacular game-playing feats (Cauteruccio & Kou, 2023; G. P. Perreault & Perreault, 2021). Lastly, the game developer, or sometimes unlicensed modders, keeps the game from going stale by reinvigorating its metagame through patches. Together, these parties co-evolve the game in a continuous metagame cycle (Kokkinakis et al., 2021).

Despite this apparent maturity, esports metagaming is still largely informal. Unlike simple metrics like the "winning rate" (Kokkinakis et al., 2021), essential criteria like "fairness" are negotiated vaguely among players and other stakeholders in the metagame cycle (Johnson & Abarbanel, 2022). Rectifying this chronic vagueness has been elusive due to the fragmentation of the esports ecosystem, which hinders governance and renders the ecosystem fragile (Nyström et al., 2022). In contrast, ludonarratification legitimizes metagames by formalizing their criteria as games in their own right, i.e., multi-universe INGs. This gamification, already emerging on platforms such as Twitch (Qian et al., 2023), can both quantify and delegate the criteria to various actors across society, somewhat in the manner of gamified e-governance (Hassan & Hamari, 2020). Indeed, this grassroots and stakeholder-driven governance model accommodates the fragmented nature of esports better than more traditional governance (Kelly et al., 2022; Nyström et al., 2022). It is then the responsibility of "metagame facilitators" to coordinate the games to advance their metagame state.

These crucial facilitators intersect with current game facilitators, who possess interpersonal, management, context comprehension, and personal competencies (Baalsrud Hauge et al., 2021). First and foremost, such a facilitator understands the game, its metagame context, its players, and how to mobilize said players to productively engage with the game, such as to support their learning, where the metagame state reflects their comprehension level. To that end, the facilitator ensures that (1) through briefing, the players enter the game well-informed of the metagame state, (2) through debriefing, they exit the game ready to advance the state, and (3) through analysis of various factors, how best to advance the metagame state, including by modifying the game's rules, is known (Klabbers,

2018; Kortmann & Peters, 2021). Sometimes, the players may also wish to move between different activities within the metagame under the facilitator's guidance. An example of this phenomenon is the Honeypot Model, where a person who encounters a public interactive system switches between "interaction zones" to become a passer-by, bystander, audience member, or participant (Wouters et al., 2016).

In addition to those competencies, metagame facilitators are adept at coordinating games and integrating their results, drawing upon the skill set of "integration and implementation experts" from today's transdisciplinary projects (Bammer et al., 2020). These experts serve such a project by coordinating it, maintaining collaboration between its main actors, and integrating their results into the end product. The potential conflicts between the actors call for expertise in conflict resolution, whose methods revolve around nurturing metacognition (Ku & Ho, 2010). Metacognitive assessments of a conflict lead to a clearer view of its tangled web of factors (Rollwage et al., 2018), resulting in incremental cohesion and synergy (Auerbach, 2009). Since metacognition heavily drains cognitive capacity (Norman, 2020), entrusting its facilitation to metagame facilitators is reasonable, doubly so in the context of planet-wide ludonarratification.

3.5 Meta-meta-ING Facilitators

This profession manages meta-meta-INGs as nexus points of meta-INGs from across the future society. Within "meta-meta-ING cycles," they mediate the tension between meta-INGs hosting a diverse collection of INGs, some of which do not share anything operation-wise. Meta-meta-ING facilitators achieve this goal primarily by being "facilitators of facilitators," assisting meta-ING facilitators in optimizing their meta-ING cycles, including by adjusting the rules of the meta-INGs. Such adjustments flow downward to modify each meta-ING's INGs, sometimes so substantially as to virtually replace the INGs.

Meta-metagaming is a curious topic within today's games scholarship and gaming culture. Although professional and amateur game designers often explore novel game rules and even game genres (Jagoda, 2020), they seldom systematically plan the resulting metagames, especially as part of a meta-metagame (Boluk & LeMieux, 2017). Consequently, "meta-metagame facilitators" are still a purely speculative role. That being said, some existing professions do wrestle with "what game to play" and other philosophical problems, the most notable being scholars of game studies and game science

(Klabbers, 2018; Stenros & Kultima, 2018). By following these scholars' footsteps, meta-meta-ING facilitators may materialize in a ludonarratified world to handle its top-level governance. Reflecting on the engineering-arts dichotomy problem in game development (Engström et al., 2018), these professionals must equally be experts in two contrasting yet complementary issues: (1) grounding the philosophy of science, science, and application of INGs (Klabbers, 2018), and (2) recognizing the rich diversity of ING cultures and fostering their collaboration (Stenros & Kultima, 2018). This expertise allows meta-meta-ING facilitators to mobilize the entire ludonarratified society to engage in collective "rule finding" (Pies et al., 2010), treating INGs not just as "problem solvers" but also as "problem makers" through which we expand our limits (Jagoda, 2020).

4. Conclusion

We have theoretically explored one possible evolution path for current game-related professions following the ludification and narratification of society, which may transform every activity into an "informative narrative game" or ING, much like what the metaverse aspires to achieve (Dwivedi et al., 2022). We have based our theorization on a literature review covering many relevant fields, including game development, serious games, esports, and systems science. These contemporary professions, including game designers and esports athletes, may have future counterparts that far surpass them in knowledge, skills, and work ethics. On the other hand, the immense complexity of a society-wide ING network and its governance also necessitates some new professions, which may be rooted in today's transdisciplinary endeavors in games and beyond.

Among many possible future scenarios, ours tells an idealized trajectory of games, where their steady growth culminates in a utopia. Other game-related scenarios may be more dystopian, casting games and gamification as mere authoritarian shackles (Boland, 2024). Regardless of such contrasting scenarios, ours integrates principles from various bodies of knowledge into a coherent whole, making it plausible and thus worth preparing for.

We leave many things related to ludonarratification and its professions for future research. Among these is the full extent of ludonarratification itself: if it does gamify and narratify every activity, then it should include the creation of INGs and their infrastructure. What may the "ING of ING creation" look like, and does this ING require "out-of-game" maintenance? Another thing worthy of deeper inquiry is the hierarchy of gaming space. Although we have assumed meta-

metagaming as the top-level governance in a ludonarratified society, it may not be the highest that the society can or needs to reach, especially since our brain is capable of meta-meta-metacognition (Recht et al., 2022).

Finally, the roles of AI in the ludonarratified future are an exciting and timely topic. Currently, advancements in AI have opened up possibilities for AI to be a co-creator (Mirowski et al., 2023), although challenges regarding trust in AI have hindered this approach's realization (Saßmannshausen et al., 2022). Assuming that the ludonarratified society successfully solves this trustworthiness problem, how may AI serve ludonarratification? Will AI replace humans in some ING-related professions? What human-AI teamwork patterns may emerge among the professions?

About the Authors

Pratama Wirya Atmaja is a lecturer in the Digital Business Program at the University of Pembangunan Nasional (UPN) "Veteran" Jawa Timur, Indonesia, with a background in games and software engineering. His research focuses on educational games, interactive digital narratives, and gamification. He has been a member of ARDIN (Association for Research in Digital Interactive Narratives) and COST Action INDCOR (Interactive Narrative Design for Complexity Representations) since 2022. Within UPN "Veteran" Jawa Timur, he leads the "Game" research group and is a member of the Digital Business Program's "Appropriate Immersive Technology for SMEs" research unit.

X: @pratamawirya
LinkedIn: pratama-atmaja-2ab451174

Sugiarto is a lecturer in the Digital Business Program at the UPN "Veteran" Jawa Timur. His expertise lies in software development, database development research, and digital entrepreneurship development. His evolving research focus centers around software development for marketing and product development of SMEs and local communities. He currently leads the "Appropriate Immersive Technology for SMEs" research unit, whose roadmap focuses on the metaverse as a powerful yet economical solution for local SMEs.

Hendra Maulana is a lecturer in the Digital Business Program at the UPN "Veteran" Jawa Timur. He has expertise in software engineering, digital image processing, the Internet of Things (IoT), and digital business. He researches hardware and software for agriculture, tourism, and SMEs, especially as a member of the "Appropriate Immersive Technology for SMEs" research unit.

Dhian Satria Yudha Kartika is a lecturer in the Digital Business Program at the UPN "Veteran" Jawa Timur. His expertise lies in data mining, image processing, software engineering, and digital business. As a member of the "Appropriate Immersive Technology for SMEs" research unit, he specializes in supporting SDGs through local smart farming.

Yisti Vita Via is a lecturer in the Informatics Program at the UPN "Veteran" Jawa Timur. Her research interests include nature-inspired optimization algorithms for intelligent systems, including metaverse-based ones.

References

Abtahi, P., Hough, S. Q., Landay, J. A., & Follmer, S. (2022). Beyond Being Real: A Sensorimotor Control Perspective on Interactions in Virtual Reality. *CHI '22: Proceedings of the 2022 CHI Conference on Human Factors in Computing Systems*, 1–17. https://doi.org/10.1145/3491102.3517706

Agusdinata, D. B., & Lukosch, H. (2019). Supporting Interventions to Reduce Household Greenhouse Gas Emissions: A Transdisciplinary Role-Playing Game Development. *Simulation & Gaming, 50*(3), 359–376. https://doi.org/10.1177/1046878119848135

Atmaja, P. W., & Sugiarto. (2022). When Information, Narrative, and Interactivity Join Forces: Designing and Co-designing Interactive Digital Narratives for Complex Issues. In *Interactive Storytelling. ICIDS 2022. LNCS, vol. 13762* (pp. 329–351). https://doi.org/10.1007/978-3-031-22298-6_20

Auerbach, Y. (2009). The Reconciliation Pyramid-A Narrative-Based Framework for Analyzing Identity Conflicts. *Political Psychology, 30*(2), 291–318. https://doi.org/10.1111/j.1467-9221.2008.00692.x

Baalsrud Hauge, J., Söbke, H., Bröker, T., Lim, T., Luccini, A. M., Kornevs, M., & Meijer, S. (2021). Current Competencies of Game Facilitators and Their Potential Optimization in Higher Education: Multimethod Study. *JMIR Serious Games, 9*(2), e25481. https://doi.org/10.2196/25481

Baker, M. (2019). Reframing Conflict in Translation. In *Researching Translation in the Age of Technology and Global Conflict: Selected Works of Mona Baker* (pp. 111–129). Routledge.

Bammer, G., O'Rourke, M., O'Connell, D., Neuhauser, L., Midgley, G., Klein, J. T., Grigg, N. J., Gadlin, H., Elsum, I. R., Bursztyn, M., Fulton, E. A., Pohl, C., Smithson, M., Vilsmaier, U., Bergmann, M., Jaeger, J., Merkx, F., Vienni Baptista, B., Burgman, M. A., … Richardson, G. P. (2020). Expertise in research integration and implementation for tackling complex problems: when is it needed, where can it be found and how can it be strengthened? *Palgrave Communications, 6*(1). https://doi.org/10.1057/s41599-019-0380-0

Bányai, F., Zsila, Á., Griffiths, M. D., Demetrovics, Z., & Király, O. (2020). Career as a Professional Gamer: Gaming Motives as Predictors of Career Plans to Become a Professional Esport Player. *Frontiers in Psychology, 11*. https://doi.org/10.3389/fpsyg.2020.01866

Berardo, R., & Lubell, M. (2019). The Ecology of Games as a Theory of Polycentricity: Recent Advances and Future Challenges. *Policy Studies Journal, 47*(1), 6–26. https://doi.org/10.1111/psj.12313

Berg Marklund, B., Engström, H., Hellkvist, M., & Backlund, P. (2019). What Empirically Based Research Tells Us About Game Development. *The Computer Games Journal, 8*(3–4), 179–198. https://doi.org/10.1007/s40869-019-00085-1

Berry, G. R. (2011). A cross-disciplinary literature review: Examining trust on virtual teams. *Performance Improvement Quarterly, 24*(3), 9–28. https://doi.org/10.1002/piq.20116

Boland, T. (2024). Dystopian Games: Diagnosing Modernity as the Scene of Tests, Trials and Transformations. *Cultural Sociology, 18*(1), 72–90. https://doi.org/10.1177/17499755221143835

Boluk, S., & LeMieux, P. (2017). *Metagaming: Playing, Competing, Spectating, Cheating, Trading, Making, and Breaking Videogames*. University of Minnesota Press. https://doi.org/10.5749/j.ctt1n2ttjx

Breslin, D., & Gatrell, C. (2023). Theorizing Through Literature Reviews: The Miner-Prospector Continuum. *Organizational Research Methods, 26*(1), 139–167. https://doi.org/10.1177/1094428120943288

Bryant, J. (2021). From Game Theory to Drama Theory. In *Handbook of Group Decision and Negotiation* (pp. 485–504). Springer International Publishing. https://doi.org/10.1007/978-3-030-49629-6_14

Buruk, O. "Oz," Salminen, M., Xi, N., Nummenmaa, T., & Hamari, J. (2021). Towards the Next Generation of Gaming Wearables. *CHI '21: Proceedings of the 2021 CHI Conference on Human Factors in Computing Systems*, 1–15. https://doi.org/10.1145/3411764.3445785

Cabot, J., & Vallecillo, A. (2022). Modeling should be an independent scientific discipline. *Software and Systems Modeling, 21*(6), 2101–2107. https://doi.org/10.1007/s10270-022-01035-8

Cai, X., Cebollada, J., & Cortiñas, M. (2022). From traditional gaming to mobile gaming: Video game players' switching behaviour. *Entertainment Computing, 40*, 100445. https://doi.org/10.1016/j.entcom.2021.100445

Cardona-Rivera, R. E., Zagal, J. P., & Debus, M. S. (2023). Aligning story and gameplay through narrative goals. *Entertainment Computing*. https://doi.org/10.1016/j.entcom.2023.100577

Cauteruccio, F., & Kou, Y. (2023). Investigating the emotional experiences in eSports spectatorship: The case of League of Legends. *Information Processing & Management, 60*(6), 103516. https://doi.org/10.1016/j.ipm.2023.103516

Chang, Y. K., Chen, K., & Li, Z. (2024). Systematic Framework for Esports Training: Informing eSports Training with the Learning Sciences. *Simulation & Gaming, 55*(1), 82–108. https://doi.org/10.1177/10468781231219938

Cheng, R., Wu, N., Varvello, M., Chen, S., & Han, B. (2022). Are we ready for metaverse?: a measurement study of social virtual reality platforms. *IMC '22: Proceedings of the 22nd ACM Internet Measurement Conference*, 504–518. https://doi.org/10.1145/3517745.3561417

Cole, C., Parada, R. H., & Mackenzie, E. (2023). Why and How to Define Educational Video Games? *Games and Culture*. https://doi.org/10.1177/15554120231183495

Conroy, E., Toth, A. J., & Campbell, M. J. (2022). The effect of computer mouse mass on target acquisition performance among action video gamers. *Applied Ergonomics, 99*, 103637. https://doi.org/10.1016/j.apergo.2021.103637

Daneels, R., Bowman, N. D., Possler, D., & Mekler, E. D. (2021). The 'Eudaimonic Experience': A Scoping Review of the Concept in Digital Games Research. *Media and Communication, 9*(2), 178–190. https://doi.org/10.17645/mac.v9i2.3824

Denisova, A., Cairns, P., Guckelsberger, C., & Zendle, D. (2020). Measuring perceived challenge in digital games: Development & validation of the challenge originating from recent gameplay interaction scale (CORGIS). *International Journal of Human-Computer Studies, 137*, 102383. https://doi.org/10.1016/j.ijhcs.2019.102383

Deterding, S., Andersen, M. M., Kiverstein, J., & Miller, M. (2022). Mastering uncertainty: A predictive processing account of enjoying uncertain success in video game play. *Frontiers in Psychology, 13*. https://doi.org/10.3389/fpsyg.2022.924953

Dettmer, P. (2005). New blooms in established fields: Four domains of learning and doing. *Roeper Review, 28*(2), 70–78. https://doi.org/10.1080/02783190609554341

Ding, Z., Gong, W., Li, S., & Wu, Z. (2018). System Dynamics versus Agent-Based Modeling: A Review of Complexity Simulation in Construction Waste Management. *Sustainability, 10*(7). https://doi.org/10.3390/su10072484

Donaldson, S. (2016). Towards a typology of metagames. *ACSW '16: Proceedings of the Australasian Computer Science Week Multiconference*, 1–4. https://doi.org/10.1145/2843043.2843474

Dopfer, K., Foster, J., & Potts, J. (2004). Micro-meso-macro. *Journal of Evolutionary Economics, 14*(3), 263–279. https://doi.org/10.1007/s00191-004-0193-0

Dörner, D., & Funke, J. (2017). Complex Problem Solving: What It Is and What It Is Not. *Frontiers in Psychology, 8*. https://doi.org/10.3389/fpsyg.2017.01153

Dwivedi, Y. K., Hughes, L., Baabdullah, A. M., Ribeiro-Navarrete, S., Giannakis, M., Al-Debei, M. M., Dennehy, D., Metri, B., Buhalis, D., Cheung, C. M. K., Conboy, K., Doyle, R., Dubey, R., Dutot, V., Felix, R., Goyal, D. P., Gustafsson, A., Hinsch, C., Jebabli, I., … Wamba, S. F. (2022). Metaverse beyond the hype: Multidisciplinary perspectives on emerging challenges, opportunities, and agenda for research, practice and policy. *International Journal of Information Management, 66*, 102542. https://doi.org/10.1016/j.ijinfomgt.2022.102542

Echeverri, D., & Wei, H. (2023). Exploring the experience with tangible interactive narrative: Authoring and evaluation of Letters to José. *Entertainment Computing, 44*. https://doi.org/10.1016/j.entcom.2022.100535

Ekdahl, D., & Ravn, S. (2022). Social bodies in virtual worlds: Intercorporeality in Esports. *Phenomenology and the Cognitive Sciences, 21*(2), 293–316. https://doi.org/10.1007/s11097-021-09734-1

El Outa, F., Marcel, P., Peralta, V., da Silva, R., Chagnoux, M., & Vassiliadis, P. (2022). Data Narrative Crafting via a Comprehensive and Well-Founded Process. *Advances in Databases and Information Systems. ADBIS 2022. LNCS, Vol. 13389*, 347–360. https://doi.org/10.1007/978-3-031-15740-0_25

Engström, H., Berg Marklund, B., Backlund, P., & Toftedahl, M. (2018). Game development from a software and creative product perspective: A quantitative literature review approach. *Entertainment Computing, 27*, 10–22. https://doi.org/10.1016/j.entcom.2018.02.008

Ezzeddine, A., & García de Soto, B. (2021). Connecting teams in modular construction projects using game engine technology. *Automation in Construction, 132*, 103887. https://doi.org/10.1016/j.autcon.2021.103887

Friedewald, M., & Raabe, O. (2011). Ubiquitous computing: An overview of technology impacts. *Telematics and Informatics, 28*(2), 55–65. https://doi.org/10.1016/j.tele.2010.09.001

Funk, D. C., Pizzo, A. D., & Baker, B. J. (2018). eSport management: Embracing eSport education and research opportunities. *Sport Management Review, 21*(1), 7–13. https://doi.org/10.1016/j.smr.2017.07.008

Gazzard, A., & Peacock, A. (2011). Repetition and Ritual Logic in Video Games. *Games and Culture, 6*(6), 499–512. https://doi.org/10.1177/1555412011431359

Hanna, F. (2022). Planner Systems for Historical Justice? A Case Study of a People's History of Lebanon. In *Interactive Storytelling. ICIDS 2022. LNCS, vol. 13762* (pp. 159–170). https://doi.org/10.1007/978-3-031-22298-6_10

Harviainen, J. T., & Lieberoth, A. (2012). Similarity of Social Information Processes in Games and Rituals: Magical Interfaces. *Simulation & Gaming, 43*(4), 528–549. https://doi.org/10.1177/1046878110392703

Hassan, L., & Hamari, J. (2020). Gameful civic engagement: A review of the literature on gamification of e-participation. *Government Information Quarterly, 37*(3), 101461. https://doi.org/10.1016/j.giq.2020.101461

Hemmingsen, M. (2023). What is a Metagame? *Sport, Ethics and Philosophy*, 1–16. https://doi.org/10.1080/17511321.2023.2250922

Hong, H. J. (2023). eSports: the need for a structured support system for players. *European Sport Management Quarterly, 23*(5), 1430–1453. https://doi.org/10.1080/16184742.2022.2028876

Höök, K., Benford, S., Tennent, P., Tsaknaki, V., Alfaras, M., Avila, J. M., Li, C., Marshall, J., Roquet, C. D., Sanches, P., Ståhl, A., Umair, M., Windlin, C., & Zhou, F. (2021). Unpacking Non-Dualistic Design: The Soma Design Case. *ACM Transactions on Computer-Human Interaction, 28*(6), 1–36. https://doi.org/10.1145/3462448

Hooker, T. B., & Karnes, M. S. (2022). More than serious: Medicine, games, and care. *Computers and Composition, 65*. https://doi.org/10.1016/j.compcom.2022.102727

Ip, B. (2011). Narrative Structures in Computer and Video Games: Part 1: Context, Definitions, and Initial Findings. *Games and Culture, 6*(2), 103–134. https://doi.org/10.1177/1555412010364982

Jagoda, P. (2020). *Experimental Games: Critique, Play, and Design in the Age of Gamification.* University of Chicago Press. https://doi.org/https://doi.org/10.7208/9780226630038

Johansson, B., Berggren, P., & Leifler, O. (2023). Understanding the challenge of the energy crisis – tackling system complexity with megagaming. *ECCE '23: Proceedings of the European Conference on Cognitive Ergonomics 2023*, 1–7. https://doi.org/10.1145/3605655.3605689

Johnson-Bey, S., Nelson, M. J., & Mateas, M. (2022). Exploring the Design Space of Social Physics Engines in Games. In *Interactive Storytelling. ICIDS 2022. LNCS, vol. 13762* (pp. 559–576). https://doi.org/10.1007/978-3-031-22298-6_36

Johnson, M. R., & Abarbanel, B. (2022). Ethical judgments of esports spectators regarding cheating in competition. *Convergence: The International Journal of Research into New Media Technologies, 28*(6), 1699–1718. https://doi.org/10.1177/13548565221089214

Jungherr, A., & Schlarb, D. B. (2022). The Extended Reach of Game Engine Companies: How Companies Like Epic Games and Unity Technologies Provide Platforms for Extended Reality Applications and the Metaverse. *Social Media + Society, 8*(2), 205630512211076. https://doi.org/10.1177/20563051221107641

Kahila, J., Valtonen, T., López-Pernas, S., Saqr, M., Vartiainen, H., Kahila, S., & Tedre, M. (2023). A Typology of Metagamers: Identifying Player Types Based on Beyond the Game Activities. *Games and Culture*. https://doi.org/10.1177/15554120231187758

Karhulahti, V.-M. (2015). Defining the Videogame. *Game Studies, 15*(2).

Kelly, S. J., Derrington, S., & Star, S. (2022). Governance challenges in esports: a best practice framework for addressing integrity and wellbeing issues. *International Journal of Sport Policy and Politics, 14*(1), 151–168. https://doi.org/10.1080/19406940.2021.1976812

Keogh, B. (2021). The Cultural Field of Video Game Production in Australia. *Games and Culture, 16*(1), 116–135. https://doi.org/10.1177/1555412019873746

Keogh, B., & Hardwick, T. (2023). Creative, Technical, Entrepreneurial: Formative Tensions in Game Development Higher Education. *Games and Culture*, 155541202311768. https://doi.org/10.1177/15554120231176874

Klabbers, J. H. G. (2018). On the Architecture of Game Science. *Simulation & Gaming, 49*(3), 207–245. https://doi.org/10.1177/1046878118762534

Klein, J. H. (2000). Telling stories: a metagame description of a conflict. *Omega, 28*(1), 1–15. https://doi.org/10.1016/S0305-0483(99)00028-6

Knoller, N., Roth, C., & Haak, D. (2021). The Complexity Analysis Matrix. *Interactive Storytelling. ICIDS 2021. Lecture Notes in Computer Science, Vol 13138*, 478–487. https://doi.org/10.1007/978-3-030-92300-6_48

Koenitz, H., Roth, C., & Dubbelman, T. (2021). Educating Interactive Narrative Designers: Cornerstones of a Program. *Transactions of the Digital Games Research Association, 5*(3). https://doi.org/10.26503/todigra.v5i3.125

Kokkinakis, A., York, P., Patra, M. S., Robertson, J., Kirman, B., Coates, A., Chitayat, A. P., Demediuk, S., Drachen, A., Hook, J., Nolle, I., Olarewaju, O., Slawson, D., Ursu, M., & Block, F. O. (2021). Metagaming and metagames in Esports. *International Journal of Esports, 1*(1).

Kortmann, R., & Peters, V. (2021). Becoming the Unseen Helmsman - Game facilitator competencies for novice, experienced, and non-game facilitators. *Simulation & Gaming, 52*(3), 255–272. https://doi.org/10.1177/10468781211020792

Krath, J., Schürmann, L., & von Korflesch, H. F. O. (2021). Revealing the theoretical basis of gamification: A systematic review and analysis of theory in research on gamification, serious games and game-based learning. *Computers in Human Behavior, 125*, 106963. https://doi.org/10.1016/j.chb.2021.106963

Ku, K. Y. L., & Ho, I. T. (2010). Metacognitive strategies that enhance critical thinking. *Metacognition and Learning, 5*(3), 251–267. https://doi.org/10.1007/s11409-010-9060-6

Laamarti, F., Eid, M., & El Saddik, A. (2014). An Overview of Serious Games. *International Journal of Computer Games Technology*. https://doi.org/10.1155/2014/358152

Larsen, L. J. (2022). The Play of Champions: Toward a Theory of Skill in eSport. *Sport, Ethics and Philosophy, 16*(1), 130–152. https://doi.org/10.1080/17511321.2020.1827453

Lehtonen, A., Salonen, A., Cantell, H., & Riuttanen, L. (2018). A pedagogy of interconnectedness for encountering climate change as a wicked sustainability problem. *Journal of Cleaner Production, 199*, 860–867. https://doi.org/10.1016/j.jclepro.2018.07.186

Li, K., Lau, B. P. L., Yuan, X., Ni, W., Guizani, M., & Yuen, C. (2023). Toward Ubiquitous Semantic Metaverse: Challenges, Approaches, and Opportunities. *IEEE Internet of Things Journal, 10*(24), 21855–21872. https://doi.org/10.1109/JIOT.2023.3302159

Li, T., Yang, C., Yang, Q., Lan, S., Zhou, S., Luo, X., Huang, H., & Zheng, Z. (2023). Metaopera: A Cross-Metaverse Interoperability Protocol. *IEEE Wireless Communications, 30*(5), 136–143. https://doi.org/10.1109/MWC.011.2300042

Liming, D., & Vilorio, D. (2011). Work for Play: Careers in Video Game Development. *Occupational Outlook Quarterly, 55*(3), 2–11.

Lukosch, H. K., Bekebrede, G., Kurapati, S., & Lukosch, S. G. (2018). A Scientific Foundation of Simulation Games for the Analysis and Design of Complex Systems. *Simulation & Gaming, 49*(3), 279–314. https://doi.org/10.1177/1046878118768858

Lyytinen, K., & Yoo, Y. (2002). Issues and challenges in ubiquitous computing. *Communications of the ACM, 45*(12), 62–65.

Marín-Lora, C., Chover, M., Sotoca, J. M., & García, L. A. (2020). A game engine to make games as multi-agent systems. *Advances in Engineering Software, 140*, 102732. https://doi.org/10.1016/j.advengsoft.2019.102732

Mattlin, M. (2018). Adapting the DIPLOMACY Board Game Concept for 21st Century International Relations Teaching. *Simulation & Gaming, 49*(6), 735–750. https://doi.org/10.1177/1046878118788905

Meng-Lewis, Y., Wong, D., Zhao, Y., & Lewis, G. (2022). Understanding complexity and dynamics in the career development of eSports athletes. *Sport Management Review, 25*(1), 106–133. https://doi.org/10.1016/j.smr.2020.08.003

Mirowski, P., Mathewson, K. W., Pittman, J., & Evans, R. (2023). Co-Writing Screenplays and Theatre Scripts with Language Models: Evaluation by Industry Professionals. *CHI '23: Proceedings of the 2023 CHI Conference on Human Factors in Computing Systems*, 1–34. https://doi.org/10.1145/3544548.3581225

Moloney, K., & Unger, M. (2014). Transmedia Storytelling in Science Communication: One Subject, Multiple Media, Unlimited Stories. In *New Trends in Earth-Science Outreach and Engagement: The Nature of Communication* (pp. 109–120). https://doi.org/10.1007/978-3-319-01821-8_8

Nagorsky, E., & Wiemeyer, J. (2020). The structure of performance and training in esports. *PLOS ONE, 15*(8). https://doi.org/10.1371/journal.pone.0237584

Neller, T. W. (2019). AI education matters: data science and machine learning with magic: the gathering. *AI Matters, 5*(2), 8–10. https://doi.org/10.1145/3340470.3340474

Norman, E. (2020). Why Metacognition Is Not Always Helpful. *Frontiers in Psychology, 11*. https://doi.org/10.3389/fpsyg.2020.01537

Nygren, N. V., Kankainen, V., & Brunet, L. (2022). Offsetting Game—Framing Environmental Issues in the Design of a Serious Game. *Simulation & Gaming, 53*(6), 615–644. https://doi.org/10.1177/10468781221126786

Nyström, A.-G., McCauley, B., Macey, J., Scholz, T. M., Besombes, N., Cestino, J., Hiltscher, J., Orme, S., Rumble, R., & Törhönen, M. (2022). Current issues of sustainability in esports. *International Journal of Esports, 1*(1).

Parker, F., Whitson, J. R., & Simon, B. (2018). Megabooth: The cultural intermediation of indie games. *New Media & Society, 20*(5), 1953–1972. https://doi.org/10.1177/1461444817711403

Pereira, L. S., & Bernardes, M. M. S. (2022). Reporting on the project development practices of total conversion game mod teams. *Creative Industries Journal*, 1–23. https://doi.org/10.1080/17510694.2022.2077590

Pérez-Colado, V. M., Pérez-Colado, I. J., Freire-Morán, M., Martínez-Ortiz, I., & Fernández-Manjón, B. (2019). Simplifying the creation of adventure serious games with educational-oriented features. *Educational Technology and Society, 22*(3), 32–46.

Perreault, G. P., & Perreault, M. F. (2021). eSports as a news specialty gold rush: Communication ecology in the domination of traditional journalism over lifestyle journalism. In *Handbook of Research on Pathways and Opportunities Into the Business of Esports* (pp. 303–320). https://doi.org/10.4018/978-1-7998-7300-6.ch014

Perreault, M. F., Perreault, G., & Suarez, A. (2022). What Does it Mean to be a Female Character in "Indie" Game Storytelling? Narrative Framing and Humanization in Independently Developed Video Games. *Games and Culture, 17*(2), 244–261. https://doi.org/10.1177/15554120211026279

Pies, I., Beckmann, M., & Hielscher, S. (2010). Value Creation, Management Competencies, and Global Corporate Citizenship: An Ordonomic Approach to Business

Ethics in the Age of Globalization. *Journal of Business Ethics, 94*(2), 265–278. https://doi.org/10.1007/s10551-009-0263-1

Pihkala, P. (2022). Toward a Taxonomy of Climate Emotions. *Frontiers in Climate, 3.* https://doi.org/10.3389/fclim.2021.738154

Politowski, C., Petrillo, F., Ullmann, G. C., & Guéhéneuc, Y.-G. (2021). Game industry problems: An extensive analysis of the gray literature. *Information and Software Technology, 134*, 106538. https://doi.org/10.1016/j.infsof.2021.106538

Potanin, R., & Davies, O. (2011). Designing the Designer. *Proceedings of DiGRA 2011 Conference: Think Design Play.*

Qian, T. Y., Yu, B., Matz, R., Luo, L., & Xu, C. (2023). Gamification for consumer loyalty: An exploration of unobserved heterogeneity in gamified esports social live streaming. *Telematics and Informatics, 85*, 102062. https://doi.org/10.1016/j.tele.2023.102062

Raile, E. D., Shanahan, E. A., Ready, R. C., McEvoy, J., Izurieta, C., Reinhold, A. M., Poole, G. C., Bergmann, N. T., & King, H. (2022). Narrative Risk Communication as a Lingua Franca for Environmental Hazard Preparation. *Environmental Communication, 16*(1), 108–124. https://doi.org/10.1080/17524032.2021.1966818

Recht, S., Jovanovic, L., Mamassian, P., & Balsdon, T. (2022). Confidence at the limits of human nested cognition. *Neuroscience of Consciousness, 2022*(1). https://doi.org/10.1093/nc/niac014

Reer, F., Wehden, L.-O., Janzik, R., Tang, W. Y., & Quandt, T. (2022). Virtual reality technology and game enjoyment: The contributions of natural mapping and need satisfaction. *Computers in Human Behavior, 132*, 107242. https://doi.org/10.1016/j.chb.2022.107242

Rollwage, M., Dolan, R. J., & Fleming, S. M. (2018). Metacognitive Failure as a Feature of Those Holding Radical Beliefs. *Current Biology, 28*(24), 4014-4021.e8. https://doi.org/10.1016/j.cub.2018.10.053

Saßmannshausen, T., Burggräf, P., Hassenzahl, M., & Wagner, J. (2022). Human trust in otherware – a systematic literature review bringing all antecedents together. *Ergonomics*, 1–23. https://doi.org/10.1080/00140139.2022.2120634

Simons, J. (2008). Complex narratives. *New Review of Film and Television Studies, 6*(2), 111–126. https://doi.org/10.1080/17400300802098263

Steegen, S., Tuerlinckx, F., Gelman, A., & Vanpaemel, W. (2016). Increasing Transparency Through a Multiverse Analysis. *Perspectives on Psychological Science, 11*(5), 702–712. https://doi.org/10.1177/1745691616658637

Steinkuehler, C., Anderson, C. G., Reitman, J. G., Lee, J. S., Wu, M., Wells, G., & Gardner, R. T. (2023). Enriched Esports: The Design and Four-Year Examination of a School-Affiliated Competitive Videogame Program for Youth. *Journal of Interactive Learning Research, 34*(1), 59–119.

Stenros, J., & Kultima, A. (2018). On the Expanding Ludosphere. *Simulation & Gaming, 49*(3), 338–355. https://doi.org/10.1177/1046878118779640

Sterman, J. (2018). System dynamics at sixty: the path forward. *System Dynamics Review, 34*(1–2), 5–47. https://doi.org/10.1002/sdr.1601

Thaicharoen, S., Gow, J., & Drachen, A. (2023). An Ecosystem Framework for the Meta in Esport Games. *Journal of Electronic Gaming and Esports, 1*(1). https://doi.org/10.1123/jege.2022-0045

Tharchen, T., Garud, R., & Henn, R. L. (2020). Design as an interactive boundary object. *Journal of Organization Design, 9*(1). https://doi.org/10.1186/s41469-020-00085-w

Toftedahl, M., & Engström, H. (2019). A Taxonomy of Game Engines and the Tools that Drive the Industry. *Proceedings of the 2019 DiGRA International Conference: Game, Play and the Emerging Ludo-Mix.*

Toth, A. J., Ramsbottom, N., Constantin, C., Milliet, A., & Campbell, M. J. (2021). The effect of expertise, training and neurostimulation on sensory-motor skill in esports. *Computers in Human Behavior, 121,* 106782. https://doi.org/10.1016/j.chb.2021.106782

Turakhia, D. G., Mueller, S., & DesPortes, K. (2022). Identifying Game Mechanics for Integrating Fabrication Activities within Existing Digital Games. *CHI '22: CHI Conference on Human Factors in Computing Systems,* 1–13. https://doi.org/10.1145/3491102.3517721

van Krieken, K., & Sanders, J. (2021). What is narrative journalism? A systematic review and an empirical agenda. *Journalism, 22*(6), 1393–1412. https://doi.org/10.1177/1464884919862056

Wardaszko, M. (2018). Interdisciplinary Approach to Complexity in Simulation Game Design and Implementation. *Simulation & Gaming, 49*(3), 263–278. https://doi.org/10.1177/1046878118777809

Wijman, T. (2021). *Global Games Market to Generate $175.8 Billion in 2021; Despite a Slight Decline, the Market Is on Track to Surpass $200 Billion in 2023.* Newzoo. https://newzoo.com/insights/articles/global-games-market-to-generate-175-8-billion-in-2021-despite-a-slight-decline-the-market-is-on-track-to-surpass-200-billion-in-2023

Williams, K. (2020). Gaming for the Greater Good: The North American Scholastic Esports Federation Sets Students on a STEM Trajectory. *IEEE Women in Engineering Magazine, 14*(2), 22–26. https://doi.org/10.1109/MWIE.2020.3020451

Wouters, N., Downs, J., Harrop, M., Cox, T., Oliveira, E., Webber, S., Vetere, F., & Vande Moere, A. (2016). Uncovering the Honeypot Effect: How Audiences Engage with Public Interactive Systems. *DIS '16: Proceedings of the 2016 ACM Conference on Designing Interactive Systems,* 5–16. https://doi.org/10.1145/2901790.2901796

Wu, J. (2013). Hierarchy Theory: An Overview. In *Linking Ecology and Ethics for a Changing World* (pp. 281–301). Springer Netherlands. https://doi.org/10.1007/978-94-007-7470-4_24

Yang, L. (2023). Recommendations for metaverse governance based on technical standards. *Humanities and Social Sciences Communications, 10*(1), 253. https://doi.org/10.1057/s41599-023-01750-7

Zendle, D., Flick, C., Halgarth, D., Ballou, N., Demediuk, S., & Drachen, A. (2023). Cross-cultural patterns in mobile playtime: an analysis of 118 billion hours of human data. *Scientific Reports, 13*(1). https://doi.org/10.1038/s41598-022-26730-w

Zioga, P., Pollick, F., Ma, M., Chapman, P., & Stefanov, K. (2018). "Enheduanna—A Manifesto of Falling" Live Brain-Computer Cinema Performance: Performer and

Audience Participation, Cognition and Emotional Engagement Using Multi-Brain BCI Interaction. *Frontiers in Neuroscience, 12*. https://doi.org/10.3389/fnins.2018.00191

Zyda, M. (2022). How Do I Get a Position in the Games Industry? The FAQ. *Computer, 55*(5), 102–108. https://doi.org/10.1109/MC.2022.3151459

V. THE COMMODIFICATION OF GAMES AND ITS COSTS

AFTER THE STACK OPAQUE

CLOUD GAMING INFRASTRUCTURE AND ENVIRONMENTAL OUTSOURCING METABOLISMS

Eduardo Luersen, Bibiana da Silva de Paula

This paper discusses the environmental implications of cloud gaming and the sustainability strategies employed by infrastructure providers underpinning this gaming model. At present-day, such an analysis needs to recognise the increasing presence of other agents from the ICT sector in the gaming ecosystem in specific, and the digital entertainment economy at large. To understand the inherent infrastructural and environmental challenges to operationalise cloud gaming in this setting, the paper examines the intricate geo-distributed architecture required to offer the real-time experience of gaming through cloud-based services, while observing the growing concerns with the resource consumption associated with cloud platforms. As a result, the analysis unfurls the prevailing adoption of energy efficiency and carbon offsetting strategies by cloud infrastructure providers. Under environmental compensation methods, heat dissipation and water excess are not merely emblems of an accursed climatic share, but also valuable assets for trade. The paper highlights the significance of taking a step back to re-evaluate discourses on gaming and sustainability, to observe more closely how the environmental problems associated to the industry take shape under a cloud-based platform model.

Keywords: gaming-as-a-service, media infrastructure, cloud gaming, sustainability imagery, environmental media

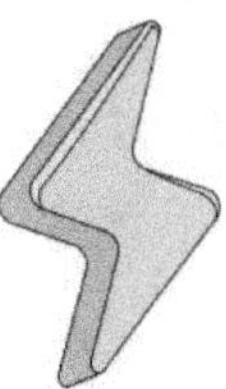

1. Introduction

The prevalence of cloud gaming within the jargon of the digital entertainment economy has witnessed a notable upsurge (Newzoo, 2021), as cultural industry observers see big tech conglomerates exhibiting substantial interest in fostering gaming as services (Cai, Chen and Leung, 2014), with titles being offered through platforms such as Microsoft xCloud, Amazon Luna, Nvidia GeForce Now, or the now already obsolete Google Stadia (Di Domenico et al., 2021). The attempt to provide on-demand content through platforms is said to be especially challenging in a technical sense, though, due to the intricate and highly specialised infrastructure required to foster the effective, real-time performance of games through streaming to large audiences (Willett, 2019). Concomitantly, the rapid escalation of cloud-based media services of different sorts has drawn attention to a series of ecological concerns (Brennan, 2019), from energy consumption to a surge in water usage. The latter issues are not specific to games, as they refer more widely to the data processing facilities that underpin the cloud model. Such a potential transition in the business model of the gaming industry, with the worldwide audience of players that would rely upon it, can significantly contribute to intensifying tensions over the subject. In this paper, we will discuss the interconnectedness between these two challenges, namely the infrastructural and the environmental, which lie at the heart of an operatively functional cloud platform model for gaming. The successful accomplishment of the former would largely add up pressures over the latter, making it necessary to establish wider debates on the topic.

As recent discussions on environmental sustainability in the Information and Communication Technology (ICT) sector point out (Freitag et al., 2021; Pasek, Hunter and Starosielski, 2023), there is an increasing concern with the use of carbon compensation strategies and energy efficiency discourses to justify business-as-usual approaches to development. The rationale behind this is that such incentives would stabilize growth as the primary driver of the sector, while disregarding potential collateral and deleterious environmental effects. Therefore, further in the analysis we outline some of the problematic sustainability strategies adopted by cloud infrastructure providers, pointing out how, at the present state, they may just render the environmental effects of outsourced media processing more opaque.

2. Entanglements: why (and how) infrastructure matters

In simple terms, and on a surface level, cloud gaming lets players experience games without needing to install them on their machine. Without demanding expensive hardware from players, games can be played via streaming, akin–at first glance–to the experience of film streaming services. On the surface, this operation may give the impression that the infrastructure underpinning cloud gaming would be somewhat equivalent to what is necessary to stream other media content, and that the gaming industry could easily operate the same business transition that led other media industries in the past to successfully establish themselves upon a service-based model.

However, this perception is not utterly accurate. In an operative level, gaming platforms make their content available in servers geographically distributed in decentralised data centres. The location of servers influences the routes from-where-to-where data circulates. If game servers are in a data centre far from the player, it takes more time for information to travel, potentially incurring more latency. Without a proper, functional infrastructure across different geographies, it is not reliable to scale cloud gaming services, as latency is particularly worrisome for playing most of the triple-A titles which drive the market, and which are based on consistent real-time interaction. As an employee from an Internet Exchange Point in Germany affirmed to us in a recent, but still unpublished interview, "to provide services from banking to gaming, latency is the currency of the data centre industry".

However, even if reducing latency is important to the wider array of online activities, the infrastructural needs required for gaming are not directly comparable to that of other media services. Still, considering that cloud-streamed games rely on video traffic similar to other audiovisual media, and all game processing occurs on industrial supercomputers, why does the infrastructure present greater challenges when compared to streaming video content? It turns out that gaming demands differ in at least three factors (Ball, 2020). In the video streaming for movies: 1) The content is fully encoded, analysed, and compressed well before delivery; 2) Live streaming with precise timing is seldom necessary, as milliseconds typically have negligible perceptible impact; and 3) Since media files have a predetermined endpoint, the content remains consistent for all viewers and is notwithstanding predictable. On the other hand, in the data traffic for games, if a data packet is missing it requires cueing or skipping the missing video frame, which causes jittery. Buffering can be annoying when streaming a movie, but in a digital game it will make the player fail in its most fundamental operations.

Players acknowledge this through the phenomenological experience of gaming, of course, but theory on game interfaces can help shed light on further details of this problem. The continuous iteration between player actions and the images and sounds of gameplay establishes videogames as *operative media.* This "interface mises-en-scène" (Distelmeyer, 2022), with its visual, acoustic, and kinetic qualities, provides a familiar framework for non-specialised individuals to perform the high-level operation of digital media. Such interfacing condition conveys the ready-made possibilities of entertainment software, turning the human-computer relationship more functional. Interfaces, therefore, offer conducting and guiding principles for the actions of users, or players, interacting with the machine. If this command-response mise-en-scène is periodically impaired by infrastructural problems, the thorough experience of gaming through the cloud model is jeopardised. As most Triple-A games demand precise, synchronous movements, the interfacing disruptions caused by latency and jitter become ultimately intolerable.

The surface-level interfaces of monitors, loudspeakers and controller peripherals are, nevertheless, only gateways to much larger and intricate technical systems, and the failures in the interfacing operations provide us with a valuable opportunity to interrogate the larger infrastructures that underpin them. Latency brings infrastructure to the foreground, as a form of infrastructural inversion (Bowker and Star, 2000), showing why it is particularly challenging to implement gaming as a cloud-based service. Particularly in the case of the cloud gaming model, these operative problems run from the user interface down to the lower levels of critical infrastructure and all the way back. They re-articulate in the digital media ecology one of the most basic functions of the infrastructures for providing physical products and goods: transportation. To mitigate the risk of latency, which is ultimately an expression of geography over the contrivances of telematics, the closest bet for platforms is geo-distributing several game servers across countries and the globe, whether in privately owned or, as in most cases, leased data centres. This means expanding horizontally the density of data processing facilities, enabling the logistics of the cloud gaming model to multiply the available pathways and route the traffic more efficiently. Furthermore, for the gaming industry, maintaining engagement, and therefore, the processing, is naturally a key objective. The service-oriented business model itself shows how the sector seeks to create incentives for gaming modes where the gaming opportunities are seldom truly over (Ochsner et al., 2023).

Moreover, in terms of their technical and spatial implementation, the logic and logistics of cloud gaming data traffic function on the principle of outsourcing computational processing from personal devices to these geographically distributed server halls, which are equipped with substantially more potent hardware. Beyond the technical requirements of household computing apparatus, this model demands the provisioning of power to sustain entire on-premise or colocation data centres (inclusive of auxiliary utilities such as air conditioning and power generators). Considering its resource metabolism, this whole operation is an energy colossus that draws resources on a macro scale.

As outlined by researchers from the Lawrence Berkeley National Laboratory (Mills et al., 2019), to ensure that it can operate fully functionally, cloud-based gaming emerges as the most energy-intensive facet of internet-based gaming. In this sense, it is important to understand gaming activities in the cloud through a broader scope, aiming at the overarching environmental concerns intrinsic to the demands of its vast-scale infrastructure, which is poised to exacerbate as the demand for entertainment software continues to surge. In the present-day scenario, data centres collectively consume already an estimated 200-terawatt hours (TWh) of energy annually (Jones, 2018). That is to say that, if one were to treat the cloud as a country, it would rank as the sixth-largest global electricity-consuming nation-state [1] (Ensmenger, 2018). But that treatment would lead to a misrepresentation, as cloud applications are more often merging with state plans, and not just adding to them. Just as importantly, their environmental effects transcend matters of computing power, electricity consumption and carbon dioxide emissions, as cloud computing extends to a more complex and multifaceted interaction with Earth systems. For instance, in the United States,

---

[1] Just for the sake of illustration, we could also mention the environmental pressures posed by the computational workload of Artificial Intelligence applications. It is not simple to estimate a representative average of the electricity consumption of AI model training and consumer use, as they are largely variable according to the tasks and parameters used to run it, as well as the technical conditions of data processing. AI represents one of the most significant workloads in data centres and, according to a recent study (de Vries, 2023), based on the performance of AI servers shipped by market-leading company NVIDIA (which currently retains 90–95% of the market share for graphic processors used in data centres), estimates are that global AI demand could consume around 85–134 terawatt-hours (TWh) of electricity by 2027. If this scenario is confirmed, the estimation of water withdrawal for operating AI applications would amount to circa 4.2–6.6 billion cubic meters globally–roughly half of the total annual water withdrawal of the United Kingdom (Li et al., 2023).

data centres currently rank among the top ten water-consuming industrial sectors and are witnessing an upward trajectory (Siddik, Shehabi and Marston, 2021). Conventional cooling methods employed within relatively modest 1-megawatt data centres–that is, with an electricity demand equivalent to that of 1,000 households–can consume as much as 26 million litres of water annually (Mytton, 2021).

By connecting this secondary data to the materialities of media (Parikka, 2015; Luersen and Fuchs, 2021), one can say that the energy usage and management within the facilities running cloud-based computer applications are always dependable on the continuous interaction between computational and non-computational resources. Especially when following the techno-aesthetic standards of computer-demanding triple-A titles, gaming through the cloud necessarily entails the support of a comprehensive, planetary-scale computational infrastructure (Bratton, 2015) to furnish real-time gameplay experiences across global audiences. Even though its initial customer base continues to be based on class privilege and access (Hogan, 2021), the several investments in developing gaming-specific racks and utilities for geo-distributed data centres suggest that it is very likely that such an infrastructure is going to keep escalating both vertically and horizontally.

In recent years, several researchers have started to observe the nexus between gaming and climate change (Preisinger and Endl, 2023; Fizek et al., 2023; Abraham, 2022; Chang, 2019; Navarro-Remesal, 2019; Raessens, 2018; Woolbright, 2017). At the industry level, new organisations concerned with the environmental effects of gaming have emerged to channel environmental policies and advise best practices to game developers and publishers (Whittle et al., 2022; Patterson and Barratt, 2019). This is the case of the Playing for the Planet Alliance (P4P), backed by the United Nations Environment Programme, and the special interest group on climate of the International Game Developers Association (IGDA Climate SIG). Moreover, these initiatives can effectively encourage class action among developers and help establish climate councils in the industry.

Nevertheless, even if such initiatives are important, comparatively limited attention has been directed to scrutinising the environmental implications intrinsic to the infrastructure needed for gaming through the cloud. And there is a fundamental reason why this should not be neglected: if gaming services unfurl more aggressively towards the cloud, the major environmental pressures of gaming in the coming years may not be assessed by monitoring developers and publishers alone, but the more fundamental level of critical infrastructure provided by cloud assemblages. Estimations from life cycle assessments project that if the demand for cloud storage and processing keeps its current growth tendency, the electricity usage for communication technologies could contribute to circa 23% of the globally released greenhouse gas emissions by 2030 (Andrae and Edler, 2015). Data centres alone are expected to consume from 5 to 10% of the global electricity demand, in comparison to circa 1% as of today.

Therefore, it is necessary to point out this important gap in scholarly discourse and environmental advisory within the gaming industry. As models based on the outsourcing of computational demands unfurl, it is important to take a step back to underscore the telematic infrastructure supporting cloud gaming, which spans from the electricity grids sustaining data centres to the intricate mesh of cables and satellites interconnecting servers within a transcontinental overflow of networked devices. Networked synchronous media traffic, although portrayed with the use of seemingly ethereal metaphors, is inexorably tethered to terrestrial, atmospheric, and aquatic realms (Parikka, 2015; Peters, 2015; Starosielski, 2015). As a composite construct derived from Earth's elemental reserves, the cloud concentrates and distributes resources at once. Likewise, digital distribution platforms turn game production and consumption into a process that is "both inherently global and intensely localized" (Sotamaa and Švelch, 2021, p. 9). Hence, discussions on the sustainability of activities such as cloud gaming cannot focus solely on the micro level, such as stimulating game developers to adapt their studios to sustainability standards. Focusing on the support systems that underpin the practices of ambient supercomputing appears more promising. Measuring the footprint of game developing studios is important, but scratches only the surface of the problem. In our view, inquiring the infrastructure underpinning gaming platforms can provide a deeper understanding of the environmental implications of gaming, especially as the industry transitions toward a cloud service paradigm.

3. Growings crops, planting trees: on compensations

Currently gaming is roughly estimated to make up 7% of global network demand (Marsden, Hazas and Broadbend, 2020). Cloud gaming still refers to an indeterminate part of this signal traffic. As data centre providers do not discriminate, or at least do not disclose publicly, how each activity in the cloud is responsible for this consumption, providing an estimation of the cloud gaming share would be reckless. Notwithstanding, as a popular computer-intensive activity which is outsourced to data centres, gaming can be ascribed as a significant activity participating in this resource metabolism. As an ongoing, constantly renewed trend in the industry, it is important to document the development of gaming in the cloud as it unfolds, as these services have been gaining a lot of traction with the infrastructure provided by corporations such as Amazon, Alphabet, Microsoft, and so on. Even with the recent failures of projects such as Google Stadia, it is still important to keep track of the provision of infrastructure to support game streaming services as they develop.

As such evolution is path-dependent, it is also important to think about what the arguments in favour of cloud gaming could be. Many advances are being made to improve the energy efficiency of cloud computing facilities, for instance, and energy specialists often have to recalculate the energy expenditure of the devices every year due to such improvements (Masanet et al., 2020). It is also true that fewer consoles being manufactured means fewer in landfills after they are outmoded and discarded. If there are also no discs to make, the environmental burden of transporting them to physical stores vanishes. As Benjamin Abraham argues (2022), this would be beneficial to mitigate the overall carbon cycle involved with digital gaming, as the emissions involved in the distribution of physical products are very high.

However, what can be observed more prominently at least since the COVID-19 pandemic is that the implementation of digital infrastructures has been growing at a much faster pace than the discontinuation of analogous offline, carbon-intensive logistical operations (Freitag et al., 2021). More often than not, online and cloud-based applications are used not as a substitute, but as a redundant infrastructure. In practice, this means that the steady growth of cloud-based gaming services and the infrastructure to support them is stacked upon prevailing models of manufacturing and shipping of game disks and downloadable gaming content. In this sense, the environmental pressures associated to established gaming infrastructures are accumulated instead of being mitigated.

While it is true that the energy efficiency of cloud computing facilities has demonstrated improvement trends, these advancements are contingent upon the cleanliness of local energy mixes and other parts of the remaining infrastructures. More importantly, they are completely path-dependent, what makes any estimation highly volatile to broader macroeconomic and political trends. A well-argued, optimistic view of such developments was conveyed by Jonathan Koomey, an experienced researcher in the field of energy and sustainability, who posed more than a decade ago that peak-output computing efficiency was doubling every 1.5 years (Koomey et al., 2011). From this data, Koomey inferred that the total energy consumption of ICT would constantly decrease over time in line with industry tendencies. Indeed, since 2010 the energy intensity of data centres has decreased by approximately 20% per year, leading the International Energy Agency (IEA) to project significant growth in the sector *coupled with* reduced energy demand (International Energy Agency, 2020). This was particularly noticeable in the data centres designed to accommodate higher volumes of data storage and processing, called hyperscale. These facilities require a lower energy consumption per unit of data–although processing *more data*. This condition suggests imagining a scenario in which the infrastructures to support cloud gaming are expanded without amplifying environmental pressures.

However, it is highly questionable whether this efficiency tendency in enough to guarantee the long-term sustainability of the sector. Energy efficiency, for instance, is constrained by the physical limitations of silicon semiconductors (Freitag et al., 2021), which eventually reach a point in which further miniaturisation compromises performance. As the ongoing improvements in energy efficiency are contingent on the densification of microchips, the more optimistic forecasts are difficult to meet. Nowadays we already see the predictions from more than a decade ago compromised, as the rate of peak-output energy efficiency slowed down, now taking 2.7 years, instead of 1.5, to double (Pasek, Vaughan and Starosielski, 2023).

Moreover, besides the uncertainty itself, another problematic aspect of the most optimistic discourses on energy efficiency is that, ultimately, they may just incentivise more growth without serious carbon mitigation commitments. It is not difficult to predict that computer-intensive activities of data centres, such as game processing, can serve to feed into the very same logic. When looking to reality on the ground, beyond the modelling of projections, one can see platforms already using this rhetoric to justify unsustainable growth, by using the heat produced by the increased consumption in data-processing facilities as an additional financial asset.

The constant refrigeration of data centres, for instance, is a systemic source of heat dissipation. Circa 40% of the energy consumed in data centres goes for air conditioning, as the facilities are normally recommended to maintain a temperature between 20 and 25 degrees Celsius to operate properly, keeping the process-intensive servers from overheating (Zhang, Li and Wang, 2023). Even personal computers, from old machines to consoles of different generations, have heat prevention systems that shut the device down when a certain internal temperature is reached, in order to protect the delicate hardware from heat overexposure, which could melt or damage the components irreversibly. More sophisticated computer systems have configurable automatic shutdown temperatures, while simpler home entertainment systems have a pre-established factory setting [2].

As a scalable thermocultural technique, though, artificial cooling has much more radical effects in the case of supercomputing infrastructures available to operate 24/7. In order to keep their internal server halls at an ideal temperature, data centres need a lot of air conditioning, and end up generating a lot of excess heat. To take advantage of the excess heat produced, some data centres have used increased air temperature as a commercial asset, incorporating the transfer of heat into their sustainability portfolios in different ways: Amazon and other companies with proprietary data centres invest in projects to channel the heat produced in their server farms to heat their own offices (Oró and Salom, 2022), and Amazon reported to have drastically reduced the projected greenhouse gas emissions from their offices by these means. In partnership with local energy cooperatives, several projects are underway to transfer the heat generated inside Amazon Web Services (AWS) data centres to other commercial buildings (Amazon, 2021). Waste heat from data centres is increasingly traded with municipalities to provide domestic heating. The *thermopolitical strategy* (Velkova, 2021) of transferring the heat produced by intense computer processing in data centres to municipalities and businesses is repeated in Rotterdam, Basel, Mantsaala and Dublin, and in more and more cities around the world [3].

Another way to profit from the excess heat produced is to grow plants in greenhouses near data centres. Projects from data centre operators in Sweden

---

[2] This is a personal anecdote, but one of the most tangible examples we have of this type of system is our experience a couple of decades ago with an old PlayStation console, which used to work perfectly for several hours in winter, in the subtropical-temperate climate of southern Brazil, but during the hottest summer nights rarely operated for many hours straight without the frustration of shutting down unexpectedly. Unless, of course, the user could resort to artificial cooling of the room.

[3] The growing interest to incorporate energy sources in urban planning also generated compelling gamification methods to identify and report sources of waste heat in industrial infrastructures. See Wernbacher et al. (2022).

and Canada are expected to grow crops of leafy green in greenhouses warmed with the excess heat transferred from their server halls (Cáceres et al., 2022; Frenzel and Ruder, 2023). Another example of a combination between cultivation and the use of excess heat is the White Data Centre in Hokkaido. In addition to cultivating mushrooms and spinach, the company harnesses the heat generated by its data centre to rear eels, as the fish is valued in the Japanese seafood market. The company raises 300,000 eels a year for the gastronomy sector (Judge, 2022). The waste heat is used to warm water tanks to an adequate temperature for breeding the fish. Green Mountain, a data centre operator from Norway, also channels the heat from its data centres to warm the water they use to grow lobsters and trouts for restaurants (Judge, 2021; Swinhoe, 2021).

Other data centres prefer to take measures targeted at biodiversity, hosting beekeeping or tree planting programs to improve their sustainability indicators. Stack Infrastructure hosts circa 200,000 bees on the roof of its data centre in Milan (Swinhoe, 2022b). A CyrusOne data centre has installed *bee hotels* and so-called *bee-friendly landscapes* on its data campus in Dublin, the same city where Equinix grows orchards and raises pollinators (Swinhoe, 2022a), allegedly for the same environment-friendly reasons.

While at a first glance most of these examples might look like promising cases of efficiency derived from computer-intensive activities, one needs to hold their expectations about their viability as a pathway to reduce the environmental impacts of the industry. More than an ecological motivation, the rationale underpinning these initiatives points towards a financial strategy that nurtures continuous growth. Instead of being seen as an environmental burden, the heat from data centres becomes a strategic asset to be traded on energy markets, on carbon markets, on food markets, as well as on markets for voluntary environmental compensation. In the meantime, the cumulative heat generated, and the overall CO2 emitted, some of the biggest environmental problems with data centres, are not properly addressed. As data centres establish themselves as the factories of Industry 4.0, such practices grant more productivity through the efficient use of the systemically supplied heat, which is incentivised to increase.

Aside from the involvement in the computer processing happening in proprietary and leased data centres, the gaming industry invests in other sorts of projects with rather similar problems. These include the several reforestation initiatives that are recommended and implemented by actors in the gaming industry. In recent years, discourse about forestry has begun to to abound in gaming industry conventions, as game developers seek strategies to offset the carbon dioxide emissions produced by their studios. One of the most widely adopted initiatives for this purpose is reforestation. In Germany, for instance, non-profitable organisations such as *GamesForest.Club* encourage industry actors to contribute to forest protection and reforestation enterprises as part of a carbon sequestration strategy. The goal of the initiative is to harness the influence of games and compassionate individuals within the industry to safeguard and rejuvenate nature (Games Forest, 2023). When accessing the website of the organisation, one starts to hear the playback of bird vocalisations and other compositional elements of an archetypal forest soundscape. Nevertheless, even if these initiatives convey persuasive enunciations and messages about an idyllic (albeit engineered) nature, there are arguments suggesting that carbon compensation strategies deliver more in terms of corporate rhetoric than of practical, eco-conscious achievements. Scholars in Earth System Governance advise that tree-planting might not be an adequate way to offset emissions (Blum and Lövbrand, 2019). Depending on the species, trees require a significant amount of time to grow and begin sequestering carbon from the atmosphere. In worst-case scenarios, which are not uncommon, forests may also become susceptible to wildfires during heat waves or as an outcome of active anthropogenic deforestation activities. This situation can cause forests to shift from carbon sinks to significant carbon emitters, suddenly reversing any previously alleged "compensation" for emissions. Additionally, numerous tree-planting initiatives have been issuing redundant certifications for different venues (Romm, 2023), complicating the efforts to accurately assess the potential positive impacts of these incentives.

Of course, investments from the gaming industry in the breeding of bees and reforestation (and, naturally, in securing that forests also keep standing) are more than welcome, but it is misleading to think of them as intrinsically beneficial environmental initiatives, especially from the perspective of carbon offsetting. More importantly, by using heat as a financial asset, as in the other cases shown during the paper, the ICT sector is focusing on the benefits of energy efficiency. The argument is that efficiency gains will *compensate* for the growth in consumption driven by cloud-based services, such as cloud gaming. However, if we look deeper into the history of the energy sector, there are reasons to be sceptical. A similar argument was made in relation to coal-dependent industries already during the first Industrial Revolution. Industrialists argued that by investing in greater energy efficiency, the increase in productivity could happen with less collateral environmental damage, allowing the industry to grow faster without polluting more (Clark and Foster, 2001). In 1865, economist William Jevons wrote *"The Coal Question"*, a book in which he questions the longevity of economies based on coal usage. Jevons observes, in particular, how the steam engine improved energy efficiency compared to previous designs, making it possible to produce more with fewer resources. However, Jevons also noticed that as efficiency increased, the cost of energy fell, which led to an increase in consumption. This phenomenon is nowadays called the *Jevons Paradox*. In summary, it highlights that improvements in resource efficiency can lead to a potential *rebound effect*. By stimulating economy-wise growth, efficiency can lead to higher overall resource consumption. This challenges the assumption that efficiency alone would lead to environmental benefits and reduced use of resources.

While Jevons developed his argument within the framework of non-renewable energy, which is not at all a negligible aspect, the significance of his argument still resonates strongly today. While the preference for renewable energy sources over fossil fuels is self-evident, and hastening the energy transition remains paramount, it is nonetheless concerning to rely solely on this strategy, ignoring potential collateral effects. The prevailing discourse within the ICT sector often emphasises efficiency as the main driver of solutions to environmental challenges, and this extends to sectors like data centres and gaming. As we move further away from the goals of the Paris agreement (that is, to reduce greenhouse gas emissions by 45% by 2030, compared to 2010 levels) (United Nations Environment Programme, 2023), relying on energy efficiency and compensation strategies is not enough, and these trends often extend further business-as-usual approaches. The current financial architecture systemically incentivises the proliferation of heat dissipation infrastructures.

If the games industry is serious about promoting more sustainable practices, it will have to move beyond reliance on compensatory measures. This does not affect only the strategy for cloud gaming, but also hardware choice, support for repairing and recycling, and end-of-life services–exceeding the criteria of TCO Gold certification, which promotes sustainability standards in ICT products. Sustainability analysts at the ICT sector suggest that to act in a truly environmentally responsible way, all stakeholders should be enacting policies on a much larger scale, while adopting a radically different management rationale, such as putting a price on carbon emissions or a global constraint on consumption (Freitag et al., 2021), which would push for more innovation in resource usage alternatives. This is a big challenge, of course, because taking the suggested pathway requires adaptation and potential reductions, meaning a broader restructuring of the sector and the whole resource metabolism.

On a conceptual level, this paper modestly aims to contribute to the discussion by suggesting that some improvement can be achieved by taking a step back to acknowledge the impossibility of mitigating planetary-scale problems without a more comprehensive, macrosystemic approach. To address environmental issues at their proper scale, it is necessary to examine the entangled infrastructure that underpins the gaming ecology of both today and the future.

4. Challenges to assessing the future and the reality of gaming's environmental entanglements: infrastructure and opacity

There is much work to do on the infrastructure level. Game studios have been collaborative in participating in intersectoral research initiatives, but the same cannot always be said about other actors in the ecosystem of cloud gaming.

An illustrative practical example can shed light on the delicate intricacies of the current situation. As part of a recent research project, we have contacted via email 25 large-to-hyperscale data centre operators providing cloud services in Germany, Austria, and Switzerland. The intention was to inquire about the possibility of visiting the facilities to interview managers and workers to discuss aspects of sustainability related to their businesses, as well as to photograph the physical facilities that process gaming data. Although not all gaming platforms disclose transparently which data centres are leased to host their servers[4], one can have a general idea of the companies that have the apt facilities to provide such services. As we mentioned earlier, cloud gaming is a highly computing-demanding and therefore resource-demanding activity, engaging all layers of the computational stack, from the physical hardware and network infrastructure to the software and user interface. Thus, facilities need to provide not only a stable and reliable high-speed connection but also a very robust non-computational infrastructure of air conditioners, generators, and software systems. As not all data centres at all are capable of processing computing-costly games, the ones that can do it tend to advertise it openly on their website.

[4] Contracts of confidentiality very often prevent private enterprises in the sector from revealing the activities their customers develop within the leased facilities.

Based on this publicly available information, we have contacted cloud infrastructure providers inquiring whether they would be open to receiving our visit. Before doing this, though, we asked individually to each of them whether they could confirm whether they provided any kind of gaming-related services. Most operators never responded to any of the attempts to establish contact. Some of the few answers we had in these private correspondences are rather curious, nevertheless. The most common response provided was that there was not any interest in taking part on the research, with no further reason given. Some companies alleged that unfortunately it was not possible for "external personnel" to visit their data centres for "several, but private reasons". Some companies phrased their replies stressing that they "could not" fulfil our request to visit the facilities in person. Another data centre administrator straightforwardly mentioned that the company "didn't want" to support the request. A less laconic response was given by another provider, which operates a colocation data centre in Frankfurt. The alleged reason was that the company had no insight into what activities their customers developed in the servers hosted in their data centres, as they simply provide the core infrastructure to them, and are by no means involved with the content of these activities.

This may sound surprising, but in fact it could be expected as a fair response from colocation data centre operators, which only rent the space in their facilities to the server owners. And here things start to get more delicate. Such a secrecy regime, although understandable from a cybersecurity standpoint, is also very problematic, not only from the perspective of our failed attempts to start a research collaboration. It is comprehensible that companies that deal with confidential private and state-level data take secrecy as a matter of principle. The main contradiction, nevertheless, is that in the current situation, when cloud infrastructure is merging with resource-intensive software services that escalate to a planetary dimension, the auditability of such support systems becomes more and more a matter of commonly shared, public concern.

From this vantage point, the case of cloud gaming encapsulates a paradoxical scenario. It reflects a society striving to adapt individual and collective action by identifying sustainable management strategies, while at the same time exacerbating environmental pressures through digital interconnectedness and virtual environments.

As Lisa Parks (2014) notoriously put it, engineers often refer to infrastructure as *stuff you can kick*–robust physical apparatus that are dispersed and assembled to compose a system for the distribution of materials of value. But the environmental entanglements of infrastructure may show us the other way around: infrastructures can also kick you (and us all) back. As cloud infrastructures interact broadly with the earthly metabolism through the technical management of water, air, and temperature (Jue, 2020; Furuhata, 2019; Vonderau, 2019; Starosielski, 2016; Velkova, 2021), the pressure in scale impelled by cloud platforms cannot be understood by monitoring studios alone, nor its accountability can be delegated to the voluntary disclosure by companies. As global-scale infrastructures, cloud services are not only meant to provide social goods to the public in a sustainable way, but should also be available for public scrutiny. Due to issues of privacy and secrecy involving data centre operations, researchers and civil society at large have problems with understanding, let alone auditing them, in a way that is more reliable than accessing self-disclaimed reports. The challenge starts with the difficulty in assessing the facilities to conduct research (Vonderau, 2019). In this sense, questions on gaming and environment-wise polity also arise: how are cloud-based gaming services meant to serve the public in the face of planetary environmental upheavals? Are cloud gaming platforms publicly auditable in the first place?

Notwithstanding, these questions may sound naïve without a wider comprehension of the cloud's stack infrastructure that stretches beyond regional regulatory frameworks. Considering present-day developments, cloud infrastructures have been working on a very different techno-political spectrum. As Yannis Varoufakis (2023) asserts, the proliferation of cloud platforms is not merely a technological advancement but a pivotal driver of a predominantly self-contained rental economy, in a global level. This transformation gives birth to what Varoufakis terms *cloud capital*, a concept that is emblematic of the cloud colocation paradigm, wherein access to and control over digital infrastructure increasingly rely on power dynamics centred on ownership, concentration, resource extraction, and rental. As such, platforms and colocation providers control the access and terms of use of services, managing the servers, networks, and data centres that form the backbone of gaming practices. Moreover, as only a few large cloud infrastructure providers dominate the market, monetising the data traffic generated from users, they wield grand influence over platform economics and the management of resources in the digital realm.

Considering this, it is relevant to reassess this infrastructure and the services that rely upon the cloud from a perspective of the environmental risks involved in the wider geo-distribution of its architecture. In Paul Virilio's worn out expression, "to invent the train is to invent derailment; to invent the ship is to invent the shipwreck" (Virilio and Der Derian, 1998). Accidents are inherent to all technical systems, and each new technology nourishes its own specific and novel kind of accident, Virilio would advise. Cloud infrastructure is not at all new, however. The idea of data processing as a ubiquitous utility distributed from centralised computing units is as old as computer science itself, being traceable back to the development of the UNIX system in the 1970s, which synchronized computers across networks (Bratton, 2015). The main difference from then to nowadays, though, is that the horizontality of the network gave way to the conversion of several activities, and sometimes entire sectors, to a model based on proprietary platform services. Such services are largely available, yet also largely opaque.

One could say, still with Virilio, that the larger the infrastructure, the larger the accident. While in general infrastructures are understood as support systems that allow human agents to extrapolate certain physical limitations, providing societies with mid to long-term stability, the very same infrastructures may also create unforeseeable systemic vulnerabilities (Edwards, 2003). This may happen because of the inseparable metabolic connections that exist between technology and nature, through which the embeddedness between organic and inorganic systems (Schneider, 2018) comes to the fore, backlashing from fuel consumption, intensive video rendering, or computer heat dissipation–from smaller events to the point of anthropogenic global climate change.

In a more hopeful note, Gabriele Schabacher (2022) observes that although we usually focus on their more immediate and tragic dimension, disasters also have an epistemic significance: they can provide us with *infrastructural learning* about emerging sociotechnical systems. With this term, Schabacher emphasises the importance of understanding infrastructures not just as technical systems, but also as dynamic entities shaped by social, economic, and political factors. Accidents are diagnostic: amid their looming presence, infrastructural learning can be a pathway to the continuous adaptation that is necessary to effectively manage and govern the sociotechnical support structures of a world that is rapidly changing due to anthropogenic action, global interconnectedness, and resource-intensive planetary-scale systems. As argued in preliminary work (Luersen, 2023), this is even more reason to reframe the analysis of the environmental entanglements of cloud platforms from a perspective of their infrastructures: thinking along these lines, one can evaluate the challenges and the very failures to establish cloud gaming infrastructure so far as valuable cautionary tales for the future development of entertainment software. More so, one can think of the actual and potential environmental pressures outlined in the previous sections as analytical onsets, epistemological vantage points that can nurture future developments in the face of emerging gaming platforms.

5. Final considerations

The development of gaming towards a cloud service model raises questions on how to evaluate the environmental pressures associated to the gaming industry. Significant concerns involve, for instance, the energy and water consumption of data centres, which are increasingly utilised to process the intensive data traffic of games, let alone the widespread deployment of machine learning algorithms and artificial intelligence models. In this scenario, we discuss the need to address the infrastructure and ecological issues of cloud gaming platforms, emphasising the importance of further approaching the extent to which the gaming industry intersects with developments in the data centre sector. In this context, we highlight concerns related to questionable sustainability strategies adopted by cloud computing infrastructure providers, pointing out gaps in the understanding of the environmental problems associated to the support systems of media distribution services.

Throughout the analysis, we point out that the environmental problems associated to gaming are, likewise, increasingly intersecting with power dynamics centred on ownership, concentration, and resource extraction in the development of cloud infrastructure. The influence exerted by on-premise and colocation data centres over access and service conditions places a few major cloud computing facility providers in a position of substantial influence and control over platform economies and resource management.

We emphasise the significance of intersectoral research involving cloud infrastructure providers, as we understand that it can help identifying the new synergies between activities which are, otherwise, normally understood as constitutively separate. Initially, this may not contribute to mitigating adverse impacts of cloud gaming infrastructures, but it can help preventing that unsustainable innovation in the information technology ecosystem takes place inadvertently. As one can infer by observing how energy efficiency measures and carbon offset strategies are rhetorically used as synonyms of sustainable practices, the current developments often contribute to maintaining business as usual, outsourcing environmental pressures while increasing consumption.

As global-scale problems could hardly be mitigated without a macro approach, in the first place it is important to map and re-evaluate the wider ecology of machines and environments where digital gaming is processed, considering the complex techno-economic support system in which data centres and cloud gaming platforms overlap. In order to do this, however, it is necessary to acknowledge the significance of scrutinising both the existing gaming infrastructures and those currently in development with a broader ecosystemic view, and a higher degree of autonomy.

Acknowledgments

Funded by the Federal Ministry of Education and Research (BMBF) and the Baden-Württemberg Ministry of Science as part of the Excellence Strategy of the German Federal and State Governments.

The researchers would like to further acknowledge the financial and non-financial support of the Zukunftskolleg for this research.

About the Author

Eduardo Luersen is a postdoctoral fellow at the Zukunftskolleg at the University of Konstanz, where he develops the research project "Cloud Gaming Atlas: from Earth's metabolism to the longing for radiant infrastructures". Affiliated with the Department of Literature, Art, and Media Studies at the same institution, he has conducted research into the theory and analysis of visual and aural media, as well as on the internet in its different manifestations, with a focus on the interconnectedness between media infrastructures and environmental systems.

Social: @EL_Harry0
Website: https://eduardohluersen.weebly.com/

Bibiana da Silva de Paula holds a master's degree in Communication Sciences awarded by Unisinos University, specialising in Visual Poetics at Feevale University. She pursued her undergraduate studies in Journalism at the Federal University of Pelotas. She is a visual artist working at the confluence of art and technology, with a particular emphasis on media archaeology. Her artistic activities have been distinguished by the Dana Visual Arts Award in 2018 and 2019, as well as the Goethe-Institut Porto Alegre Printed Art Award in 2020.

Social: @bya.de.paula
Website: https://www.byadepaula.com/

References

Abraham, B. (2022). Digital games after climate change. Cham: Palgrave Macmillan.

Andrae, A. and Edler, T. (2015). On global electricity usage of communication technology. Challenges, 6(1), 117–157. https://doi.org/10.3390/challe6010117

Amazon. (2021). Amazon sustainability 2020 report: further and faster, together. https://sustainability.aboutamazon.com/amazon-sustainability-2020-report.pdf

Blum, M. and Lövbrand, E. (2019). The return of carbon offsetting? The discursive legitimation of new market arrangements in the Paris climate regime. Earth System Governance, 2. https://doi.org/10.1016/j.esg.2019.100028

Bowker, G. and Star, S. L. (2000). Sorting things out: classification and its consequences. Cambridge: MIT Press.

Bratton, B. (2015). The stack: on software and sovereignty. Cambridge: MIT Press.

Brennan, S. (2015). Making data sustainable: backup culture and risk perception. In J. Walker and N. Starosielski (Eds.). Sustainable Media. New York: Routledge, 57–76.

Cáceres, C. R. et al. (2022). Data-center farming: exploring the potential of industrial symbiosis in a subarctic region. Sustainability 2022, 14(5), https://doi.org/10.3390/su14052774

Cai, W., Chen, M. and Leung, V. (2014). Toward gaming as a service. IEEE Internet Computing, 18(3), 12–18.

Chang, A. Y. (2019). Playing nature: ecology in video games. Minneapolis: University of Minnesota Press.

Clark, B. and Foster, J. B. (2001). William Stanley Jevons and the coal question: an introduction to Jevons's "Of the Economy of Fuel". Organization and Environment, 14(1), 93-98.

De Vries, A. (2023). The growing energy footprint of artificial intelligence. Joule, 7(10), 2191–2194. https://doi.org/10.1016/j.joule.2023.09.004

Di Domenico, A. et al. (2021). A network analysis on cloud gaming: Stadia, GeForce Now and PSNow. Network, 1(3), 247–260. https://doi.org/10.3390/network1030015

Distelmeyer, J. (2022). Critique of digitality. Wiesbaden: Palgrave MacMillan.

Edwards, P. N. (2003). Infrastructure and modernity: force, time, and social organization in the history of sociotechnical systems. In T. J. Misa, P. Brey and A. Feenberg (Eds.). Modernity and technology. Cambridge: MIT Press, 185–226.

Ensmenger, N. (2018). The environmental history of computing. Technology and Culture, 59(4), 7–33. https://doi.org/10.1353/tech.2018.0148

Fizek, S. et al. (2023). Teaching Environmentally Conscious Game Design: Lessons and Challenges. ACM Games 1(1). https://doi.org/10.1145/3583058

Freitag, C. et al. (2021). The real climate and transformative impact of ICT: a critique of estimates, trends, and regulations. Patterns, 2(9), 1–18. https://doi.org/10.1016/j.patter.2021.100340

Frenzel, J. and Ruder, S. (2023). Can the heat from running computers help grow our food? It's complicated. The University of British Columbia Magazine. https://magazine.alumni.ubc.ca/2023/life-technology/can-heat-running-computers-help-grow-our-food-its-complicated

Furuhata, Y. (2019). Of dragons and geoengineering: rethinking elemental media. Media and Environment, 1(1). https://doi.org/10.1525/001c.10797

Games Forest (2023). Games Forest Club. https://gamesforest.club/

Hogan, M. (2021). The data center industrial complex. In M. Jue and R. Ruiz (Eds.). Saturation: an elemental politics. Durham: Duke University Press.

International Energy Agency (2020). Global data centre energy demand by data centre type, 2010–2022. https://www.iea.org/data-and-statistics/charts/global-data-centre-energy-demand-by-data-centre-type-2010-2022

Jevons, W. (1865). The coal question. London: Macmillan and Co.

Jones, N. (2018). How to stop data centres from gobbling up the world's electricity. Nature, 561(7722), 163–166. 10.1038/d41586-018-06610-y

Judge, P. (2021). Crustacean cultivation: Lobsters and data centers. Data Center Dynamics. https://www.datacenterdynamics.com/en/analysis/crustacean-cultivation-lobsters-and-data-centers/

Judge, P. (2022). Japanese snow-cooled data center opens an eel farm. Data Center Dynamics. https://www.datacenterdynamics.com/en/news/japanese-snow-cooled-data-center-opens-an-eel-farm/

Jue, M. (2020). Wild blue media: thinking through seawater. New York: Duke University Press.

Koomey, J. et al. Implications of historical trends in the electrical efficiency of computing. IEEE Annals of the History of Computing, 33(3), 46–54. https://doi.org/10.1109/MAHC.2010.28

Li, P. et al. (2023). Making AI Less "Thirsty": Uncovering and Addressing the Secret Water Footprint of AI Models. ArXiv, abs/2304.03271.

Luersen, E. H. (2023). Every cloud has a silver lining: seeing through the cracks of cloud gaming infrastructure. Conference Proceedings of the Digital Games Research Association (DiGRA) 2023.

Luersen, E. H. and Fuchs, M. (2021). Ruins of excess: computer game images and the rendering of technological obsolescence. Games and Culture, 16(8), 1087–1110. https://doi.org/10.1177/15554120211005363

Marsden, M., Hazas, M. and Broadbent, M. (2020). From one edge to the other: exploring gaming's rising presence on the network. Proceedings of the 7th International Conference on ICT for Sustainability, ACM, 247–254.

Masanet, E. et al. (2020). Recalibrating global data center energy-use estimates, Science, 367(6481), 984-986. https://doi.org/10.1126/science.aba3758

Mills, E. et al. (2019). A plug-loads game changer: computer gaming system energy efficiency without performance compromise. California Energy Commission. Publication Number: CEC-500-2019-042.

Mytton, D. (2021). Data centre water consumption. NPJ Clean Water, 4(11), 1–6. https://doi.org/10.1038/s41545-021-00101-w

Navarro-Remesal, V. (2019). Pixelated nature: ecocriticism, animals, moral consideration, and degrowth in videogames. Logos, 26(2), 13–26. https://doi.org/10.12957/logos.2019.46108

Newzoo (2021). Global cloud gaming report. Technical Report. https://newzoo.com/insights/trend-reports/global-cloud-gaming-report-2021-free-version

Ochsner, B. et al. (2023). "Serious Gaming" oder spielen ernst nehmen: ein Forschungsprogramm. ZfM - Zeitschrift für Medienwissenschaft, 15(28-1), 121–136. https://doi.org/10.14361/zfmw-2023-150112

Oró, E. and Salom, J. (2022). Data centre overview. In J. Salom, T. Urbaneck and E. Oró (Eds.). Advanced concepts for renewable energy supply of data centres. New York: River Publishers.

Parikka, J. (2015). A geology of media. Minneapolis: University of Minnesota Press.

Parks, L. (2014). Stuff you can kick: toward a theory of media infrastructure. In D. T. Goldberg and P. Svensson (Eds.). Between Humanities and the Digital. Cambridge: MIT Press, 355–373.

Pasek, A., Vaughan, H. and Starosielski, N. (2023). The world wide web of carbon: toward a relational footprinting of information and communications technology's climate impacts. Big Data and Society, 10(1). https://doi.org/10.1177/20539517231158994

Patterson, T. and Barratt, S. (2019). Playing for the planet: how video games can deliver for people and the environment. UN Environment/GRID-Arendal. https://gridarendal-website-live.s3.amazonaws.com/production/documents/:s_document/506/original/gamingpub2019.pdf?1569241220

Peters, J. D. (2015). Infrastructuralism: Media as Traffic Between Nature and Culture. In M. Näser-Lather and C. Neubert. Traffic: media as infrastructures and cultural practices. Leiden: Brill, 31–49.

Preisinger, A. and Endl, A. (2023). Gaming on climate change: discursive strategies of environmental problems in strategy games. In J. Friedmann (Ed.). Narratives crossing boundaries: storytelling in a transmedial and transdisciplinary context. Bielefeld: Transcript Verlag, 225–246. https://doi.org/10.1515/9783839464861-010

Raessens, J. (2018). Ecogames: playing to save the planet. In T. Meireis and G. Rippl (Eds.). Cultural sustainability: perspectives from the Humanities and Social Sciences. London: Routledge, 232–245.

Romm, J. (2023). Are carbon offsets unscalable, unjust, and unfixable–and a threat to the Paris Climate Agreement? White Paper, Penn Center for Science, Sustainability and the Media.

Schabacher, G. (2022). Infrastruktur-Arbeit: Kulturtechniken und Zeitlichkeit der Erhaltung. Berlin: Kadmos.

Schneider, B. (2018). Entangled trees and arboreal networks of sensitive environments. ZMK Zeitschrift für Medien- und Kulturforschung, 9, 107–126. https://doi.org/10.28937/ZMK-9-1

Siddik, A. B. M., Shehabi, A. and Marston, L. (2021). The environmental footprint of data centers in the United States. Environmental Research Letters, 16(6). https://doi.org/10.1088/1748-9326/abfba1

Sotamaa, O. and Švelch, J. (2021). Introduction: why game production matters? In O. Sotamaa and J. Švelch (Eds.). Game production studies. Amsterdam: Amsterdam University Press.

Starosielski, N. (2015). The undersea network. Durham: Duke University Press.

Starosielski, N. (2016). Thermocultures of geological media. Cultural politics, 12(3), 293–309. https://doi.org/10.1215/17432197-3648858

Swinhoe, D. (2022a). CyrusOne joins orchard initiative in Ireland. https://www.datacenterdynamics.com/en/news/cyrusone-joins-orchard-initiative-in-ireland/

Swinhoe, D. (2021). Green Mountain to heat land-based trout farm. Data Center Dynamics. https://www.datacenterdynamics.com/en/news/green-mountain-to-heat-land-based-trout-farm/

Swinhoe, D. (2022b). Stack deploys beehives at data center campus in Milan. Data Center Dynamics. https://www.datacenterdynamics.com/en/news/stack-deploys-beehives-at-data-center-campus-in-milan/

United Nations Environment Programme (2023). Emissions Gap Report 2023: Broken Record – Temperatures hit new highs, yet world fails to cut emissions (again). Nairobi. https://doi.org/10.59117/20.500.11822/43922.

Varoufakis, Y. (2023). Technofeudalism: what killed capitalism. London: The Bodley Head.

Velkova J. (2021). Thermopolitics of data: cloud infrastructures and energy futures. Cultural Studies, 35(4–5), 663–683. https://doi.org/10.1080/09502386.2021.1895243

Virilio, P. and Der Derian, J. (1998). Is the author dead? – An interview with Paul Virilio. In J. Der Derian (Ed.). The Virilio Reader. Malden: Blackwell Publishers, 16–21.

Vonderau A. (2019). Storing data, infrastructuring the air: thermocultures of the cloud. Culture Machine, 18, 1–12.

Wernbacher, T., et al. (2022). HotCity—A gamified token system for reporting waste heat sources. In A. Dingli et al. (Eds.). Disruptive technologies in media, arts and design: a collection of innovative research case-studies that explore the use of artificial intelligence and blockchain within the media, arts and design sector. Cham: Springer, 15–27. https://doi.org/10.1007/978-3-030-93780-5_2

Whittle, C. et al. (2022). The environmental game design playbook (presented by the IGDA Climate Special Interest Group). International Game Developers Association.

Willett, S. R. M. (2019). When infrastructure becomes failure: a material analysis of the limitations of cloud gaming services. Culture Machine, 18, 1–14.

Woolbright, L. (2017). Game design as climate change activism. Ecozon@, 8(2), 88–102.

Zhang, W., Li, H. and Wang, S. (2023). The global energy impact of raising the space temperature for high-temperature data centers. Cell Reports Physical Science, 4(10). https://doi.org/10.1016/j.xcrp.2023.101624

MONETISING NOSTALGIA

ARTIFICIAL SCARCITY OF RETRO GAMES AND HOW IT INFLUENCES PLAYERS BEHAVIOUR

Maximilian Stefan Mohr

This paper will look at the organizational force that Super Mario 64, or rather its legacy and developer Nintendo's dealing with said legacy, expresses onto fans of the game and players in general. As a very much still sought after and popular game, Super Mario 64 will be representative of many games that might have been lost to time amidst questions of intellectual property, cultural heritage, legality vs morality and profit driven market interests. Players have been forced into different ways, e.g. emulation or flee market hunting, of dealing with such tactics and formed communities because of such factors. The paper identifies both academic and public efforts to combat the loss of games and maintain a broader access to them for all.

Keywords: Mario, Nintendo, Video Games, Ownership, Emulation

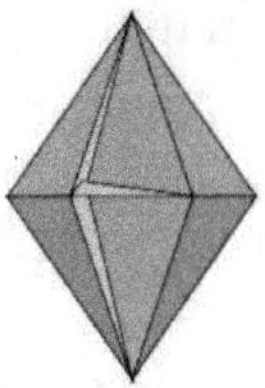

1. Introduction

Video Games are in a somewhat weird position. They combine a multitude of audio-visual medial expressions with an interactive component and create a new experience through that practice. Their special relationship not only to these such media, but also to analogue games has been coined the 'Double Alterity of Digital Games' before, as they are neither something totally else, but also not the exact same as their counterparts (Freyermuth 2015, 93). As one of the younger forms of entertainment media, it is just understandable that many analyses of them, be they journalistic or academic in nature, focus on one of their specific parts, such as the often-included narrative or their graphical fidelity. Reviews in popular media magazines are for example often structured around that compartmentalization by judging each individual part separately; scholars on the other hand frequently pick out something that their original discipline favours, such as narratives and symbolisms, just as historian and political scientist Eugen Pfister does in "On Infected and the Collapse of Society (Case Study: The Last of Us)", in which he, amongst others, examines the myths of a post-apocalyptic collapse of society and the romanisation of nature against culture (Pfister 2021).

This paper will not be an exception to that phenomenon. But rather than on the building blocks that make up the games people play, it will focus on a specific form of materiality and ownership, how game studios handle questions resulting from it and how gamers are affected by their actions.

Super Mario 64 (Nintendo 1996) released in 1996 as a launch title for Nintendo's third big home console, the Nintendo 64, for about $60. It was instantly hailed as a revolutionary game that introduces 3D platforming into the world, even though that honour technically belongs to other games (Wirtanen 2017). Nonetheless, it remains one of the most influential games of its (and today's) time, having led many others to follow its example and take inspiration. This includes 1998's *Banjo-Kazooie* (Rare 1998) and *Spyro the Dragon* (Insomniac Games 1998) as almost all of Nintendo's later mainline 3D Mario titles. The *Super Mario* franchise remains one of the bestselling game series (Clement 2023) and has led to countless publications across all types of media. Most notably for this paper may be the machinima, a narrative video most often produced through hacks of the in game-engine, "filmed" by environmental organisation Greenpeace in 2007, where in Mario, together with the playable characters from other system mascots *Halo* and *God of War*, *Master Chief* and *Kratos* respectively, is faced with the electronic waste produced by the never ending cycle of consoles being released and made obsolete a few years later when their successor arrives (Milburn 2018).

We won't dwell on the ecological implications of that short film, but rather on the idea of release cycles. It is natural for each new console to come with their own line-up of games that the predecessor is not able to utilise and vice versa. This also holds true for the next title in the Super Mario Series, *Super Mario Sunshine* (Nintendo EAD 2002), which was released for Nintendo's next console, the GameCube, and could only be played on it, while *Super Mario 64* was not playable on it. This is a simple question of hardware used; the Nintendo 64 games were shipped on cartridges, while the GameCube used optical minidiscs; only recently, with the newest generations of Sony's PlayStation and Microsoft's Xbox, notably not Nintendo's consoles, did these circumstances change. Now hardware that is built on the same logic as its former counterpart means that backwards compatibility is becoming way easier to achieve and almost the whole catalogue can be transferred to the new system (Sony Interactive Entertainment, no date).

This is where we backtrack, just as if a new door opened up in a previous level, to the beginning of this text. Games like *Super Mario 64* share another 'Double Alterity' with other media, and that is their (for the longest time at least) dependence on their corresponding hardware. Books for example consist, in maybe to broken down terms, of letters on a page, and while the production may have changed from copywriting to manual typesetting to laser printer, that is what they had to work with. The "content" of the medium book always remained the same, text made up of individual letters (McLuhan 1994, 8). Similar was the change from analogue to digital, movies "just" had to be transferred. Games though, they are, as we now showed, build in tune with the console(s) they are produced for and only play on that hardware. And with the releases of new consoles and new games, older ones fall out of the commercial interest of the developer and are as such no longer produced and / or available to be bought through official means. Unless they are ported.

2. Tracing Marios Footsteps

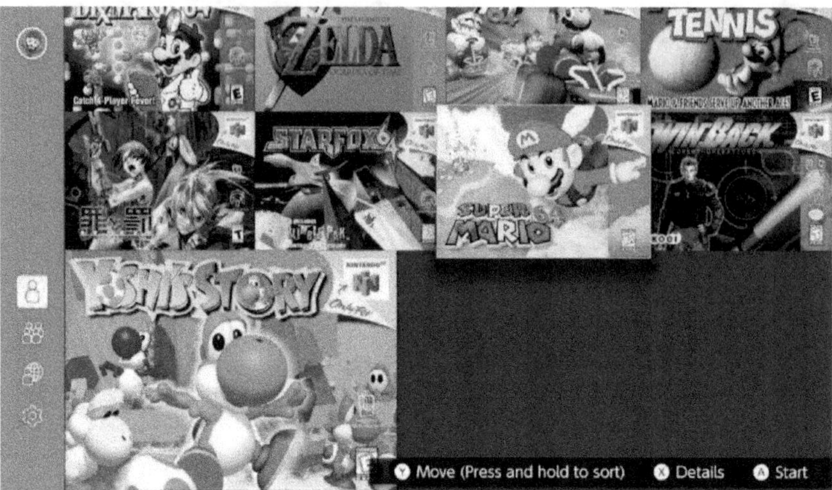

Figure 2: Super Mario 64 in the Nintendo Switch Online Service

Super Mario 64 represents a somewhat special case in this regard. The game has seen multiple versions on different platforms. In 2004 Nintendo released a remade version together with its newest handheld console, the Nintendo DS, at a price of around $40; costing $10 in 2006, the original version was brought to the Virtual Console, a digital store for specific titles on the Nintendo Wii, the successor to the GameCube; and its successor, the Wii U, saw $15 releases of both versions on its own Virtual Console in 2015. The Game was also part of *Super Mario 3D All-Stars* (Nintendo EPD and 1-UP Studio 2020), a $60 collection of three 3D Super Mario titles, which came out in September of 2020. None of these versions are officially obtainable anymore. The Nintendo DS and all its versions were officially discontinued in 2020 (BBC News 2020), while the Virtual Consoles both for the Wii (Nintendo 2019) and the Wii U (Nintendo 2023) were shut down. As for *Super Mario 3D All-Stars*, the collection was only available digitally up until the end of March 2021("Super Mario 3D All-Stars leaves Nintendo eShop on March 31st - News - Nintendo Official Site," 2021), physical versions were not reproduced. As of now, the only official way to play the game is through Nintendo's Switch Online Subscription Service for the price of $50 annually. This also requires an active Internet connection and once someone ends their subscription, they lose access to the game, a notable difference to the previous offered online versions.

Table 1. Total Cost of playing Super Mario 64 throughout the years

Game	Price (+ Price of Console at Release)
Super Mario 64	$60 ($200)
Super Mario DS	$40 ($150)
Wii Virtual Console Release	$10 ($249)
Wii U Virtual Console (Versions of both the 64 and DS Games)	2 * $15 ($299)
Nintendo Switch Online (Subscription, annual as example)	$50 ($299)
3D All-Stars	$60 (also on Switch)
Total Cost	$1447

All of this has led players who want to play the game but do or did not own the corresponding console of the time, into different strategies. On the physical side, the retro and used video game market was born. Depending on circulation and preserved quality, retro games on flea markets and auction sites like eBay can go for everything between five and multiple thousands of euros, although the latter ones are more a case for the collector aficionados. There are also whole stores that only deal in used games or exchange events organised that it has sprawled event lists onto the internet (retroplace 2021). An economy of its own and all of this going on largely untouched by companies like Nintendo.

The ways players move on the digital side are a little more complicated. On the one hand, the uncertainty of when games, especially digital only releases, are taken offline can lead to impulse buying due to FOMO (fear of missing out, exemplified in (Zhang et al. 2022) in context of scarcity during the Covid-Pandemic). It also entices the use of emulators, software that mimics a different hardware than the one it runs on to play the original code of a given game, usually referred to as a ROM (read only memory) (Dor 2023). For this, there are multiple websites which share these ROMs to download, often free of charge. While some might describe this practice as a "legal grey area" (Mosqueda 2016), there is judicial precedent of its illegality in form of lawsuits won by Nintendo, further limiting the options of players who do not want to risk repercussions for their wish to play old video games (Stedman 2019)

The organisational force is therefore only indirectly emitting from the games like *Super Mario 64* themself. Much rather it is an economic and political practice on the side of rights holders like Nintendo that forms a struggle for players, and while it might not be quite the same as being part of a newly emerging industrial machinery, the sites of power (Beyes et al. 2022, 1009–1010) become even more apparent if we consider the question of academic organisation and game preservation.

Game Studies are, in principle, interested in all forms of games. That includes, to a non-minimal degree, the historic emergence of them. To be able to study said emergence, access to the games themself is non-negotiable. In times of digital storefronts, it should not be a problem to either make game files, if they have survived of course, available to buy or, in case of abandonment, give people and institutions the possibility to archive them. Such calls have been made, also in academia, over ten years ago (Newman 2012. They also talk about artistic practices possible through access to the game files.). Another argument is made insofar as that games as they gain more and more in popularity build up a form of 'cultural heritage' (Barwick et al. 2010) which would get lost if not properly preserved. A claim supported by the wish of many players to relive nostalgia, by the already shown sales figures, but also by the companies themselves celebrating the "birthdays" of their characters and their own cultural history through their releases. ("The official home of Super Mario – History," n.d.). And finally, games harbour the potential to function as an 'interactive archive' themselves, expressing unique ways of conveying historical circumstances and possibly creating understanding of psychological situations. An often brought in example is Ubisoft Montpellier's Valiant Hearts: The Great War (Ubisoft, 2014), which shows the dire situations both soldiers and civilians found themselves in during the First World War (Hartman et al. 2021). Of course, academics have not been sitting idle. Projects such as *The International Computer Game Collection* are actively collecting information and actual games to preserve them and have secured funding, in this case even from political partners. ('About Us - Internationale Computerspielesammlung (EN)', n.d.)

The aforementioned closing of Nintendo's Wii U eShop has once more reignited the ongoing debate. While game scholars try to find solutions in tandem with Nintendo, their position remains steadfast for the given moment. They oppose any attempt at the organisation of an online library and so far have been given the legal right to do so (Orland 2023).

There are still efforts brought on by these business practices to combat the loss of games and game knowledge. Individuals create podcasts ("Stay Forever" 2023) or try to save games being taken offline (The Completionist 2023). Studies like the 'Survey of the Video Game Reissue Market in the United States' (Salvador 2023) re-shine the light on the issue and also manage to gather some public support and visibility ("Video Game History Foundation on Twitter," 2023).

For the time being, the everyday player faces fewer options yet. There are repeated calls for Nintendo to release their old games (GameCentral 2021), showing that the players are, through their wish of playing old favourites, willing to enter a 'symbolic order' (Siegert and Peters 2012, 10) that would then be established by Nintendo. In the case of *Super Mario 64*, they admittedly have the chance (hidden behind a costly console, see the table further up), but for many other games, that is not the case. For those seeking these, there is a game itself afoot, almost like a hunt, which can be thrilling, but also stressful (Battaglia 2022). In some cases, where games offer the possibility of multiplayer, either co-operational or versus, players come together and organise events like the yearly Evolution Championship Series to come together and compete while raising money for charity. In 2013, Nintendo also tried to prevent the streaming of their fighting game Super Smash Bros. Melee (HAL Laboratory 2001), but caved after fan backlash (Summerley 2020, p. 62). The game went on to collect the most donations of all participants. (Shoryuken 2016).

Another case for games being pulled from stores is licensing, something that doesn't initially point to corporate greed, but in the end follows similar patterns. Exemplary, let's shortly look at the Lord of the Rings games published by Electronic Arts between the years 2002 and 2009. During this time, EA brought seven titles in total to the market, more, if one is to account for the in part big differences between release platforms. These games were based on the Peter Jackson film trilogy and thus had to be licensed accordingly. Since then, the rights to publish games based on the films and literary works by J.R.R Tolkien have, with a small stint at Warner Bros. Entertainment, moved to the Embracer Group, which is at the moment the owner of Middle-Earth Enterprises (Prescott

2022). The games published by Electronic Arts, which especially in the case of the *Battle for Middle-earth* series still experiences active modding support by its fans, are since stuck in "licensing hell" and no longer available in physical stores, not to begin digital storefronts, where they never appeared to begin with. This situation probably could be solved by a partnership between the companies, but presumably won't happen in the foreseeable future due to various factors, not the least the question who would reap in the bulk of profits.

This paper may read a tad activistic, but to recap in the end it will go a step further and divide. There are two forces of organisation being pushed on players and archivists in this constellation, one neutral or even positive by the games themselves, which is passive. This force expresses itself through the practices of people trying to preserve games in a playable state, for reasons such as cultural archiving or simply nostalgic feelings towards them. The second force is of a hindering, or negative, nature, and it is the active counterpart to the first one. As newer generations join the greater gaming community, this also means they struggle more and more to join into discussions around older titles. We can just hope that a solution can be found, before games face the same fate as early Silent Films, where an estimated 70 percent of them have been lost to time (Ohlheiser, 2014).

About the Author

Maximilian Stefan Mohr is enrolled in the master program Media and Digital Studies at Leuphana University in Lüneburg where he also works as a student assistant at the Leuphana Institute for Advanced Studies in Culture and Society. His main research interests include critical theory, phenomenological and social impacts of media and technology, as well as game studies, where Mohr is still trying to find his niche. His favourite games combine artful presentation with strong gameplay ideas, such as Brothers: A Tale of Two Sons (2013) and Ori and the Blind Forest (2015).

Socials: @legilian

References

Barwick, J., J. Dearnley, and A. Muir (2010) 'Playing Games With Cultural Heritage: A Comparative Case Study Analysis of the Current Status of Digital Game Preservation'. Games and Culture, December.

Battaglia, N. (2022) 'Collecting Memories: A Chat With Retro Game Collectors About The Future Of Their Hobby'. DualShockers. https://www.dualshockers.com/retro-game-collectors-interview/

BBC News (2020) 'Nintendo 3DS Discontinued after Almost a Decade'. BBC News, sec. Technology. https://www.bbc.com/news/technology-54191058

Beyes, T., W. H. K. Chun, J. Clarke, M. Flyverbom, and R. Holt (2022) 'Ten Theses on Technology and Organization: Introduction to the Special Issue'. Organization Studies 43 (7): 1001–18.

Bungie (2001) 'Halo: Combat Evolved'. Xbox. Microsoft Game Studios.

Clement, J. (2023) 'Best-Selling Video Game Franchises 2022'. Statista. https://www.statista.com/statistics/1247964/best-selling-video-gaming-franchises/.

Dor, S. (2023) 'Emulation'. In The Routledge Companion to Video Game Studies, edited by Mark J.P. Wolf and Bernard Perron, 2nd ed. Routledge.

Freyermuth, G. S. (2015) Games | Game Design | Game Studies: An Introduction. Games | Game Design | Game Studies. Bielefeld: transcript Verlag.

GameCentral (2021) 'Nintendo Need to Do Better at Selling Their Old Games - Reader's Feature'. Metro (blog). https://metro.co.uk/2021/03/20/nintendo-need-to-do-better-at-selling-their-old-games-14273083/.

HAL Laboratory (2001) 'Super Smash Bros. Melee'. GameCube. Nintendo.

Hartman, A., R. Tulloch, and H. Young (2021) 'Video Games as Public History: Archives, Empathy and Affinity'. Game Studies 21 (4).

Insomniac Games (1998) 'Spyro the Dragon'. PlayStation. Sony Computer Entertainment.

McLuhan, M. (1994) Understanding Media. The Extensions of Men. First MIT Press edition. Cambridge, Massachusetts. London, England: The MIT Press.

Milburn, C. (2018) Respawn : Gamers, Hackers and Technological Life. Experimental Futures. Technological Lives, Scientific Arts, Anthropological Voices. Durham: Duke University Press.

Mosqueda, A. J. (2016) 'The Grey Area Behind Emulators'. Houstonian News. https://houstoniannews.com/2016/10/18/the-grey-area-behind-emulators/.

Naughty Dog (2013) 'The Last of Us'. Playstation 3. Sony Interactive Entertainment.

Newman, J. (2012) 'Illegal Deposit'. Convergence.https://doi.org/10.1177/1354856512456790.

Nintendo (1996) 'Super Mario 64'. Nintendo 64. Nintendo.

——— (2019) 'Nintendo Support: Wii Shop Channel Discontinuation'. https://en-americas-support.nintendo.com/app/answers/detail/a_id/27560/~/wii-shop-channel-discontinuation.

——— (2023) 'Nintendo Support: Wii U & Nintendo 3DS EShop Discontinuation Q&A'. https://en-americas-support.nintendo.com/app/answers/detail/a_id/57847/~/wii-u-%26-nintendo-3ds-eshop-discontinuation-q%26a.

Nintendo EAD (2002) 'Super Mario Sunshine'. GameCube. Nintendo.

——— (2004) 'Super Mario 64 DS'. Nintendo DS. Nintendo.

Nintendo EPD, and 1-UP Studio (2020) 'Super Mario 3D All-Stars'. Nintendo Switch.

Nintendo R&D1, and Intelligent Systems (1986) 'Metroid'. Nintendo Entertainment System. Nintendo.

Ohlheiser, A. (2014) 'Most of America's Silent Films Are Lost Forever'. The Wire. https://web.archive.org/web/20141105020735/http://www.thewire.com/culture/2013/12/most-americas-silent-films-are-lost-forever/355775/.

Orland, K. (2023) 'Why Game Archivists Are Dreading This Month's 3DS/Wii U EShop Shutdown'. Ars Technica. https://arstechnica.com/gaming/2023/03/why-game-archivists-are-dreading-this-months-3ds-wii-u-eshop-shutdown/.

Pfister, E. (2021) 'On Infected and the Collapse of Society (Case Study: The Last of Us)'. Horror - Game - Politics (blog). https://hgp.hypotheses.org/1545.

Prescott, S. (2022) 'Embracer Goes on Spending Spree: Buys Lord of the Rings IP Rights, Tripwire Interactive, and More'. PC Gamer,. https://www.pcgamer.com/embracer-goes-on-spending-spree-buys-lord-of-the-rings-ip-rights-tripwire-interactive-and-more/.

Rare. (1998) 'Banjo-Kazooie'. Nintendo 64.

retroplace. (2021) 'Börsenticker'. retroplace.com. https://www.retroplace.com/de/feature/boersenticker/165.

Salvador, P. (2023) 'Survey of the Video Game Reissue Market in the United States'. Zenodo.

Santa Monica Studio (2005) 'God of War'. PlayStation 2. Sony Computer Entertainment.

Shoryuken (2016) 'Fighting Game Fans Raise over $225,000 for Breast Cancer Research. Smash Wins! | Shoryuken'. https://web.archive.org/web/20160130090146/http://shoryuken.com/2013/02/01/fighting-game-fans-raise-over-225000-for-breast-cancer-research-smash-wins/.

Siegert, B., and J. D. Peters. (2012) 'Doors: On the Materiality of the Symbolic'. Grey Room 47 (April): 6–23.

Sony Interactive Entertainment. 'Backward Compatibility: PS4 Games Playable on PS5 Consoles'. no date. https://www.playstation.com/en-gb/support/games/ps5-backward-compatibility-games/.

'Stay Forever' (2023) Stay Forever. https://www.stayforever.de/.

Stedman, K. D. (2019) 'Sue for Mario Bros.: Nintendo vs. Emulation'. In The 2018 Intellectual Property Annual. Intellectual Property Standing Group of the Conference on

College Composition and Communication, edited by Clancy Ratliff, 16–20. UC Santa Barbara: Writing Program: The Intellectual Property Standing Group of the Conference on College Composition and Communication.

Summerley, R. (2020) 'The Development of Sports: A Comparative Analysis of the Early Institutionalization of Traditional Sports and E-Sports'. Games and Culture 15 (1): 51–72.

'Super Mario 3D All-Stars Leaves Nintendo EShop on March 31st - News - Nintendo Official Site'. (2021) https://www.nintendo.com/whatsnew/super-mario-3d-all-stars-leaves-nintendo-eshop-on-march-31st/.

The Completionist, dir. (2023) I Bought EVERY Nintendo Wii U & 3DS Game before the Nintendo EShop Closes. https://www.youtube.com/watch?v=ujHUMG0Uovs.

'The Official Home of Super MarioTM – History'. https://mario.nintendo.com/history/.

Ubisoft (2014) 'Valiant Hearts: The Great War'

'Video Game History Foundation on Twitter' (2023) Twitter. https://twitter.com/GameHistoryOrg/status/1678419548326772737.

Wirtanen, J. (2017) 'The 3D Platformer: How 1996 Witnessed the Birth of a Genre – Retrovolve'. https://retrovolve.com/the-3d-platformer-how-1996-witnessed-the-birth-of-a-genre/.

Zhang, J., N. Jiang, J. J. Turner, and S. Pahlevan-Sharif. (2022) 'The Impact of Scarcity on Consumers' Impulse Buying Based on the S-O-R Theory'. Frontiers in Psychology 13. https://www.frontiersin.org/articles/10.3389/fpsyg.2022.792419.

Internationale Computerspielesammlung (EN) (n.d) 'About Us' https://www.internationale-computerspielesammlung.de/en/about-us.

GAME CULTURE BETWEEN FINE ARTS AND CRUDE ECONOMIES

Simon Huber

The perception of the contemporary habits of gaming as cultural affair has consequences. This essay explores different meanings that emerge, when the socio-economical practices surrounding digital media are supposed to be more than mere entertainment. The campaigning for acceptance of games as cultural asset produces in different contexts a wide array of connotations: historical schemes of technological development, social mobility, national competition, just to tap into a few. For a conclusion about how to deal with these ambiguities the paper is focusing on the Ludology vs. Narratology-debate (cf. Mukherjee 2015), as a central part of the disciplinary struggle, that arises from similar questions in the academic field. In this specific case, the ludological approach offers an inverted perspective, that is gained from the object of interest and is not borrowed by an established discipline, like economics, literature, media or art history that formalize games as phenomena according to the applied methods. Going beyond a binary classification of games as either art or models for quantification, we aim to cultivate a truly ludic perspective on financial transactions, from which knowledge emerges that is embedded within the dynamic of the game form and its procedurality (Rautzenberg et al. 2021).

Keywords: games culture, cultural techniques, game art, ludology, material culture

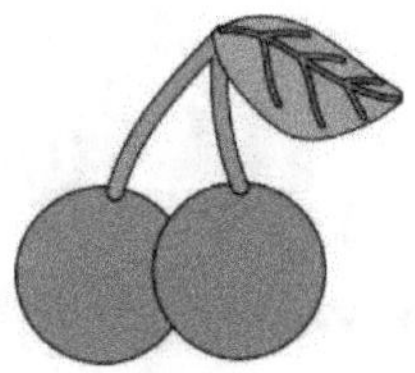

1. Prima facie: games as cultural goods

In 2020 the *Handbuch Gameskultur* is published and the mere existence of such a book is interesting for observers of our times. As the historian of sciences Ludwik Fleck pointed out in his influential book about the *Genesis and development of a scientific fact* (2021[1935]), hand books are an important medium, through which scientific communities reproduce themselves: that means reproducing the ways they see; the ways they choose what is observed; the ways they interpret; and the ways they communicate their findings — in short: how any scientific community produces facts.

He differentiated between various sciences, depending on whether they're relying on the popularization, journals or — indeed – handbooks. So as a consequence, it seems just right, that the editors plotted this publication itself as milestone into this overview that is published with the texts (fig. 1). One could argue that we're witnessing an attempt of game scholars to consolidate their field of research through a book.

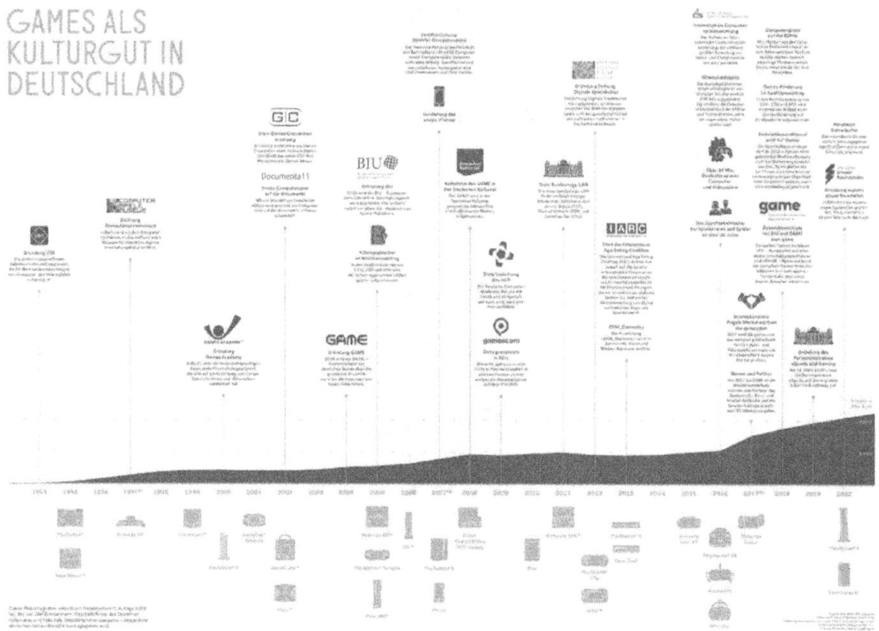

Figure 1. Poster „Games as cultural good in Germany" attached to the Handbuch Gameskultur (2020), reprinted with permission of the owner.

The main object of interest is framed as a cultural good („Kulturgut") via a poster included in the print version. It shows a diagram, that charts the rise of gaming culture in tracing the the computational goods flooding the market; they are causing remarkable economic effects, that the viewers can see continuously rising up to more than € 4.000 Million as the handbook is released.

This chart is not plain „facts'n'figures". Besides the impressive sales volume, it tells a lot in a graphically implicit manner: The blue shapes visualize the growing market like a wave. It surfaces in the early 1990s and continuously is becoming more. Some might come to conclusion that we need to prepare! Above the value generated, one can trace the establishment of institutions as punctual, significant milestones in a somewhat naturally growing and continuously evolving development of cultural goods. The color red shows its material basis: the timeline itself and when precisely innovative gaming devices and products hit the market, contributing to this growth. They add specific forms to the rather vague term of cultural goods and the fluid impression of revenue streams.

These are the visuals to the story that's been told over and over again in the past decades: It emphasizes the importance of games. It stresses the fact, that they deserve our attention. Game researchers are doing an important job; they are not only ‚into games' because of the fun of playing them. Also gaming is not a childish activity that only kids do. (Certainly, most game designs are created by adults, even though they might address children.) It's a ‚cultural good' and needs research that is legit and serious. Probably any game scholar can remember a moment, when she emphasized the well-known fact, that the revenue that games make, exceeds globally speaking any other segment of the entertainment industry.

Tonio Schachinger, a young Austrian writer, who recently received the *Deutscher Buchpreis,* spoke about his latest novel and used exactly this formula in an interview to promote his new book. [1] The protagonist of this coming-of-age novel *Echtzeitalter* (2023) is a gamer. The author — himself a relevant player in the

[1] At the moment of writing this paper, the video can be watched here: https://www.servustv.com/kultur/v/aa4sleqlkt5hmynlkn2t/ But besides the actual statement in this interview (at the time point 9:09) the novel over all seems to matter because of this juxtaposition. The justification text of the jury hints again at the opposition of computer games to the canonical literary tradition exercised in school (cf. https://www.deutscher-buchpreis.de/nominiert/)

cultural field of fiction writing — felt the need to explain this to listeners of literature shows.

2. A cultural force on the rise

This chart displays an economic development and a fight for its acceptance as relevant part of the cultural department. That means a massive change, and this deserves our attention: It deserves the museums, that save gaming heritage from oblivion; it deserves the media coverage, that reflect on the best practices to cultivate this societal good; it deserves the mentioned juries and the prices, that tell us which games are actually outstanding among the mass production in full steam; it deserves the the attention of politicians, therefore the attendance of the chancellor Angela Merkel herself at the *Gamescom* in 2017. It deserves a handbook and the academic controversy.

It's not just a plain data projection, there are also attempts to flesh out storytelling-wise, what this rise means on a personal level: not only the young play games, also the adults, who grew up with them as important part of their lives. Games are woven into their childhood memories, they are part of their nostalgic feelings, so ultimately those are used to interact differently with the story worlds, they are familiar with.

Maybe they even learned a different skill set to express themselves: I paraphrase Csongor Baranyai, who was verbally making an important point: He argued that adolescent children used to pick up their guitar and write a punk song about their frustration. Nowadays teenagers might make a game to articulate their protest. Apart from the question, whether this is true, it obviously must be a different protest with a different audience, that is receiving the message differently. So, gaming produces as a new media form a new youth culture — maybe even another youth per se: through the smart phone the line between personal autonomy and parental control is renegotiated.

With the understanding of games as cultural good a new medium for self-expression emerges. This implies several questions, questioning the state of game design as established art form: Is it only popping up at the documenta, within the art scene; or is it a discourse on its own, with its own codes, rules and institutions? What are the premises, that we can accept a new cultural good on its own terms? What does it mean, when after decades of struggle game design and gaming practices are finally attributed to the domain of culture? If we figure this new subsection of culture rising, when is its climax to be expected? How is its fall to be imagined?

3. Popular culture vs. canonical culture

With the everyday use of the term culture historical schemes come along. Looking at the cinemas, the record labels, the print publishers, the network stations, the theaters, all those cultural institutions which are more or less in crisis, one can compare the changes witnessed there with the established gaming practices. How are those corresponding with the digital circumstances we're living in? This new digital regime is at the same time laying ground for the economic success of gaming. [2]

If somebody stresses the point that games have outrun the movies, I usually answer: Game studios hire screenwriters for their products. The game industries are depending on the knowledge that those storytellers incorporate, in spite of the fact that the cinematic style of narration is outmoded by games. Still they are needed to produce artifacts that are culturally compatible and cater to a visual comprehensible form. Embedded in such interdependencies games appear just as another layer of popular culture. [3] Are games no culture after all, but just another technological effect of media convergence? This traces back to the question of nowadays „platform economies" (cf. Seemann, 2019) and their industry standards.

The notion of culture at hand has not only a historical dimension in which technological progress becomes visible. Culture was used to describe national differences in contrast to scientific and technical development: Differences that shine through the artwork; features that can't be separated from a specific artistic expression, so the well-educated could tell the difference of German and French

---

[2] The overarching cultural change stimulated by computational technology is addressed more precisely as „digital culture" in a way that Felix Stalder (2018) defined it as it affects other media-cultural areas like music, film and entertainment.

[3] As such it is defined by its opposition to what is traditionally considered as cultural value and therefore the fight for acceptance inherited by the popular discourse (cf. Fiske, 1989).

style, or they can argue whatever makes this piece of fine art by Michelangelo paramount for the understanding of Italian nationality.

How would this kind of thinking apply to games culture? In a near future, children at school would not have to play any instructive game to cover a certain part of the curriculum, but maybe *Valve*'s original *Half-Life*. This game might be considered so special because of the impact it had: There are sequels, mods and spin-offs and other games running on the same engine. In a first-person-shooter genealogy *Half-Life* could be considered the point where other important genres and iconic titles branch out from: *Counterstrike*, a tactical multiplayer shooter and early title to be played in tournaments; and *Portal*, another title that advanced the puzzles given in the virtual settings of the original *Half-Life* relying on the innovative physics engine. Also the platform *Steam* belongs to the company *Valve*. So in this exemplary reasoning *Half-Life* lead arguably to economically, academically and culturally significant output that added up to the public controversy. This title would be necessary to understand the age around 2000 und the cultural context in which it emerged and contributed to.

So there's a difference within our conception of culture, regarding whether our own context is thematized or some time and place we consider as foreign. The distance to other eras and epochs gives the culture considered extinct an opaque and superficial touch. For example, thinking of ancient Egyptians, one likes to think of pyramids, papyrus, sphinxes, hieroglyphs. One's own immediate cultural sphere is inhabited, decorated, and decoded fairly along the intended ways. So we are immersed in our own culture that appears transparent as we are engaged in it through the cultural techniques we apply, without thinking about it: contemporary culture is addressed as infra-structural matter; the line between form and function blurs. It is crucial to keep in mind, what the philosopher Robert Pfaller (2002) calls „illusions of perspective": the assessment of a culture, we don't consider ourselves a part of, establishes an ideologically distorted view in which meaning is attributed. To use a positive term, one could also refer to Bruno Latour's concept of a „symmetrical anthropology" (1995), that does not treat the own modern, scientifically structured and mediated culture in the biased way. This again is not (only) a critique of current practices of xenophobic othering, but principally a matter of thinking about how processes of transformation within the cultural sphere can be discursively described, imagined and theorized.

What are common ways to reflect on gaming culture in our age? Accepted as a cultural good it is allowed to think about it in at least three ways: games as piece of artwork, games as popular culture embedded in the community surrounding it and games as technically extended economic relationship:

Firstly, there are numerous academic papers that cover specific games in order to extract the cultural meaning in ways similar to those used by sophisticated critics of fine art. Tobias Unterhuber (2020) analyzed thoroughly the difficulties of establishing a canonical relationship to games. Secondly, newspapers and magazines approach the matter as popular culture or youth culture. These journalists do service to the community of gamers, as they report and discuss the variety of new releases. Thirdly, the established economic relationships are simply read out loud: You buy this game, so you are a part of it. If you also play it, you will get continuously better at it. In contrast to the traditional clubs that compete in tournaments one needs to buy a whole digital game — not just some of the parts you need to play: the equipment, access to the playing field or membership fees in associations — whatever is needed to partake in any given community of players of that specific game.

In the first case there is nowadays probably more economic and sociological knowledge involved, when it comes to excavating a certain cultural tendency in the design of games. This is because cross-disciplinary work has become the standard of game studies. So scholars include this sort of knowledge and attribute certain differences in the game to the cultural context in which the game was designed.

But when culture is emerging from the communication between producers, players and fans then it's regarded as residue from the use of technology. If someone is ‚into games', and so are his friends and playmates from Sweden, Britain and Albania, their nationalities and local differences don't matter as much anymore, as they are consuming the same media products; they're interacting via the designed channel; they're using the same lingo to chat about it, and so on.

That reminds us also about a rather bad connotation that comes nowadays with the term culture. In scandalous times of #meetoo and #gamergate one is used to the fact that culture can contain, hide or foster toxic behavior like chauvinism. Next to the heavily contested border between civilized ‚high culture' and clandestine ‚low culture', we find morally devious culture located on this spectrum.[4]

4. Cultural hegemony and critical interventions

Such graphics (fig.1) might trace a German footprint within game culture, as the displayed milestones are events happening specifically in Germany. But at the same time, it corresponds to a global trend. We can expect it to represent American history as well — actually we might expect it to represent an even bigger effect on market affairs there, as it's originating there.

This rise of games culture could as well be read as an expression of the hegemony of American culture in our neo-liberal age acted out through entertainment systems, that serves us accordingly with the ideology that we need to misjudge our own economic situation.

Still, even though this seems valid, this critical take on the economic status-quo is grounded in left-wing theory. The question remains: What terminology can game scholars and researchers refer to, when it comes to formulating a critique in their own terms? This brings us back to the *Narratologist vs. Ludologist*-debate, that some say never took place. The antagonism between those two positions is often exaggerated, as these camps can't be found in this distinctness. Still, the controversy has become canonical because it roots in the struggle for a disciplinary identity. So for several decades we witness the appearance of new research programs, the assembling of fitting methods to tackle a new cultural phenomenon, that some would like to call a discipline on their own (cf. Mukherjee, 2015).

Ludologists claim that games don't tell stories, so it is at least problematic to apply frameworks, methods and tools we have at hand from other established disciplines (linguistics, literature, art history, etc.). We can't do research about this new medium, like we designed our investigations about theatre, books,

---

[4] This seems sketchy to those anyone who refined their notion of culture – because it is. Nonetheless this schematic thinking is crucial for connecting the academic discussion of the term *culture* with its everyday usage, which is the aim of this paper.

newspaper, films. This must lead to misunderstandings, because one misses what's actually new about these Games.

Now turning back to the figure, one can see this diagram as an arrangement of economic data with historical facts added, and therefore not necessary a ludological, but a standardized economic perspective on games culture. From a ludologist's standpoint, this is just a chart that shows how computational media developed new forms of monetization of human play. Because humans played games before there were computers.

Proper ludologists investigate critically by stripping away any decoration, anything non-essential, everything accidental, like an interchangeable color and ultimately also the stories that are embedded in rule-based structures. The understanding of games that is left by analyzing is commonly known as „mechanical", although it doesn't concern only interaction with machines, but also basic human action at play like throwing a ball.

5. The simple pleasure of inserting coins

Rules that allow players to interact through a ball do not constitute a story. For some game scholars this is convincing enough to call themselves ludologists. Stories don't seem necessary for games. Sometimes they are added to give context that helps to engage with the game mechanic. [5]

On the other hand, products like *Assassin's Creed* obviously tell a story; they are even fictionalizing a computational technology that allows us to get an accurate account of the historical fact in form of an immersive experience (cf. Huber 2014a). As historian I'm not very much concerned with the ontological enigma

[5] „The floor is lava!" is much shorter than any instruction in this game of ‚not touching the floor under any circumstances, ideally with an exaggerated amount of enthusiasm, because you are pretending to be dealing with an obviously fictional matter of life and death', could possibly be. As this game is played on the same ground that supports us in daily life, this game seems to be a good example of how the formal separation from the profane world can be completely contained in the narrative. The magic circle equals solely the shared phantasy obtained by the players.

whether games tell stories, but rather simply ask: „Since when do games tell stories?"

I already presented my findings to this question in great detail as a media archeological excavation of the emergence of cutscenes (cf. Huber 2014b): With the widespread use of home computers the new games were made for households rather than arcade halls. So to monetize the desire to play different strategies emerged: Formerly players who just failed were offered another shot by inserting a coin. So they were allowed to aim for the new high score, that was then displayed on the local machine's scoreboard. On your own computer at home, one could have as many shots as one wanted to. Games needed to come to an end, so the demand for another one can be artificially created. To put this cultural change into a catchy formula: *happy end instead of highscore.*

Thus, the quarter I have to insert is like a bet I take on: I can place myself on top of the scoreboard and the local game community with the amount of tries I buy. The money I pay for a game to play at home is the price of a story I consume through the interface of my computer, instead of a book, for example. So the narratologist's view is based on many more preconditions: the basic capacities of computational devices for home use, the possibilities to distribute games per data carriers (like the CD-ROM); also hardware like graphic cards that set the standard for ‚realistic' representations and also indirectly for independent games that are now renouncing those features. In a ludological framework these forms of exchange (of coins, packaged goods and bootlegs) that predetermine the in-game action become part of the gameplay analysis.

Narratology focusses on how gameplay is adapted to discourse; how it is translated into language and this happens in many ways inside and outside the game, as discussed above. Whereas Ludology is decentralizing the game product itself and is able to reconfigure games at a fundamental level within their context. This broadens the area of research but comes with a price as the lines between different games — board games, digital games, sports — becomes blurry and the cultural sub-texts gets very difficult to decode.

Let's consider this urban legend: the first Pong machine that was placed in a pub needed technical support just a day after it was set up. The producer, who went there to see what the problem was, found the machine so full of coins that it wasn't capable of taking any more money. It wasn't broken, the builders just didn't anticipate the extend of success (Berlin 2017).

That makes a good story. As such it's useful for marketing and the chronicles, typically written by winners. Besides that it might be not true (cf. Smith 2013), it's remarkable how it doesn't objectify the success through facts and figures. It emphasizes the enormous number of coins, several handfuls adding up to some 100$. It comes from the realm of myth. Unlike the chart from the start, it doesn't calculate the return of investment. It recalls the material culture and the specific effect it had on the people trying this machine, that could have made a magical appearance to them. It focuses actually on a flawed design of this early version, because it turned out that it wasn't fit for the demand it created immediately.

At the *Vienna Maker Fair* in June 2023 a hobbyist exhibited his reconstruction of the original *Pong*, giving closest attention to every detail: He was taking great care to use the right buttons and switches and also the original slot. To try out his replica, he handed over a coin. There was no need to pay, but still to insert a coin, because this act set in motion the video game. The money handling is part of the play experience.

Considered by many as the first video game on the market, *Pong* is complete with the insertion slot where players need to put loose change into, simply because of its circuit diagram. Such an illustrative piece creates evidence about how people received new media forms and adapted to it; how traditional economic cycles and new technologies were hard wired and culturally connected in the first place. People are familiar with handling money but are new to video games. Basically the exchange of a real world currency for in-game currencies — balls, lifes, gold, experience points, etc. — is established.

6. A genuinely ludological view on cultural exchange

The goal of this essay is to offer an inverted perspective: Neither looking upon games culture through an economic lens as a growing market, nor emphasizing games culture as a form of artistic expression that is becoming more and more common because of its increasing popularity. Instead focusing on the handling of money with a ludological lens means tackling the opaque material culture that underpins the virtualizations and augmentations that are normally addressed as meaningful interactions through games. The digital culture they form seems to be so transparent and continuously converging with our everyday life, in so-called extended realties. But our habits of everyday trading, the handling of goods and money, the mathematical practices have also a ludogical aspect to them that can be uncovered in their materiality.

Our ordinary life is still full of transactions fueled by small change: public transport ticketing, lotteries, tip jars, fully automated coffee vendor machines; all these transactional moments, that make your time in a specific place worthwhile and maybe even special in a very rudimentary way.

There are arcade halls with slot machines run by coins, but economically speaking casinos are more important. They exchange real life currencies into shiny jetons, that seduce one to engage into gambling. Money is turned into something that makes it fun to play with. Such tokens have their own feel to it, so the croupiers can handle it in a magically precise way to place bets for the customers they are serving.

Also, we tend to forget about toys from childhood like marbles.[6] On one hand this is a game mastered in the yard, but at the same time it's a toy that is collected. As such a dear thing it is at stake in each game. From here it's not far to the layered game experience of trading card games. They are not only about the designed competition, but also about collecting, trading and the depicted story worlds. Here again the ongoing acts of exchange play an important part in the game experience.

If bargaining doesn't involve cash, we still can find material aspects in their ludic set up: Think about auctions and their bidding processes, which use a game mechanic to determine the price for a piece of art. Here the price is not determined by bargaining about its actual value, or by the usual context of a competitive market for commodities.7 It follows its own set of rules, that is

---

[6] If it weren't for entertainment series like *Squid Game* (2021). This fictional game show reminds us of children's game culture that is not monetized, simply acted out in the yard, the parks, on the street. It is actually creating horror just by pointing towards the brutality that can emerge from child's play. Played by adults these games are presented bare of any nostalgic bias.

[7] Also this case can easily be illustrated by an iconic moment from the movies: In *Monty Python's Life of Brian* (1979) the protagonist is on the run fleeing from soldiers. He wants to buy a bottle that should help him escape, but the merchant insists on extensive negotiations, bevor he can receive the money and hand over the product. Like any playful communication also haggling tends to excessive dynamics.

gaining its energy for playful interaction through information-asymmetry, resulting from the uniqueness of the art object.

On a sidenote, there is another tricky case whether a game culture is a valuable asset for the cultural identity: sports. Cash is not involved in the games themselves. (Of course, there is betting and gambling surrounding it.) But the public matter of sport adds another layer of national interest and fandom. South Korea is a common example for a seemingly progressive political decision to foster their national e-sports capacities. According to Yu (2018) this is now again contested by China. An international competition about cultural hegemony arises. In more classical sports money serves as for achieving what can be called „meta-game balance" in technical terms of game designers: the salary caps for players guarantee that the amount of available money alone is decisive for their in-game success: because of these rules „a wealthy team can't just outbid everyone else for the best players." (Schreiber & Romero, 2022, p.41)

So money is woven into the brick and mortar of stadiums and the tournament taking place within: a society pays for the infrastructure to host the game events on a larger level; as well as it is part of the social event, taking place and being monetized again (sponsorships, advertisement, etc.) These cultural forms allow the audience to partake in the games as sporting events by showing their support. For all these habits the fans need to trust the established procedure to determine the winner.

7. Coins, commodities, and accounts

Originally loose change puts games into the loop of the entertainment industries. The handling of money can be understood by game designers, artists and scholars as part of the play experience. Also nowadays the immersion into expansive story worlds is an effect designed for the monetization of material culture we're already accommodated with.

Considering the money handling as part of the game experience, like in slot machines, we find gaming practices together with the according story worlds themselves optimized for widespread circulation through the past decades: At first, the narratives were packed into game machines, then cartridges, CDs and other data carrier until they have been obsolete because of all surrounding data streams and wireless internet connection. The container is now the legal subtext, the license, the terms and conditions that spell out under what circumstances when and how I'm able to play. So what becomes continuously uniform is the material culture of the gaming market, which is run on platforms.

Board games are an interesting exception: Since *Monopoly* (originally *The Landlords' Game*) there is a heavily diversified spectrum of different games. They can't rely on the common knowledge embedded in everyday culture to play these very different games. For example, it might be considered as part of proper education being able to play *Chess* or *Go*. Those modern board games [8] on the other hand ultimately need to provide the material basics with the rulebook in a box. While the DVD-Covers are disappearing these boxes are stacked and shelved like a book. This way it employs themes and narratives that become a relevant part in over-all aesthetics of a non-digital game.

In-App payments on the other hand are the ultimate entanglement of paying and playing, where the money does not buy me more past-time — i.e. another round. In-App purchases mean advantages in an ongoing game, called out in resentment as pay-to-win. The player's banking account is intertwined with the artificial economic cycles of the games.

The many investments, turns, rounds, games add up to a history of gaming culture. It falls short to consider the recent development as an exemplary story for commercial success which is enforced through computational media. Neither are games works of art, even though they might be discussed in terms of aesthetics (cf. Lantz, 2023). The informal games we play in everyday life on the other hand have not only playful aspects, but some can also be described in rule-bound game mechanics. Therefore, further ludogical research should focus on cultural techniques through which the possibility space of games is navigated without a word — not to mention a story: the handling of money (inserting coins, handing over cash, placing bets, etc.) is an ideal starting point for such investigations.

[8] Brougère (2021) proposes the French term „jeux d'edition", in German we like to say „Autorenspiele" which both link the uniqueness of a game to the production that is tied to legal entities like an author, producer or publisher as they are accustomed from book culture.

About the Author

Simon Huber studied History and Educational Science at the University of Vienna. His doctoral thesis (promoted at the University of Applied Arts) was honored with the *Award of Excellence* by the Federal Ministry of Education, Science, and Research. He is currently running a research project funded by the INTRA-program „Ludological Investigations. Game Design in terms of Cultural Techniques" to explore the differences in media culture. Additionally, he is teaching *the Anatomy of Games,* thus fostering a creative and analytical perspective among students and has also initiated a venture centered around coffee and everyday culture, titled *Second Sunrise.*

Website: https://www.secondsunrise.at

References

Begründungstext der Jury für den Roman des Jahres (2023). Retrieved 2 March 2024, from https://www.deutscher-buchpreis.de/

Berlin, L. (2017). The Inside Story of 'Pong' and Nolan Bushnell's Early Days at Atari. Wired. Retrieved 17 February 2024, from https://www.wired.com/story/inside-story-of-pong-excerpt/

Brougère, G. (2021). Des jeux et des sociétés. Sciences du jeu, 14.

Fiske, J. (1989). Reading the Popular. Routledge.

Fleck, L. (2021). Entstehung und Entwicklung einer wissenschaftlichen Tatsache: Einführung in die Lehre vom Denkstil und Denkkollektiv (13. Auflage). Suhrkamp.

Huber, S. (2014a). The Remediation of History in Assassin's Creed. In T. Winnerling & F. Kerschbaumer (Eds.), Early Modernity and Video Games (pp. 162–174). Cambridge Scholars Publishing.

Huber, S. (2014b). Zur Geschichte der Cutscenes. In T. Winnerling & F. Kerschbaumer (Eds.), Frühe Neuzeit in Computerspielen (pp. 55–70). Transcript.

Lantz, F. (2023). The Beauty of Games. The MIT Press.

Latour, B. (1995). Wir sind nie modern gewesen: Versuch einer symmetrischen Anthropologie. Akademie-Verlag

Merkel, A. (2017). Rede von Bundeskanzlerin Merkel zur Eröffnung der gamescom am 22. August 2017. https://www.bundesregierung.de/breg-de/aktuelles/rede-von-bundeskanzlerin-merkel-zur-eroeffnung-der-gamescom-am-22-august-2017-392398

Mukherjee, S. (2015). Video Games and Storytelling: Reading Games and Playing Books (1st ed. 2015 Edition). Palgrave Macmillan.

Pfaller, R. (2002): Die Illusionen der anderen. Über das Lustprinzip in der Kultur. Suhrkamp Verlag.

Romero, B., & Schreiber, I. (2021). Game balance (1st edition). CRC Press.

Schachinger, T. (2023). Echtzeitalter (1st ed.). Rowohlt.

Seemann, M. (2021). Die Macht der Plattformen: Politik in Zeiten der Internetgiganten. Ch. Links Verlag.

Smith, K. (2013, May 30). The Golden Age Arcade Historian: Video Game Mythbusters?? - The Malfunctioning Pong. The Golden Age Arcade Historian. https://allincolorforaquarter.blogspot.com/2013/05/video-game-mythbusters-malfunctioning.html

Stalder, F. (2018). The digital condition. Polity Press.

Theodora Bauer trifft Tonio Schachinger. (2023). https://www.servustv.com/kultur/v/aa4sleqlkt5hmynlkn2t/

Tonio Schachinger erhält den Deutschen Buchpreis 2023 für „Echtzeitalter". (2023). Retrieved 17 February 2024, from https://www.deutscher-buchpreis.de/

Unterhuber, T. (2020, July 16). Mit Kanones auf Spiele schießen? – Die (Un)Möglichkeit eines Computerspielkanons und die Rolle der Game Studies - Paidia. https://paidia.de/mit-kanones-auf-spiele-schiessen-die-unmoeglichkeit-eines-computerspielkanons-und-die-rolle-der-game-studies/

Yu, H. (2018). Game On: The Rise of the eSports Middle Kingdom. Media Industries Journal, 5(1). https://doi.org/10.3998/mij.15031809.0005.106

Zimmermann, O., Falk, F., & Deutscher Kulturrat e.V. (2020). Handbuch Gameskultur. Deutscher Kulturrat. https://www.kulturrat.de/publikationen/handbuch-gameskultur/

www.ingramcontent.com/pod-product-compliance
Lightning Source LLC
LaVergne TN
LVHW060837170826
845678LV00007B/1780

* 9 7 8 3 9 0 3 4 7 0 1 4 9 *